Praise for
THE BEST *of the* MARSHALL MEMO

"I've long admired Kim Marshall's dedication to improving teaching, leadership, and learning as a principal, principal-mentor, and writer. For more than 15 years, the *Marshall Memo* newsletter has been a vital resource for educators across the country. Now Kim has partnered with Jenn David-Lang to curate the very best Memo summaries and add specific action recommendations. With tips that range from the practical to the aspirational and even inspirational, *The Best of the Marshall Memo* is a veritable treasure trove full of gems for every educator who wants to better their schools, districts, and themselves."

—John B. King Jr., President and CEO, The Education Trust; formerly tenth US Secretary of Education

"The Marshall Memo has long been the go-to guide for teachers and school administrators seeking sound advice about research that informs their work. Now, in this skillfully curated compendium of first-rate articles, Marshall and David-Lang provide readers with a trove of insight and commentary about key challenges that educators face in leadership, school organization, and instructional practice. The book brims with issues that will strike a professional chord, findings that will confirm and challenge educators' beliefs, and resources to support individual learning and collegial growth. Keep this book within easy reach; you'll use it often."

—Susan Moore Johnson, Jerome T. Murphy Research Professor, Harvard Graduate School of Education

"Kim Marshall, in collaboration with Jenn David-Lang, has reviewed, synthesized, and updated nearly 800 Marshall Memos he has written over the last fifteen years and produced an absolutely invaluable guide for school leaders. Under three broad headings—the leadership toolkit, more teaching in more classrooms more of the time, and structures for student success—this book provides school leaders an unprecedented amount of wisdom, drawing on research, of course, but also interpreting that research in the light of experience about how research can be implemented in real schools. Add in the clear signposting provided by the chapter headings, and this is, quite simply, a book that no school leader can afford to be without."

—Dylan Wiliam, Emeritus Professor, University College London

"Whether we are principals, superintendents, coaches, or master teachers, we often find ourselves wishing we had a guardian angel on our shoulder helping us navigate the abundance of ideas and research on educational practice. Once we find great ideas and research in a particular area of practice we then wonder, "How can I use this effectively to polish my practice?" *The Best of the Marshall Memo* offers those of us engaged in the field practical solutions and key insights, as well as cautionary notes about ineffective practices in K–12 settings. A must-read for all leaders of teaching and learning!"

—Mary Nash, Superintendent, Maine School Administrative District No. 35/Eliot, ME; 2018 Maine Superintendent of the Year

"Kim Marshall has become a clarion voice in the crowded, murky field of educational leadership, identifying what matters most and sharing it in bite-sized form for educators across the globe. Kim's and Jenn's combination of real-world experience and visionary thinking creates a needed resource for every educator. Thank you—we've been waiting for this for a long time!"

—Paul Bambrick-Santoyo, Founder and Dean, Leverage Leadership Institute; Chief Schools Officer, Uncommon Schools

"I can't overstate the contribution the Marshall Memo has made to my work over the years, with its exquisitely-written weekly summaries of the most important educational articles. Now comes *The Best of the Marshall Memo*, the very "best of the best" of those summaries, with helpful activities and advice for how to apply their contents. This book is masterfully-organized around the most critical issues of instruction and leadership. There is more practical, concentrated wisdom in its pages than in all of the education courses I have ever taken. *The Best of the Marshall Memo* should be given to every teacher and leader who enters the education profession."

—Mike Schmoker, Author, Speaker, Consultant

"Kim Marshall and Jenn David-Lang have always provided an invaluable service to educators, condensing all the complex information on what works in education into digestible bites, so we can quickly learn what we need to learn and then get back to the business of teaching. And now, like a single pearl produced by an oyster over many years, we get the very best of their curation in one powerful book."

—Jennifer Gonzalez, *The Cult of Pedagogy*

"I often speak of the amazing "teacher in 206," whose combination of belief and instructional skill gets amazing results with all students. *The Best of the Marshall Memo* is founded on the same formula: *belief* that our students can learn and our teachers can teach them. Marshall and David-Lang have produced a highly organized set of topical, research-based summaries of *instructional practice* that, taken together, set a comprehensive foundation for practical classroom application. This is a crucial handbook for educator proficiency."

—Jeffrey Howard, Founder and CEO, Efficacy Institute

"Kim and Jenn have given busy school and district leaders exactly what we need—a thoughtful review and summary of relevant research and concrete ways for us to share this knowledge with our school-based practitioners. The selected themes and essential questions will transform meetings into professional learning sessions. This is a must-have resource for any school or central office leader."

—Joan Dabrowski, Assistant Superintendent of Teaching and Learning,
Wellesley Public Schools/Wellesley, MA

"*The Best of the Marshall Memo* is an essential resource for the modern educator. Teachers and school leaders alike will benefit from the thoughtfully curated analysis and review of recent educational research and articles. The book's format helpfully lends itself to deep dives on key topics relevant to every school in America. Leaders can use this book to foster reflection, dialogue, and staff-wide engagement on important challenges facing their school communities. Smart educators will use this resource to deepen the effectiveness of their practices and build capacity in their schools."

—Nicholas Tishuk, Executive Director, Bedford Stuyvesant New Beginnings Charter School/Brooklyn, NY

"As a school leader for the last 20 years, I have been both inspired and overwhelmed by the countless books, articles, research, and ideas out there that can make me and my school better. Being a principal feels like two full-time jobs; sifting and sorting through all of the learning and professional development materials could easily feel like a third. Over the years, Kim Marshall and Jenn David-Lang have saved me immeasurable time by leading me directly to the best resources and thinking in education and providing me with thoughtful, effective, and efficient ideas and tools to turnkey and share my growth and learning. I could not be more excited about this new book and brilliant collaboration."

—Mark Federman, Principal, East Side Community School/New York, NY

"Drawn from almost 800 Marshall Memos, this new volume represents yet another impressive and deeply appreciated service, *curating the curation* into a gold mine of the best thinking on some of the most challenging K–12 issues. Added to this meta-curation are Jenn's pragmatic step-by-step instructions for how staff can apply these ideas right away. A truly fabulous effort, Kim and Jenn!! You have us all spoiled."

—Elizabeth Imende-Cooney, International Educational Consultant, Advancing Educators

"Kim Marshall and Jenn David-Lang are unquestionably the most eminent summarizers of articles and books in education today. In this volume they take their unique and inimitable talents to a new level, combining their works on topics at the forefront of nearly every education improvement initiative. The works they summarize range from persuasively argued opinions to careful research syntheses—and the authors of these works don't reach the same conclusions or offer the same recommendations. So while readers may not come away with definitive answers to their most probing questions, they will gain a deeper understanding of the issues involved and the voices most influencing the discussion."

—Thomas R. Guskey, Senior Research Scholar, University of Louisville;
Professor Emeritus, University of Kentucky

"Change is vital and difficult. Kim Marshall and Jenn David-Lang show us the way. In this gift of collective wisdom from decades of service, Marshall and David-Lang offer all of us who care deeply about children, social justice, schools, districts, and systems a toolkit and roadmap to assist us in leading-for-improvement—on behalf of students' achievement and growing leaders on the ground. This book is, indeed, a treasure chest. A must buy. You will feel very wise to gain from it and its practical wisdom and accessible tools to improve your noble work and build capacity each and every day."

—Ellie Drago-Severson, Professor of Education Leadership and Adult Learning and Leadership,
Teachers College–Columbia University

"The *Marshall Memo* has played an indispensable role for years now in helping educators and school leaders to access cutting-edge research that can inform their work. With this new volume, Marshall and David-Lang have developed a resource to allow educators and school leaders to dive thoroughly and deeply into the research on a set of topics and themes crucial to their success. This book promises to be an invaluable text for powerful professional development and learning."

—Scott Seider, Associate Professor, Boston College–Lynch School of Education and Human Development

"I highly recommend Kim Marshall and Jenn David-Lang's *The Best of the Marshall Memo*, a terrific and well-organized collection of article summaries and professional development suggestions. I have greatly benefited from the Marshall Memo over the years—while in PK–12, and now as a professor—and more recently I gained further appreciation while studying the Memo as a key resource, a bridge that can span and connect the too-often disparate worlds of research and practice. Marshall and David-Lang, focusing intently on ideas and practices that can improve teaching and learning, do a great service for educators."

—Joel Malin, Assistant Professor, Department of Educational Leadership,
Miami University/Oxford, OH

"For leaders who smile each time they see a Marshall Memo or The Main Idea in their inbox, this book will be a treasure! Jenn David-Lang and Kim Marshall demonstrate their mutual commitment to leaders as learners, providing rich resources drawn from thousands of articles found in the Memo. Jenn David-Lang offers substantive, thoughtful ideas for professional learning connected to each chapter, allowing leaders to transfer and apply the concepts to their own unique needs. *The Best of the Marshall Memo* will serve as a powerful catalyst for professional growth, and will provide leaders with positive, creative ideas that are so needed in our schools today."

—Debbie McFalone, Author, Educational Leadership Consultant

"Discover actionable insights to improve teaching, deepen learning, and strengthen leadership. This first-ever collection of the best of the Marshall Memo and the Main Idea is a must-have for busy educators who want effective ideas, strategies, and techniques they can use to enhance their own practice and expand student outcomes."

—Mary Grassa O'Neill, Senior Lecturer on Education; Faculty Director, School Leadership, Harvard Graduate School of Education

"This unique book presents key insights from the education literature through the lens of two lifelong educators. Marshall and David-Lang skillfully interweave summaries of leading education research with case studies and narratives from practitioners about what it really means to implement change on the ground. It is sure to be a powerful new resource for engaging in evidence-based conversations about how to improve leadership and instruction in our nation's schools."

—Matthew A. Kraft, Associate Professor of Education and Economics, Brown University

"*The Best of the Marshall Memo* is a must-have-at-your-fingertips tool. This book contains information for what you have to know to lead effectively; it also has what you need to do to be an efficient and impactful leader. Kim and Jenn curate resources for what, why, and a healthy dose of how leaders will close the Knowing-Doing Gap and positively impact student learning. The 'what' is with current research articles across fields; the 'why' is with reflective questions for leaders to connect the information and explore implications for their practices; and the 'how' is in the form of a detailed PD plan to apply the knowledge for each topic."

—Hoa Tu, Deputy Superintendent, Brooklyn North High Schools/Brooklyn, NY

"This amazing book reminds me of my favorite childhood haunt: Mary's Candy Store. Jam-packed with an eclectic mix of tantalizing treats, Marshall and David-Lang's digest is simply irresistible."

—Jerome T. Murphy, Dean Emeritus, Harvard Graduate School of Education

THE BEST
of the
MARSHALL MEMO

―――――― *BOOK ONE* ――――――

Ideas and Action Steps to Energize Leadership, Teaching, and Learning

Kim Marshall & Jenn David-Lang

EPIGRAPH BOOKS
RHINEBECK, NEW YORK

The Best of the Marshall Memo: Book One: Ideas and Action Steps to Energize Leadership, Teaching, and Learning © 2019 by Kim Marshall and Jenn David-Lang

Paperback ISBN 978-1-948796-83-5
Hardcover ISBN: 978-1-948796-88-0
eBook ISBN 978-1-948796-84-2

Library of Congress Control Number: 2019911681

Book design by Colin Rolfe

Epigraph Books
22 East Market Street, Suite 304
Rhinebeck, New York 12572
(845) 876-4861
epigraphps.com

To the 195 researchers and practitioners featured in this book.
Their insights benefit educators and students around the world.

Acknowledgments

Kim and Jenn want to thank those who supported and improved this book from its earliest conception to last-minute suggestions: Justin Baeder, Paul Bambrick-Santoyo, Joanne Bragalone, Lee Bromberg Andrew Bundy, Rudd Crawford, Mike Doughty, Karen Drezner, Alex Estrella, Sarah Fiarman, Kate Gagnon, Amelia Gorman, Tom Guskey, Linda Hartzer, Bill Henderson, Jeff Howard, Elizabeth Imende, Shahara Jackson, Barry Jentz, the Jewish Education Project Study Group, Mike Lupinacci, Nick Marinacci, Maisie McAdoo, Jay McTighe, Mary Nash, the New York City District 4 Principals' Study Group, Mary Grassa O'Neill, Rob Ramsdell, Doug Reeves, Douglas Rife, Josh Roth, Kate Roth, Jon Saphier, Mike Schmoker, Mark Shellinger, Sue Szachowicz, Nick Tishuk, Betsey Useem, David Vazquez, David Ward, Bob Weintraub, Dylan Wiliam, and Sara Zrike.

Kim gives special thanks to Jon Saphier and Jon Schnur, who played a key role in launching the Marshall Memo in 2003; to Lillie Marshall, David Marshall, and Colin Turner, who have helped shape the Memo in innumerable ways; and to Rhoda Schneider, who works with me to polish the Memo every week, and provides the love, support, brilliance, and common sense that make all things possible.

Jenn is deeply grateful to her family. To my parents, Patricia and Simeon David, who are thoughtful, gracious, and loving leaders in so many aspects of their lives. To my daughters, Zoe and Alexa—each day I am deeply moved by your warm and giving souls—my relationship with each of you is precious. And most definitely to my husband, Tim, who is my lodestar and best friend, at the same time.

Contents

Introduction

Both of us—Kim Marshall and Jenn David-Lang—have devoted our professional lives to making schools a force for learning, collegiality, and social justice. After a combined total of forty-eight years of classroom teaching and school leadership, we are now coaching principals, consulting with schools and districts, and spreading the word about what works in two online publications. Kim's weekly Marshall Memo, www.marshallmemo.com, summarizes the best articles from more than sixty journals, magazines, and newspapers. In The Main Idea, www.themainidea.net, Jenn writes a detailed synopsis of a carefully selected education book each month, accompanied by professional development suggestions. We're "designated readers," curating ideas and research for busy front-line educators.

This book is the resource we both wish we'd had throughout our careers: a compact set of the very best insights on teaching, leadership, and learning. To write the book, our first step was deciding on eleven topics that are front-of-mind for PreK–12 educators (a second volume, coming soon, will tackle eleven more). We then scoured the eight thousand-plus article summaries in the Marshall Memo archive, asking which would be the most thought-provoking and helpful for principals, leadership teams, teachers, instructional coaches, consultants, district leaders, and those who train and support educators. We looked for articles that had

- practical and solution-oriented ideas with convincing evidence of impact;
- vivid stories and quotes from successful classrooms and schools;
- key insights from thought leaders; and
- cautionary notes about ineffective practices.

Having located the very best Memo summaries for each chapter, we sorted them into logical groups, picked a good lead-off quote, posed some essential questions, and crafted a set of professional development suggestions to help you make immediate use of the ideas and close the "knowing-doing gap."

Each chapter of this book is like a theme issue of an educational journal, but with four important advantages: (a) We were able to cast a much wider net, choosing from almost two decades of articles in numerous publications. (b) Marshall Memo summaries are usually much shorter than the original articles, making it possible to read the key ideas in under an hour. (c) At the end of each chapter are tailor-made PD suggestions to put the ideas into action. (d) The book has eleven themes under one cover, putting at your fingertips an extraordinary amount of useful information—visionary and practical, provocative and hands-on, and readily accessible as you and your colleagues wrestle with the myriad challenges of running an effective school.

The chapters fall into three sections. *The Leader's Toolkit* presents the foundational knowledge any school leadership team needs for strategic planning, making the best use of limited time, and managing emotions and interpersonal relationships. The second section, *More Good Teaching in More Classrooms More of the Time*, covers interviewing and hiring, effective coaching of teachers, conducting difficult conversations, providing effective feedback, and key issues with teacher evaluation. The third section, *Structures for Student Success*, focuses on positive classroom discipline, planning curriculum units and lessons, effective use of assessments, and new thinking on grading student work.

What are the best ways to use this book? You may read it from cover to cover, but it's more likely that you'll use certain chapters when you face an issue on which you'd like more ideas, research, and recommendations. Some examples:

- A school working on improving student discipline practices;
- A math department preparing to adopt standards-based grading;
- A grade-level team designing curriculum units and lesson plans;
- A department head preparing for a difficult conversation with a colleague;
- An instructional coach strategizing how best to support rookie teachers;
- A committee working to make the school's strategic plan a living document;
- A school leader struggling with HSPS (hyperactive superficial principal syndrome);
- An external consultant giving administrators insights on emotional intelligence;
- A superintendent aiming to improve the district's interviewing and hiring practices;
- A school board rethinking policies on teacher supervision and evaluation;
- A professional development retreat focused on a particular issue;
- A graduate course preparing aspiring school leaders.

You may also want to share individual article summaries with colleagues and have teacher teams read and think through articles or a whole chapter. Another idea is to ask the leadership team or the entire faculty to read article summaries "live," use a protocol for small-group discussion, and then plan action steps. Or you may want to use the PD ideas at the end of a chapter to structure discussions, reflection, collaborative activities, and overall professional learning opportunities for you and your colleagues.

We hope this book will help foster reflection on your school's purpose and goals, lead you to rethink old assumptions, spark productive debates, elevate the level of discourse, and lead to action steps that improve what students experience in classrooms every day.

Kim Marshall and Jenn David-Lang, July 2019

A. THE LEADER'S TOOLKIT

Chapter One: **Planning with a Purpose**

Chapter Two: **Managing Time for Impact**

Chapter Three: **Leaders' Emotional Intelligence**

Chapter One: Planning with a Purpose

Simply put, words have power. And a powerful vision statement is one that gives everyone in the organization a vivid sense of purpose in the work they do.
—BEN OWENS

Writing a school improvement plan is often an onerous task, and many of us have had the experience of working for hours on an elaborate document, only to have it sit on a shelf gathering dust. Searching the Memo archive turned up a number of helpful articles and also clarified four stages in crafting and implementing a plan that really improves teaching and learning: prerequisite steps; the plan itself; what makes the plan compelling; and rolling it out. Here are brief capsules of what the authors of these articles advocate:

Setting the Stage – Herb Childress says that before schools draft an improvement plan they should imagine the qualities of their ideal graduates, including creativity, bravery, a love of reading, and the ability to work with others. Tony Wagner urges planners to start by asking: What is the problem? What's our theory of action? Who do we need to include? Who's accountable? And how will we measure success? And Ben Owens contrasts the fluff of all too many mission statements with exemplars of bold, simple statements that direct and motivate action.

The Plan – Lew Allen decries empty mission statements that serve more as a symbol than as a catalyst of real change in schools. He suggests focusing on a few principles and actionable steps, and then ensuring that those guide daily actions and spark ongoing debate. Mike Schmoker also criticizes long, complicated mission statements and plans that don't produce results, but his solution is different; he proposes a few measurable goals linked to student assessments, with rigorous monitoring by teacher teams. And Nicholas Morgan and Nathan Levenson provide even more specific advice on thinking through an if/then theory of action for each initiative.

Making the Plan Compelling – David Collis and Michael Rukstad use the analogy of a magnet aligning iron filings; in the same way, a good plan rallies and focuses colleagues around a common purpose. Chip Heath and Dan Heath describe a medical intervention that saved more than one hundred thousand lives, and show how the same process can apply in schools: a clear goal, compelling personal stories, proven methods, faithful implementation, and constant checking on results.

Implementation – Steve Benjamin suggests specific ways to keep the mission statement alive by setting a few clear goals, measuring progress, selecting improvement strategies, and monitoring progress. John J-H Kim and Kriti Parashar caution leadership teams about ten mistakes often made as plans are formulated and rolled out. And Gary Klein suggests that planners conduct a "pre-mortem" in which they imagine that their plan failed spectacularly; then they brainstorm everything that could have produced that result and plan backwards so the plan will succeed.

Questions to Consider

• Are school improvement plans worth the trouble?
• Are we "walking the talk"? Do our policies, priorities, and actions reflect our beliefs?
• Do stakeholders in our school know the *why* and *how* of key initiatives?

Setting the Stage

1

A Vision of What a High-School Graduate Should Look Like

In this *Phi Delta Kappan* article, Herb Childress (then at Boston Architectural College) criticizes the "additive" approach he sees in many high schools "in which each certified specialist takes an assembly under construction and screws on a particular component and then passes the material along to the next specialist. One teacher takes 150 kids and screws on some algebra, another screws on some world history, a third screws on some Hemingway. Over the course of four years, each successful kid gets more than twenty components screwed on. And in the end, they're screwed, indeed.

"They're encased in this educational armor and have no experience in encountering and challenging their own communities, futures, or desires, because all of that has been sublimated to the repetitive and mechanical structures they've endured," says Childress. "This additive education is an education of fear. It's an effort to avoid disaster rather than to reach for a dream—to avoid a career at McDonald's rather than to pursue a deep personal mission."

Childress then presents a vision for the graduates of his ideal high school with commentary on each one:

- Graduates should love to read. That involves being open to new ideas and constantly reinventing themselves.
- They should enjoy numbers. Being able to do mental arithmetic, says Childress, "has served me well all the way through calculus and physics, it's a skill that helps me navigate the everyday world of taxes and budgeting, of saving and knowing when I can indulge in an extravagance, and it's a skill that helps me evaluate the accuracy and pertinence of information that's offered to me."
- They should enjoy physical exertion and activity. Physical activity needs to be a lifelong pursuit.
- They should have some well-developed outlet for their creative desires. This might be visual arts, music, or physics.
- They should know how to work in groups, and they should know how to teach a skill to someone else. "We are social animals," says Childress, "and we need to quit pretending that individual performance is the only thing that really matters."
- They should be brave and take risks. That means experiencing failure and coming through the other side.

- They should understand and take an interest in their community. They should know something about real estate, local government, services, industries, the landscape, and climate.

- They should be compassionate and care about people they don't know. "They should understand that a lot of what happens in people's lives isn't their fault, and that even things that are someone's fault usually are mistakes that can be recovered from, rather than a sign of a core moral failing that leaves people irredeemable and dismissible."

Can a school like this exist in the real world? Childress admits that his vision is, well, visionary. What he's calling for is "subtractive" education—the way Michelangelo saw sculpture: "I saw the angel in the marble and carved until I set him free." In schools, this means getting to know students, listening to and believing in them, and helping fulfill each child's potential.

"We are better than our systems," concludes Childress. "We are better than our structures. We can be brave, help our kids discover who they are, help them go where they want to go, and wish them Godspeed as they leave us behind."

"A Subtractive Education" by Herb Childress in *Phi Delta Kappan*, October 2006 (Vol. 88, #2, pp. 104–109), summarized in Marshall Memo 156.

2 | Key Questions to Guide School Improvement

In this article in *Education Week*, Harvard leadership specialist Tony Wagner says that many educators fall into the trap of becoming reactive to countless over-the-transom crises, compliant to various faddish initiatives from their central office, and isolated from their colleagues. When confronted by difficult problems, he says they ask "safe" questions and give "warm" feedback. He suggests asking the following questions to get to the heart of the matter:

- What is the problem we are trying to solve or the obstacle we are trying to overcome, and what does it have to do with improving teaching and learning?

- What is our "theory of action"—our strategy for solving this problem and why it will bring about the desired outcome?

- Who needs to understand what? How can teachers, parents, students, and the community "own the problem" and support the strategies we're implementing?

- Who is accountable for what? For this strategy to be successful, what do these key people need in order to be successful?

- What data (observable changes in short-term outcomes or behaviors) will we track to tell us whether our strategies are working?

"Leading for Change: Five 'Habits of Mind' That Count" by Tony Wagner in *Education Week*, August 15, 2007 (Vol. 26, #45, pp. 29, 32), summarized in Marshall Memo 197.

3 Vision and Mission Statements That Actually Inspire

In this article in *Education Week Teacher*, North Carolina teacher Ben Owens describes how he and his principal challenged a group of two hundred educators at a conference to write down their school's or district's vision statement (without looking). Less than 10 percent were able to recall the gist of their statements, let alone write them down verbatim. What people did remember was that their vision and mission statements were full of broad, ambiguous, meaningless statements that looked good hanging on the wall but didn't motivate anyone to strive for excellence. Here was the prize-winner:

> *To create 21st-century learners through the development and delivery of a diverse set of strategic teaching and learning strategies in a way that is targeted to enhance the individual growth pathway for each learner so that learning outcomes are maximized for the long-term benefit of the communities we serve.*

If their schools have verbiage like this, no wonder most educators can't remember their vision and mission statements!

Here are some much more eloquent and helpful statements of purpose that Owens found in his search of the business, nonprofit, and K–12 worlds.

- Habitat for Humanity: *A world where everyone has a decent place to live.*
- Google: *To organize the world's information and make it universally accessible and useful.*
- Disney: *To make people happy.*
- Cleveland Heights–University Heights School District: *Preparing all students for success in a global economy.*

"Simply put," says Owens, "words have power. And a powerful vision statement is one that gives everyone in the organization a vivid sense of purpose in the work they do." Any school that is serious about changing the status quo for its students, he believes, "has to start with a thorough evaluation of its core beliefs and how those may be articulated in a clear mission and vision statement."

That's step one. The next step is having your vision/mission statement pass the "red face test": If an outside observer reads your statement and then walks around the school, does he or she see evidence of the statement in the actions of adults and students? If there's no reason for embarrassment after this exercise, says Owens, "then you are indeed on the way to creating a culture of shared purpose – a culture where common goals and common language can be the catalyst that closes the gap between the current reality for the school and the future that all stakeholders desire .... If what you do is clearly aligned with your inner purpose, then you will be passionate about the work you do. You will eagerly collaborate with others, you will find ways to share ideas and resources to help yourself and others reach your common goals, and you will have a relentless focus on continuous improvement and innovation."

"Do You Know Your School's Vision? Tips on Making a Meaningful Mission Statement" by Ben Owens in *Education Week Teacher*, November 21, 2017, summarized in Marshall Memo 713.

The Plan

4 Making the Mission Statement *Real*

Every school has a mission statement, says University of Georgia educator Lew Allen in this *Phi Delta Kappan* article. That's because the literature universally supports the importance of a covenant, vision, mission, guiding statement, philosophy, or set of values to guide the work of teachers, administrators, students, and parents. But Allen has found that very few educators can quote the mission statement of the schools they attended as children, in which they currently work, or that their own children attend. "Guiding statements are rarely used for anything other than an occasional, symbolic group hug," he writes.

What's the problem? Allen and his colleagues have identified five reasons why mission statements are so hard to craft—and even more difficult to bring to life.

• Mission statements are usually so general that nobody can tell what success looks like. Slogans like *We want our students to reach their full potential mentally, physically, and socially*—or *We seek excellence in all we do*—are doomed to be forgotten, says Allen. "A school can never know if its students are reaching their 'full potential' or if they are seeking more 'excellence' this year than last. Such statements are probably meant to set a tone and to inspire people. Instead, they encourage people to ignore them."

- Guiding statements seldom link desired results with specific teaching and assessment practices. "This leaves the statements void of any practical implications for what people actually do on a day-to-day basis," writes Allen. They may clarify beliefs, at least in the beginning, but they don't guide actions.

- Mission statements are generally too long and complicated. "In an effort to cover all bases," says Allen, "people often include every good thing they want for their students. In doing so, they overwhelm themselves with words, water down what is of bottom-line importance to them, and encourage members of the school community to ignore the entire document."

- Some schools put a bunch of sayings, mottos, and quotes in offices, corridors, and classrooms. This confuses people about what a school is really committed to doing.

- Few people in the school are part of writing the mission statement. "People will not work hard to implement guiding statements that are simply handed to them," says Allen, "Moses being a notable exception."

- The hectic pace of life in schools is not conducive to reflective, ongoing dialogue. "Everyone is consumed by the issues of the day," writes Allen, "and there is little time or energy for thinking about visions and missions."

Allen goes on to make a series of recommendations to counteract the cynicism-producing effects of these problems:

- Look at your mission statement line by line and cut out anything that isn't measurable—anything for which you can't hold yourselves accountable. This includes phrases like *We will create a dynamic educational environment*, or *We will provide a quality educational program*, or *We will develop and support all human resources.*

- Include statements that articulate a theory of action about teaching and learning—for example, *Students learn best when they apply their learning in real-world situations*, or *Students learn best when they ask critical, probing questions on the subject matter*, or *Students learn best when they are actively engaged in their own learning.* These statements that would *not* guide action would therefore tend to be ignored: *We will provide courses that will challenge and enlighten all students*, and *Our courses will include instruction and experiences that will enhance reading, writing, speaking, listening, and presentation skills.*

- Keep the dialogue going to deepen staff understanding of the mission statement's content. "Without structures that help people explore what is meant by guiding statements," says Allen, "many will conclude that their own actions already embody the beliefs in the statements and won't give them any further thought …. Guiding statements should be seen as catalysts for deep reflection about beliefs and practices—not as vague reminders to do the right thing."

- Ensure that the mission truly guides action—including hiring, mentoring, staff development, student assessment, teacher evaluation, and relationships with parents. This doesn't mean that everyone has to do the same things in lockstep—innovation and experimentation should still be encouraged—but all efforts should be informed by the same principles and ideals. "Guiding statements should be provocative and challenging, not prescriptive and limiting," says Allen. "They should spark debate and inform action, not encourage compliance and unquestioned routines."

- Principals should make sure mission statements inform people's actions, including their own, by using mission language frequently and walking the talk.

- Periodically look at data to see if the school's mission is becoming a reality. "A cycle of learning needs to be put in place," says Allen, "that ensures that people in groups and as individuals (a) translate their school's guiding statements into action, (b) link their actions to the effect they have on student learning, (c) reflect on what they have learned, (d) share what they are learning with the entire school community, and (e) plan their next steps."

"From Plaques to Practice: How Schools Can Breathe Life into Their Guiding Beliefs" by Lew Allen in *Phi Delta Kappan*, December 2001 (pp. 289–293), summarized in Marshall Memo 194.

5 Making the Shift from Annual to Embedded Improvement Planning

In this article in *Phi Delta Kappan*, author/consultant Mike Schmoker remembers that for two decades as a district administrator, he and his colleagues did traditional strategic planning, complete with

- conducting wide-ranging needs assessments;
- writing lofty-sounding vision, mission, and belief statements;
- holding lengthy meetings to get buy-in from multiple constituencies;
- listing goals, action steps, and objectives;
- designating persons responsible, resources needed, evaluation, and timelines;
- producing a fat, impressive published plan that got pro forma approval.

Principals and teachers were then asked to commit to far more activities and initiatives than they could possibly monitor, much less complete. One guess is that less than 10 percent of what gets planned actually gets implemented.

Over time, Schmoker noticed that, despite all this hard work, instructional quality and student achievement rarely budged. He likens the hundreds of school plans he has seen to "beautiful but badly leaking boats" doomed to sink with little effect on teaching and learning. He's concluded that traditional planning "separates thought from action" (Kouzes and Posner, 1995); it "presumes that the most vital, high-leverage thinking is done primarily by 'planners' before the school year begins, rather than by teaching practitioners throughout the school year." Worse still, many initiatives aren't vetted on the basis of their proven impact on learning, but are often adopted for personal or political reasons.

Schmoker has a radical alternative: focus on the "on-going, messy work of improving teaching." Boil everything down to a few simple, measurable statements linked to student assessments. The heart of a school plan, he says, should guide how "teams of teachers will implement, assess, and adjust instruction in short-term cycles of improvement—not annually, but continuously." It's important that teams have a good deal of professional autonomy in the context of clear accountability for meeting explicit goals for student learning. "Effective teachers must see themselves not as passive, dependent implementers of someone else's script," he says, "but as active members of research teams—as 'scientists who continuously develop their intellectual and investigative effectiveness.'"

And what do these "scientists" do? They focus on areas where assessments reveal that students are having the most difficulty and craft "plans that focus on actual teaching lessons and units created in true 'learning communities' that promote team-based, short-term thought and action …. The key is for teams of professionals to achieve and celebrate a succession of small, quick victories in vital areas …. The cumulative effect of such small, ongoing 'wins' is the surest route to annual achievement gains."

Judith Warren Little has documented what happens when teachers collaborate in this way:

- There are higher-quality solutions to instructional problems.
- Teachers become increasingly confident in their own efficacy.
- Teachers are more able to support one another's strengths and accommodate each other's weaknesses.
- Beginning teachers get more systematic help.
- Teachers have a continually expanding pool of ideas, methods, and materials to draw upon.

Schmoker says these practices are not rocket science; they can be implemented by any leader, not just the rare individual with great charisma. The result will be "remarkable gains" in student achievement.

"Tipping Point: From Feckless Reform to Substantive Instructional Improvement" by Mike Schmoker, *Phi Delta Kappan*, February 2004 (Vol. 85, #6, pp. 424–432), summarized in Marshall Memo 25.

6 Developing Theories of Action

In this article in *The District Management Journal*, Nicholas Morgan and Nathan Levenson describe theories of action as "If-then" statements that embody testable hypotheses about how change will occur. Answering three questions helps create a good theory of action:

- What do we believe?
- What do we look like now, and what do we want to look like?
- How do we get there? What needs to change?

Ideally, a school district has several theories of action linked together in a causal pathway to improvement. Incomplete or illogical chains do not produce results. For example, a district leader who says that "professional learning communities" or "response to intervention" are the theory of action is not going to get results.

Losing weight provides an example of good and bad theories of action. Saying "I will eat less and thus will lose weight" is not a theory of action—it's just a hope. Here is a real theory of action from a weight-loss program:

- Create a baseline—know your starting weight.
- Set a goal—decide on the desired end weight.
- Tightly control calorie intake.
- Adhere to an exercise schedule—physical activity is required for success.
- Have a weekly weigh-in—this provides motivation and monitors progress.
- Adjust as needed—mid-course corrections are based on weekly weigh-ins.
- Celebrate success—plan for end of services.

The program is revised based on successes and failures of all participants, and new program improvements are rolled out each year.

Here are some examples of possible school-district theories of action that hang together as an overall strategy:

• *Teacher quality*—By setting expectations for what is "effective teaching" and providing frequent feedback to teachers through classroom observations and verbal feedback, teacher instructional practice will improve and student achievement will rise.

• *Principal autonomy*—By shifting resource allocation and decision-making to the building level, where employees are most equipped to make decisions that benefit children, student achievement will increase.

• *Earned autonomy*—By allowing principals to earn autonomy over certain domains when they are successful in their buildings, the district can continue to hold all building leaders to certain standards but reward successful practices. As a result, the district will focus attention where it is needed most, and student achievement will rise.

• *Professional learning communities*—Frequent collaboration among teachers in a grade or subject—coupled with clear standards, measuring progress through common interim assessments, and frequently reviewing student achievement data—will improve instructional practice, and student achievement will rise.

• *High expectations*—By increasing and standardizing expectations for students and staff, they will be pushed harder to achieve great things, creating a culture of high performance and increasing teacher effectiveness and student achievement.

Morgan and Levenson conclude with one theory of action that seems to make sense: If we hold class sizes down, then individual attention between teachers and individual students will increase and student learning will improve. They then show how it can ripple into some unarticulated theories of action, given finite resources. In effect, the implementation of the class-size theory of action means: "Cutting professional development, reducing support for principals to be instructional leaders by having fewer assistant principals, and decreasing teachers' access to data by having fewer staff members in IT and the accountability office will not harm student learning."

"Theories of Action: Aligning Priorities and Resources" by Nicholas Morgan and Nathan Levenson in *The District Management Journal*, Fall 2011 (Vol. 8, pp. 38–46), summarized in Marshall Memo 399.

Making the Plan Compelling

7 The Importance of a Clear, Concise Strategy Statement

Can you summarize your organization's strategy in thirty-five words or less? If so, would your colleagues describe the strategy in similar terms? Most corporate leaders flunk this test, say David Collis and the late Michael Rukstad in this *Harvard Business Review* article. Very few businesses, they write, have a well-articulated theory of action that is known throughout the organization—this despite the distribution of beautifully worded, framed mission and vision statements. "In an astonishing number of organizations, executives, frontline employees, and all those in between are frustrated because no clear strategy exists for the company or its line of business." Could this be true in schools?

Collis and Rukstad argue that this is a major impediment to success in any organization. "The value of rhetoric should not be underestimated," they say. "A thirty-five-word statement can have a substantial impact on a company's success. Words do lead to action." They ask us to think of the employees in a business [or school district] as a mound of ten thousand iron filings on a piece of paper, pointing every which way. People can be working hard and making what they think are good decisions, but the net result is confusion and incoherence. A well-understood statement of strategy is like passing a magnet over the iron filings. They line up! "It allows everyone in the organization to make individual choices that reinforce one another," say Collis and Rukstad, "rendering those ten thousand employees exponentially more effective."

The authors put strategy in the context of a hierarchy of other guiding statements, from the lofty and abstract to the concrete and organization-specific.
- Mission: why we exist.
- Values: what we believe in and how we will behave.
- Vision: what we want to be.
- Strategy: what our competitive game plan will be.
- Balanced scorecard: how we will monitor and implement that plan.

The strategy statement has three vital components:
- The objective—What is the strategy designed to achieve in terms that are specific, measurable, time-bound?
- The scope—What are the boundaries beyond which the organization will not venture (e.g., geographically, type of customer)?

- The means—What does the organization do differently that sets it apart from others? For example, Walmart's "values proposition" is providing a broad range of goods that are always in stock at low prices at convenient geographic locations while de-emphasizing ambiance and sales help, which makes lower prices possible.

How does an organization go about developing an effective strategy statement? Step one is a careful analysis of customer needs, competitors, market conditions, and internal capabilities. "The creative part of developing a strategy," say Collins and Rukstad, "is finding the sweet spot that aligns the firm's capabilities with customer needs in a way that competitors cannot match given the changing external context." [In schools, one of the key competitive contexts may be the ongoing struggle to recruit and hold onto effective teachers.]

"The wording of the strategy statement should be worked through in painstaking detail," recommend the authors, so that it reflects the three key elements (objective, scope, and means) and clears up any possible ambiguities. "In fact, that can be the most powerful part of the strategy development process. It is usually in heated discussions over the choice of a single word that a strategy is crystallized and executives truly understand what it will involve."

"Can You Say What Your Strategy Is?" by David Collis and Michael Rukstad in *Harvard Business Review*, April 2008 (Vol. 86, #4, pp. 82–90), summarized in Marshall Memo 227.

---

8 A Formula for Transformational Change in Hospitals and Schools

In this article in *School Administrator*, authors Chip Heath and Dan Heath describe how physician Donald Berwick went about saving more than one hundred thousand lives. Berwick and his colleagues at the Institute for Healthcare Improvement knew what all medical practitioners know—that the "defect" rate in most hospitals is as high as 10 percent. For example, about 10 percent of patients don't get their antibiotics at the right time and in the right dosage. Because of errors like these, tens of thousands of patients die each year.

Berwick had studied Total Quality Management in corporations and wondered why the methods that have reduced errors to one in one thousand at Toyota plants couldn't be applied to health care. He identified areas of patient care where specific procedures had been shown to reduce the error rate to zero—for example, elevating the heads of patients in ventilators thirty to forty-five degrees prevents oral secretions from getting into the windpipe.

On December 14, 2004, Berwick gave a speech at a large industry convention and challenged an audience of hospital administrators to save some of their patients' lives soon. "Some is not a number," he continued. "Soon is not a time. Here's the number: one hundred thousand. Here's the time: June 14, 2006, 9:00 a.m."—exactly eighteen months away.

Berwick then introduced the mother of a girl who had died because of a medical error. "I'm a little speechless," she said, "and I'm a little sad, because I know that, if this campaign had been in place four or five years ago, my daughter Josie would be fine …. But, I'm happy—I'm thrilled to be part of this, because I know you can do it."

Berwick made it easy to sign up for the program, and more than one thousand hospitals quickly did so. The Institute for Healthcare Improvement gave hospital staffs step-by-step training and manuals on six specific procedures. They held conference calls in which hospital leaders shared ideas. Some doctors were irritated by the new procedures, saying they were overly constricting, but as the months went by, hospitals began to see dramatic improvements in infection rates and mortality. The word spread and more hospitals joined the campaign.

Exactly eighteen months after his initial speech at 9:00 a.m. on June 14, 2006, Berwick announced the results. The hospitals in the campaign had collectively prevented 122,300 deaths and had put in place procedures that would continue to save lives and improve health-care outcomes into the future.

How was Berwick able to get hospitals to change entrenched procedures when he had no positional power and only a small staff? The Heaths attribute this dramatic success to the following factors:

- setting a crystal-clear goal and timeline (one hundred thousand lives saved in eighteen months);
- putting a human face on medical errors by having the mother speak, engaging the hospital leaders' emotions;
- proposing six proven methods for accomplishing the goal (versus talking about "evidence-based medicine" or "bringing Total Quality Management to health care");
- maintaining a laser-like focus on the faithful implementation of the six procedures;
- shaping the pathway to success—making it easy to enroll, providing training, and getting hospitals talking to and supporting each other.

The Heaths use the metaphor of a *rider* trying to guide an *elephant* down a *path* to explain how change happens. We have to appeal to the *rider* (people's intellectual side) and the *elephant* (people's emotions), and we need to show a *path* to success.

The Heaths believe this applies to education as well as medicine. They tell the story of Molly Howard, who in 1995 became principal of a three-thousand-student high school in rural Georgia where only 15 percent of students typically went on to postsecondary education and many teachers had the attitude that "some children *can* and some children *can't*." Howard quickly made several changes:

- She abolished a two-track system that had separated "college-bound" from "vocational" students.
- She matched students with on-campus advisors who stayed with them all four years of high school.
- She beefed up assessments and tutorial programs.
- She changed the A-B-C-D-F grading system to A-B-C-NY (Not Yet).
- She had teachers explain to students exactly what A, B, and C work look like.

The school made dramatic progress in achievement, graduation rates, and climate. In 2008, Howard was selected as national Principal of the Year by NASSP.

"The changes you face may feel daunting," conclude the Heaths, "but there is tremendous hope in change stories like those of Donald Berwick and Molly Howard. Both walked into situations where bad behaviors were so entrenched that no one was trying to change. Yet both of them systematically addressed the weaknesses of *rider* and *elephant*. And they both succeeded where no one thought success was possible."

"Overcoming Resistance to Change" by Chip Heath and Dan Heath in *School Administrator*, March 2011 (Vol. 68, #3, pp. 28–32), summarized in Marshall Memo 378. The article is based on the Heaths' book, *Switch: How to Change Things When Change is Hard* (Broadway, 2010).

Implementation

9   Eight Steps to High-Achieving Schools

In this article in *EDge* magazine, leadership consultant and former principal Steve Benjamin bemoans the fact that many principals are caught up in basic tasks (e.g., student discipline, teacher contentment, a clean school) and function as middle managers implementing directives from above. He urges school leaders to get beyond these important basics and focus on the two activities that are essential to getting students to achieve at high levels: (a) setting direction, and (b) regularly checking on progress. Here are the lessons he's learned from working with successful—and unsuccessful—leaders:

• *Set a clear, measurable direction.* Benjamin has found that many school mission statements do little to move a staff forward. He believes that more concrete, measurable mission statements make a huge difference. Imagine, he asks, if a school declared: WE TEACH KIDS TO READ. "The key performance reflected in this mission statement can be measured," he says. "It is easier to conceive of the nature of important work in a 'we teach kids to read' school… organizational vision becomes 20/20." Benjamin doesn't advocate a mission statement as spare as this one, but he does believe that everything in the mission should be focused and measurable. "Mission should not be allowed to creep," he declares.

• *Decide on a few key metrics and keep them at the center of your daily work.* Benjamin says that the information on a car's dashboard provides a good analogy to the data that educators should have at their fingertips. A driver can see, at a glance, the car's speed, RPM, engine temperature, fuel level, mileage, and (through warning lights) whether there are problems with the oil pressure and battery level. Educators should decide on no more than five to seven key data points and regularly monitor them. Here are a few possible candidates:

- percentage of students reading at or above grade level;
- percentage of students writing at the proficient or advanced level;
- percentage of students mastering state standards in ELA, math, and science;
- percentage of students participating in extracurricular activities;
- number of service/learning hours per student;
- number of bullying incidents per month.

What's vital, says Benjamin, is that these measure results, not processes. For example, "number of staff members trained to use balanced literacy techniques" is process data, not results data. To be sure, school leaders should collect and monitor information on processes, says Benjamin, "But the last ten years should have taught us that establishing vague process or procedural goals in the absence of clear, concrete learning goals is foolish."

It's also important that the school's metrics be aligned with the district's and external stakeholders' expectations. "For example," writes Benjamin, "if a high school's list of performance indicators failed to include 'writing ability,' it would suggest a lack of awareness of post-secondary stakeholder expectations."

A special challenge for principals is preventing activities that are not aligned to the key indicators from gobbling up precious time—for example, spending more time with troublesome, high-maintenance parents than visiting classrooms and meeting with teacher teams to monitor and improve the reading performance of struggling first graders. "An 'open-door policy' may seem like good public relations," says Benjamin, "but operating in this manner suggests that you are not in control of your most valuable resource—time."

• *Develop frequent formative measures for each "dashboard" performance indicator.* What good would a fuel gauge be, asks Benjamin, if it gave you a reading only once a year? Similarly, principals need frequent assessment data to inform decisions in real time, not when the school year is over. Such data should be timely enough to

- tell which students need additional help,
- help evaluate which programs and strategies are working and which aren't,
- indicate what additional resources and training are needed.

Benjamin recounts a role-play he does with superintendents. He asks them to imagine a school board meeting in which a member abruptly asks for the percentage of students who read at or above the target instructional level for their grade level. Most superintendents sheepishly admit that most of their teachers and principals don't have that information—but readily agree that it's vital to the success of their schools and should be on everyone's "dashboard."

• *Set a long-term goal for each performance indicator.* Many schools have goals like "Improve our reading scores." Benjamin suggests that a more focused goal might read: "Increase the percentage of free- and reduced-price students who read at or above the target instructional level from 55 percent to 85 percent, as measured by the Developmental Reading Assessment by May 2010."

• *Conduct a gap analysis.* Once baseline data are available and a long-term goal has been set, it's easy to spot the gaps—for example, the chasm between 55 percent of low-income students currently meeting the target reading level and the long-range goal of 85 percent. These cry out for explanation—and this is where schools need to use root cause analysis, fishbone diagramming, cause-and-effect thinking, and other techniques to figure out why a performance gap exists and how it can be closed.

The problem, says Benjamin, is that most educators haven't been trained in gap analysis and tend to jump straight to solutions that turn out to be ineffective. Teachers are often told to go into a room for two hours and come up with ideas to put in the school improvement plan. "If data do not guide improvement efforts," say Heritage and Chen (2005), "schools will continue to base decisions on a mixture of intuitions, beliefs, philosophy, and hypotheses."

One school, for example, set a goal of improving student attendance from 93 percent to 97 percent in two years' time, and decided to use incentives—pizza and iPods—to motivate students to come to school more regularly. The school didn't come close to reaching the goal. Why? A more careful analysis would have revealed that low attendance was disproportionately caused by a small number of chronically absent students for whom pizza and iPods had no allure. To improve these students' attendance and meet the goal, the school would need to create individual attendance plans that included mentoring, improved home-school communication, differentiated instruction, alternative learning environments, and involvement of the legal system.

• *Clearly specify improvement strategies and key action steps.* For example, if a school's goal is to provide staff development in the district's balanced literacy model for all teachers and principals within eighteen months, it's wise to "begin with the end in mind," visualizing the action having been successfully completed and working backwards to the present. "Creating effective action plans," writes Benjamin, "requires a mix of past, present, and future verb tenses rumbling around in your head." He recommends keeping plans simple, breaking them into specific tasks, making sure everyone knows what they are supposed to do, and patiently keeping at it until results can be harvested.

The implementation stage, of course, is where the most debate, resistance, and even obstructionism is likely to occur. "No one will disagree that reading is important or that we should produce more students who are capable of reading at or above grade level," says Benjamin. "But conflict will arise when the system requires all faculty members to be trained to implement the very best reading practices that can be identified and teachers are actually observed implementing the new processes at a highly proficient level." This is when principals really earn those big bucks—by tenaciously keeping at it and using actual student learning data to inform necessary mid-course corrections.

• *Conduct regular data meetings.* Benjamin says that none of this will produce results if leaders aren't highly disciplined about devoting serious time to regularly sitting down with their teams, reviewing the most current data, and discussing in detail how things are going and what needs to be improved. This is part of what he calls a tight-loose-tight management strategy: "tight around agreed performance indicators and goals, loose regarding day-to-day implementation of strategies designed to close the gaps, and tight regarding frequent checking of interim performance." Without regular, hard-nosed results-and-improvement meetings, teachers will rightly conclude that the big "reading push" (for example) is just a lot of hot air.

Benjamin suggests these guidelines for leaders as they run these meetings with their teams:

- Ask good questions and refrain from providing answers too quickly. Benjamin quotes Heifetz and Laurie (1997): "Responsibility must shift to the collective intelligence when facing adaptive challenges." Thoughtful questions about the data and processes can get teachers rethinking "old habits that previously have been either off-limits or simply so routine as to make them invisible."

- Keep the same agenda structure in these meetings, he suggests, "focusing unwaveringly on the formative results of performance indicators and the degree of strategy implementation."

- Work on keeping the conversation direct and honest. The key is getting team members to look in the mirror and then speak the truth.

• *Maintain a sense of continuous improvement.* In the real world, the path of improvement is not linear. The leader's challenge is keeping a "virtuous cycle" going, with data constantly feeding improvement and growth.

Benjamin closes by exhorting school leaders to keep a laser-like focus on the academic success of students and constantly monitor and respond to these gaps:

- the results gap, which becomes clear when we know current and desired performance levels;

- the strategy-implementation gap, as new processes are put in place and staff are trained to use them;

- the personnel gap, as the need arises to replace staff who are ineffective even after attempts to support their growth;

- the resources gap, as staff demand materials and time to implement the improvement strategies.

"Mind the Performance Gap: Focusing Leaders on the Vital Few Competencies" by Steve Benjamin in *EDge*, January/February 2007 (Vol. 2, #3, pp. 1–19), summarized in Marshall Memo 169.

---

10 Avoiding Common Mistakes in Strategic Planning

In this *District Management Journal* article, John J-H Kim and Kriti Parashar describe the strategic planning process they have developed working with numerous school districts.

- Mission and vision: long-term district aspirations;
- Theory of action: fundamental beliefs about what will lead to long-term success;
- Priorities: broad areas of focus to support the theory of action;
- Measurable goals: specific and measurable targets related to district priorities;
- Initiatives: projects related to priorities to achieve the measurable goals;
- Action steps: an articulation of what steps need to occur, by when, and by whom.

Kim and Parashar conclude with ten mistakes to avoid in the strategic planning process:

- Don't start without first gaining a clear, fact-based understanding of the district's current strengths and challenges.
- Don't draft a plan that skims the surface; address the root causes by asking *Why* five times to get at the underlying issues.
- Don't shortchange developing a cogent theory of action. "The strongest theories of action are focused, easily understood by virtually all district stakeholders, and guide critical tasks and workflows, organizational arrangement, and culture in the district," say the authors.
- Don't treat every idea as a good idea; develop a list of fewer than five high-impact priorities. "Manage expectations that not all ideas may find their place in the final plan," say Kim and Parashar.
- Don't forget to include specific, measurable action plans. This includes the roles and responsibilities of school and central staff, key milestones, and necessary budget shifts.
- Don't forget to include many parts of the organization, not just academics. Although student achievement is the ultimate outcome, other departments such as finance, human resources, and operations play key roles.
- Don't just engage in open-ended discussions with stakeholders about their concerns and hopes. Elicit specific, actionable feedback on a draft of the strategic plan.
- Don't forget to include lagging (output-oriented) as well as leading (input-oriented) metrics to track progress.
- Don't just layer new initiatives on top of existing ones. "Seek to leverage and build upon the work being done in the district and create a coherent and aligned approach to moving the work forward," say the authors.

- Don't forget to establish clear implementation and monitoring processes. "Effective implementation requires detailed planning and communication, cultivation of leadership capacity, and the analytics to monitor progress," conclude Kim and Parashar. "The implementation plan and monitoring process must also be tailored to the district's strengths, weaknesses, and available resources."

"Strategic Planning for Today's Challenges" by John J-H Kim and Kriti Parashar in *The District Management Journal*, Spring 2016 (Vol. 19, pp. 12–27), summarized in Marshall Memo 638.

11 "Pre-Mortems" Are Better than Post-Mortems

"Projects fail at a spectacular rate," writes Ohio-based business expert Gary Klein in this *Harvard Business Review* article. "One reason is that too many people are reluctant to speak up about their reservations during the all-important planning phase." The remedy, says Klein, is to mobilize "prospective hindsight" through the "pre-mortem"—a special meeting that makes it safe for dissenters and worriers to identify risks before a project is launched.

Pre-mortems are at the opposite end of the spectrum from post-mortems, in which medical professionals investigate what caused a patient's death. Pre-mortems also differ from meetings in which managers ask their subordinates to critique a project before it's launched, asking them to think about what might go wrong. Here's the pre-mortem protocol:

-   The team is briefed on a project plan.
-   The leader then asks everyone to imagine that the project has failed spectacularly.
-   Team members are asked to take a few minutes to reflect silently and write down every reason they can think of for the project's failure—especially the kinds of problems they wouldn't ordinarily mention.
-   Team members then take turns reading one reason from their lists; someone records each reason on a flip chart.
-   The process continues until all reasons have been shared.
-   After the meeting is over, the project manager reviews the list and looks for ways to strengthen the plan.

Klein says that companies using the pre-mortem process have found that it's a highly effective way to nip unseen problems in the bud. Here's why:

- It helps teams escape the damn-the-torpedoes momentum that develops when people get overinvested in a project. By visualizing the project's failure, team members are more likely to identify problems.

- When team members describe a weakness that no one else had mentioned, they feel valued for their intelligence and experience, and others learn from them.
- The pre-mortem process sensitizes the team to the things that might go wrong, and as the project gets underway members are more likely to notice if there are early signs of trouble.

"In the end," concludes Klein, "a pre-mortem may be the best way to circumvent any need for a painful post-mortem."

"Performing a Project Pre-mortem" by Gary Klein in *Harvard Business Review*, September 2007 (Vol. 85, #9, pp. 18–19), summarized in Marshall Memo 199.

Professional Learning Suggestions for Chapter One Planning with a Purpose

How to Develop and Sustain Your Own Living Mission

A common problem Kim and Jenn have seen in countless schools is that when asked about the school's mission, staff give such varied responses! While the articles in this section all emphasize different aspects of strategic planning, one strong common thread is that, in order to truly set the direction for your school, you need to do much more than craft a perfectly-worded mission statement. Instead, you need a living, breathing plan along with active follow-through to make sure everyone is on the same page. Along with reading this chapter, the ideas below will help you develop a living mission and put the structures in place to lead your school forward.

I. The Ideal Graduate

These two activities are best done with the entire staff before the first day of school. Note that this is about more than thinking through the school's mission—by involving the entire staff, it is about enhancing culture and building teams. It moves staff away from their day-to-day tasks and encourages them to dream bigger and remember why they entered the field of education in the first place.

A. What adult skills are you most proud of?
Have teachers look back at the first article by Herb Childress, and in particular, about the characteristics he would hope for in a high school graduate (should enjoy physical exertion, know how to work in groups, etc.).

Now ask staff to think of their own skills, habits, dispositions, and abilities that they value and that enrich their adult lives. Have them individually brainstorm and create a list: for example, read the New York Times daily, do my own taxes, empathize with colleagues, play in a weekly basketball game, etc.

B. Brainstorm skills for students to have an "attractive adulthood."
Now have staff think on which of the above skills their school should foster in students. Hand out large pads of newsprint paper and organize staff into groups of four to six people. Have each group

draw an outline of a bubble stick figure (like the one below—with a graduation cap!) to represent a graduate (this can be an elementary-, middle-, or high-school graduate). Now have the groups brainstorm the skills they would want their students to acquire by the time they graduate by putting each skill on a sticky note and attaching it to the "graduate."

C. Gallery walk to choose top skills for a graduate.
Have groups hang their "graduates" on the wall and ask everyone to walk around, voting for five of the skills they believe to be most important by placing check marks on those sticky notes. Turn over the most voted-for skills to a smaller committee to create a few versions of a mission to share with staff at a later date.

II. Components of an Effective Mission

The activities below are best to do with your leadership team or with a committee working on writing the school's mission.

A. Discuss compelling aspects of a school mission.
The articles emphasize different aspects of creating an effective mission to guide improvement efforts. With your leadership team, discuss which aspects of creating a strong mission resonated with you.

B. Evaluate your school mission with a rubric.
The following rubric contains highlights of what makes for an effective mission from the articles in the chapter. Use it with your leadership team to rate your own mission. Next decide which of the nine mission components in the rubric are most important to your school. Collaboratively fill in the Highly Effective (4.) column with descriptions of what this component would look like so your team has a common understanding of what a highly effective mission would look like. Once you have come to consensus, be sure to share what you've written with the committee working to create drafts of your school mission (see above).

	MISSION COMPONENTS	4. Highly Effective	3. Effective	2. Developing	1. Novice
Mission Wording	The mission addresses a problem we are trying to solve.				
	The mission prepares students for an "attractive adulthood."				
	The mission paints a specific and quantifiable picture of what success looks like.				
	The mission is short enough for people to remember (few goals and few words).				
	The mission includes theories of action—hypotheses about *how* change will occur.				
Mission Implementation	Before launching the mission, a "pre-mortem" is conducted to identify potential obstacles.				
	There is a plan to keep dialogue about the mission alive throughout the year.				
	Throughout the year, the mission guides decisions about teaching, learning, hiring, PD, assessment, community relations, and more.				
	We have a plan to use data to track progress toward the mission.				

III. Keeping the Dream Alive—How to Sustain the Mission

These are some activities to do on your own, as the leader, to help you keep the mission of your school alive.

A. Practice your own elevator speech.

Whether you have a new mission or not, it's helpful for you to be able to articulate your school's mission in a concise and compelling way. Review the Collis and Rukstad (Article 7). Whether you are speaking with a parent or the superintendent, your job is to promote the school and communicate what it is that makes your school your school. Take some time to prepare and then look in the mirror and explain the heart of your school in thirty to sixty seconds (the time it takes to speak to a new person in an elevator)!

B. Create your own dashboard.

Like in the dashboard of a car (review Benjamin, Article 9), what are the most important pieces of data you would like to review regularly to determine your school's progress toward the mission? Benjamin provides a few examples: percentage of students reading at or above level, percentage of students participating in extracurricular activities, etc. First, choose which data points you want access to (Benjamin suggests fewer than seven). Next, decide on a model you will use to display this data. You can use a simple Word document or spreadsheet, or you can Google companies (like iDashboards) or templates (search for "school dashboard templates").

For a simple example, see this data dashboard from the New York City Charter School Center: http://www.nyccharterschools.org/sites/default/files/resources/Sample_Data_Dashboard.pdf

For a more complex model of a dashboard, take a look at this one from the Alexandria City Public Schools: http://idashboard.acps.k12.va.us:6700/idashboards/idb/html5?CMD=viewer-Login&loginType=guest&embedded=true&username=guest&c=0&dashID=10

C. Remember to walk the walk.

As leader, it is your job to keep the mission alive throughout the year. If your initiatives lead you in a different direction—or worse, contradict your school's mission—then the mission becomes a nominal piece of paper. Take some time now to think about some recent initiatives or changes you've made at the school. How well do these align with your mission? Now think about some upcoming initiatives. If these are not fully aligned to the mission, is there a way to tweak them? Or should they be scrapped?

Chapter Two: Managing Time for Impact

The job of the principal is 'undoable' in the sense that all the work never gets done.
So the principal who thrives must have a clear sense of which activities produce the most student gains.
—Daniel Duke

Managing time is a perennial challenge for school leaders, who are uniquely vulnerable to interruptions and distractions that pull them away from the core work of instructional leadership. The articles in this chapter address three levels of the challenge: setting big-picture priorities, being proactive about preventing unnecessary work, and specific techniques that maximize effectiveness.

Priorities – Kenneth Freeston and Jonathan Costa say school leaders spend their time in three ways: value-added work, necessary work, and waste work. They argue that the key to effective leadership is maximizing time on work that improves teaching and learning, doing necessary work as quickly and efficiently as possible, and reducing waste work to an absolute minimum. Kim Marshall also highlights the ways school leaders can prioritize the most important work and avoid HSPS (hyperactive superficial principal syndrome): focus on a few "big rocks;" organize around them; be systematic about getting into classrooms; and take care of yourself. William Powell and Ochan Kusuma-Powell reprise Stephen Covey's four quadrants model (1989) as a way to help school leaders think about time and priorities: concentrate on actions that are in Quadrant II—not urgent but central to student learning.

Systems – Justin Baeder believes principals have a lot to learn from today's firefighters, who spend less time heroically carrying people out of burning buildings because they invested in preventing fires from happening in the first place. In schools, this means setting up systems that handle routine matters and allow leaders to focus on their core work, so they won't get burned out.

William Oncken, Jr. and Donald Wass say the wise manager builds initiative in subordinates so they will take responsibility for their core work and stop unnecessarily shifting tasks to the boss.

Techniques – James Fallows summarizes the recommendations of time management guru David Allen, including writing a master to-do list, reviewing the list once a week, and dealing quickly with items that take less than two minutes. James Surowiecki explores the psychology of procrastination—avoidance, denial, and sometimes a rational aversion to working on something that's not important—and shares some time-tested methods for getting started on work that's truly a priority. Verena von Pfetten cites research on how multitasking degrades performance and results in less being accomplished. The antidote: paying attention to one task or one person at a time.

Questions to Consider

- How can school leaders make time for what's truly important?
- Which leadership tasks have the biggest impact on teaching and learning?
- How can leaders be accessible without taking on everyone else's problems?

Priorities

1 Valuable Work, Necessary Work, and Waste Work

In this article in *Educational Leadership*, Connecticut educators Kenneth Freeston and Jonathan Costa channel the frustration of school leaders who know they aren't spending enough time on activities that improve teaching and learning. There are three common reactions: wishing there were more hours in the day; believing that "just getting organized" will lead to more efficient use of time; and thinking that being busy is the same as being productive.

None of these go to the heart of the matter, say Freeston and Costa. The solution is using the time we have more wisely. But how? The work of business expert William Conway (1992) is instructive. Conway spent twenty years helping corporate leaders use their time more thoughtfully and found that the first step is coming to a shared understanding of what *value* is. In the business world, value is a product or service the customer is willing to pay for. Having defined value, Conway divided the daily work of a corporate leader into three categories:

- *Value-added work* produces things that the customer wants; the value of the work is greater than the work itself.
- *Necessary work* is time spent on things that an organization must do to function but that have no direct value to the customer.
- *Waste work* is time spent on things that the customer will *not* pay for—errors, rework, problems, redundancies.

Conway's studies revealed that the average corporate leader spends 40 percent of the time doing waste work. Effective leaders, on the other hand, "... do not allow waste to accumulate. They systematically teach their employees to eliminate waste and streamline necessary work in order to maximize the time spent on value-added work."

Can this construct be applied to school leadership? The first challenge is defining value. "Business leaders have it easy when it comes to defining their primary goal," say Freeston and Costa. "They sell stuff. With education, it may seem more ambiguous, but it is nonetheless certain: The goal of a school is to create *learning*." From that starting point, it's possible to transpose Conway's three kinds of work to schools:

- *Value-added work* is any activity that leads directly to improvements in student learning—for example, research on effective instructional practices; observing and supporting classroom learning; keeping professional dialogues focused on learning.

- *Waste work* is any activity that doesn't contribute to learning and could have been avoided if it had been done properly the first time—for example, correcting one's own mistakes or those of others; dealing with teacher, parent, or student complaints; conducting a meeting without the right people present.

- *Necessary work* is any activity that keeps the school running but has no direct impact on learning—for example, signing purchase orders; ordering supplies; supervising bus duty.

Freeston and Costa say the principal's challenge is reducing waste, improving efficiency, and aligning the work of the school with its primary goal. Sounds simple—right? Not so much! They go right to the thorniest issue: teaching. "The value of teaching is equivalent to the learning it creates," they write. "To anyone who purports that teaching has intrinsic value, we say yes it does—to the extent that it creates learning. After all, from an educational consumer's point of view, if something is taught and not learned, does it really matter that it was taught?" This creates a high bar for principals as they analyze how much of their daily work truly adds value.

How can a principal get an accurate sense of the proportion of time spent on value-added work? Freeston and Costa did studies in which they beeped school leaders at random intervals and had them write down what kind of work they were engaged in at that moment—value-added, waste, or necessary. Principals found that after jotting down their activities for five to seven weeks (about eight hundred entries), value-added work made up only 10–20 percent of their time. They were horrified, and began looking much more critically at whether certain activities were really contributing to improved student learning.

Principals in the studies zeroed in on two arenas with a lot of waste work: school governance council meetings and faculty meetings (Freeston and Costa said the latter are often "a dead zone of value-added work.") With this new consciousness, principals became much more aggressive about pre-screening agenda items for direct links to student learning, delegating necessary work to others, and driving out waste by implementing problem-solving and group-facilitation strategies.

Freeston and Costa then had the school leaders in their studies calculate their VQ—value quotient. This was the amount of value-added work divided by the amount of waste work (assuming a reasonably efficient percent of necessary work— less than 40 percent of each week). It turned out that a VQ of 1.0 was a threshold:

- Principals with a greater than one-to-one ratio of value-added to waste work "feel a great sense of worth and pride in their work."

- Principals with less than a one-to-one ratio "tend to be numb to innovation, suspicious of new ideas, dispassionate toward improvement, and not willing to find challenge in their work. A cycle of chronically low VQ is characteristic of burnout."

In short, the challenge of every school leader is increasing the proportion of time spent on value-added work, doing necessary work as quickly and efficiently as possible, and cutting down on waste work. Freeston and Costa have found that when principals are successful in moving in this direction, there is a ripple effect in the school. When school leaders improve their value quotient, the VQ of their staff improves as well, resulting in fewer grievances, lower absenteeism, less resistance to academic initiatives, and better morale, motivation, and performance. VQ, they believe, "is an excellent measure of an educational institution's ability to grow and sustain itself."

"Making Time for Valuable Work" by Kenneth Freeston and Jonathan Costa in *Educational Leadership*, April 1998 (Vol. 55, #7, pp. 50-52), summarized in Marshall Memo 146.

2 Ten Keys to Managing Time and Priorities

"How can a dedicated principal work really, really hard but fail to get significant gains in student achievement?" asks Kim Marshall in this *Principal Leadership* article. "The answer is obvious: by spending too much time on the wrong things and not enough on the right things." H.S.P.S. (Hyperactive Superficial Principal Syndrome) is a perennial problem for principals; it's a constant struggle to identify and work effectively on the right stuff and avoid being consumed by things that don't really make a difference. Based on front-line experience and extensive reading, Marshall offers these pointers:

• *Identify a few "big rocks."* In his book, *First Things First* (1996), Stephen Covey tells the story of a time management expert who put three big rocks into a mason jar and asked his listeners if it was full. Sure, they said. He then poured in a bucket of gravel and asked again. Probably not, was the response. He then poured in sand, and finally water. The moral? If you don't put the big rocks in first, your time will be filled with smaller things, and you'll never get to what matters most. "The key," says Covey, "is not to prioritize what's on your schedule, but to schedule your priorities."

So, what are the big rocks for principals? Marshall offers the following list, saying that it's possible to focus effectively on only two or three, and those need to be chosen after a careful diagnosis of the school's situation.

- Mission: Staff, students, and parents know that the goal is to get all students on track for college and career success.
- Climate: The school is safe, respectful, and culturally competent.

- Learning goals: Each teacher is working toward clear, detailed, rigorous, manageable state-aligned end-of-year student learning outcomes.
- Resources: Teachers have high-quality materials and tools.
- Informative data: Teacher teams use both on-the-spot and interim assessment results to continuously improve instruction, give students feedback, and reteach.
- Safety nets: Struggling students get prompt, effective support, both academic and non-academic, inside and outside regular school hours.
- Supervision and evaluation: Teachers get frequent, honest feedback on their performance, all keyed to what's producing student learning (and what's not).
- Professional growth: Teachers are constantly improving their craft through individual, small-group, and whole-staff activities—all informed by student learning results.
- Hiring: Every staff vacancy is filled with a top-notch performer.
- Parent involvement: Parents are optimally involved in their children's education.

"Once you've put your lean, mean strategic plan in place," says Marshall, "it's much easier to say no to off-mission activities, to be present for students and staff members, and to roll with the punches (because there will still be those crazy days)."

• *Set clear expectations.* It's essential that all teachers have a clear idea of what their students must know and be able to do by the end of the year, as well as schoolwide guidelines on which discipline infractions must be referred to the office and which must be handled by teachers.

• *Decide on a planning system.* "The tug of H.S.P.S. is so constant and so inexorable that principals need a foolproof ritual to bring year-end goals down to the ground level," says Marshall. The best time managers have a system for organizing priorities by the year, the month, the week, and the day—and a weekly planning time is essential. There also has to be a portable daily format that reminds the principal of the big rocks as well as daily obligations. At the end of most days, only half of these things will have been checked off—and then it's time to think about what's really important and plan for the next day.

• *Schedule key meetings.* "People are busy," says Marshall. "Students are demanding. There's always too much to do." If key meetings aren't in everyone's calendars, they won't happen. Especially important are weekly meetings of grade-level and subject-area teacher teams, where the all-important work of planning curriculum units and looking at student work and assessment data takes place.

• *Write it down.* "The challenge for principals is remembering and acting on the myriad items that flood their brains every day," says Marshall. It's essential to have a system for recording things and following up—otherwise the leader's credibility with teachers, students, and parents will plummet, and the stress level will spike. Some suggestions:

- Wear practical clothes that have pockets for a pen and paper or a holster for an all-purpose electronic device. Some women's fashions are unhelpful (no pockets!), and many men refuse to put anything in their shirt pockets after hearing junior-high-school peers called nerds. Marshall's advice to the men: Get over it!

- Consider writing must-remember items on different index cards so they are pre-sorted at the end of the day (e-mails on one, staff memo ideas on another, etc.).

- Attack in-basket items every hour and/or apply a fifteen-second rule: if it can't be signed, delegated, filed, or thrown away in that amount of time, put it in the pile for late afternoon or evening. "During the day," says Marshall of his years as a principal, "I was a people person, not a paper pusher."

- Do e-mail in efficient bursts early in the morning and late in the afternoon. "The beauty of e-mail is that it's asynchronous," says Marshall. "You can answer at your convenience (but hopefully within twenty-four hours)." The key to sanity is not using the audible signal that announces the arrival of each new e-mail (it's not a ringing phone!) and resisting the urge to stay on top of e-mails (on your desktop computer or smartphone) during the day. One way to signal this approach to colleagues is to always have an automatic response message on your computer: "I'm in classrooms during school hours and check e-mail each weekday afternoon after 3:00 p.m. If your message is urgent, please call me at (617) 555-0105."

- Be aware of the areas in which you're likely to fall victim to PAUT (Putting Aside Unpleasant Tasks). "Be honest: what are the things that you hate to do and creatively avoid?" asks Marshall. Financial stuff? Notes from upset people? Filing? Once you're clear on what they are, analyze why and develop a system for forcing yourself to do them—and reward yourself when they're done.

• *Delegate, delegate, delegate.* Some principals have the urge to do everything themselves and can't stand when things aren't done just right. "The key to long-range sanity and effectiveness," says Marshall, "is hiring good people, nurturing them, and refraining from micromanagement.… The goal is clear: teachers handling instruction and virtually all discipline problems, teacher teams using data to continuously improve teaching and learning, counselors preventing or dealing with students' emotional problems, custodians handling the physical plant, students taking increasing responsibility for their own learning—and the principal freed up to orchestrate the whole process and focus relentlessly on the big rocks (while occasionally picking up trash in the corridors)." Marshall also believes that teachers and principals should be pulled from classrooms and schools as little as possible and that it's important for the principal to be physically present as students enter the building in the morning, for at least one lunch period, and when students leave in the afternoon.

• *Get into classrooms.* Conventional, announced teacher evaluations have four built-in flaws, says Marshall: They don't give principals a very accurate picture of day-to-day instruction; they put a premium on pleasing the boss, not on long-term student learning; they rarely improve teaching and learning; and they are so daunting and time-consuming that they prevent principals from being in classrooms on a regular basis. "Except for gathering evidence to dismiss an ineffective teacher," he writes, "conventional evaluation is a poor use of a principal's valuable time." But what's the alternative? Marshall suggests mini-observations—two to three short, unannounced classroom visits a day with a candid, informal face-to-face feedback conversation with each teacher within twenty-four hours. This creates hundreds of substantive conversations about teaching and learning each year, keeps the principal in close touch with what's really happening in classrooms, and saves time and energy for the biggest rock of them all—orchestrating a low-stakes process of teacher teams using interim assessment data to continuously improve teaching and learning.

• *Avoid time-wasters.* "A key to committing time to the right stuff is preventing or deflecting time-consuming crises and activities," says Marshall. Walking down a corridor when he was principal, Marshall once overheard a teacher utter the word "jackass," but was too distracted to follow up. The price for not addressing this immediately was more than twenty hours of wasted time dealing with the fallout when an angry parent stormed into the school the next day and had to be restrained from punching out the teacher for calling her daughter a jackass. "It's truly astonishing how much time a screw-up can consume," says Marshall ruefully. Other ways to cut down on wasted time include: organized meeting agendas and crisp closure; multi-tasking (within reason); and being out and about and spending very little time in the office for those frequent *Got-a-minute?* drop-ins. "A sitting principal is a sitting duck," he says.

• *Take care of yourself.* Burning out is not a good leadership strategy, says Marshall: "Good time management includes knowing your limits; planning for the long haul; and finding ways to fuel your physical, emotional, mental, and spiritual energy." (Patterson, 2007) This means exercising regularly (three times a week is plenty); eating the right foods (breakfast being the most important meal); getting enough sleep; carving out regular times for relaxation and fun (e.g., a movie most Friday nights); building a support system; and orchestrating small wins (success boosts optimism and energy).

• *Take stock.* Regularly evaluate your progress in the areas above, suggests Marshall. Effective practices will translate into better teaching and learning throughout the school.

"The Big Rocks: Priority Management for Principals" by Kim Marshall in *Principal Leadership* (Middle and High School Editions), March 2008 (Vol. 8, #7, pp. 16–22), summarized in Marshall Memo 225.

---

3   Spending More Time on the Right Stuff and Less on the Wrong Stuff

In this *Journal of Staff Development* article, William Powell and Ochan Kusuma-Powell (Education Across Frontiers) grapple with the challenge of leaders managing time in hyper-busy schools. "Unfortunately," they say, "busy-ness doesn't always equate with high-quality learning. In fact, once a school becomes too busy, that overload of activity often serves as a barrier to deep learning—for both students and adults. Some well-meaning schools suffer from organizational attention deficit disorder."

The authors believe Stephen Covey's four quadrants model (1989) is a helpful model for thinking about time and priorities. Picture a square divided into four quarters, with the vertical axis being urgent/not urgent, the horizontal axis important/not important.

- Quadrant 1 (top left): Important and urgent—pressing issues and problems, genuine crises, deadline-driven projects, health and safety issues;
- Quadrant 2 (top right): Important, not urgent—professional learning, inquiry, planning, structured reflection, preventive activities, relationship building, recreation;
- Quadrant 3 (bottom left): Urgent, not important—interruptions, some meetings, many phone calls, e-mails, and social media interactions;
- Quadrant 4 (bottom right): Not urgent, not important—trivia, some mail and e-mail, some phone calls, time wasters.

Quadrant 1 activities demand our attention and can be all-consuming, but spending too much time there leads to unhealthy stress and burnout. "Quadrants 3 and 4 are the domains of those who live irresponsible lives," say Powell and Kusuma-Powell. "The tasks in these arenas are simply not important, and, in Quadrant 3, the urgency is coming from someone else—not from our own deeply held values and beliefs." Quadrant 2 is the time management sweet spot where we get control of the torrent of urgent activities and focus on long-term accomplishments. It's hard to force Quadrant 2 activities into our calendars, but that's where "our actions are deeply aligned and congruent with our values. It is the home of responsibility and integrity."

Powell and Kusuma-Powell point to three supremely unproductive activities that take up far too much time in schools:

• *Giving students feedback that isn't used* – Conscientious teachers spend countless hours writing comments on students' papers and projects, only to see students glance at the grade and toss the work aside. "Teacher feedback that isn't used by students squanders billions of hours of teacher time each year," say the authors.

• *Poorly-run meetings* – "Many of the meetings we attend are enormous wastes of time," say Powell and Kusuma-Powell. Their suggestions: First, come to grips with the fact that some tasks, such as drafting a document, don't lend themselves to group collaboration (better to have one person create a draft, and then edit as a group). Second, meetings need to be guided by protocols "that focus the group's attention and provide structure to the conversation."

• *The traditional teacher-evaluation process* – Powell and Kusuma-Powell have asked hundreds of teacher groups if significant professional learning and growth has ever resulted from a formal evaluation. "The positive response is minuscule," they say. "Most teachers (and many administrators) have come to perceive the annual process of teacher evaluation as an enormous waste of time—something mindlessly forced upon the evaluator and the evaluated. If the purpose of traditional teacher evaluation is to develop professional learning that results in enhanced performance in the classroom, it has been a miserable failure. Not only has it not produced meaningful professional learning and not enhanced student learning, it has served to create dependency relationships and has infantilized teachers. It has also done much to undermine the vital culture of relational trust that must form the fabric of culture in high-quality schools."

Taking a hard look at time-wasting activities is difficult, conclude Powell and Kusuma-Powell. Many educators are too busy to step back and see the bigger picture. But, as Bob Garmston and Bruce Wellman have said, "Any group that is too busy to reflect on how it is working together is a group that is too busy to improve."

"Make the Most of Every Day" by William Powell and Ochan Kusuma-Powell in *Journal of Staff Development*, October 2015 (Vol. 36, #5, pp. 40–43, 46), summarized in Marshall Memo 610.

Systems

4   Defining and Protecting School Leaders' Core Work

In this article in *The Principal Center*, former principal Justin Baeder weighs in on the perennial issue of work-life balance for school leaders. "Evidence is starting to emerge that stress isn't just endemic to leadership," he says, "—it's an epidemic .... Many hard-working educators seem to feel a strong sense of guilt around the idea of self-care, as if a 'whatever it takes' attitude toward student learning rules out any effort to limit one's own stress." This is a formula for overwork and burnout. To have a positive impact on student learning over time, says Baeder, principals need to pace themselves as professionals, not damage their health by acting like heroes.

An interesting parallel is what has happened in firefighting, a line of work with a long history of heroism. Rushing into burning buildings, carrying out gasping victims, and dousing raging fires—all this epitomizes bravery and self-sacrifice. But starting in the middle of the twentieth century, firefighters turned to a much more effective way to save lives: prevention. Firefighters now spend most of their time visiting schools, supervising fire drills, and checking on sprinkler and alarm systems, fire doors, and smoke detectors. According to Steven Pinker in his book, *Enlightenment Now* (Viking, 2018), firefighters now see a burning building every other year; 96 percent of 911 calls to fire stations are for cardiac arrests and other medical emergencies, and most of the rest are for small fires. "Professionalism outperforms heroism, every time," says Baeder. "It's not flashy, but it works far better." So what's the equivalent in the world of schools?

• *Define and protect the leader's work.* That means staying focused on a well-defined leadership agenda designed to maximize student learning and having systems to prevent and deal with things that pull principals away from the core work. "If you're fighting fires all day, every day," says Baeder, "it's time to step back and look at the system you're dealing with. Do you have a wooden building with no sprinklers, metaphorically speaking? Are you plagued with perpetual emergencies that could and should be prevented by proactive leadership?"

One example is substitute teachers—calling them, assigning them, dealing with problems when they can't handle classes, covering classes yourself when there aren't enough subs or they arrive late. Baeder suggests putting some serious time into solving the problem up front: consulting colleagues in other schools who have a better system; recruiting a strong pool of subs; getting a staff member to train and handle subs; and delegating the daily business of calling and assigning replacement teachers to a competent person in the office.

"Ninety percent of schools have already done this," says Baeder, "and you can too. In fact, we have the knowledge and the ability to solve virtually every problem that's currently stressing principals out. The key to sharing that knowledge and implementing it everywhere is to drop the pretention of heroism. We must instead adopt a mindset of professionalism, stop tolerating the endless cycle of burning buildings, and install the 'sprinkler systems' we need."

• *Build low walls with gates.* If you don't protect your core work from all the other agendas that compete for your time, says Baeder, you won't be effective for students. Working with principals over the last decade, he's noticed that "the most overwhelmed and stressed-out principals seem to be in a constant state of emergency. It's not just that they're dealing with a few emergencies. It's that *everything* is an emergency all the time." But in other schools, the same phenomena aren't emergencies; they're handled by systems. In the school where Baeder was principal, for example, there was already a good system for handling substitutes before he arrived—a combination of technology, delegated responsibilities, and resources that made subs "a permanently solved problem" that rarely demanded his attention.

Baeder likes the analogy of a low wall around a pasture. When teachers needed a substitute, they connected with the school's online SubFinder system. If that didn't arrange for a sub, they called the school's office manager, who worked her magic with glitches in the automated system. If that failed, teachers could "jump over the wall" and bring the problem to him. Importantly, the "wall" was low enough that Baeder could see what was on the other side and intervene if necessary. The result: subs took very little of his time.

• *Designate exception-handlers.* Of course, not all problems can be solved with systems. How can principals keep from being pulled off agenda by unique situations that demand an immediate response? An example: there's a traffic-flow issue out front at dismissal time. This kind of problem could come straight to the principal, but a better process (unless it's a real emergency) is asking the safety committee to address it at the next meeting. "Again, the 'wall' protecting our time shouldn't be so high that we're fully insulated from every issue," says Baeder. "But the wall should gently guide issues to the right 'gate'.... 'Let's put that on the agenda' is a magical phrase. It shows responsiveness and concern, but also a disciplined, measured response—you're not dropping everything in response to someone else's issue."

Another example: a parent comes to the principal and says, "My kid is being bullied. What are you going to do?" The best scenario is that the school has a PBIS program in place and there's a structured response ready to be implemented—a "gate" to which the principal can direct the parent. If such a program isn't in place, the principal's work is getting a program up and running, which will take time now but pays big dividends in the long run. That's the macro work that prevents lots of inefficient micro stopgaps. "Again," says Baeder, "think of these as low walls … to keep people from dumping too many of their issues on us too easily. Some issues are big enough to get over them, and interrupt you immediately, like if there's a fight, or a serious complaint about a teacher, or some other emergency. But other issues aren't big enough to go over the wall, so you route them to the 'gate.' They walk around for a bit, come to a gate, and try to get in."

Does this sound bureaucratic? Sure, but it's bureaucracy in the best sense of the word—systems to get routine things done efficiently. It seems bureaucratic when the fire marshal comes around with a clipboard and scolds a principal for using door stops on fire doors and asks to see the fire drill logs. "Would it be more 'heroic' to carry people out of burning buildings?" asks Baeder. "Absolutely … but which saves more lives—the professional process, or the heroic rescue?"

• *Keep regular working hours.* Even with good systems and low walls in place, leaders still get a lot of other people's issues. That's because there's one leader and lots of stakeholders, and it's very easy for them to buttonhole the leader or send an e-mail. "It's important to recognize that this work is endless," says Baeder. "There is no hope of ever being free from this work, or ever finishing it all …. You're the bottleneck in your organization. So how can you keep these pressures from eating you alive?"

Step one, says Baeder, is recognizing that, "If you're willing to stay at school until 9:00 p.m. every night, your work will oblige you by expanding to fill whatever time you give it …. If you feel guilty leaving at 5:00 p.m., just remember this: you're never going to get everything done, and the longer you work, the more time you waste. You'll approach each additional task with less mental energy, and you'll be working on less and less important tasks as the evening wears on. Do the most important work first, and give yourself a hard deadline for going home. You'll work faster and more efficiently, you'll prioritize more rigorously, and you'll be more effective."

• *Don't use text messages for tasks.* In recent years, there's been a big increase in texting in professional contexts, accompanied by less use of e-mail, which Baeder believes is a big reason for leaders' stress and overwork. Texts are great for quick questions, he says, but a very poor way to manage work. Why?

- Texts can't be marked as unread.
- They're difficult to forward or copy people on.
- They're difficult to manage on your computer and other devices.
- They don't integrate well with productivity tools like Outlook and Google Calendar.

The solution: Don't let people text you at 10:00 p.m. and expect an immediate response, and don't let people text you random requests that you'll struggle to keep track of. Institute a clear policy that people may e-mail you if they need you to do something, and model this by using e-mail the same way yourself.

"How Instructional Leaders Can Create Healthy Work-Life Balance" by Justin Baeder in *The Principal Center*, March 2018, summarized in Marshall Memo 729.

---

5. Managers: Don't Let Subordinates Delegate Work to You!

In this *Harvard Business Review* article, management consultants William Oncken Jr. and Donald Wass tackle the perennial time management challenge of delegation. They start by delineating three types of work.

- Boss-imposed: A manager can't ignore these tasks without immediate consequences.
- System-imposed: These must be accomplished, but the penalties for not doing them are less direct and swift.
- Self-imposed: Some of these are discretionary, but some are imposed by subordinates.

The manager's goal, say Oncken and Wass, is to minimize or eliminate subordinate-imposed work, get control of boss- and system-imposed work, and maximize discretionary time.

The big problem, however, is that subordinates have a way of shifting work to the boss. "Most managers spend much more subordinate-imposed time than they even faintly realize," say the authors. How does this happen? A manager is walking along a corridor and encounters a subordinate. "Good morning," says the underling. "By the way, we've got a problem. You see …" The manager quickly realizes two things: he knows enough to get involved, but doesn't know enough to solve the problem on the spot. "So glad you brought this up," he says. "I'm in a rush right now. Meanwhile, let me think about it and I'll let you know."

What just happened? Before this encounter, the monkey (the problem) was on the subordinate's back. When the subordinate said, "We've got a problem," the monkey was astride both backs. After the encounter, it was on the manager's back. "Subordinate-imposed time begins the moment a monkey successfully executes a leap from the back of a subordinate to the back of his superior," say Oncken and Wass, "and does not end until the monkey is returned to its proper owner for care and feeding. In accepting the monkey, the manager has voluntarily assumed a position subordinate to his subordinate …. The manager has accepted a responsibility from his subordinate, and the manager has promised him a progress report. The subordinate, to make sure the manager does not miss the point, will later stick his head in the manager's office and cheerily query, 'How's it coming?' (This is called 'supervision.')"

In this and countless other interactions, the monkey starts as a joint problem but quickly ends up on the manager's back. Pretty soon the manager is overwhelmed by subordinate-imposed tasks that require follow-up, develops a reputation as a bottleneck, takes weeks to get to things, gets stressed-out, makes his family unhappy by working all weekend, and leaves subordinates spinning their wheels waiting for direction. "Worst of all," say Oncken and Wass, "the reason the manager cannot make any of these 'next moves' is that his time is almost entirely eaten up in meeting his own boss-imposed and system-imposed requirements. To get control of these, he needs discretionary time that is in turn denied him when he is preoccupied with all these monkeys. The manager is caught in a vicious cycle."

A wise manager, say Oncken and Wass, will call each subordinate in, put the monkey on the table between them, "and figure out together how the next move might conceivably be the subordinate's. For certain monkeys, this will take some doing. The subordinate's next move may be so elusive that the manager may decide—just for now—merely to let the monkey sleep on the subordinate's back overnight and have him return with it at an appointed time the next morning to continue the joint quest for a more substantive move by the subordinate. (Monkeys sleep just as soundly overnight on subordinates' backs as on superiors')." But most subordinates will leave the manager's office with monkey firmly on their backs and a deadline to produce an answer. The manager might use some of his newfound discretionary time strolling around, sticking his head into people's offices asking, "How's it coming?"

The point, say the authors, is to develop *initiative* in subordinates. They won't take it until they *have* it. If the manager has all those monkeys on his back, "he can kiss his discretionary time goodbye." Here are the five degrees of initiative that people can exercise in an organization, from the lowest to the highest:

- Wait to be told what to do.
- Ask what to do.
- Recommend, then take appropriate action.
- Act, but advise at once.
- Act on one's own, then routinely report.

People working at the lowest levels have no control over their time. Those working at the third, fourth, and fifth levels can increasingly manage their own time. "The manager's job, in relation to his subordinate's initiatives, is twofold," say Oncken and Wass. "First, to outlaw the use of initiatives 1 and 2, thus giving his subordinates no choice but to learn and master 'Completed staff work'; then, to see that for each problem leaving his office there is an agreed-upon level of initiative assigned to it, in addition to the agreed-upon time and place of the next manager-subordinate conference."

"Get control over the timing and content of what you do," conclude Oncken and Wass. Eliminate subordinate-imposed time. Use the newfound discretionary time to see to it that subordinates take the initiative. And then get control over boss-imposed and system-imposed work. "The result of all this is that the manager will increase his leverage, which will in turn enable him to multiply, without theoretical limit, the value of each hour that he spends in managing management time."

"Management Time: Who's Got the Monkey?" by William Oncken, Jr. and Donald Wass in *Harvard Business Review*, November/December 1974 (Vol. 52, #6, pp. 75–80), summarized in Marshall Memo 441.

Techniques

6 Mastering Workflow

In this article in *The Atlantic*, James Fallows admits that he was a highly disorganized person who nonetheless got things done. A few years ago, he heard about David Allen, a consultant on time management and personal organization, and was intrigued enough to read his book, *Getting Things Done: The Art of Stress-Free Productivity* (Penguin revised edition, 2015), attend several seminars, and interview Allen and a number of people who had been through his program. Despite initial skepticism, Fallows found Allen's ideas very helpful and was even successful at digging through the archeological layers of stuff on his own desk.

Allen's aim is not to help people get more work done but to get them to feel less anxious and racked with guilt about what they can and cannot do. This comes from his belief that the difference between done and undone tasks is more stressful than we realize. When our ancestors worked (harvesting wheat, chopping wood, etc.) there was a sense of completion and work produced visible results every day. For modern people "each day is a fog of constantly accumulating open-ended obligations, with little barrier between the personal and the professional and few clear signals that you are actually 'done.' E-mail pours in. Hallway conversations end with 'I'll get back to you.' The cell phone rings. The newspaper tells you about movies you'd like to see, recipes you'd like to try, places you'd like to go. There are countless things that everyone really 'should' do more of—exercise, read, spend time with the family, have lunch with a contact, be 'better' at work. The modern condition is to be overwhelmed, … to feel not just tired but chronically anxious because so many things you have at some level committed to do never get done." (Fallows paraphrasing Allen.) Here is Fallows's summary of six key points from Allen's program:

• *Get everything out of your head by making a complete list of everything you want to, have to, or are expected to do.* Only when you are sure that all your obligations are written down and retrievable can you stop waking up at 3:00 a.m. A small-scale example of this principle is a date-book. Most people don't worry about forgetting appointments because they write them in their date-books and know that they will check their books frequently. Allen says that busy people need a "leak-proof collection system" for *all* their obligations—a way in which all the old stuff and any new thoughts, chores, and plans get *written down*. He recommends carrying a pad, smartphone, or some other device and recording ideas the minute they pop into our heads—the errand to run, the call to make, etc. Fallows has started doing this himself, thinks it's helped a lot and reduced his anxiety level, and says he now gets nervous when people tell him they're going to do something and don't write it down.

• *Identify the "next action" toward a demanding goal.* This is Allen's version of the homily about a journey of a thousand miles beginning with a single step. "The more important a goal is (fix your marriage, get a better job)," says Fallows, "the easier it is to procrastinate, because people don't know just where to start. Allen emphasizes that almost any undertaking involves a specific and manageable *next* thing to do." Often this is as simple as making a phone call or setting up an appointment. Thinking in terms of next actions and listing them all "reduces each new challenge or commitment to a series of specific steps. As a corollary [Allen] says that meetings should never end without an agreement on what next step each participant is expected to take."

• *Set up reminders and tricks to increase the chances that all the little to-dos actually get done.* What do people do when they want to be *absolutely* sure they don't forget to bring something with them in the morning? They put it in front of the door so they can't miss it on the way out. Grouping tasks by context (where and when you might actually do them), rather than by their importance to you, is a basic difference between Allen's system and Stephen Covey's "four quadrants" approach. Covey recommends that we match our long-range goals with our hour-by-hour activities in order to spend as much time as possible doing the most important tasks. Allen says that his system is more flexible and less likely to be swamped by e-mail, phone calls, interruptions, and new tasks.

• *Develop the habit of review.* Allen recommends a regular "weekly review" of an hour or so to go over the list of all long-term projects and short-term next actions. "… If you apply the habit of looking over everything once a week," says Fallows, "you can feel comfortable about never being more than a week behind in tending to important matters."

• *Apply the "two-minute rule" to over-the-transom stuff.* When you are going through mail, phone messages, e-mails, etc., do immediately the things that can be completed in less than two minutes. Allen explains: "That's more or less the point where it starts taking longer to store and track an item than to deal with it the first time it's in your hands. In other words, it's the efficiency cutoff. If the thing's not important enough to be done, throw it away. But if it is important enough that you are *ever* going to do it [and it can be done in less than two minutes], the efficiency factor should come into play, which means doing it right now. This rule is magic."

• *Get your e-mail in-box back to "empty" each day.* This doesn't mean that every single e-mail is fully dealt with by the end of the day. It means that those that could be done in under two minutes are answered and filed, that the Viagra ads are thrown away, and that important items are printed out or stored in an "Action" folder on the desktop—some place where you're sure you'll get to them at a time you've blocked out. Allen says that this approach is the key to keeping e-mail under control.

The goal of Allen's overall system is to reduce stress, and Fallows says it works (as did the people he interviewed who had been through the program). Fallows also likes Allen's recommendation to look at life from different vantage points at different points in the day and week: the "runway level" at times when we're applying the two-minute rule, the fifty-thousand-foot level, where we're contemplating the meaning of life. The loftiest level interests Allen the most at this point in his life: "My perspective is that until you have fully fulfilled your destiny as a human spirit on the planet, you'll probably be in some level of stress." Fallows describes himself shying away from this line of thinking in a conversation with Allen and returning to the safer realm of e-mail management. "You want to operate just at the runway level?" replied Allen. "That's fine! Let's see how things can get done with the least effort. But if you're interested in where all this came from, where we came from, then we can have another conversation." Fallows's reaction: "I'll put it on my list."

"Organize Your Life!" by James Fallows, *Atlantic Monthly*, July/August 2004 (Vol. 294, #1, pp. 171–176), summarized in Marshall Memo 41.

7 The Psychology of Procrastination

In this article in *The New Yorker*, James Surowiecki explores the reasons for procrastination, which he calls "a basic human impulse." The word comes from Latin—"to put off for tomorrow"—and consists of not doing what we think we should be doing—"a mental contortion that surely accounts for the great psychic toll the habit takes on people," he says. "This is the perplexing thing about procrastination: although it seems to involve avoiding unpleasant tasks, indulging in it generally doesn't make people happy." And it seems to be creating increasing anxiety in the modern era, judging by more-frequent references to it in literature and popular culture. Procrastination can be costly: Americans waste hundreds of millions of dollars by filing their tax returns late and forgo vast sums by not getting around to signing up for a retirement plan.

The basic problem is that we tend to do what is in front of us rather than what is out of sight, however positive and attractive future rewards may be. "Our desires shift as the long run becomes the short run," says Surowiecki. There's also the "planning fallacy"—the tendency to underestimate the time it will take to complete a task by ignoring how long similar tasks have taken in the past. "When I was writing this piece, for example, I had to take my car into the shop, I had to take two unanticipated trips, a family member fell ill, and so on," he says. "Each of these events was, strictly speaking, unexpected, and each took time away from my work. But they were really just the kinds of problems you predictably have to deal with in everyday life. Pretending I wouldn't have any interruptions to my work was a typical illustration of the planning fallacy."

Avoidance and denial aren't the only reasons for procrastination. We often tend to do things "whose only allure is that they aren't what we should be doing," says Surowiecki. "My apartment, for instance, has rarely looked tidier than it does at the moment."

Another cause of procrastination is "lack of confidence, sometimes alternating with unrealistic dreams of heroic success," he continues. Civil War General George McClellan was a classic example of this. He dithered and dallied, planned incessantly, and constantly asked for more troops and better equipment. "Viewed this way," says Surowiecki, "procrastination starts to look less like a question of mere ignorance than like a complex mixture of weakness, ambition, and inner conflict." It's as though there were different parts of ourselves debating with each other—"jostling, contending, and bargaining for control …. In that sense, the first step to dealing with procrastination isn't admitting that you have a problem. It's admitting that your 'yous' have a problem."

Surowiecki says the philosopher Don Ross framed the problem correctly: "For Ross, the various parts of the self are all present at once, constantly competing and bargaining with one another—one that wants to work, one that wants to watch television, and so on. The key, for Ross, is that although the television-watching self is interested only in watching TV, it's interested in watching TV not just now but also in the future. This means that it can be bargained with: working now will let you watch more television down the road. Procrastination, in this reading, is a result of a bargaining process gone wrong."

The idea of the divided self suggests the best ways to deal with procrastination, says Surowiecki: employing "external tools and techniques to help the parts of ourselves that want to work." The classic example is Ulysses ordering his men to tie him to the mast of his ship so he wouldn't be able to steer into the rocks when the Sirens' song wafted their way. Similarly, Victor Hugo would write in the nude and have his valet hide his clothes so Hugo couldn't go outside while he was supposed to be writing. A contemporary example: a program that cuts off your Internet access for eight hours so you can focus on a project.

Another approach is trying to strengthen your will. "This isn't a completely fruitless task," says Surowiecki. "Much recent research suggests that will power is, in some ways, like a muscle and can be made stronger." But the same research says we have a limited supply of will power and it can be used up quite quickly. One experiment found that people who resisted the temptation to eat forbidden chocolate-chip cookies had less will power left when asked to persist with a challenging task.

Which brings us back to one of the most common external devices for dealing with procrastination: deadlines. Here's an interesting experiment: Students are required to complete three papers by the end of the semester. They can submit them all on the last day, or they can set three deadlines, with a grading penalty for missing any of them and no advantage for early submission. The rational thing is to stick with the end-of-semester deadline and hope to finish one or two of the papers early. But most students choose to set three deadlines. "This is the essence of the extended will," says Surowiecki. "Instead of trusting themselves, the students relied on an outside tool to make themselves do what they actually wanted to do."

A final way of dealing with procrastination is reframing the task in front of you. "Procrastination is driven, in part, by the gap between effort (what is required now) and reward (which you reap only in the future, if ever)," says Surowiecki. "So narrowing the gap, by whatever means necessary, helps." One way is to divide large, long-term projects into short-term projects with discrete deadlines. This is the approach recommended by time-management guru David Allen (author of *Getting Things Done*): "the vaguer the task, or the more abstract thinking it requires, the less likely you are to finish it." Reduce your choices, and you're more likely to make the right one.

Surowiecki closes with a confounding thought: sometimes we procrastinate because what we're supposed to be doing is not worth doing at all. So the deepest challenge is knowing which kind of procrastination we're confronted with: "the kind that's telling you that what you're supposed to be doing has, deep down, no real point," or the kind that's telling you to get to work and DO IT! "The procrastinator's challenge, and perhaps the philosopher's, too," says Surowiecki, "is to figure out which is which."

"Later: What Does Procrastination Tell Us About Ourselves?" by James Surowiecki in *The New Yorker*, October 11, 2010, summarized in Marshall Memo 491.

8 | The Virtues of Single-Tasking

In this *New York Times* article, Verena von Pfetten reviews some findings from the research on multitasking:

- Interruptions as brief as two or three seconds double the number of errors people make on a task they're performing.
- We have finite neural resources that are depleted every time we switch between activities, which can happen more than four hundred times a day.
- Multitasking is cognitively exhausting; it's one reason people feel tired by sundown.
- The more we multitask, the more distractible we are.

- Multitasking is self-reinforcing; the more we allow ourselves to be distracted, the more we feel the need to be distracted.
- Switching between activities decreases our enjoyment of any one of them.
- Having a cell phone in view markedly reduces empathy and rapport between two people having a conversation.
- The counterintuitive bottom line: multitaskers actually get less done.

What does all this imply? Von Pfetten defines *single-tasking* (sometimes called monotasking or unitasking): "Not the same as mindfulness, which focuses on emotional awareness, monotasking is a twenty-first-century term for what your high-school English teacher probably just called 'paying attention.'" Psychologists have documented a number of advantages to focusing on one thing, including the obverse of the list above: fewer errors, less distractibility, more enjoyment, deeper and more satisfying conversations, less fatigue, and improved productivity. "Almost any experience is improved by paying full attention to it," says author Kelly McGonigal. "Attention is one way your brain decides, 'Is this interesting? Is this worthwhile?'"

Very busy people—parents and teachers, for example—may find single-tasking challenging because they're constantly pulled in so many different directions. "In those cases, try monotasking in areas where you can," suggests von Pfetten, "—conversations with your children, reading a book in bed before going to sleep, dinner or drinks with friends." Exercise is also helpful for focusing. Another strategy is starting small, giving yourself just one morning a week to experience again what it's like to immerse yourself in one thing. And in conversations, concludes McGonigal, "Practice how you listen to people. Put down anything that's in your hands and turn all your attentional channels to the person who is talking. You should be looking at them, listening to them, and your body should be turned to them."

"Drop Everything and Read This" by Verena von Pfetten in *The New York Times*, May 1, 2016, summarized in Marshall Memo 638.

Professional Learning Suggestions for Chapter Two Managing Time for Impact

How Leaders at *Your* School Can Improve Time Management

It's one of the easiest things for school leaders to read about and yet one of the most difficult things to implement regularly: managing time! To ensure that the ideas in this chapter truly take root after you read them, below are two suggestions:

• Get *another leader* (a colleague) to commit to reading and engaging in the professional learning activities below in order to hold each other accountable, or

• For an extra boost in productivity at your school, conduct the professional learning activities below with your entire leadership/cabinet/district *team*. This way, instead of being the only leader who becomes skilled in time management, you can raise the productivity level of your entire leadership team. This will, in turn, greatly benefit your entire school.

I. Three Essential Time-Management Subskills to Master

While the articles in this section focus on different aspects of time management, three larger subskills emerge:

> A. The ability to prioritize what is most important
> B. The ability to organize tasks and get them done
> C. The ability to delegate and maximize the use of teams

With a colleague or team of leaders, discuss the difference between the three abilities above and how they interrelate.

Next, look back at the chapter and discuss how the varying approaches to time management fit into these three categories. Some of the approaches include:
  • (Article 1) William Conway's division of work into three categories as they apply to schools: *value-added work* (leads to improvement in student learning); *waste work* (doesn't

contribute to learning and could be avoided, like mistakes); and *necessary work* (keeps the school running, like ordering supplies)

- (Article 2) Kim Marshall's "big rocks" for principals (such as mission, climate, learning goals, etc.)

- (Article 3) Steven Covey's division of tasks into four quadrants (Quadrant 1: important and urgent; Quadrant 2: important, not urgent; Quadrant 3: urgent, not important; and Quadrant 4: not urgent, not important)

- (Article 4) Justin Baeder's ideas to define and protect the leader's work

- (Article 5) Oncken and Wass's goal to "get the monkey off your back" by helping subordinates develop initiative

- (Article 6) Having a system for being organized and getting things done, based on the ideas of David Allen

- (Article 8) The importance of engaging in "monotasking" rather than multitasking, as Verena von Pfetten suggests

II. Self-Assess Your Own Time Management Skills

Individually, have your leadership team members or just you and your accountable colleague assess your own time management skills by filling in Kim Marshall's Instructional Management Rubric (see Article 2) on the next page:

Instructional Management Rubric

Kim Marshall, revised 2016

	4 Highly Effective	3 Effective	2 Developing	1 Novice
A. **Focus**	I have a laser-like focus on student achievement and my strategic plan for the year.	I keep student achievement and my strategic plan in mind every day.	I periodically remind myself of my strategic plan and the goal of student achievement.	Each day is driven by events, not by my long-term goals.
B. **Planning**	I have an effective personal planning system for the year, month, week, and day.	I write down a list of what I want to accomplish each week and day.	I come to work with a list of what I want to accomplish that day.	I have a list in my head of what I want to accomplish each day but sometimes lose track.
C. **Monitoring**	I regularly evaluate progress toward my goals and work on continuous improvement.	I periodically review how I am doing on my weekly goals and try to do better.	I try to keep track of how I am doing on my goals.	I occasionally berate myself for not accomplishing my long-range goals.
D. **Expectations**	Staff know exactly what is expected of them in terms of classroom instruction and discipline.	Most of my staff know what is expected in terms of classroom instruction and discipline.	I often have to remind teachers of policies on instruction and discipline.	I am constantly reminding staff to use better procedures for instruction and discipline.
E. **Collaboration**	All key teams are scheduled and regularly do high-quality work together.	Key team meetings are scheduled and take place regulary.	Each month I have to schedule key meetings because they are not in people's calendars.	I call grade-level, curriculum, and other meetings when there is a crisis or an immediate need.
F. **Instruction**	I visit 2-3 classrooms a day and give face-to-face feedback to each teacher within 24 hours.	I get into some classrooms every day and give personal feedback to each teacher.	I try to get into classrooms as much as possible but many days I don't succeed.	I am so busy that I rarely visit classrooms.
G. **Follow-Up**	I have a foolproof system for writing things down, prioritizing, and following up.	I almost always write important things down and follow up on the most critical ones.	I try to write things down but am swamped by events and sometimes don't follow up.	I trust my memory to retain important tasks, but I sometimes forget and drop the ball.
H. **Delegation**	I have highly competent people in key roles and delegate maximum responsibility to them.	I give key staff people plenty of responsibility for key items.	I have trouble letting go and delegating a number of key tasks.	I end up doing almost everything myself.
I. **Prevention**	I have effective strategies for preventing or deflecting time-wasting crises and activities.	I am quite good at preventing or deflecting most time-wasting crises and activities.	I try to prevent them, but crises and time-wasters sometimes eat up large chunks of time.	Much of each day is consumed by crises and time-wasting activities.
J. **Balance**	I am sharp and fresh because I attend to family, friends, fun, exercise, nutrition, sleep, and vacations.	I am mostly successful in balancing work demands with healthy habits and a life outside school.	I'm not always attending to family, health, exercise, sleep, and vacations.	Work and/or personal life are suffering because I rarely exercise, don't sleep enough, and am in poor health.

Next, record your scores by subskill below:

- The ability to prioritize (enter the average of your scores on A. Focus, D. Expectations, and F. Instruction): _____
- The ability to organize tasks and get them done (enter the average of your scores on B. Planning and G. Follow-Up): _____
- The ability to delegate and maximize the use of teams (enter the average of your scores on E. Collaboration and H. Delegation): _____
- The ability to self-monitor and maintain a work-life balance (enter the average of your scores on C. Monitoring and J. Balance): _____

Based on your average scores for each of the four areas above, choose the professional learning activities below that best match the areas you would like to improve.

III. If You Need Improvement in Prioritizing
(A. Focus, D. Expectations, and F. Instruction)

A. Distinguish which tasks are highest priority for you as the leader.
You cannot choose to engage in the highest priority tasks if you do not know which tasks are most important.

With your colleague or leadership team, review the articles that address prioritization (Articles 1, 2, 3, and 5).

These articles each describe different ways to think about high-priority tasks (the Quadrants, "big rocks," etc.). Choose the one that makes the most sense to you, and then discuss and sort the tasks in the box below into different priority-level categories.

For example, here are the categories of tasks from Article 2:
> *Value-added work* (leads to improvement in student learning)
> *Waste work* (doesn't contribute to learning and could be avoided, like mistakes)
> *Necessary work* (keeps the school running, like ordering supplies)

Examine the following tasks, discuss them with your colleague/team and sort them into the proper categories.

Common School Leader Tasks

planning professional learning, ensuring buses run smoothly, addressing bullying, balancing the budget, going to the gym regularly, providing supports for struggling learners, dealing with complaints, finding substitute teachers, getting buy-in for the school mission, improving parent involvement, setting up systems for clear communication with staff, observing and coaching teachers, picking up litter from hallways, responding to parent complaints, infusing the school with technology, ordering supplies, developing a strong culture, dealing with traffic at dismissal time, supporting teacher teams, engaging in personal professional development, redoing a task because it was done improperly the first time, hiring, greeting families in the morning, ensuring even implementation of the discipline policy, scheduling, conducting meetings that consist of announcements

Value-added work	*Waste work*	*Necessary work*

B. Determine which activities currently take up most of your time.
It is hard to become more efficient if you don't know exactly how you are spending your time right now.

Have your leadership team or you and your colleague take a week to code all of your activities according to the six categories below from a large-scale study of principals' use of time (for more information about the study, see Marshall Memo 349 or access it here: https://web.stanford.edu/~sloeb/papers/Principal%20Time-Use%20%28revised%29.pdf)

(If you have a clear understanding of your time use and don't want to spend a week doing this, just rate yourself as high, medium, or low for each category.)

1. **Administration** – discipline, lunch duty, attendance, student records, compliance
2. **Organization Management** – budget, school facilities, school schedule, safety, managing non-instructional staff

3. **Day-to-Day Instruction** – observations, coaching, evaluations, feedback, PD, data-informed instruction
4. **Instructional Program** – summer school, afterschool, evaluating curriculum, using assessment results for program evaluation, planning PD
5. **Internal Relations** – interactions with staff, interactions with students, communicating with parents, attending school events (sports, arts, etc.)
6. **External Relations** – interactions with the community, interactions with the district, fundraising

---

Results from the study—how principals use their time:

27% on administration
21% on organization management
19% on other tasks—lunch, bathroom, transitions
15% on internal relations
7% on the instructional program
6% on day-to-day instruction
5% on external relations

After a week, discuss your own results with your colleague or your team. How do your results compare to the results from the study? How well do your results align with the tasks you want to prioritize?

C. Determine your priorities and bring them to life.
If you are not spending the most time on tasks that will improve student learning, now is the time to start.

Before meeting with your colleague or leadership team, gather some quantitative and qualitative (surveys, observations) data that will illuminate student learning gaps.

Next, come to the meeting prepared to think through the questions in the second column and create a plan in the third column in the following chart. For example, if the data reveal that vocabulary is a particularly weak area across the school, you may want to create a SMART goal for this area, focus every PD session on this topic, and schedule biweekly coaching meetings with teachers that include vocabulary as a standing agenda item.

From the Instructional Management Rubric	Think	Plan
A. **Focus** – laser-like focus on student achievement	Based on quantitative and qualitative data, what is your student achievement goal?	Write your goal here:
D. **Expectations** – staff know exactly what is expected to meet the student achievement goal	How will you convey this goal to everyone? How will you help teachers learn what they need to do to meet the goal?	Write your plan here:
F. **Instruction** – leader observes for movement toward student achievement goal in 2-3 classes a day and gives teachers feedback and coaching in this area	How will you ensure that you focus on this goal when observing and debriefing with teachers?	Write your plan here:

IV. If You Need Improvement in Organizing Tasks and Getting Them Done (B. Planning and G. Follow-Up)

Sometimes time management issues stem from being unsure about priorities (addressed above), and sometimes they result from not having a clear organizational system. Given the demands of the job of school leader, it is impossible to truly be effective without being organized. The activities below will help.

A. Discuss your current organizational system.

With your colleague or leadership team, take a few minutes to reread Article 7 (Mastering Workflow) in the chapter. Next, discuss how you currently stay organized and which parts of the article sparked ideas for you.

B. Prepare to fully implement an organizational system.

If your leadership team has time to delve further into David Allen's system, you should consider conducting a study group with his book, *Getting Things Done: The Art of Stress-Free Productivity*. As an alternative, you can start now with the following simplified version.

At the heart of the organizational system described in Fallows's article are four key (CORE) steps:

__Capture__ – You must collect every task you need to complete in one place.

__Organize__ – You need to organize these tasks in a logical way.

__Review__ – You need to regularly review these tasks so you know when to do what.

__Execute__ – You need to actually *do* the tasks!

Here are a few activities to do with your team to get started on the first two parts of the system:

__Capture__ – You may want to have leaders research different electronic tools so they can discuss the choices that exist. Or they can simply discuss the tools they currently use to capture every task. Once you have done this, have everyone on the team commit to just *one* capturing tool and record commitments below:

School Leader Name	Which tool will you use to capture all to-do items-- paper (like index cards or notebook) or electronic (apps like OneNote or Notability)?

__Organize__ – The goal is to be able to know where to put every task. David Allen suggests that you organize all tasks into one of the eight "buckets" listed below. Have each member of your leadership team learn about two of these categories (from Allen's book) and what is needed to set them up. At the next meeting, jigsaw and have everyone share what they've learned and make sure everyone knows what to do to set up each bucket.

Next Actions – These include all of the one-step actions we need to take by ourselves, such as call Jim Smith, draft ideas for the conference, etc. Most of us have around 50–150 of these items.

Calendar – The calendar should *only* be used to remind you of those items that are time-specific or day-specific (can happen any time but *must* be on a certain day). Your to-do items should *not* appear here (they belong in *Next Actions* above) otherwise they cloud what absolutely must get done on each day.

Waiting For – When you decide to delegate tasks, this list will remind you of what you are waiting for and from whom.

Projects List – This is a list of all projects, requiring more than one action step, that can be accomplished in a year. This is simply an index of the *names* of the projects, such as: get new staff member on board, update will, upgrade computers, etc.

Project Materials – While the *Projects List* is the list of the *names* of the projects, this category includes the actual file folders or computer files that will hold all of the materials for each project.

Trash – These are the things you want to quickly throw away, delete, shred, or recycle.

Someday/Maybe – This is a list of useful and inspiring items you might do someday. Let's say you read an article that gives you an idea, but you can't do it now. That idea goes on this list. It could be anything from *Learn Spanish* to *Set up a foundation*.

Reference – You probably receive a lot of useful information that you would like to reference someday. Whether you receive a menu for a local café or an article to keep on file, you need to set up a way to store and file these items—both paper and electronic—that can be easily accessed when required.

Next, do the following activity so that everyone understands exactly which tasks fit in which categories.

As a group, simulate what happens with a few sample to-do items. For example, you pass a teacher in the hall and she says, "You had mentioned that interesting Marshall Memo article about writing across the curriculum—would you mind sending it to me?" As a group, discuss the path this task would take. (You would "capture" it on paper or electronically, then later you would need to decide if takes less than two minutes—remember the article?—and just do it or put it on your *Next Actions* list.)

Have the group do the same for these tasks—which buckets would these land in?
1) You need to ask your administrative assistant to fill out a form due to the district by Friday.
2) You need to co-plan next Monday's staff PD with your Assistant Principal.
3) You would like to research new ways to recruit teachers for next year's hiring season.

V. If You Need Improvement in Delegation and Maximizing the Use of Teams (E. Collaboration and H. Delegation)

Clearly delineate roles and responsibilities.
Several of the articles (Marshall, Article 2; Baeder, Article 4; and Oncken and Wass, Article 5) mention *delegation* as an essential key in helping school leaders manage their time. However, part

of why leaders don't delegate is that they don't have a clear enough idea of whose wheelhouse a task belongs in.

Take some time before the school year begins to meet with your leadership team and outline *the major responsibilities* of each school leader and each team at your school. For example, if there is a Green Team at your school, when the district outlines new recycling policies you can delegate these to the team rather than adding them to your responsibilities.

Use the chart below to map out all responsibilities. In addition, decide how the leadership team will divide up oversight for these responsibilities *and* how the rest of the school community will be informed of these responsibilities. (It will save a lot of time if parents go directly to the Green Team rather than schedule a meeting with you to discuss ideas to celebrate Earth Day!)

Person/ Team	Major responsibilities	Who from the leadership team will regularly check in with this person/team?	How will someone on the leadership team *convey* these responsibilities to the person/team and the school?
Seventh-grade math team	-Map out curriculum pacing maps -Provide support for struggling students during intervention time -etc., etc.	Math department chair	Math department chair will meet with the seventh grade math team once a month and will post a list of the team's responsibilities in the math department and on the school's website
Etc.			
Etc.			

Chapter Three: Leaders' Emotional Intelligence

Organizational cultures that cling to the ideal of an all-knowing, omnicompetent executive will pay a high cost in time, resources, and progress, and will be sending the message to managers that it is better to hide their confusion than to address it openly and constructively.
—BARRY JENTZ AND JEROME MURPHY

In addition to nuts-and-bolts management skills, school leaders need a broad repertoire of interpersonal and intrapersonal skills and the wisdom to match them to different situations. They have to be able to do everything from facing down an adult bully to helping a kindergartner deal with the loss of a pet rabbit. The articles in this chapter address four aspects of emotional intelligence: what we want in leaders; building trust; handling stress; and recognizing cognitive biases.

Desirable Qualities – Daniel Goleman believes the key to high performance is the ability to recognize and manage our own feelings, be aware of the inner life of others, and skillfully manage the emotional life of the workplace. Tasha Eurich also argues for the benefits of developing emotional intelligence and describes two ways to know ourselves: introspection, and an awareness of how others see us. Todd Kashdan, David Disabato, Fallon Goodman, and Carl Naughton report that curiosity, an important dimension of emotional intelligence, has several dimensions, including interest in others, wonder about the world, and the quest for solutions. And David Brooks describes the qualities of people he truly admires—humility, self-knowledge, devotion to a noble cause—and contrasts those with the "résumé virtues" embraced by many, himself included.

Building Trust – Barry Jentz and Jerome Murphy say that when we face a crisis and are uncertain what to do, the best approach is to say we're confused and then structure interactions with colleagues to make sense of the situation and think through solutions. Amy Cuddy, Matthew Kohut, and Jon Neffinger argue that in initial encounters with colleagues leaders should project warmth, then understated displays of strength and competence. John Ritchie suggests a moral compass to guide principals through the job's outsized expectations, drama, exhilaration, fear, confusion, and loneliness. His north star: creating the best possible environment for teaching and learning.

Dealing with Stress – David Holmes has ten pieces of advice for dealing with the relentless demands of school leadership; they include reaching out to a few trusted colleagues, getting enough sleep, and engaging in professional reading and writing. John Tierney reports on the phenomenon of "decision fatigue"—how our ability to make good decisions is degraded when we are overloaded with choices and hungry or tired.

Cognitive Quirks – Jena Pincott says we must recognize and manage a number of common tendencies by, for example, worrying less about what others think of us, reframing disappointments, finding ways to tackle tasks we avoid, and tolerating ambiguity. Cari Romm suggests ways to get past our natural but unproductive desire to be liked, identifying our biases, considering all the things we don't know, and not making assumptions.

Questions to Consider

- Which "soft" skills are most important to school leadership?
- Which cognitive biases are most problematic?
- How can principals fulfill all their responsibilities without burning out?

Desirable Qualities

| 1 | **Deconstructing Emotional Intelligence** |

"Emotional intelligence, a different way of being smart, is a key to high performance at all levels, particularly for outstanding leadership," says Daniel Goleman in this article in *More Than Sound*. "Emotional intelligence is the capacity to recognize our own feelings and those of others, and to manage emotions effectively in ourselves and our relationships." Research by Goleman, Richard Boyatzis, and colleagues has identified four dimensions of emotional intelligence:

• *Emotional self-awareness:*
- The ability to understand our own emotions and their effects on our performance.

• *Self-management:*
- Emotional self-control – The ability to keep disruptive emotions and impulses in check and maintain our effectiveness under stressful or hostile conditions;
- Achievement orientation – Striving to meet or exceed a standard of excellence; looking for ways to set challenging goals, take calculated risks, and do things better;
- Positive outlook – The ability to see the good in people, situations, and events; persistence in pursuing goals despite obstacles and setbacks;
- Adaptability – Flexibility in handling change, juggling multiple demands, and modifying ideas or approaches when needed.

• *Social awareness:*
- Empathy – The ability to sense others' feelings and perspectives, take an active interest in their concerns, and pick up cues about what they feel and think;
- Organizational awareness – The ability to read a group's emotional currents and power relationships; identifying influencers, networks, and organizational dynamics.

• *Relationship management:*
- Influence – The ability to have a positive impact on others, persuading or convincing them in order to gain their support;
- Coach and mentor – The ability to foster the long-term learning or development of others by giving feedback, guidance, and support;
- Conflict management – The ability to help others through emotional or tense situations, tactfully bringing disagreements into the open and finding solutions all can endorse;

- Inspirational leadership – The ability to inspire and guide individuals and groups toward a meaningful vision of excellence, and to bring out the best in others;
- Teamwork – The ability to work with others toward a shared goal; participating actively, sharing responsibility and rewards, and contributing to the capability of the team.

These competencies, says Goleman, aren't just innate; they can be developed through introspection, feedback from others, and effective effort.

"Emotional and Social Intelligence Leadership Competencies: An Overview" by Daniel Goleman in *More Than Sound*, April 2017, summarized in Marshall Memo 684.

2 Self-Awareness 101

In this *Harvard Business Review* article, organizational psychologist Tasha Eurich says that people with good self-awareness are more confident and creative, communicate more effectively, build stronger relationships, make sounder decisions, and are less likely to lie, cheat, and steal. These insights came from four years of research with almost five thousand subjects. An initial takeaway: although most people believe they are self-aware, only 10–15 percent really are. This led the researchers to look more closely at the whole subject. The major findings:

• *There are two ways of knowing ourselves.* The first is internal self-awareness—how clearly we see our own values, passions, aspirations, fit with our environment, reactions (thoughts, feelings, behaviors, strengths, weaknesses), and impact on others. People with good internal self-awareness have higher job and relationship satisfaction, personal and social control, and happiness. Those who don't have good internal self-awareness are more prone to anxiety, stress, and depression.

The second is external self-awareness—understanding how other people view us on the dimensions above. Those with good external self-awareness are better at showing empathy and taking the perspective of others, and their colleagues have better relationships with them, feel more satisfied with them, and see them as more effective.

Surprisingly, the researchers found virtually no relationship between internal and external self-awareness. Teasing out the permutations, they defined four types of leaders:

- *Seekers (low internal and low external self-awareness)* – They don't yet know who they are, what they stand for, or how their teams see them—and may feel stuck or frustrated with their performance and relationships.

- *Pleasers (low internal and high external self-awareness)* – They can be so focused on appearing a certain way to others that they could be overlooking what matters to them and over time make choices that don't serve their own success and fulfillment.
- *Introspectors (high internal and low external self-awareness)* – They're clear on who they are but don't challenge their own views or search for blind spots by getting feedback from others.
- *Aware (high internal and high external self-awareness)* – They know who they are, what they want to accomplish, and seek out and value others' opinions.

"The bottom line," says Eurich, "is that self-awareness isn't one truth. It's a delicate balance of two distinct, even competing, viewpoints." The most effective leaders consciously cultivate both types.

• *Experience doesn't improve self-awareness.* Quite the contrary, as leaders became more experienced and powerful, their self-awareness became less and less accurate. "Contrary to popular belief," says Eurich, "studies have shown that people do not always learn from experience, that expertise does not help people root out false information, and that seeing ourselves as highly experienced can keep us from doing our homework, seeking disconfirming evidence, and questioning our assumptions."

Why does this happen? First, as people rise in the hierarchy there are fewer people above them who can provide candid feedback. Second, the more powerful a leader is, the less comfortable people are giving critical feedback (for fear of their own status). And third, as one's power increases, one's willingness to seek out and listen to feedback shrinks.

"But this doesn't have to be the case," says Eurich. The most successful leaders in the study pushed back on all three tendencies: they actively sought feedback, encouraged those around them to speak honestly (they actually loved their critics!), listened, checked in with others when they got critical feedback, and continuously improved their internal and external self-awareness.

• *Introspection doesn't always lead to self-awareness.* It turns out that navel-gazers "are *less* self-aware and report worse job satisfaction and well-being," says Eurich. But the problem isn't with introspection itself; it's that most people are doing it wrong. A prime example—asking "why" to understand our emotions:

- *Why don't I like this person?*
- *Why did I fly off the handle?*
- *Why am I so against this idea?*

"As it turns out," says Eurich, "'why' is a surprisingly ineffective self-awareness question. Research has shown that we simply do not have access to many of the unconscious thoughts, feelings, and motives we're searching for. And because so much is trapped outside our conscious awareness, we tend to invent answers that *feel* true but are often wrong …. We tend to pounce on whatever 'insights' we find without questioning their validity or value, we ignore contradictory evidence, and we force our thoughts to conform to our initial explanation." Sometimes anger or self-doubt is the result of something as simple as low blood sugar, but people caught in a self-awareness loop may obsess about their fears, shortcomings, and insecurities.

A better self-awareness question than Why? is *What?* "'What' questions help us stay objective, future-focused, and empowered to act on our new insights," says Eurich. A manager who hated his job didn't ask himself, "Why do I feel so terrible?" Rather, he asked, "What are the situations that make me feel terrible, and what do they have in common?" The answers led him to quit his job and pursue a far more fulfilling career in another field.

Eurich's conclusion: "Leaders who focus on building both internal and external self-awareness, who seek honest feedback from loving critics, and who ask *what* instead of *why*, can learn to see themselves more clearly—and reap the many rewards that increased self-knowledge delivers. And no matter how much progress we make, there's always more to learn. That's one of the things that makes the journey to self-awareness so exciting."

"What Self-Awareness Really Is (and How to Cultivate It)" by Tasha Eurich in *Harvard Business Review*, January 4, 2018, summarized in Marshall Memo 719.

3   Are You a Curious Person? If So, in What Ways Are You Curious?

In this *Harvard Business Review* article, Todd Kashdan, David Disabato, and Fallon Goodman (George Mason University) and Carl Naughton say that curiosity is an important trait for work and life success. Psychologists have found that curiosity enhances intelligence, increases perseverance, and propels people toward deeper engagement, superior performance, and setting more-meaningful goals.

But it turns out that curiosity is not a single trait. Kashdan, Disabato, Goodman, and Naughton synthesized decades of research into five dimensions: social curiosity, joyous exploration, thrill seeking, deprivation sensitivity, and stress tolerance. They also created the curiosity self-assessment included below. People rate themselves on each line within a range of 1 (*doesn't describe me at all*) to 7 (*completely describes me*). The last dimension is reverse-scored.

Social Curiosity: talking to, listening to, and observing others to learn what they're thinking.

- I like to learn about the habits of others.

- I like finding out why people behave the way they do.
- When other people are having a conversation, I like to find out what it's about.
- When around other people, I like listening to their conversations.
- When people quarrel, I like to know what's going on.

Joyous Exploration: being consumed with wonder about the intriguing features of the world.

- I view challenging situations as an opportunity to grow and learn.
- I am always looking for experiences that challenge how I think about myself and the world.
- I seek out situations where it is likely that I'll have to think in depth about something.
- I enjoy learning about subjects that are unfamiliar to me.
- I find it fascinating to learn new information.

Thrill Seeking: being willing to take risks to acquire varied, complex, intense experiences.

- The anxiety of doing something new makes me feel excited and alive.
- Risk-taking is exciting to me.
- When I have free time, I want to do things that are a little scary.
- Creating an adventure as I go is much more appealing than a planned adventure.
- I prefer friends who are excitingly unpredictable.

Deprivation Sensitivity: recognizing gaps in knowledge and wanting to reduce them

- Thinking about solutions to difficult conceptual problems can keep me awake at night.
- I can spend hours on a single problem because I just can't rest without knowing the answer.
- I feel frustrated if I can't figure out the solution to a problem, so I work even harder to solve it.
- I work relentlessly at problems that I feel must be solved.
- It frustrates me to not have all the information I need.

Stress Tolerance: a willingness to accept and harness the anxiety associated with novelty.

- The smallest doubt can stop me from seeking out new experiences.
- I cannot handle the stress that comes from entering uncertain situations.
- I find it hard to explore new places when I lack confidence in my abilities.
- I cannot function well if I am unsure whether a new experience is safe.
- It is difficult to concentrate when there is a possibility that I will be taken by surprise.

Administering this assessment internationally—Kashdan, Disabato, Goodman, and Naughton have found that two dimensions are most strongly associated with work success:

- Social curiosity (high scores) – Those who score high on this dimension are better at resolving conflicts; they receive social support and build connections, trust, and commitment on their teams.

- Stress tolerance (low scores) – "Without the ability to tolerate stress," say the authors, "employees are less likely to seek challenges and resources and to voice dissent and are more likely to feel enervated and to disengage."

The dimension that has the weakest association with work success is thrill seeking.

In a separate article in *Psychology Today* (January 2018), Kashdan uses scores on this self-assessment to sort people into four categories:

- The Fascinated—high on all dimensions of curiosity, especially Joyous Exploration;
- Problem Solvers—high on Deprivation Sensitivity, medium on the other dimensions;
- Empathizers—high on Social Curiosity, medium on the others;
- Avoiders—low on all dimensions, particularly Stress Tolerance.

"The Five Dimensions of Curiosity" by Todd Kashdan, David Disabato, Fallon Goodman, and Carl Naughton in *Harvard Business Review*, September-October 2018 (Vol. 96, #5, pp. 58–60), summarized in Marshall Memo 752.

---

4   "Résumé Virtues" versus "Eulogy Virtues"

"About once a month I run across a person who radiates an inner light," says David Brooks in this *New York Times* column. "They seem deeply good. They listen well. They make you feel funny and valued. You often catch them looking after other people and as they do so their laugh is musical and their manner is infused with gratitude. They are not thinking about what wonderful work they are doing. They are not thinking about themselves at all. When I meet such a person it brightens my whole day."

Brooks confesses he's not one of those people. Distinguishing between "eulogy virtues" (like the ones he just described) and "résumé virtues," he believes he has more of the latter than the former. In the final analysis, of course, eulogy virtues are more important. "But our culture and our educational systems spend more time teaching the skills and strategies you need for career success than the qualities you need to radiate that sort of inner light," says Brooks. "If you live for external achievement, years pass and the deepest parts of you go unexplored and unstructured. You lack a moral vocabulary. It is easy to slip into a self-satisfied moral mediocrity.… Gradually, a humiliating gap opens between your actual self and your desired self, between you and those incandescent souls you sometimes meet."

The big question is whether truly virtuous people are born or made. Brooks did some research and concluded that those he admires most have gone through what he calls a moral bucket list of experiences that take them to a higher level (which means that if you've taken the résumé approach, it's still possible to change):

• *The humility shift* – Our culture encourages us to puff ourselves up, but "all the people I've ever deeply admired are profoundly honest about their own weaknesses," says Brooks. "They have identified their core sin, whether it is selfishness, the desperate need for approval, cowardice, hard-heartedness, or whatever."

• *Self-defeat* – Dwight Eisenhower realized that his temper was his Achilles heel, so he worked on projecting a moderate, cheerful exterior while using specific tricks to control anger—for example, writing the names of people he hated on pieces of paper, tearing them up, and throwing them in the trash.

• *The dependency leap* – The key is acknowledging that you can't do anything significant alone and identifying the people who support you.

• *Energizing love* – Deep devotion "decenters the self," says Brooks. "It reminds you that your true riches are in another. Most of all, this love electrifies. It puts you in a state of need and makes it delightful to serve what you love."

• *The call* – Brooks describes how Frances Perkins watched the Triangle Shirtwaist fire—women trapped in a burning factory and hurling themselves to their deaths—and was transformed into a lifelong civic activist.

• *The conscience leap* – Some virtuous people come to a crossroads and boldly take a path that defies their upbringing and social norms but liberates them to be more than they could be before.

The standard graduation speech, says Brooks, urges us to be true to ourselves. "This is a vision of life that begins with self and ends with self," he says. "But people on the road to inner light do not find their vocations by asking, what do I want from life? They ask, what is life asking of me? How can I match my intrinsic talent with one of the world's deep needs? Their lives often follow a pattern of defeat, recognition, redemption. They have moments of pain and suffering. But they turn those moments into occasions of radical self-understanding.... The people on this road see the moments of suffering as pieces of a larger narrative. They are not really living for happiness, as it is conventionally defined. They see life as a moral drama and feel fulfilled only when they are enmeshed in a struggle on behalf of some ideal .... Those are the people we want to be."

"The Moral Bucket List" by David Brooks in *The New York Times*, April 12, 2015, summarized in Marshall Memo 583.

Building Trust

5   Can a Leader Admit Confusion and Still Lead?

"Confusion is not a weakness to be ashamed of but a regular and inevitable condition of leadership," say Barry Jentz and Jerry Murphy in this article in *Phi Delta Kappan.* They describe a five-step process for taking advantage of "Oh, no!" moments to "embrace confusion," open up better lines of communication, test old assumptions and values against changing realities, and develop more-creative approaches to problem solving.

Jentz and Murphy present a case study of a school leader confronted with unexpectedly low test scores (25 percent of eighth graders scored as non-readers), demands from parents and community groups to *do something,* and defensive reactions from teachers who resented being blamed for low student achievement. Like others in this kind of predicament, the leader felt under tremendous pressure to act and churned with these emotions:

- shame and loss of face—*I'll look like a fool!*
- panic and loss of control—*I've let this get out of hand!*
- incompetence and incapacitation—*I don't know what I'm doing!*
- shame—*I'm at a loss here. I'm not fit to lead.*

The last thing the leader was inclined to do was admit confusion, which seemed like weakness. Of course, for the school leader's subordinates, the last thing they wanted to see was a principal who:

- instinctively blames circumstances or other people when things go wrong,
- claims to be open to input but sees feedback as criticism and doesn't listen,
- hates uncertainty and opts for action even when totally confused,
- believes that anything less than take-charge decision-making is weak,
- habitually resorts to the "art of the bluff" to avoid looking stupid.

Yet when leaders are disoriented and confused by developments that just don't make sense and have no idea what to do, these are the very tendencies that take hold. After all, leaders are supposed to know what to do! In a crisis, they tend to deny their confusion and reflexively and unilaterally impose quick fixes to solve the problem. Shoot-from-the-hip decisions like these, say Jentz and Murphy, "rarely address underlying causes. More often, they lead to bad decision-making, undermine crucial communication with colleagues and subordinates, and make managers seem distant and out of touch. In the long run, managers who hide their confusion also damage their organizations' ability to learn from experience and grow."

How can a leader get out of this box? Jentz and Murphy suggest a five-step process for turning confusion into a resource, maintaining authority, avoiding premature closure, and enlisting the team in finding the best way forward:

• *Embrace your confusion.* "When confronted with disorienting problems," they say, "you need to do the one thing you least want to do—acknowledge to yourself that you are confused *and* that you see this condition as a weakness .... You might take a deep breath and say to yourself, 'I'm confused and that makes me feel weak.' Paradoxically, fully embracing where you start will not lead you to wallow in your confusion, but rather frees you to move beyond your inner conflict." Doing this is difficult, and Jentz and Murphy recommend developing a personal mantra for crisis moments, for example, "Leadership is not about pretending to have all the answers but about having the courage to search with others to discover solutions."

• *Assert your need to make sense.* Sit down with your colleagues and say something like, "This new information just doesn't make sense to me. Before I can make a decision, I need help in understanding this situation and our options for dealing with it." It's critically important to 'fess up to your confusion: "Unless you unambiguously assert, with conviction and without apology, your sense of being confused, others will fulfill your worst expectations—concluding that you *are* weak—and they will be less willing to engage in a shared process of interpersonal learning." If the leader is faking confidence and competence as the ship goes down, the crew will be in no mood to admit their own distress and find new ways to plug the leaks.

• *Structure the interaction.* "Without skipping a beat," say Jentz and Murphy, "you must next provide a structure for the search for new bearings that both asserts your authority and creates the conditions for others to join you." The leader needs to state the purpose for the joint inquiry, lay out specific steps to fulfill that purpose, provide a timetable, and identify the criteria and methods by which decisions will be made. These actions show colleagues that although you have admitted you are confused, you are not incapacitated; you may not know what course to take, but you know the next step, you are "asking for directions" (difficult for some guys) but you are still in charge of a process that will produce a clear outcome, and you give suggestions about the type of data you need to clarify and resolve the problem.

Jentz and Murphy illustrate this point with another case study of a leader in a pickle. *The alarm sounds in a nuclear power plant, signaling that something is seriously wrong. The manager makes an educated guess about what the problem might be, but then a team member reports a piece of data from the reactor that doesn't fit the manager's hypothesis—in fact, it's the exact opposite of what it should be. The manager is stunned and sits starting at the console as the team anxiously awaits a decision.*

Following Step 3, here is what the manager might say: "Listen up! We've got two minutes, and then you'll get my decision. Between then and now, I'm going to talk about what's got me confused, and you are going to give me new information, feedback, or explanations for what is going on." The key steps embodied in this response are:

• *Listen reflectively and learn.* As your team begins to respond with data, ideas, and pushback, the leader needs to shift gears and engage in what Thomas Gordon called "active listening"—putting yourself in other people's shoes and with an open mind really listening to what they are saying (often reflecting it back to be sure you have heard it accurately). For example:

- "You seem to be saying that x caused y. Do I have that right?"
- "You're torn between two explanations. On one hand, you think x accounts for z; on the other hand, you think y does?"
- "So you're angry because I am saying one thing and yet doing quite another?"

Reflective listening doesn't come naturally and takes lots of practice, like hitting a backhand in a fast-paced tennis game.

The opposite of active listening is reflexive responding, which bad listeners do all the time; they immediately judge the worth of what was said and say whether they agree or disagree. "This typically leads to a confrontation, not a joint inquiry" say Jentz and Murphy. "Indeed, our habit of responding in kind is such a powerful force that it has a name: The Norm of Reciprocity. ('If you don't listen to me, I'll be damned if I'll listen to you.')"

• *Openly process your effort to make sense.* Having heard what your colleagues have to say (some of which may be puzzling and upsetting), it's important to think through your responses *out loud*. This works much better than what we usually do, which is think it through silently and then announce our decision. Here are some examples of open processing:

- "That's news to me. I haven't heard that before."
- "That really throws me. How did you get to that from what you were saying?"
- "That helps me a lot by pointing out x."

"When you find the courage to externalize your intellectual process," say Jentz and Murphy, "you invite others to engage in interpersonal learning. Working together, you can discover the limitations of one another's thinking—limitations that you cannot know as long as you process privately."

Returning to the case of the bad test scores, here is how these five steps might be applied. The leader meets privately with all parties (administrators, teachers, union representatives, board members) and asserts his confusion about the test scores. Listening reflectively to accusations, explanations, and demands from all sides (*More phonics! Remedial reading for all students! A "shape up" memo to teachers!*), he argues that they should not take action until they understand the reasons for such low scores. He uses a similar approach with parents, media, and community leaders (although with them he is not quite as open about his confusion). The leader then sets up a committee to analyze student achievement data and evaluate competing explanations for the results. The group is confused at first; none of their assumptions or preconceptions seem to explain the low test scores. Having admitted their confusion, members of the group keep working and finally figure out that:

- Most of the non-reading eighth graders entered the district after third grade, missing the district's exemplary phonics program.
- The non-readers all come from a particularly impoverished neighborhood.
- As students moved from one grade to another, remedial services were totally uncoordinated and these students fell through the cracks.

Based on this deeper and more nuanced understanding of the problem, the team implements a series of targeted programs that brings about significant gains in student achievement the following year.

Jentz and Murphy conclude with a broader message for leaders: "In the 21st century, as rapid change makes confusion a defining characteristic of management, the competence of managers will be measured not only by *what they know* but increasingly by *how they behave* when they lose their sense of direction and become confused. Organizational cultures that cling to the ideal of an all-knowing, omnicompetent executive will pay a high cost in time, resources, and progress, and will be sending the message to managers that it is better to hide their confusion than to address it openly and constructively …. Managers can be confused yet still be able to exercise competent leadership by structuring a process of reflective inquiry and action."

"Embracing Confusion: What Leaders Do When They Don't Know What to Do" by Barry Jentz and Jerome Murphy in *Phi Delta Kappan*, January 2005 (Vol. 86, #5, pp. 358–366), summarized in Marshall Memo 70.

6 Projecting Warmth and Strength as a Leader

In this *Harvard Business Review* article, Amy Cuddy (Harvard Business School) and Matthew Kohut and Jon Neffinger (KNP Communications) address an age-old question of leadership: Is it better to be loved or feared? The answer for leaders, say Cuddy, Kohut, and Neffinger, is to project both warmth *and* competence—but that doesn't come naturally. They recommend a one-two punch: start with warmth, closely followed by competence.

It turns out that more than 90 percent of our social judgment upon meeting someone new comes from two areas:

- The person's warmth, communion, and trustworthiness—*What are his or her intentions toward me?*
- The person's strength, agency, and competence—*Is he or she capable of acting on those intentions?*

Interestingly, most people think it's important to project strength toward others—but what they look for in others is warmth. "Most leaders today tend to emphasize their strength, competence, and credentials in the workplace, but that is exactly the wrong approach," say the authors. "Leaders who project strength before establishing trust run the risk of eliciting fear, along with a host of dysfunctional behaviors. Fear can undermine cognitive potential, creativity, and problem-solving, and cause employees to get stuck and even disengage."

"A growing body of research," they continue, "suggests that the way to influence—and to lead—is to begin with warmth. Warmth is the conduit of influence: It facilitates trust and the communication and absorption of ideas …. Prioritizing warmth helps you connect immediately with those around you, demonstrating that you hear them, understand them, and can be trusted by them …. Without a foundation of trust, people in the organization may comply outwardly with a leader's wishes, but they're much less likely to conform privately—to adopt the values, culture, and mission of the organization in a sincere, lasting way."

How does a leader project warmth in a way that doesn't seem phony? Cuddy, Kohut, and Neffinger suggest the following:
- Don't speak too loudly. Talking at a lower pitch conveys the feeling of confiding and trusting. It's also helpful to share an appropriate personal story.
- Validate people's feelings. "Before people decide what they think of your message, they decide what they think of *you*," say the authors.
- Smile. Genuine smiles are self-reinforcing, both for you and for others. Because people can see through a false smile, it helps to think of positive things and focus on one person in the group.

How does a leader project strength?
- Feel in command. "Warmth may be harder to fake, but confidence is harder to talk yourself into," say Cuddy, Kohut, and Neffinger. If you feel like an imposter, others will feel it. Hold your body in a way that expresses confidence, facing directly toward people you're talking to, and avoid cutting gestures, a furrowed brow, or an elevated chin. Balance your weight primarily on one hip to avoid appearing rigid or tense. Tilt your head slightly and keep your hands open and welcoming.
- Stand up straight. "It is hard to overstate the importance of good posture in projecting

authority and an intention to be taken seriously," say the authors. This doesn't mean standing rigidly at attention, military style. "It just means reaching your full height, using your muscles to straighten the S-curve in your spine rather than slouching."

- Be poised. "When you move, move deliberately and precisely to a specific spot rather than casting your limbs about loose-jointedly," say Cuddy, Kohut, and Neffinger. "And when you are finished moving, be still. Twitching, fidgeting, or other visual static sends the signal that you're not in control. Stillness demonstrates calm."

"Is It Better to Be Loved or Feared?" by Amy Cuddy, Matthew Kohut, and Jon Neffinger in *Harvard Business Review*, July/August 2013 (Vol. 91, #7/8, pp. 54–61), summarized in Marshall Memo 492.

7 A Principal Shares His Moral Compass

In this *Phi Delta Kappan* article, former Massachusetts principal and superintendent John Ritchie quotes Emily Dickinson: *The sailor cannot see the north—but knows the needle can.* "On countless occasions," says Ritchie, "I felt lost in a sea of complex challenges, conflicting expectations, and vexing problems—compounded by expectations that the principal always knows what to do. I came to rely more than anything else on my own compass to guide me." Every new principal needs to develop a reliable compass, he says, and every veteran principal needs to be careful not to lose it.

Ritchie says his guiding principles had less to do with educational vision and goals than with "attitudes, behaviors, and modes of operation." He focused less on strategies for solving problems than on ways of approaching them; on treating people with respect, being a good listener, even with angry and unhappy people, and noticing and appreciating good deeds.

The principalship was "immensely rewarding, enjoyable, and entertaining," he says. "There was always something unexpected, hilarious, unbelievable, or quirky going on." However, "it is a cold fact that every principal will face dark and tough times, deal with tragedy, make painful decisions about cutting valuable programs, and conduct difficult conversations with students, teachers, or parents. The principalship is often a draining job, and there is always the danger of psychic exhaustion that results from being at the center point of a school, where the No. 1 requirement seems to be to do more, listen better, and be more places than any person could ever do or be.

"The tide of visitors that washes into a principal's office almost any week brings with it an astonishing array of human stories of pain, frustration, pride, loneliness, or hope," Ritchie continues, "the overtly angry and aggressive parents who in reality are simply terrified by not knowing how to handle their child; the teacher who has lost a loved one and is struggling just to stay afloat, let alone teach; the student whose troublesome behavior is a mask for sadness, fear, anxiety, and for whom school is a daily nightmare…. Everyone has a story to tell, everyone wants their story to be heard, and one of the principal's responsibilities is to hear and respond meaningfully to these stories."

One of the basic paradoxes of the principalship, says Ritchie, is that on the one hand school leaders are the public face of the school every day, at a school dance, on the soccer field, and at the dry cleaner. "Simultaneously, being a principal is a solitary position," he says. "No one else in a school has exactly the same job as the principal, knows the daily demands of the job or the many directions in which one is constantly pulled. No one knows about all the information that must be kept confidential, the tough decisions, the emotionally charged conversations. Since there's only one principal, there really isn't anyone else in the school available to share what it is like being principal, which is inevitably isolating. Solitariness is not the same as loneliness, but it can easily turn into loneliness, especially when paired with the tiring public demands of the job."

An important release from this isolation is communing with other principals, who know exactly what their fellow school leaders are talking about.

Ritchie says he struggled with the expectation that he be the disciplinarian-in-chief, dispensing punishment for students' errors and misdeeds. But school is a place to learn from mistakes, he believes, and punishment is often ineffective. He often tried to be "the chief dispenser of mercy and kindness, which is a difficult and sometimes risky balance to strike."

Ritchie is skeptical about the expectation that principals be decisive—exhibiting "boldness, lack of equivocation, the courage to make tough decisions quickly—and deal with the consequences without flinching." But he believes this macho expectation often gets in the way of good decision-making. Schools are complex. Students are in a continual state of flux. "As a result, and quite wonderfully, ambiguity is part of the landscape of any school …. A very different kind of decisiveness is often better suited to meet goals or solve problems. Being decisive isn't only or mainly about acting. Being decisive is about approaching problems or decisions with a clear head and open mind, a willingness to examine all sides of an issue, and an ability to contemplate the possible unintended consequences of any choice. In this conception, being decisive often means having the courage not to make a decision until a problem has been thoroughly examined and understood."

One of the biggest traps of the principalship, Ritchie continues, is trying to please everyone— parents, students, teachers, the community, the central office: "Trying to meet everyone's expectations is a fool's errand, and it takes a great deal of fortitude not to forget it."

Ritchie questions the expectation that principals need to have a destination in mind, a clear sense of where they are taking the school (a standard interview question for aspiring school leaders). "My experience was that this conventional concept of vision turns out to be limiting rather than energizing and can even distract a school from its real mission," he says. "The fundamental work of a school leader is simple: engender and sustain the best possible environment for teaching and learning …. Hire the best teachers you can find, support them in every way possible, help them grow, evaluate them fairly, set and exemplify high expectations for everyone, and create and insist on a climate and culture where students feel safe, known, and challenged. That's the only vision a principal needs."

"The Effective and Reflective Principal" by John Ritchie in *Phi Delta Kappan*, May 2013 (Vol. 94, #8, pp. 18–21), summarized in Marshall Memo 485.

Dealing with Stress

8 Managing the Stresses of School Leadership

In this article in *Independent School*, David Holmes (Community School, Idaho) says the pressures of school leadership take their toll, and too many principals have an abbreviated tenure—five or fewer years, definitely suboptimal. Holmes believes the loneliness of the principalship plays a major part in turnover. Not having someone to talk to and/or the social-emotional skills to deal effectively with stresses can lead to:

- unhealthy habits—poor sleep patterns, insufficient exercise, alcohol abuse;
- acting out in anger and frustration;
- developing a pattern of avoidance;
- not making good use of sources of emotional sustenance like friends, colleagues, and loved ones.

The bottom line, says Holmes, is that what's healthy for the principal is healthy for the school. He suggests ten rules for school leaders to manage their inner lives and remain effective, confident, enthusiastic, and satisfied with their work:

• *Accept the situation as it is.* "You need to do this in order to deter a pattern of complaining that is so easy to begin," says Holmes. "The discipline of dealing with 'what is,' not what you wish things to be, is an important principle."

• *Sometimes you need to vent.* This should be done with someone you can trust and who doesn't have a direct stake in your work. In almost all cases, it shouldn't be your spouse or partner.

• *Don't take it personally.* It's easier to handle in-your-face emotional complaints, criticisms, and venting when you believe it's about the other person, not you.

• *Keep the intensity of the job in perspective.* School leadership is uniquely demanding, but try to be as healthy as possible, both physically and psychologically. One strategy is to have a non-school "subplot" to your life, for example—writing, mindfulness, or becoming proficient at a sport.

• *Develop friendships with a few trusted colleagues.* "There is nothing like a good laugh," says Holmes. "Friendships, heart-to-heart discussions, and humor can sideline day-to-day stresses and provide emotional sustenance and enjoyment."

• *Engage in professional reading and writing.* "Days filled with administrative tasks and problem solving will ultimately wear you down," says Holmes. The key is to read about what others are doing in the field, put your own stresses and anxieties in a wider frame of reference, and carry those insights into your work.

• *Get enough sleep.* "Whether it is makeup sleep on Sunday morning or a regular schedule of seven hours," says Holmes, "leaders must play the 'long game,' and sleep is fundamental to longevity."

• *Attend to the home front.* "If family life is tension-filled or infused with resentment, you carry this with you every day," says Holmes, "—and it will affect both your family life and your ability to lead the school."

• *Adopt a posture of fearlessness.* Rather than allowing yourself to be paralyzed worrying what can go wrong, say to yourself: *I am on the right course; there are inherent risks, but the odds are with me; wise people around me agree with what we are doing; and no matter what happens, I can live with the consequences.*

• *If necessary, get help.* Not all problems can be solved alone, and there are times when a leadership coach, a psychologist, a cardiologist, or an addiction counselor is essential.

"The Inner Life of School Leaders" by David Holmes in *Independent School*, Fall, 2016 (Vol. 76, #1, pp. 52–56), summarized in Marshall Memo 656.

How Making Too Many Decisions Can Erode Their Quality

9 In this *New York Times* article, John Tierney explores "decision fatigue"—the research finding that having to make lots of decisions degrades people's ability to decide wisely. This can happen, for example, to judges, quarterbacks, and couples preparing for a wedding (the decision-fatigue equivalent of Hell Week, says Tierney).

In one experiment, college students were offered the chance to keep one item from a store's going-out-of-business sale. The treatment group (deciders) had to make choices among numerous items. The control group (non-deciders) looked over the same items for a similar amount of time but didn't have to make any choices. Afterward, all the students were subjected to a classic test of self-control: how long they could hold their hand in ice water. Those who had been required to make lots of decisions gave up much sooner (twenty-eight seconds, on average) than the non-deciders (sixty-seven seconds). Making all those decisions had sapped the deciders' willpower.

Similar experiments with people who'd been making purchasing decisions in a suburban mall, deciding on multiple features on a tailor-made suit, and deciding on extra features on a new car produced similar results. The most intriguing experiment looked at the parole decisions made by judges at different times of day. It turned out that prisoners had a much lower chance of being paroled just before lunch and late in the afternoon, when judges had been making difficult decisions for hours. At those points, they were more likely to make the non-decision of keeping a prisoner locked up. "Once you're mentally depleted," says Tierney, "you become reluctant to make trade-offs, which is a particularly advanced and taxing form of decision-making."

"Decision fatigue helps explain why ordinarily sensible people get angry at colleagues and families, splurge on clothes, buy junk food at the supermarket, and can't resist the dealer's offer to rustproof their new car," says Tierney. "No matter how rational and high-minded you try to be, you can't make decision after decision without paying a biological price. It's different from ordinary physical fatigue—you're not consciously aware of being tired—but you're low on mental energy." That leads people to take shortcuts—acting impulsively, taking the easy way out, or deciding not to act (the judges not granting parole). It seems that people have a finite amount of decision-making energy, and when it's depleted, they're less able to make good decisions.

Tierney offers another case study: Julius Caesar's dilemma as he returned from Gaul in 49 BC and had to decide whether to cross the Rubicon River with his army. (Bringing his troops with him was forbidden and would lead to civil war.) The three phases of the decision were: (a) pre-Rubicon—weighing the options; (b) deciding to cross the river, at which point the die would be cast; and (c) what to do after crossing. Modern researchers have found that the second step in a Rubicon-type decision is by far the most mentally taxing.

Making choices when grocery shopping is particularly challenging for the poor, says Tierney. Multiple trade-off decisions with very limited resources deplete mental energy, leaving people vulnerable to impulse buying when they get to the cash register—which is, of course, why the sweet snacks are displayed there. And there's a reason that sugary products are temptingly available at that location: glucose restores mental energy very quickly. The problem, Tierney says, is that it's short-term mental energy, not the kind of wise decision-making energy that serves people best. That's why dieting is a decision-making Catch 22: In order not to eat, the dieter needs willpower; but in order to have willpower, especially after resisting temptation all day, the dieter needs to eat, and sweets are tempting—but not helpful. Protein and other more-nutritious foods eaten throughout the day are better.

Even with better food choices, decision fatigue is still a factor. The study of the parole judges found that just after a mid-morning snack, they made more merciful decisions—but an hour or so later, they were back to harsher decisions, keeping prisoners locked up, even with exactly the same characteristics. The same was true just after lunch—more mercy—and late afternoon—slim chances of being paroled.

"To Choose Is to Lose" by John Tierney in *The New York Times*, August 17, 2011, summarized in Marshall Memo 764.

Cognitive Quirks

10 Managing Feelings, Values, and Expectations

In this *Psychology Today* article, science writer Jena Pincott lists correctives for some common cognitive biases:

• *Understand that not everything that happens to you is about you.* "At the very least, the egocentric bias causes us to misread others," says Pincott. "It undermines empathy and tolerance. It also traps us in a bubble; we waste vast amounts of psychic energy recovering from insults that were never targeted at us in the first place. To live a life that is less reactive, more directed, it is necessary to put the ego in its place."

• *Worry less about what others think of you.* It turns out that people are much less aware of our competence, awkwardness, verbal flubs, facial expressions, even what we wear—than we imagine. "When we care less about our curated self-image, we open the door to interacting more genuinely," says Pincott. "We can let down our guard. Others may respond in kind, focusing less on their own self-image and opening up."

• *Realize that you don't have to act the way you feel.* Pincott advises "self-distancing" to keep disappointments and negative emotions from spilling into everyday interactions. This involves processing our feelings from an outsider's point of view, addressing ourselves in the third person to normalize and make meaning of disturbing experiences. This makes it possible to preserve our dignity, privacy, and self-respect when we're not at our best.

• *Reframe and manage disappointment and adversity.* "There is nothing good or bad, but thinking makes it so," said Hamlet. Social psychologists have confirmed Shakespeare's wisdom, showing that although there are differences in people's innate ability to handle stressful events, mental fortitude can be acquired. This means learning how not to jump to conclusions, overgeneralize, catastrophize, personalize, and engage in black-or-white thinking. "Resilient people do not define themselves by their adversity," says Pincott. "They understand that bad times are temporary affairs."

• *Solicit honest feedback.* It's possible to be internally self-aware (in touch with our own values and passions) and not externally self-aware (knowing how others see us). "External self-awareness allows us to be more in sync with others," says Pincott. "It makes us more effective leaders because we have more empathy, which comes from understanding other people's perspectives." She advises identifying several "critical friends" and periodically asking them questions like: *What am I doing that I should keep doing? What should I stop doing? What about me annoys you?*

• *Stay true to your own values despite what others expect.* There's sometimes a tug-of-war between what we want and what others expect—parents, teachers, love partners. "People high in both internal and external self-awareness can navigate competing expectations," says organizational psychologist Tasha Eurich. They value authenticity and integrity, knowing what they want to do and illuminating it with other perspectives.

• *Be open to revising your thinking.* "The world doesn't stand still," says Pincott. "Situations change. Available information changes. However much we get emotionally attached to our own decisions, however much our opinions and perspectives may have once served us, there comes a point at which constancy can curdle into rigidity." Studies show that we're most open to change when we're feeling good about ourselves, most resistant to change when we feel threatened and uncertain. Hanging out with a four-year-old is a good way to see what cognitive flexibility looks like.

• *Find ways to tackle tasks you want to avoid.* Pincott suggests several approaches: write down how the drudgery will end with a success; gamify the activity, introducing an element of competition; use second-person self-talk (*You can crush this, Ted!*); bite off a small piece to get started (*Just twenty minutes on this and I'll do something else*); and get into a routine (for example, rising at six to exercise).

• *Zone in on your purpose in a zoned-out world.* "The two most important days in life are the day you are born and the day you discover the reason why," said Mark Twain. But a sense of big-picture purpose depends on focus and self-regulation, and that's undermined by the current obsession with checking social media every few minutes, driven by the fear of missing out on something. "You may want big ideas," says author Larry Rosen, "but if your attention is jerked away constantly, they won't come. There's no time to process anything on a deeper level." There isn't even time for the overstimulated brain to daydream. Rosen strongly recommends thirty-minute breaks from technology. Turning away from the small screen, he says, can reorient us to the big picture.

• *Tolerate ambiguity.* Uncertainty is a "sure-fire fuel of anxiety," says Pincott, but it's part of modern life, and dealing with it has many rewards. "We're more able to shift gears, experiment, be more flexible, take in new information that we'd otherwise reject, and let a situation develop before pulling the proverbial trigger," she says. "We're better able to handle risk and to make decisions without deluding ourselves into thinking we know everything there is to know. In the end, we're less anxious." Studies have shown that one way to make yourself more flexible in uncertain situations is to read fiction. "When nothing is sure," says novelist Margaret Drabble, "everything is possible."

"Lessons You Won't Learn in School" by Jena Pincott in *Psychology Today*, May/June 2018, summarized in Marshall Memo 734.

---

11 Dealing with the Desire to Be Liked

In this article in *The Cut*, Cari Romm writes about her "deep-seated, seemingly unshakable need to be liked" by everyone she encounters. Checking in with friends, she's found that this is a pretty common affliction. It's not very helpful to tell yourself it doesn't matter if people like you, says Romm. Better to heed advice she's gathered from psychologists:

• *Think of yourself as a Rorschach inkblot*. "What a person sees says more about them than it does the inkblot," says Roger Covin, a clinical psychologist and author of *The Need to Be Liked*, "and the same thing is true interpersonally. The very qualities that make you likable to one person are the exact same qualities that will make you unlikable to another person." Confidence can be seen as bossiness; honesty as rudeness; hilarious jokes as annoying. The key variable, psychologists have found, is how much your inkblot is like the other person's. "Like attracts like," says Romm, "—or, perhaps more accurately, like *likes* like. And while you can control your side of a conversation, you can't control the personality, or the preferences, of the person on the receiving end."

• *Consider all the things you don't know*. "Someone might be having a bad day at work or a bad week at home, or they might just be distracted by a growing to-do list and eager to turn their attention back to it," says Romm—or they might just be hungry. "All, again, are factors beyond your control and likely beyond your knowledge—and while they may influence how people respond to you, they're not *about* you. Sometimes it's soothing to remind yourself of your own relative insignificance."

• *Pinpoint your biases*. All of us have what psychologists call "cognitive distortions"—problematic thought patterns as we interact with others. Some examples are:

- mind-reading (assuming another person is thinking negative thoughts about you),
- personalizing (making something about you when it isn't),
- catastrophizing (imagining the worst-case outcome).

We're mostly unaware of these thought patterns, but they can generate a lot of anxiety. The key to overcoming them is being aware of what's going on in our heads. "Pay attention to where your mind goes before, during, and after conversations," Romm suggests, "and then be honest with yourself about anything that may have skewed your perception of what took place."

• *Remember the difference between negative and neutral*. Plenty of totally neutral encounters—the other person is minding their own business or texting—end up being interpreted as negative. This is especially common among people who are high in "rejection sensitivity"—anxious that others are going to shut them out.

• *Do the math.* Romm conjectures that about 30 percent of the people on the planet, if they got to know us, wouldn't like us. So the chances of running into some of those people in everyday life are very high—servers in a restaurant, clerks in a bank, people at work. "You're going to be disliked by people," she concludes. "A lot of people. And that means there's nothing left to do but suck it up …. Just tell yourself the odds are crushingly against you …."

"How to Get Over the Need to Be Liked by Everyone You Meet" by Cari Romm in *The Cut*, November 8, 2017, summarized in Marshall Memo 715.

Professional Learning Suggestions for Chapter Three Leaders' Emotional Intelligence

Understanding and Developing Emotional Intelligence

Historically, much of the literature on school leadership has focused on developing skills in areas such as supervision, evaluation, instruction, curriculum development, leading professional development, discipline, and assessment. These are the types of skills school leaders have been expected to acquire to become "competent." However, the articles in this section show that *what you know* as a school leader is not enough to be successful. Kim and Jenn have seen firsthand what happens when leaders are tone-deaf when it comes to their impact on others. You need to tune in to *how* you lead and *how* you interact with people. The first set of exercises will help you better *understand* emotional intelligence and the second set gives you suggestions to *build* these skills.

I. Understanding Emotional Intelligence

Most of the activities below can be done *on your own* as a means of reflection, but they would be even better with a leadership team or with colleagues who also serve in a leadership capacity.

A. What are the traditional notions of the role of "principal" or "leader"?
Think about and discuss the more traditional ideas some people (students, families, staff, the community, the media) might have about what the principal is *supposed* to be like. For example, Ritchie (Article 7) mentions that he believed he was expected to be the disciplinarian-in-chief, make tough decisions quickly, and try to please everybody. Reread the Goleman (Article 1) and contrast Ritchie's ideas with what the research is showing about the benefits of incorporating more "soft skills" into the role of leader.

Clearly, the role of principal is a complex one. Discuss: When might a principal need to be *tough* vs. *humane*? Note that context matters. Take the following example: A student has been absent for 25 percent of the time since the beginning of the school year. Discuss one context in which you might be tough on this student and another in which you might be more humane in approach. Context matters.

The articles also touch on the difference between *competence* and *warmth*. Discuss: When might a principal need to exhibit more *competence* than *warmth*, and vice versa? In the Cuddy, Kohut, and Neffinger (Article 6), the authors state that when we meet new people, 90 percent of our social judgment about them has to do with their *warmth* and their *competence*. Think of someone—preferably a school leader—you've met recently. How would you describe this person's *warmth*? *Competence*? Which came across more strongly and did you feel the person had the balance right? The authors suggest you should lead with warmth. How well did this person prioritize warmth?

B. What is emotional intelligence?
While Daniel Goleman (Article 1) defines emotional intelligence outright, all of the articles point to skills that fit under this important aspect of leadership. The term dates back to the 1960s and was popularized by Goleman in his 1995 book, *Emotional Intelligence: Why It Can Matter More than IQ*. Goleman defines emotional intelligence as containing four types of skills:

- self-awareness (ability to recognize our own feelings)
- self-management (how we respond to emotions)
- social awareness (ability to understand the emotions of others)
- relationship management (ability to manage conflict and form healthy relationships)

Show the team this brief six-minute video of Daniel Goleman introducing emotional intelligence: https://www.youtube.com/watch?v=Y7m9eNoB3NU

Next, return to the articles in this section and as a group, pull out any skills that fit into this definition and create a compiled list.

Now that you've done a deeper dive into the types of skills that encompass emotional intelligence, go back to the David Brooks (Article 4). He provides another way to think of "competency" versus "EI" skills by comparing "résumé" and "eulogy" virtues. On the next page, make a list of "eulogy" skills you would like to be remembered for.

_____'s Eulogy Virtues

1.

2.

3.

4.

II. Building Your Own Emotional Intelligence Skills

Another theme in the articles is that emotional intelligence is *not* something you need to be born with; it is something you can *learn*. This section focuses on developing your own EI skills as a leader.

A. Is focusing on your own emotional intelligence skills selfish? Discuss.
Do *not* think that focusing on these skills is a selfish endeavor. As David Holmes writes (Article 8), "What's healthy for the principal is healthy for the school." Discuss what this means.

B. Create a plan to strengthen one emotional intelligence skill a month.
Now it is time to put a plan in place to build your own emotional intelligence skills. This is not something that happens overnight, it requires practice and patience over time. For this reason, you will focus on strengthening just *one* skill a month for the ten months of the school year in this exercise.

Coincidentally, two of the articles in this chapter present ten skills you can focus on. Revisit the Holmes (8) and Pincott (10) articles and choose the set of ten skills that you would most like to develop (the lists are in the chart below).

1. For your chosen list of skills, you are going to do a *forced choice* activity, preferably with someone else who also chose that list. First, discuss what the skills mean so you fully understand them, and then force yourself to order them 1–10 with which you believe is most important (10) to least (1).

2. Self-assess yourself on these ten skills. Rate yourself from 1 (weakest) to 4 (strongest) on each skill.

3. Review the Tasha Eurich (Article 2) about why we might *not* be as aware of ourselves as we'd like to be. Because of this, your next step is to get some feedback about how well you perform

the ten skills you've chosen to focus on by using an anonymous survey. You can use an online tool like Survey Monkey, Zoho Survey, or Google Forms. Decide whether to send the survey to the larger staff or just to trusted colleagues. Ask for numerical ratings and any comments about how they think you're doing with these ten skills.

4. Finally, you will focus on developing *one* skill a month. Use your planner or electronic calendar to remind you to focus on one skill throughout the month. On the last day of the month rate yourself—has your rating improved from your self-assessment or from the survey results above? Below is an overview of the two sets of skills with a sample progression, but you can change the order to fit your needs.

	David Holmes's rules for school leaders to manage their inner lives (Article 8)	Jena Pincott's suggestions to address common cognitive biases (Article 10)
September	Accept what cannot be changed.	Understand that not everything that happens to you is about you.
October	Sometimes you need to vent.	Worry less about what others think of you.
November	Don't take it personally.	Realize that you don't have to act the way you feel.
December	Accept that the job is intense.	Reframe and manage disappointment and adversity.
January	Develop friendships with a few trusted colleagues.	Solicit honest feedback.
February	Engage in professional reading and writing.	Stay true to your own values despite what others expect.
March	Get enough sleep.	Be open to revising your thinking.
April	Attend to your family.	Find ways to tackle tasks you want to avoid.
May	Adopt a posture of fearlessness.	Zone in on your purpose in a zoned-out world.
June	If necessary, get help.	Tolerate ambiguity.

C. Practice addressing a crisis proactively with a five-step rocess.

Emotional intelligence is extremely important in responding to a crisis. Authors Barry Jentz and Jerome Murphy (Article 5) state that successful leaders are defined less by *what they know* than *how they behave* in response to confusion.

Using appropriate social-emotional skills to respond to a crisis is not something that will happen in the moment *unless* you have been cultivating these skills over time (like in the ten-month exercise before this). You can't just pull out skills in a crisis that you don't have deeply ingrained. That's why developing one skill a month for a year is one way to develop EI skills.

Another way to address a crisis or confusion is to follow the five-step process introduced in the Jentz and Murphy (Article 5). The article mentions that leaders often respond to crises reflexively with quick-fixes, but this rarely addresses the heart of the problem. Instead, take the time now to think of a complex or challenging dilemma (or crisis) that you need to deal with. Rather than jumping in quickly, take the time to think through the five steps *ahead of time*, using guidance from the article and filling out the following table:

5-Step Process for Turning Confusion into a Resource	Your Plan
Step 1 Embrace your confusion.	This step is just for you. Take a deep breath and acknowledge what it is you are confused about and how that makes you feel. (You can write this down if that is how you process issues.):
Step 2 Assert your need to make sense.	Now you must "fess up" to others that you are confused and will need more information to proceed. When and how will you do this? (Monday? Team meeting?):
Step 3 Structure the plan.	Provide the following to address the crisis: a) Purpose for the joint inquiry: b) The specific steps to fulfill that purpose: c) The timeline: d) The type of data you will need to clarify and resolve the problem:
Step 4 Listen reflectively and learn.	You will need to really listen with an open mind, putting yourself in others' shoes. ("You seem to be saying that x caused y, do I have that right?") Which individuals and groups will you seek out to do this:
Step 5 Openly process your effort to make sense.	Make sure to think your responses *out loud* ("This helps me a lot by pointing out x.") List the people/teams you plan to openly process with:

Chapter Four: Interviewing and Hiring

Indeed, it may be possible that a teaching career requires one set of beliefs, attitudes, and values to get hired,
another set to survive in a school bureaucracy and parent-teacher community,
and a different set altogether to be a pedagogically effective teacher.
—Scott Alan Metzger and Meng-Jia Wu

Every classroom vacancy is an opportunity to improve teaching, teamwork, adult culture, and student learning for years to come. But many principals wince remembering hiring mistakes that caused problems—often decisions made under time pressure at the end of the summer. Ideally, the hiring process begins months earlier and includes energetic outreach to expand the applicant pool; careful screening of résumés; candidate interviews; finalists teaching demonstration lessons followed by debriefs; and probing reference calls. The articles in this chapter fall into three groups: what to look for in prospective teachers; hiring strategies; and productive interview questions.

Spotting the Right Candidates – Bryan Goodwin lists nine qualities to look for in applicants for teaching positions, from experience and expertise to with-it-ness and emotional objectivity. Carol Dweck adds her insights on growth and fixed mindsets in teachers: in rookie teachers, a growth mindset fuels classroom success, while a fixed mindset spells trouble. Claire Robertson-Kraft and Angela Lee Duckworth chime in with their research on "grit" (perseverance and passion in pursuit of long-term goals)—which is a key correlate of classroom effectiveness—and suggest ways to look for it when screening candidates' résumés. Scott Alan Metzger and Meng-Jia Wu take a close look at the hiring criteria of a widely used commercial teacher-selection instrument and raise troubling concerns about their validity.

Hiring Strategy – Paul Ash advocates a three-part hiring process: screening résumés; conducting ten-minute interviews with lots of plausible applicants; then inviting the most promising candidates back for full-length interviews. Douglas Reeves says that when candidates come for an interview they should be asked to observe classrooms, look at student work and achievement data from the school, then answer follow-up questions. Claudio Fernández-Aráoz spells out the steps necessary to get the whole truth from a candidate's references.

Interview Questions – Leonard Cassuto suggests that, rather than asking prospective teachers for their philosophy of education, hiring committees should inquire about the classroom actions candidates would take if hired. Mary Clement, a leading authority on interviewing, believes that—because past performance is the best predictor of future performance. For that reason, candidates should be asked behavior-based questions—what they have done in specific situations. Susan Trimble suggests additional interview questions that get at candidates' subject-area knowledge, ability to make sense of student achievement data, and skill at planning lessons and assessing student learning. And Elena Aguilar urges schools to watch for emotional intelligence and cultural competence when hiring and suggests ways to coach teachers on those crucial skills.

Questions to Consider

- Is it possible to spot an effective teacher up front?
- Which interview questions produce the most useful answers?
- Which parts of the hiring process are problematic, and how can they be mitigated?

Spotting the Right Candidates

1   Billy Beane's Advice Applied to Teacher Hiring

In this *Changing Schools* article, Bryan Goodwin (McREL) applies the lessons of Michael Lewis's 2003 book about baseball strategist Billy Beane—*Moneyball: The Art of Winning an Unfair Game*—to the hiring and support of teachers. In his book, Beane argued that the metrics traditionally used by baseball scouts—batting average, height, and speed, for example—don't correlate well with players' contributions to winning games. Beane suggested focusing on different metrics, such as a player's ability to draw walks, as well as intangibles like self-confidence and an even temper. (When he was a player, Beane's quick temper and self-doubt undermined his performance.) Using this approach, the Oakland Athletics were able to field a team on a par with the Yankees and Red Sox on a much smaller budget.

What are the comparable metrics that educators should use to hire "winning" teachers? Goodwin lists three factors that are *not* correlated with success: licensure, credentials, and advanced degrees. Hiring certified teachers may be a requirement under the law, but it doesn't guarantee high-quality instruction in classrooms. In fact, three studies of elementary schools showed that having a master's degree was *negatively* correlated with student achievement. In high-school science and math, however, students perform better with teachers who have a master's degree in their subject area.

On the positive side, Goodwin says the research points to nine look-fors when hiring teachers. Since very few candidates will have all of them, good hiring is the art of considering several attributes and deciding which are the best fit for a particular school. To spot the intangibles, it's essential to watch candidates teach demonstration lessons.

• *Some experience* – Teachers improve rapidly in the first five years on the job, so it's definitely better to hire teachers who have taught successfully in at least one other setting. Most teachers' learning curves flatten out after five years, and although some continue to develop throughout their careers, on average, there's no great advantage to hiring a fifteen- to twenty-five-year veteran over a teacher with five to six years of experience.

• *Subject-area expertise* – It is critically important that teachers know their subject deeply, understand how children learn it, and master a range of teaching methods matched to what they are teaching—the jargon is pedagogical content knowledge.

• *Strong academic preparation* – Students do better with teachers who attended selective colleges. This effect is most pronounced in high schools and with low-income students.

• *Educational attainment* – A 2002 study showed that high teacher verbal and cognitive levels are twice as powerful at raising student achievement as poverty is at depressing it.

• *High expectations* – The research is clear about the influence of teachers' belief in students' ability to achieve.

• *Self-efficacy* – Teachers' confidence in their own ability to overcome challenges and build student achievement is also key. As Billy Beane discovered, "insidious self-doubts" can undermine formidable skills.

• *The ability to connect with students* – Effective teachers get to know students, listen to them, understand them, and care about them as individuals.

• *With-it-ness* – Effective teachers have "eyes in the back of their heads" and nip discipline problems in the bud.

• *Emotional objectivity* – "Good teachers understand the importance of keeping their cool in the classroom," says Goodwin. They deal with discipline without becoming emotionally involved or personalizing what students do.

"What Makes for a Good Teacher? Lessons from Billy Beane's Oakland A's and Research on Teacher Attributes" by Bryan Goodwin in *Changing Schools*, Summer 2008 (Vol. 58, pp. 6–8), summarized in Marshall Memo 245.

2   Fixed and Growth Mindsets in Teacher Candidates

In this article in *Educational Horizons*, Stanford professor Carol Dweck applies her "mindset" theory to the problem of teacher attrition—almost half of new teachers leave the classroom within five years. All too many teachers, she says, have a "fixed" mindset about the profession—either you're born to be a great teacher or you're not. Here are some of the agree/disagree statements that Greg Gero of Claremont Graduate University used to ascertain teachers' mindset:

- *The value of trying new teaching methods outweighs the risk of making a mistake.*
- *The kind of teacher someone is, is something very basic about them and can't be changed very much.*
- *No matter how much natural ability you may have, you can always find important ways to improve.*
- *Teachers can change the way they teach in the classroom, but they can't really change their true teaching ability.*

- *I discuss problems in my classroom teaching with others in order to learn from them.*
- *Some teachers will be ineffective no matter how hard they try to improve.*
- *Every teacher, no matter who they are, can significantly improve their teaching ability.*

Teachers who agreed with the second, fourth, and sixth statements had a "fixed" mindset and often got discouraged when they encountered difficult students and learning problems during their early weeks in the classroom. "So," says Dweck, "instead of rolling up their sleeves, using every resource at their disposal, and assuring themselves that they could only get better, they probably concluded that they didn't really have the talent in the first place or that the kids were intractable—and fled."

Teachers who agreed with the first, third, fifth, and seventh statements had a "growth" mindset. They cared more about learning than about having a good reputation as a teacher. They didn't believe that a perfect, error-free lesson defined them as a good teacher. These teachers behaved in strikingly different ways than those with a fixed mindset:

- They engaged in more professional development, read more professional literature, and constantly picked up ideas and teaching techniques.
- They observed other teachers and volunteered to have well-regarded teachers teach demonstration lessons with their students.
- They confronted their teaching problems head-on and asked for feedback from supervisors and colleagues.

Teachers with a fixed mindset, on the other hand, feared being judged negatively and were reluctant to be observed by others or collaborate with colleagues. They assumed that innate talent was the most important factor in success and it was their job to go it alone.

Dweck tells about one of her Stanford students who started teaching in a challenging New York City school and had a horrible first year. "I naively thought that since I was young, energetic, educated, and driven, I would be a rock star," this teacher wrote to Dweck. Working "maniacally long hours" and seeing no progress in her students, she thought about quitting. But she remembered growth mindset thinking and set small, measurable targets. "Instead of a goal of 'an amazing classroom with remarkable academic gains,' I had to set goals like, 'this week, everyone will line up safely for the bathroom' or 'today, the green group will identify a triangle.' The class excelled at accomplishing these little goals, and slowly, our big goal of 'an amazing classroom with remarkable academic gains' started to materialize." She began to video herself, flinching at what she saw but making daily improvements in how clear she gave directions and how often she smiled. By her fifth year of teaching, every one of her fourth-graders passed the state math test, with 90 percent of them earning the top score.

Dweck says that teachers stuck in the fixed mindset see underachieving, unmotivated, disruptive students as threats to their self-concept as good teachers. "But in a growth mindset, those students are challenges," she says; "they're opportunities to hone your skills, increase your understanding, and become a better teacher." Growth mindset teachers believe, *Each student has something to teach me*, and some even tell their students, "Every time you make a mistake, become confused, or struggle, you make me a better teacher."

Is a fixed mindset immutable? No! says Dweck: "Research has shown that it's never too late to develop a growth mindset about your abilities. The first step is to get in touch with your fixed mindset. We all have some of it tucked away somewhere, and it's important to acknowledge that." It says things like:

- *You'd be able to do this easily if you were a good teacher.*
- *You'll never be as good as that teacher.*
- *You'll never be able to get these students to learn this.*
- *If you take that risk and it doesn't work out, you'll lose your status/control/respect.*
- *You see, you took a risk and failed; don't try that again. Stick to what you know.*
- *Why not face the facts; you're just not cut out for this.*

These are thoughts from the fixed-mindset perspective. Hear them out, maybe share them in a discussion group with colleagues and realize you're not alone. Then start talking back with growth-mindset thinking:

- *Nobody is good at this right away. It takes experience.*
- *I really admire that teacher. Maybe I can ask her to observe my class and give me feedback.*
- *Maybe other teachers have some good ideas about how to teach this material more effectively.*
- *Maybe I need to find some new strategies or set different goals.*

Dweck suggests taking the mindset test http://bit.ly/MindsetTest to learn about specific areas where a shift from a fixed mindset might be helpful. "Understand that you have a choice," she concludes. "Even when you feel anxious or discouraged, you can choose to act in a growth-mindset way …. You recognize that the growth of your skills is in your hands, and you choose to make that happen."

"Teachers' Mindsets: 'Every Student Has Something to Teach Me'" by Carol Dweck in *Educational Horizons*, December 2014/January 2015 (Vol. 93, pp. 10–14), summarized in Marshall Memo 567.

3 | "Grit" As a Crucial Variable in Teachers' Longevity and Impact

"Surprisingly little progress has been made in linking teacher effectiveness and retention to factors observable at the time of hire," say Claire Robertson-Kraft and Angela Lee Duckworth (University of Pennsylvania) in this *Teachers College Record* article. "Given the urgency of closing the achievement gap between low-income and high-income children in the United States and the significant number of novice teachers in low-income schools, it is essential to improve our understanding of teacher characteristics that predict their subsequent performance."

To that end, the authors designed two studies to see if "grit" (defined as perseverance and passion for long-term goals) is a factor in teachers' tenacity and effectiveness in the classroom, and if it's possible to measure it before teachers are hired. The researchers looked at the résumés of 461 new teachers in low-income schools and used a 0-6 scale to assess their level of grit in college activities and work experience. Points were awarded for more than one year of involvement in an activity and attaining a degree of achievement. For example, one student got the highest number of points for being a member of the cross-country team for four years, being voted MVP in senior year, and being founder and president for two years of the university's Habitat for Humanity chapter (one point for multi-year cross country, two points for high achievement in that activity; one point for multi-year Habitat, two points for high achievement).

Robertson-Kraft and Duckworth found that the higher the teachers' grit scores, the less likely they were to abandon the classroom and the higher their students' achievement. No other variable—not SAT scores, college GPA, demographic characteristics, or school assignments—predicted retention or effectiveness. "We suggest that school administrators consider grit as one factor—among many—in identifying promising new teachers," conclude Robertson-Kraft and Duckworth. Much of the information can be gleaned from applicants' résumés. Since some résumés aren't specific enough about dates, the authors suggest creating a structured form that asks candidates to list college activities and work experience, dates of involvement, and associated achievement and leadership roles.

It's not surprising that grit is a critical variable in classrooms, say Robertson-Kraft and Duckworth: "Teaching is by all accounts an extraordinarily demanding profession .... Indeed, despite its many rewards, the unrelenting challenges and uncertainties of teaching can be demoralizing .... Learning their profession largely by trial and error, new teachers often take part in 'sink or swim' induction processes that can lead to feelings of isolation and ineffectiveness .... In low-income districts, the multiplicity of factors often outside a teacher's control (e.g., parental support, available resources, and poor working conditions) further obscures the link between hard work and positive student outcomes…. Moreover, beginning teachers are often asked to take on more-difficult assignments (e.g., larger classes and more challenging students) than their experienced counterparts."

Robertson-Kraft and Duckworth distinguish grit from several other closely related personality traits: resilience (successfully adapting to overwhelming adversity and stress); conscientiousness (responsibility, self-control, orderliness and traditionalism), and leadership. Grit is more about stamina, hard work, and perseverance for long-term goals, and doesn't necessarily involve organizing and managing others.

"True Grit: Trait-Level Perseverance and Passion for Long-Term Goals Predicts Effectiveness and Retention Among Novice Teachers" by Claire Robertson-Kraft and Angela Duckworth in *Teachers College Record*, March 2014 (Vol. 116, #3, pp. 1–27), summarized in Marshall Memo 534.

---

4 The Selection Criteria of the Gallup Teacher-Selection Tool

In this *Review of Educational Research* article, researchers Scott Alan Metzger and Meng-Jia Wu review the research on interviews designed to select effective teachers based on their beliefs, attitudes, and values. The theory behind such interviews—what they call the educational values hypothesis—is that the best teachers value diversity and caring, embrace patience and persistence, and have a commitment to helping all children learn—and that by assessing these qualities up front, the best candidates can be spotted. Around 10 percent of U.S. school districts use structured, scripted, commercially produced interviews to hire teachers. The appeal of these interviews is that they seem objective, efficient, and nondiscriminatory. However, very little research has been done on how effective they are at picking teachers who wind up being successful in the classroom.

Metzger and Wu set out to fill this gap by analyzing twenty-four studies of the most widely used commercial teacher selection interview, the Gallup Organization's Teacher Perceiver Interview (TPI). The TPI has evolved since the 1970s and in recent years has been used by more than twelve hundred school districts. (The Haberman Urban Teacher Selection Interview is also widely used, but there were no empirical statistics available for independent analysis.)

The TPI is based on twelve characteristics that Gallup researchers believe are present in teachers who are most successful with students. Metzger and Wu say that their summary, reproduced below, does not infringe on proprietary Gallup documents. They also emphasize that commercial teacher selection instruments like the TPI don't claim to measure effective teaching; they are designed to identify teacher candidates who communicate the same professional values and dispositions as the "best" teachers. Here is the Gallup list.

- Mission: The teacher's goal is to make a significant contribution to student growth.
- Empathy: The teacher responds to the individual student's feelings and thoughts.
- Rapport drive: The teacher likes students and promotes warm, accepting relationships.
- Individualized perception: The teacher considers the interests and needs of each student.
- Listening: The teacher tunes in to students' feelings with responsiveness and acceptance.
- Investment: Teacher satisfaction comes from the learner's response, not teacher performance.
- Input drive: The teacher searches for new ideas and experiences to share with students.
- Activation: The teacher motivates students to think, respond, and feel in order to learn.
- Innovation: The teacher is determined to implement creative new ideas and techniques.
- Gestalt: The teacher tends toward perfectionism but works from individual to structure.
- Objectivity: The teacher responds to the total situation rather than reacting impulsively.
- Focus: The teacher has models and goals and selects activities in terms of these goals.

These themes were modified somewhat when Gallup released its Urban TPI in the late 1990s and were further modified in Gallup's latest product, TeacherInsight, which candidates take online. Since 2005, this has been the company's main instrument, supplemented by a set of in-person questions.

Metzger and Wu compared TPI scores with five data points on teachers who were hired at the elementary-, middle-, and high-school level: absenteeism; ratings by trained observers from outside the school (mostly researchers); ratings by principals; ratings by students; and student gain scores. The study showed only a "modest" relationship to the indicators of teacher quality. The strongest TPI correlations were with low absenteeism and principals' ratings, with student ratings a little lower. By far the weakest correlations were with outside observers' ratings. Student gain scores couldn't be counted because so few studies measured them. Correlations were much stronger among secondary rather than elementary teachers, casting doubt on the wisdom of using the same set of characteristics for K–12.

"The TPI does seem to measure something," Metzger and Wu conclude, "but we are not convinced that what it measures relates meaningfully to what matters for teaching effectiveness." They believe it measures qualities that principals and students like—a strong work ethic and good values about teaching and learning. But the fact that trained outside observers disagreed so sharply with the other ratings casts doubt on whether this is the real essence of classroom effectiveness. Unfortunately, the test-score data were so thin that they did not contribute to the analysis.

Metzger and Wu also worry that teacher candidates could "game" the interview, saying what they thought the interview was looking for rather than what they truly believed. With the online interview, the authors note, it's easy for candidates to share and discuss the questions with others. In addition, the authors wonder whether really believing certain values necessarily translates into acting on them in a classroom setting—the gap between espoused theories and theories-in-action. "Commercial teacher interviews, by their very nature, can only assess a teacher's espoused theory, assuming that the candidate's responses to the interview prompts are both an honest reflection of personal feelings and an accurate indicator of future behavior," they write. The authors conclude that it is unwise for school administrators to rely exclusively on instruments like the TPI to make hiring decisions.

Metzger and Wu also question the wisdom of the educational values hypothesis on which interviews like the TPI (and standard what-is-your-educational-philosophy questions) are based. "The TPI is an example of how hard it is to 'prove' the efficacy of a multifaceted, slippery theory such as educational values," they say. "… The TPI's affective orientations do not appear to us to be relevant to pedagogical effectiveness—the kinds of beliefs, attitudes, and values educational researchers typically focus on."

Metzger and Wu ponder the types of questions on the TPI and the differences in the ratings of high-scoring TPI teachers and close with a provocative thought: "Indeed, it may be possible that a teaching career requires one set of beliefs, attitudes, and values to get hired, another set to survive in a school bureaucracy and parent-teacher community, and a different set altogether to be a pedagogically effective teacher."

"Commercial Teacher Selection Instruments: The Validity of Selecting Teachers Through Beliefs, Attitudes, and Values" by Scott Alan Metzger and Meng-Jia Wu in *Review of Educational Research*, December 2008 (Vol. 78, #4, pp. 921–940), summarized in Marshall Memo 267.

Hiring Strategy

5   Ten-Minute Screening Interviews

"Have you ever interviewed a teacher for a job opening and, after ten minutes, knew you would not hire the candidate?" asks former superintendent Paul Ash in this article in *The Executive Educator*. Most administrators feel they must go through with the full thirty- to forty-minute interview out of professional courtesy, but that's not a good use of anyone's time. Over the years, Ash came to believe that the normal interview process is triply inefficient: it cuts down the number of candidates who can be interviewed; it misses some high-quality candidates; and it wastes valuable time interviewing candidates who aren't a good match for the position in question.

Ash proposes a better process: after screening résumés—getting a larger number of plausible candidates in for ten minutes of screening questions, then inviting the most impressive candidates back for full-length interviews. This allows administrators to broaden their pool, discover high-quality candidates whose résumés aren't stellar, and eliminate candidates who look good on paper but aren't a good match when interviewed in person. This is especially good for discovering inexperienced teachers with real talent and promising candidates with non-traditional backgrounds—two groups that might never get an interview under normal circumstances.

When Ash launched this process in Wellesley, Massachusetts, the district was getting 50–250 applicants for each teaching vacancy. The central office asked principals and department heads to select 15–25 candidates for ten-minute screening interviews. When candidates arrived, the two-person team reminded the candidate that the interview would be brief and then asked six or seven questions, including:
- a question clarifying something on the résumé,
- a question to tap the candidate's sense of mission and enthusiasm,
- a question about curriculum knowledge,
- what the candidate thinks students should learn by June,
- what instructional strategies a visitor might see in his or her classroom in November.

Ash and his colleagues found that with questions like these, ten minutes was enough to get a sense of communication skills, knowledge of pedagogy, attitude toward children, ability to establish objectives and priorities, and beliefs about teaching. The candidates invited back for full-length interviews were higher-caliber, and interview committees rarely felt they were wasting their time. Then the finalists went through additional checks and reference calls.

Although this two-part interview process takes extra time, Ash believes strongly that it improves the quality of teachers ultimately hired.

"The 10-Minute Interview" by Paul Ash in *The Executive Educator*, March 1992 (p. 40), summarized in Marshall Memo 348.

---

6   Three Suggested Tasks for Teacher Candidates

"Those who make hiring decisions are frustrated with the limitations of interviews, which often become nothing more than sterile exercises in exchanging platitudes," says author/consultant Douglas Reeves in this *Educational Leadership* article. He quotes some responses interview committees have to sit through: "I guess I am a bit of a perfectionist." "I have a tendency to work too hard." "I like people." Reeves suggests ways to get past the baloney and really learn about aspiring educators' attitudes, beliefs, and professional practices:

• *Have candidates observe several different classrooms and ask them, "What did you notice?"* This reveals whether candidates pick up on important characteristics of instruction and classroom environment, their attitudes about student learning, whether they talk about factors that are under the school's control versus external factors like poverty, and whether they are comfortable around students.

• *Have candidates make sense of student-achievement data.* One Midwestern superintendent has teacher and principal candidates arrive an hour before the actual interview and study an array of data on student achievement and demographics from two different classrooms—one high-achieving and the other low-achieving. When the interview begins, the superintendent asks candidates to analyze the two classrooms and watches to see whether candidates focus on student characteristics or key differences in instruction, curriculum, and assessment. "Every interviewee will dutifully declare that 'All children can learn' and swear that he or she believes in equity," says Reeves. "But the candidates who are likely to be the most effective teachers or school principals will focus their attention on the actions of schools rather than demographic characteristics of students."

• *Have candidates comment on student work with respect to state or district standards.* To make this process even more telling, Reeves suggests giving interviewees samples of work from a single anonymous student, but labeling each sample with a different fictitious, racially identifiable name—Ted Hunter, Shaneequa Coleman, Jennifer Chen, and César Martinez. Interviewers can tell a lot about candidates who score the work of black and Hispanic candidates lower—or higher. "Both responses reflect the same problematic thinking dressed up in different clothing," says Reeves.

"New Ways to Hire Educators" by Douglas Reeves in *Educational Leadership*, May 2007 (Vol. 64, #8, pp. 83–84), summarized in Marshall Memo 187.

7 Getting the Whole Truth in a Reference Call

In this *Harvard Business Review* article, veteran executive Claudio Fernández-Aráoz says the best way to avoid having to fire ineffective employees is doing a good job checking references. This, he says, is "by far the most important step in making sure that you're not about to bring on someone who you'll soon want to let go."

But getting honest and helpful information from previous employers can be tricky. For a variety of reasons, they may be reluctant to tell the whole truth. This phenomenon was satirized in a book by Robert Thornton titled *The Lexicon of Intentionally Ambiguous Recommendations (L.I.A.R.)* (Sourcebooks 2003). Some examples: "You'll be lucky if you can get this person to work for you." "I am pleased to report that he is a former colleague of mine." "I assure you that no person would be better for the job."

Fernández-Aráoz claims that he's never had to fire anyone in his business career, and attributes that to the steps he always takes when calling references:

• *Agree with the candidate on a comprehensive and relevant list of references to call.* This should include former bosses, peers, and subordinates in previous jobs. Narrow the list by thinking about the specific characteristics of the job you're trying to fill.

• *Structure the conversation up front.* Say how important it is to get the full story, since the candidate won't benefit from getting the job if it's a poor fit. Say that you realize no candidate is perfect—everyone has strengths and weaknesses—and it's important that you hear about them up front so if the candidate is hired, you can provide appropriate onboarding and support. Fernández-Aráoz recommends talking in person or on the phone: "It's easier to solicit the whole truth when you can hear hesitation or emotion in a person's voice or see it on their face." And emphasize that all comments will be completely confidential.

• *Help the reference avoid common biases.* If you start by asking an overly general question ("What can you tell me about Carol?"), Carol's employer will usually trot out her best characteristics—and will then feel the need to be consistent with those positive comments when answering subsequent questions.

• *Ask about the candidate's social and emotional competence.* "We tend to hire people on the 'hard' (IQ and experience) but fire them for their failure to master the 'soft,'" he says. "References are one of the best ways to assess the latter."

• *Check values and cultural fit.* Will this candidate fit in and succeed in your organization and work collaboratively with you and your colleagues?

• *Probe for downstream qualities.* Will the candidate keep learning, adapting, and growing? "Ask for examples of situations in which the person has shown the hallmarks of potential: curiosity, insight, engagement, and determination," says Fernández-Aráoz.

"The Right Way to Check a Reference" by Claudio Fernández-Aráoz in *Harvard Business Review*, February 11, 2016, summarized in Marshall Memo 625.

Interview Questions

8   Should Applicants Be Asked for Their Philosophy of Teaching?

In this *Chronicle of Higher Education* article, Leonard Cassuto (Fordham University) says that asking applicants for college teaching positions to submit a philosophy of teaching is a waste of everyone's time. "Most of the teaching philosophies I've read have ranged from forgettable to terrible," says Cassuto. For hiring committees, they are "some of the most tiresome reading that academe has to offer (and that's saying something) …. Who ever heard of someone with fewer than five years of experience at a job having a 'philosophy' of how to perform it? … Who ever heard of young people having a well-thought-out philosophy of anything?"

Those who defend asking for such statements say it's a useful exercise for applicants, even if they haven't developed a full-blown philosophy. Cassuto disagrees: It's what writing teachers call a "bad prompt," and bad prompts "produce bad writing from good writers." That's because candidates for teaching positions don't really know what's being asked. "Asking for a 'teaching philosophy' (or a 'teaching statement') drops a grand piano of expectations out the window onto the applicant's head," he says. "It throws them into unfamiliar terrain that doesn't allow them to show their skills. They try to embrace the task, but they can't get their arms around it so their attempts look mechanical, even clumsy."

A better question for teaching candidates would be grounded in the particulars we want to see them perform on the job. How about asking for an annotated syllabus for the course they will teach? The annotations would explain the sequence of assignments, the reason for assigning particular readings, and the general rationale for the plan. This would allow candidates "to talk about their teaching in a way that they—and we—can understand and learn something from. And let's allow them to delay becoming philosophers until they have at least a grey hair or two."

"What's Your Teaching Philosophy? It's Time to Overhaul a Foolish Job-Application Requirement" by Leonard Cassuto in *The Chronicle of Higher Education*, Dec. 6, 2013 (Vol. LX, #14, p. A30), summarized in Marshall Memo 514.

9 Experience-Based Interview Questions

In this article in Phi Delta Kappa's *EDge* Magazine, veteran educator and author Mary Clement makes the case for behavior-based interview questions—asking teacher candidates what they have *done* rather than what they *believe*. Originally from the business world, behavior-based interviewing is based on the notion that "the best single predictor of a candidate's future job performance is his or her past job behavior" (Richard Deems, 1994, p. 9). It's also inspired by the scary finding in one business study that 75 percent of employee turnover can be traced to poor hiring practices—that is, hiring by gut feelings, assumptions, or intuition.

Every minute counts in interviews, says Clement, and we can't afford to waste time on questions that aren't informative—questions like, "Tell me about yourself" or "Why did you want to become a teacher?" or "Where do you see yourself in five years?" Behavior-based questions address specific job criteria and probe candidates' knowledge and experience. "Interviewers don't have to wonder about specifics if they are asking about specifics," says Clement. "When wondering about candidates' abilities to do any teaching skill, ask them about it and require them to answer with past behaviors, experiences, and situations." Interviewers should never ask a question that can't be objectively evaluated, she says.

Clement suggests these steps: assembling a representative interview team; training members on the basics (including what constitutes an illegal or unacceptable question); going over the rationale for behavior-based interviews; developing a quick scoring sheet for evaluating candidates' paperwork (cover letter, résumé, and letters of recommendation); agreeing on a set of generic questions (suitable for all positions) and more specialized questions (geared to this particular position); printing a copy of the questions for everyone; asking the same questions in the same order to all candidates for a particular position; and scoring each candidate as the interview proceeds. Here are samples of questions in three tiers—

- *An ice-breaker at the beginning of the interview:*
  - Tell me about the best teaching experience you have had.
  - Name one accomplishment from your previous teaching that characterizes your work.
- *Generic questions:*
  - Describe a lesson you taught that met state- or district-mandated standards.
  - Tell us about a lesson plan that you taught that didn't go as well as you had hoped and what you would change about that plan.
  - What are some of your best strategies to begin or end a class?
  - Describe one or two basic routines that have worked well in your class.

- Describe a common misbehavior of students and what you have done to correct it.
- How do you tell if students are "getting" the material without paper and pencil quizzes and tests?
- Describe a grading system that you have used and would implement if hired.
- How have you used and evaluated student homework?
- Describe a lesson or an activity that your students said they enjoyed, and explain why they liked it.
- How have you modified or adapted lessons to meet the needs of special-education students or English language learners?
- How have you been able to get students to use computers and/or Internet resources?
- Describe a positive form of parent communication that you have implemented.
- Tell about a positive experience working on a teaching team or committee, or with joint planning.
- What part of your teacher education preparation do you use the most?
- How have you evaluated your teaching?

• *Specialized questions for particular jobs:*

- **Preschool**—Describe how you get a child separated from the parent, into the room, and settled for the morning.
- **K–2**—Describe a math lesson that has worked well for a class you taught.
- **Grades 3–5**—How have you prepared students for standardized tests?
- **Middle School**—How have you dealt with the worries and stress that middle-school students have?
- **High School**—How have you interested students in your subject and convinced them of the importance of learning it?
- **ELA**—How have you dealt with the diversity of reading levels in your classes?
- **Math**—How have you assessed a new class with regard to students' previous math skills?
- **Science**—Tell about the use of labs in classes you have taught.
- **History**—Describe a current trend or controversy in the teaching of history and how you have dealt with this issue.
- **World Languages**—What percentage of a typical lesson do you teach in the target language? Why? (Clement suggests having the candidate speak the language to a fluent staff member.)
- **Art**—Describe how you have helped students who don't feel artistically talented.
- **Music**—Describe a successful concert or presentation and why it went well.

- **Health/Physical Education**—How have you built weight-consciousness into your courses?
- **Special Education**—Tell us about working with other teachers or professionals to help a student through collaborative consultation.

Clements believes interviewers should score candidates' responses using a 3-2-1 scale: Target, Acceptable, and Unacceptable. For example, if a candidate said that the best approach to dealing with disruptive students was to publicly humiliate them, that would be marked Unacceptable; a teacher who met the minimum standard, showing some past experience and proficiency would be marked Acceptable; and a teacher who "wowed" the committee (relating convincingly successful experiences), showed evidence of having learned from past experience, was articulate and precise, and showed promise to teach at an outstanding level would be rated Target. Clement suggests looking for short-and-sweet responses that incorporate the items in one of these acronyms: PAR—problem, action and result, or STAR—situation, task, action, and result.

What about portfolios? Clement says that the committee should not ask candidates to page through their portfolios; rather, interviewers should watch to see if the candidate uses the portfolio as an effective prop when answering behavior-based questions (e.g., showing the letter they sent home to parents describing classroom routines or a rubric they used to score students' writing). "Good portfolios are small, well-organized ones that candidates create to highlight their work and that serve as visual aids for answering questions," says Clement. "The items should include a sample lesson plan, an outline of a management plan with rules, a sample parent letter, and possibly a sample from a syllabus or curriculum map. There may be pictures of students working, or the teacher involved with students, but an interview portfolio is not a scrapbook, and pictures should be used to tell the story of how the candidate teaches rather than offer a trip down memory lane …. Bad portfolios are those four-inch notebooks containing every assignment from the candidate's teacher education program."

"Retention Begins with Hiring: Behavior-Based Interviewing" by Mary Clement in *EDge*, May/June 2007 (Vol. 2, #5, pp. 2–19), summarized in Marshall Memo 186.

10 Interview Questions to Assess Curriculum Planning and Data Savvy

In this article in *Principal Leadership*, Georgia Southern University professor Susan Trimble suggests interview questions to find out if teacher candidates know how to use assessment results to monitor and improve student learning, and if they can backwards-design curriculum.

Here are her suggested questions for a prospective middle-school teacher—and what interviewers should be looking for as candidates answer:

• *What did you notice about our school when you came in?* Trimble says this question reveals whether the candidate's primary interest is people or tasks. She suggests looking for a balanced answer that shows the teacher is aware of all aspects of the learning environment, including students and staff, student work on bulletin boards, and other visible artifacts.

• *For this job, you will be teaching seventh-grade math. How will you go about planning a unit on algebraic equations?* This question is designed to see if the candidate knows how to backwards-design curriculum, align with state standards, think about outcomes, and do a baseline assessment to find out what students know before beginning to teach.

• *Our reading test scores in sixth grade aren't the best. Take a look. How would you use these numbers in your teaching?* Trimble suggests looking for the candidate's attention to three areas: (a) which students are performing poorly in which skills; (b) which student sub-groups are having trouble; and (c) how the data can be put to work in classrooms.

• *Our school is thinking about using Project _____. As you probably know, it includes software for math practice. How do you see yourself involved with this project?* Interviewers should look for experience with schoolwide programs and assessment software. Is the candidate more focused on instruction or record-keeping? Knowledgeable about using software to generate assessments? For novice teachers, are they oriented to continuous learning?

• *The students in our eighth grade are heterogeneously grouped. What are ways you might help them learn?* Look for the teacher to see the need to identify desired outcomes, gather baseline data, use a variety of teaching strategies attuned to students' needs, and tap on-the-spot assessments.

Trimble also recommends asking candidates to submit samples of unit plans, lesson plans, interim and final assessments, and student learning results. Even brand-new teachers should have a portfolio with some or all of these artifacts. Interviewers should look for alignment with state standards, a clear link between teaching strategies, assessments, and student learning, and the candidate's own learning from teaching experiences.

"Hiring Savvy Teachers: Questions to Ask About Assessments" by Susan Trimble in *Principal Leadership* (High School Edition), May 2006 (Vol. 6, #9, pp. 35–37), summarized in Marshall Memo 136.

---

11 Watching for and Developing Emotional Intelligence in Teachers

In this article in *Educational Leadership*, consultant Elena Aguilar (Bright Morning) describes how a newly hired teacher who seemed perfectly suited for a seventh-grade science classroom cried through most of Aguilar's coaching sessions and seemed irrationally frustrated and short-tempered with her students. She'd say things like, "I can't understand why this student hates me! She looks at me with venom in her eyes," and "I just can't deal with their disrespect. I never would've talked to a teacher that way." The teacher became increasingly disengaged and at the end of the school year, she quit.

This setback made Aguilar question the school's hiring process and her own ability as a coach. Upon reflection, she concluded that something important was missing: other than passing tissues to the teacher, she hadn't dealt with the emotional side of the equation. Aguilar concluded that the school "needed to hire for emotional intelligence; coach for emotional resilience; and recognize, value, and attend to emotions in a professional setting."

To address schools' hiring and coaching challenges, she developed the *Mind the Gap* framework, designed to help schools hire more thoughtfully and do a better job supporting struggling teachers. These are the competencies, in order of importance—

- Emotional Intelligence: the ability to be aware of, manage, and express one's own feelings and recognize, empathize with, and manage other people's;
- Cultural Competence: the ability to understand, appreciate, and interact with people from cultures or belief systems different from one's own, and to navigate cross-cultural differences;
- Will: a person's desire, intrinsic motivation, passion, and commitment;
- Capacity: being able to marshal the time and resources needed to be successful, including emotional and physical capacity;
- Knowledge: a theoretical and practical understanding of the subject being taught;
- Skill: the ability to execute the technical elements of teaching, which often involves applying knowledge.

Aguilar believes emotional and cultural competence are foundational; without them, it will be much harder for a teacher to develop classroom management and close knowledge and skill gaps. All six competencies are intertwined; for example, what appears to be a will gap ("I just can't talk to that student's mother! She screams at me.") may in fact be an emotional discomfort with conflict or underdeveloped communication skills.

Good coaching may help a new teacher survive, but it's better to spot problems in the interview process. Aguilar says hiring committees should watch for two things: candidates' experience with challenges, and their methods of dealing with stress. Asked a question about stress, the best answer from a teacher candidate isn't a glass of Cabernet or an exercise program, but rather an awareness and interpretation of what's happening in a stressful classroom situation and a specific strategy for decreasing intensity and addressing the root cause. Aguilar suggests two other questions:

- *How do you recharge?*
- *Name something you've intentionally stopped doing.*

Resilient people know when to step back, do something different, and avoid overcommitting themselves.

Everyone who coaches teachers—administrators, department heads, instructional coaches, and mentors—needs to monitor and build teachers' emotional intelligence, especially the newbies. Aguilar's suggestions:

- Assign a mentor who has strong emotional intelligence.
- Be explicit about helping teachers recognize and respond to emotions and see them as a source of insight, energy, and inspiration.
- Accept emotions as a legitimate part of the workplace, weaving them into professional development.
- Set an example, such as not sending e-mails at 3:00 a.m.
- Teach and model mindfulness, including meditation. "Mindfulness helps us recognize, understand, and respond to emotions," says Aguilar, "as it strengthens our ability to recognize what we're experiencing before we react."
- Know the indicators of burnout. Telltale signs include emotional exhaustion; downplaying accomplishments; isolation; reluctance to try anything new; and blaming students or the school for lack of success. The Maslach Burnout Inventory is helpful: https://bit.ly/1qrRiMD

"Emotional Resilience: The Missing Ingredient" by Elena Aguilar in *Educational Leadership*, May 2018 (Vol. 75, #8, pp. 24–30), summarized in Marshall Memo 736.

Professional Learning Suggestions for Chapter Four Interviewing and Hiring

Getting the Best Teachers *on* the Bus

Bringing in teachers who don't fit with your mission, the skills you need, or the mindset you are looking for, is an expensive and time-consuming mistake that has grave implications for student learning. Unfortunately, most school leaders have faced this problem. To avoid hiring mistakes, the exercises below help a hiring team think through, plan, and execute a stellar approach to hiring.

I. Which Characteristics *Best* Predict Teacher Success and Longevity?

The following exercises are for a hiring team to think through what they are looking for in a teacher candidate.

A. Discuss the metaphor of the people on the bus.
In *Good to Great*, Jim Collins introduces the idea of getting the right people on the bus. (*Good to Great—Why Some Companies Make the Leap … and Others Don't* [New York: HarperCollins Publishers, 2001].) Take a look at his (emphatic) insistence on prioritizing "who" gets hired in this video and his words below: Video: "Who Before What" https://www.jimcollins.com/media_topics/media.html#*ThenWhat

---

You are a bus driver. The bus, your company, is at a standstill, and it's your job to get it going. You have to decide where you're going, how you're going to get there, and who's going with you.

Most people assume that great bus drivers (read: business leaders) immediately start the journey by announcing to the people on the bus where they're going—by setting a new direction or by articulating a fresh corporate vision.

In fact, leaders of companies that go from good to great start not with "where" but with "who." They start by getting the right people on the bus, the wrong people off the bus, and the right people in the right seats. And they stick with that discipline—first the people, then the direction—no matter how dire the circumstances.

Jim Collins

Have the hiring team discuss Collins's words and beliefs—do they agree? How does the metaphor carry over to the field of education?

*B. Given the following factors, **which** most influence teacher success and longevity?*
Write each of the following factors on an index card or Post-It note. Make two complete sets of these.

licensure	credentials	advanced degrees	emotional intelligence
cultural competence	growth mindset	grit/persistence	subject-area expertise
SAT scores	college GPA	demographic background	strong academic preparation
high expectations for students	ability to connect with students	with-it-ness	

Next, divide your hiring team into two groups, give each group one complete set of factors, and have them sort the items into the following two piles based on what they think *before* they read this chapter:

- Research shows these factors *do* influence teacher success and longevity.
- Research shows these factors *do not* correlate with teacher success and longevity.

Discuss the factors with the whole team. Which ones do you think most influence teachers' success in the classroom and longevity? Next, have them read through the articles in this chapter and determine which factors actually *do* impact teacher success. Discuss the factors they were wrong about. (As you facilitate the conversation, note that the articles in this chapter show that the following the factors do *not* correlate with teacher success: licensure, credentials, advanced degrees, SAT scores, college GPA, and demographic background. The rest do!)

C. Ask teachers to write job descriptions.
At a staff meeting, ask all teachers to write a narrative description of their job. Most teaching jobs don't have a job description—teaching seventh-grade math is assumed to mean teaching seventh-grade math! Ask your teachers to try to write as detailed an account as they can of the tasks they conduct and the skills and knowledge they need to accomplish those tasks.

D. Come to agreement about the five to seven most important candidate characteristics.
Have the hiring team look at the job descriptions teachers wrote (above) as well as the factors that research says most impact teacher performance (above that). Given this information, have the

team come to consensus about the top five to seven skills and attributes they feel are most important for a teacher candidate at your school. Then have them come up with a common definition of each one. For example, if one of the attributes is cultural competence, what does this mean? What does this look like in the classroom?

II. Plan for a Comprehensive Hiring Process

Below are a few steps your hiring team can take to plan for a more comprehensive hiring process.

A. Plan the components for a comprehensive hiring process.
Have your hiring team reread the articles in this chapter to get ideas for what they would like to include as part of a comprehensive hiring process. Some ideas from the articles include:

Possible elements of a comprehensive hiring approach

Ten-minute screening interviews (Paul Ash, Article 5)
Candidates' sample work: unit plan, lesson plan, interim assessment, student learning results
Tasks (Douglas Reeves, Article 6.)
  • Candidates observe classes and share what they notice
  • Candidates are given student data and make sense of it
  • Candidates are given student work and comment on it
Interview (Mary Clement, Article 9; Susan Trimble, Article 10)
Teaching demo
Hiring team's scoring sheets (Mary Clement, Article 9)
Reference call (Claudio Fernández-Aráoz, Article 7)

Our Comprehensive Hiring Plan:

B. Plan interview questions.

Any comprehensive hiring plan will include interview questions, either for screening on the phone or as part of an in-person meeting. While Mary Clement (Article 9) and Susan Trimble (Article 10) include sample interview questions, the other articles also provide ideas for different types of questions to ask candidates. It's not enough to simply come up with a list of questions. The hiring team needs to think about these questions:

- Are we asking interview questions about every topic we deem to be important?
- After we ask each question, what exactly are we looking for in an answer?

The chart below compiles some of the topics, questions, and look-fors mentioned in the chapter. Have the hiring team work together to fill in the holes in the following chart and add more rows for topics they want to address in interviews.

Topics	Questions	Look-Fors
Emotional intelligence	• *How do you recharge?* • *Name something you've intentionally stopped doing?*	• Awareness of own and others' feelings, look for experience with challenges and ability to manage stress
Cultural competence		• Ability to understand, appreciate, and interact with diverse people
Growth mindset	• *Do you believe that even if a teacher can change the way she teaches in the classroom, she still can't change her true teaching ability?* • *Do you think that trying new teaching methods outweighs the risk of making a mistake?*	
Grit/ perseverance and passion		• A multi-year commitment to an activity in college (e.g., four years on a team) • Attaining achievement in an activity to which are committed (e.g., becoming captain of that team)
Subject-area expertise		
High expectations of students		
The ability to connect with students	• *What did you notice about our school when you came in?*	• Whether the candidate's primary interest is in people or tasks
With-it-ness		
	• *Describe a lesson you taught that met mandated standards.*	
	• *Describe a lesson you taught that didn't go well and how you would change it.*	
	• *Describe a common student misbehavior and what you did to correct it.*	
	• *How do you tell if students are "getting" the material without a paper quiz or test?*	
	• *How have you modified lessons to meet the needs of special education students or ELLs?*	
Use of assessments to monitor student learning		
Backward planning	• *How will you go about planning a unit on algebraic equations (or whatever topic)?*	

C. Role-play with chosen interview questions or tasks.

Once the hiring team has a clear idea of the comprehensive hiring approach they want to put into effect, you don't want them to implement it the first time with a real candidate. Ask some teachers who are *not* on the hiring team to volunteer to be mock "candidates." Then have the hiring team ask them the agreed-upon interview questions or give the "candidate" the sample tasks. Afterwards, have the team:

- Norm their scores and results: Was the team on the same page in terms of what they were looking for?
- Discuss modifications: based on this mock process, does anything need to change?

Chapter Five: Coaching Teachers

Coaches can frame the job of educators as continual problem solvers who recognize that surfacing dilemmas does not indicate a teacher's deficiency; it is an essential part of teaching and learning"
—CARLA FINKELSTEIN

Instructional coaching is increasingly common in schools, but it doesn't always fulfill its potential. Some key challenges: coaches not being able to get into the classrooms of teachers who need the most support; coaches flooding teachers with too much feedback; coaches focusing too much on teaching actions and not enough on student learning; and coaches not working synergistically with the principal. The articles chosen for this chapter fall into four categories: what successful coaching looks like; striking a balance between directive and non-directive coaching; the use of peer observation and video; and whether principals can be coaches as well as evaluators.

The Elements of Successful Coaching – Atul Gawande says professionals in many fields—athletics, surgery, teaching—have greatly enhanced their performance by working with a coach. Britnie Delinger Kane and Brooks Rosenquist discuss the advantages and disadvantages of school- and district-based instructional coaches and suggest a hybrid model that makes optimal use of coaches' valuable time. And Carla Finkelstein suggests ways instructional coaches can win teachers' trust by being transparent about their role, letting teachers drive the process, and adopting a curious, problem-solving stance.

Different Approaches to Coaching – Paul Bambrick-Santoyo shares a month-by-month coaching plan for supporting the rapid professional growth of brand-new teachers. Elena Aguilar describes the less-directive approach she uses when coaching teachers: asking lots of questions, listening intently, focusing on one nugget at a time, and getting the teacher to do most of the mental work. Jennifer Abrams relates a successful coaching intervention with a ninth-grade teacher and suggests a six-question "outcome map" for instructional coaches working with resistant teachers. And Dwayne Chism argues that classroom observers get much better insights about a lesson if they ask several students what they are learning and how they will know when they're doing a good job.

Peer Observation and Video – Kathleen Sheehy and Leslie Hirsch-Ceballos see much potential in teachers observing each other's classes and suggest specific protocols for observations and ways to handle debriefs. Bradley Ermeling, Ronald Gallimore, and James Hiebert add that watching videos of lessons is one of the best ways to analyze, appreciate, and improve instruction—and describe how to make optimal use of this approach.

Principals as Coaches – Jim Knight, Christian van Nieuwerburgh, John Campbell, and Sharon Thomas believe principals can be effective instructional coaches if they treat teachers as partners, stay positive, ask good questions, and avoid the "feedback sandwich." Justin Baeder explores three types of feedback principals can give to teachers: clear mandates when things need to change; coaching to explore ways to enhance classroom practices; and follow-up when teachers point out changes that need to be made in the school.

Questions to Consider

- How can we foster productive reflection and professional growth in teachers?
- What makes for an effective coaching conversation?
- Can a principal be an instructional coach as well as an evaluator?

The Elements of Successful Coaching

1   Why Athletes, Doctors, and Teachers Need Coaches

In this *New Yorker* article, surgeon Atul Gawande says that his proficiency plateaued after eight years in the operating room. "I'd like to think it's a good thing," he says. "I've arrived at my professional peak. But mainly it seems as if I've just stopped getting better." This got him thinking about the fact that professional athletes are continuously coached and doctors aren't. Athletic coaching was an American innovation in the late 1800s, a departure from Britain's aristocratic amateur ethos in which coaching was regarded as unsporting, trying too hard. "The concept of a coach is slippery," says Gawande. "Coaches are not teachers, but they teach. They're not your boss … but they can be bossy …. Mainly, they observe, they judge, and they guide."

Athletic coaching is starkly different from the way educators look at their work; in schools it's common to think that at a certain point you're finished with your education and can thrive by yourself. Professional sports coaching considers this idea "naïve about our human capacity for self-perfection," says Gawande. Athletes know that they'll always need *deliberate practice*— "going from unconscious incompetence to conscious incompetence to conscious competence and finally to unconscious competence. The coach provides the outside eyes and ears, and makes you aware of where you're falling short."

Gawande asked world-class violinist Itzhak Perlman about coaching, and was surprised to learn that, unlike most instrumentalists, he'd been coached for forty years—by his wife. Perlman said it's difficult for a violinist to hear what the audience is hearing, and his wife has provided external judgment and constant feedback that's been vital to his success. Gawande interviewed professional singers, and they described their voice coaches in almost identical terms. "What we hear as we are singing is not what the audience hears," said soprano Renée Fleming. She relies on the "outside ears" of her coach.

Gawande's next interview was with Jim Knight, who trains and does research on K–12 instructional coaches at the University of Kansas. Studies have shown that teachers implement new practices only 10 percent of the time after hearing about them in workshops, 20 percent of the time after a practice session with demonstrations and personal feedback, and *90 percent* of the time with coaching. Teachers who are coached become more effective, and their students' results show it.

Knight trains coaches to give teachers feedback on several things in classrooms: Does the teacher have an effective plan for instruction? How many students are engaged in the material? Do they interact respectfully? Do they engage in high-level conversations? Do they understand how they are progressing or failing to progress?

But giving teachers critical feedback is tricky. "Human beings resist exposure and critique," says Gawande. "Our brains are well defended." So coaches have developed a variety of techniques, including sharing insights in seemingly casual conversations, having teachers view themselves on videotape, or getting a teacher to watch what another respected colleague does. An example of the latter: a teacher was having trouble with a very disruptive boy, and the coach suggested that she observe the boy in another classroom—where he behaved impeccably. The teacher realized that it was her teaching style that was causing the problem; she let students speak without raising their hands and go to the bathroom without asking—and then got angry when things spun out of control.

But not all instructional coaches get good results. In fact, says Gawande, "bad coaching can make people worse." He asked Knight to show him good coaching in action. In a Virginia middle school, they observed what seemed to Gawande to be a superbly taught algebra class—but the two coaches who accompanied them saw several areas where the teacher could do better. Specifically, four of the twenty students appeared to be confused. In the cooperative learning segments of the lesson, some students struggled to have a "math conversation," especially in the boy-girl pairs. In one such duo, not a single word was spoken.

At lunchtime, one of the coaches sat down with the teacher and began the conversation by asking, "What worked?" The teacher noted that she had been successful in getting students working independently more of the time (one of her goals), and was "breaking the pane" more often (getting out from the front of the room). She anticipated the coach's next question and noted that one girl clearly wasn't getting it. "How could you help her?" asked the coach. "I would need to break the concept down for her more," said the teacher. "I'll bring her in during the fifth block."

The teacher said that her second class of the day had gone better, which provided an opening for the coach to bring up the unsuccessful cooperative groups during the first-period class he'd observed. "How could you help them be more verbal?" he asked. The teacher was stumped, and so was the coach. After a silence, someone suggested putting key math words on the board. The teacher liked the suggestion. For another half hour they worked through the fine points of the observation and planned next steps.

Reflecting on the coaching session they had observed—Knight pinpointed the coach's successful practices: a low-key tone; speaking with credibility; making a personal connection; not talking about himself; listening more than talking; parceling out his observations one at a time. "It's not a normal way of communicating," said Knight, "watching what your words are doing."

Afterward, Gawande asked the teacher about the coaching. "I'd exhausted everything I knew to improve," she said. "I felt isolated, too .... So I grabbed a coach from the beginning .... My stress level is a lot less now. The coaching has definitely changed how satisfying teaching is."

All this led Gawande to recruit a retired surgeon to be *his* coach. The first time this man observed Gawande in action, he gave him a number of detailed comments in a debrief afterward. "That one twenty-minute discussion gave me more to consider and work on than I'd had in the past five years," says Gawande. He's continued the relationship and considers it more valuable than all the high-tech operating-room gear he's procured in recent years. "Since I've taken on a coach, my complication rate has gone down .... I've also begun taking time to do something I'd rarely done before—watch other colleagues operate in order to gather ideas about what I could do."

He also acknowledges that it's been difficult having the critical, judgmental eyes of his coach on him when he's made mistakes. Very few surgeons—or others—would voluntarily welcome this kind of scrutiny. "The existence of a coach requires an acknowledgment that even expert practitioners have significant room for improvement," he says. "Are we ready to confront this fact when we're in their care?"

Gawande believes that coaching professionals is a high calling with a large talent pool—the millions of recent retirees from every field. But he also says that only a few are equal to the task. "The sort of coaching that fosters effective innovation and judgment, not merely the replication of technique, may not be so easy to cultivate," he says. "Yet modern society increasingly depends on ordinary people taking responsibility for doing extraordinary things: operating inside people's bodies, teaching eighth graders algebraic concepts that Euclid would have struggled with, building a highway through a mountain, constructing a wireless computer network across a state, running a factory, reducing a city's crime rate .... Coaching done well may be the most effective intervention designed for human performance."

"Personal Best" by Atul Gawande in *The New Yorker*, Oct. 3, 2011, summarized in Marshall Memo 405.

2   Getting the Most from Instructional Coaches

In this article in *Phi Delta Kappan*, Britnie Delinger Kane (The Citadel) and Brooks Rosenquist (Vanderbilt University) say that instructional coaching would seem to be "a near-holy grail for teachers' professional learning." Why? Because it embodies three characteristics of effective PD: it's ongoing (not a one-shot workshop); it takes place in teachers' daily workplace; and coaches have content-specific expertise that's of great value to teachers.

But the evidence on coaching's impact on teaching and learning is mixed. One reason is that many instructional coaches spend only a quarter of their time working directly with teachers on instruction; the rest is spent on activities like locating curriculum materials, tutoring students, substitute teaching, collating test data, making copies, and organizing students' log-in information for software programs.

Kane and Rosenquist report on an eight-year study that provides insights on various ways of organizing instructional coaching. Researchers noticed important differences between coaches hired by schools and coaches hired and deployed by the central office:

• *School-hired coaches* worked full time in their school and had the advantage of knowing the school's personnel, students, and culture (many had been teachers in their school prior to becoming coaches). But school-hired coaches often had additional duties: teaching full classes, tutoring, substituting for absent teachers, acting as department heads or Title I coordinators, organizing assessments and curriculum materials, proctoring interim assessments, identifying students for interventions, and teaching classes created in response to low test scores. All this took 60 percent of coaches' time.

"Unfortunately," say Kane and Rosenquist, "none of these activities helps teachers improve their instructional practice, which means that school-hired coaches did not necessarily get to make the best use of the strong relationships they built with teachers." Although all the principals interviewed appreciated the coaches for their instructional expertise, they were under pressure to raise test scores and chose to allocate coaches' time to short-term activities related to test preparation and administration (as well as other immediate needs) versus the long-term goal of improving teachers' instructional effectiveness.

• *Central-office hired coaches* generally spread their time among several sites, with one day a week in each school and then Fridays attending meetings back in the office. The obvious disadvantage of this arrangement is that coaches weren't in any one school enough to build trusting relationships with teachers, especially veteran teachers whose doors are "open, but just a crack." Principals seemed to regard district-hired coaches as marginal to the school's improvement goals, often having them work with new or struggling teachers. While those teachers' needs were real, research suggests that a better use of coaches' time would be working with veteran as well as novice teachers. On the plus side, Kane and Rosenquist found that the district-based coaches spent as much as 92 percent of their time on co-teaching, modeling, observing, giving feedback, and orchestrating collaborative teamwork. That was because their district bosses viewed these activities as the core of their jobs and made sure they allocated their time accordingly.

Kane and Rosenquist believe there's a way to combine the advantages of school-based and district-based coaches, and they were fortunate enough to observe a model in the course of their study. The solution, they suggest, is hiring and directing instructional coaches centrally but having each spend full time in one school. "Because the coaches were accountable to district leaders," the authors explain, "—who were shielded to some extent from the accountability pressures that principals faced, giving them more freedom to invest in long-term instructional improvement— district-hired coaches were less likely to be assigned to non-coaching duties meant to help boost test scores. And because they now spent their time in a single building, they were able to develop stronger relationships with teachers and staff." Principals were also required to apply for an instructional coach and agree to set aside specific times when coaches and teachers would work together. During the year studied, coaches using this model spent 66 percent of their time working closely with teachers and principals—significantly more than the 40 percent spent by school-hired coaches.

"Making the Most of Instructional Coaches" by Britnie Delinger Kane and Brooks Rosenquist in *Phi Delta Kappan*, April 2018 (Vol. 99, #7, pp. 21–25), summarized in Marshall Memo 732.

3 Building Teacher Trust in Coaching Relationships

In this *Phi Delta Kappan* article, Carla Finkelstein (Towson University) examines the delicate process of instructional coaches establishing trust with teachers. There are lots of reasons that teachers resist being "helped" by a coach, she says, often manifested in shallow acquiescence, avoidance, or overt hostility, such as:

- teachers believing (not without reason) that they've been singled out as deficient,
- fear of being judged and exposed as ineffective,
- fear that deficiencies unrelated to the presenting issue will be revealed,
- a belief that the coach may report on them to the principal,
- worries about being admonished by the principal,
- discomfort examining their own practice,
- anxiety about having to change.

"The coach is responsible for mitigating resistance," says Finkelstein. "Unless the coach successfully does this, many teachers never sincerely engage in the learning process." Based on her own work as a literacy coach, she offers the following recommendations:

• *Communicate clearly and transparently.* Right from the start, coaches need to spell out key details of the partnership, including:

- the goals and time frame;
- when, why, and how the coach will observe in the classroom;
- what non-evaluative feedback will look and sound like;
- with whom the coach will (and will not) share feedback.

"Coaches must be particularly sensitive about writing down anything while visiting a classroom," says Finkelstein, "because many teachers associate this with evaluations, which are often viewed as reductive or dismissive of the rich complexity of their practice." One way out of this bind is to share with the teacher any notes taken during observations.

Coaches also need to deal with teachers suspecting they are spies for the administration. Trying to get too buddy-buddy with teachers may inadvertently reinforce that suspicion: "If you gossip about the principal with teachers, won't the teachers wonder if you gossip with the principal about them?" says author Katherine Casey. In addition, coaches need to be sensitive to the potential impact of differences in educational background, age, gender, race, ethnicity, and cultural background—compared to their coachees.

• *Let the teacher "drive" the process.* "This does not mean that the coach cedes all input," says Finkelstein, "rather that the coach's job in goal-setting is to search for points of agreement with the teacher and to direct her in ways likely to produce positive results." Finkelstein describes how she got off on the wrong foot in an early meeting with a young second-grade teacher by asking what her goals were for their work together. When the teacher hesitated, Finkelstein regrouped: "What would you like to see your students be able to do this year in reading and writing?" This got the teacher talking energetically about wanting students to read books they enjoyed, practice how good readers think, write about their reading, show deeper comprehension, and engage in meaningful conversations about their reading. "That's fantastic!" said Finkelstein. "Our coaching goals can fit right in with your ideas. I'd love for us to launch a reading workshop in your classroom. Can we talk about how that might go?"

Finkelstein notes that she had already made two low-key visits to the teacher's classroom before this discussion, one to lead a read-aloud with students and one to watch a reading lesson. This allowed her to learn more about the teacher's "turf" and acknowledge what the teacher knew about instruction and her students. "The coach also needs to respect the teacher's autonomy by offering feedback only on agreed-upon goals," adds Finkelstein. "As tempting as it can be for coaches to identify areas for improvement, unsolicited suggestions can arouse defensiveness."

• *Adopt a curious, problem-solving stance.* The coach's role, she says, "is not to fix lessons or teachers but to support teachers' abilities to meet students' needs. This view is critical to mitigating teacher resistance to feedback, which most teachers expect will be evaluative." A smart strategy is to focus on what students have learned rather than the teacher's skill executing lessons. "Collaboratively examining student performance can provide an effective third space for this kind of non-evaluative feedback," she says. "Coaches can frame the job of educators as continual problem solvers who recognize that surfacing dilemmas does not indicate a teacher's deficiency; it is an essential part of teaching and learning." It's also effective for the coach to invite the teacher to comment on lessons taught by the coach, focusing on how students reacted and behaved.

• *Walk the walk.* "Coaches need to work as hard as teachers in every phase of planning, teaching, and assessment," says Finkelstein. "It is the coach's responsibility to dispel any perception that her job is easier or more relaxed than the teacher's." This means writing lesson plans, citing standards, teaching lessons, collecting books and materials, helping with assessments, doing grading, and helping with paperwork. At the same time, the coach needs to think strategically about the teacher's growth and development and ultimate independence.

"Coaches also walk the walk by using their access to authority in schools to advocate for teachers," says Finkelstein—for example, improvements in working conditions, additional planning time, and more instructional materials. "Such actions may gain coaches credibility and build trust with often overburdened teachers."

"Trust is not something coaches can achieve at some magical point and then ignore," Finkelstein concludes. "These recommendations are ongoing, recursive, and interconnected. Effective coaches attend to trust building at all times."

"Thank You So Much for the Truth!" by Carla Finkelstein in *Phi Delta Kappan*, April 2016 (Vol. 97, #7, pp. 19–24, summarized in Marshall Memo 633

Different Approaches to Coaching

4 Coaching Key Skills in a Teacher's First Ninety Days on the Job

In this article in *Phi Delta Kappan*, New Jersey author/school leader Paul Bambrick-Santoyo says the opening months of a new teacher's career are a critical window of opportunity to accelerate classroom effectiveness. The mistake many principals make is pushing rookie teachers to master every element of teaching from Day One. A much better strategy, says Bambrick-Santoyo, is to focus on coaching a small number of building-block skills in the first three months and then broaden the agenda. Here are some of his suggested priorities for new teachers—

- Covered in professional development meetings before the first day of school:
  - Management routines and procedures 101. These are specified down to the smallest detail—exactly what is said and done—and the teacher plans how and when to roll out routines and procedures in the classroom.
  - Rigorous lesson plans. These include data-based objectives and pre-planned questions that students will be asked.
- By September 30:
  - Strong voice 101. When giving instructions, the teacher stands still, squares up, strikes a formal pose, uses formal tone and word choice, and uses as few words as possible.
  - Checking for understanding. The teacher monitors student work conscientiously, noting student errors, and assigns and reviews brief end-of-class mini-assessments to see who has mastered the material and who hasn't.
- By October 30:
  - Individual student corrections. The teacher redirects students, choosing the right spot on a continuum from the least to the most invasive: proximity, eye contact, body language, saying the student's name quickly, small consequence; the teacher anticipates student off-task behavior and rehearses what to do next; the teacher restates expectations while looking at students who are not complying.
  - Data-driven instruction 101. The teacher analyzes why students answered incorrectly; plans days and times to reteach what students didn't understand; scripts desired student responses; annotates in lesson plans which questions to ask students based on the analysis and calls on those students.

- By February 15:

  - Pacing 101. The teacher creates a brisk pace so students feel constantly engaged; uses brief fifteen- to thirty-second turn-and-talks; allows no more than two or three seconds between student responses and continuing with instruction.

  - Data-driven instruction 201. The teacher scripts what will happen when students don't answer correctly; repeats wrong answers, giving time for the teacher and student to reflect; asks scaffolded questions that break the problem into smaller chunks; after correcting an error, asks the student who made the error to summarize the correct answer.

Crucial to mastering these developmental steps are frequent classroom visits, feedback conversations, and role-playing to practice effective questions and moves. Supervisors and instructional coaches push teachers to think through what happened in classroom interactions, sometimes viewing videos: *Why was this student's answer unsatisfactory? What was missing in the teacher's questioning? What would have worked better? Let's try it.*

This process, concludes Bambrick-Santoyo, "is an incredible boon to rookie teachers. It empowers them to get to the bottom of nagging worries about how effectively students are really learning, to master those practices that will lock in student success, and to do it all while honing their own instincts about what will make their teaching great."

"Rookie Teachers: The First 90 Days" by Paul Bambrick-Santoyo in *Phi Delta Kappan*, November 2013 (Vol. 95, #3, pp. 72–73), summarized in Marshall Memo 510.

5 Exercising Restraint as a Coach

"Ideally, coach-talk should account for somewhere between 10 percent to 33 percent of a conversation," says Elena Aguilar in this *Education Week* article. "The ability to do this emerges from a deep understanding and belief that your role as a coach is not to fill someone else's head with ideas, advice, or direction. Your role is to facilitate reflection." Sharing too much feedback and too many opinions is unlikely to get coachees focusing on their growth areas and untangling instructional or leadership problems when they're on their own. Oversharing also communicates a lack of trust in a coachee's ability to figure things out. Better to start from a position of confidence in people's smarts and commitment, get them talking through their challenges and dilemmas, and limit advice-giving to one nugget per session.

The key is what Aguilar calls a "safe learning space," with well-framed questions and patience, since change usually won't be immediate. She recorded a coaching conversation and was able to capture her questions and prompts:

- *Where would you like to start today?*
- *That sounds really hard. What else came up for you?*
- *What do you hope you'd do next time something like this happens?*
- *Tell me more.*
- *What did you learn about yourself?*
- *What else did you learn?*
- *And what else?*
- *I remember when this happened a year or so ago and how you responded then. What's your memory of that time, and how do you see your response then as different from now?*
- *Tell me more about that.*
- *How did you see your growth?*
- *How do you wish you'd responded?*
- *What do you think affected how you responded to her?*
- *I agree with your thoughts. Yes, try that.*
- *What's most important for you to remember from this conversation?*

As she posed questions, Aguilar had to listen intently and guide the conversation to deeper thinking. "But then I didn't have to do too much," she says. "It felt remarkably easy." Her coachee, on the other hand, said at the end of our conversation, 'Wow, that felt like a mental workout!'"

"Improve Your Coaching with One Move: Stop Talking" by Elena Aguilar in *Education Week*, July 20, 2017, summarized in Marshall Memo 696.

6 Preparing to Coach a Resistant Teacher

In this *Educational Leadership* article, author/consultant Jennifer Abrams describes a ninth-grade social studies class taught by Terry, a rookie teacher. Before class, students chatted about homecoming and clubs as Terry wrote on the board. When the bell rang, she unsmilingly had students write down the homework, take notes on a thirty-minute PowerPoint, and do small-group work. At the end of the class, Terry collected papers, reminded students of the homework, and had them push in their chairs.

Terry's instructional coach complimented her on a competent class and asked why she didn't ask students about homecoming. Defensive, Terry said, "With so much content to cover, I don't have time to *chat*."

How to deal with situations like this? Abrams suggests an "outcome map" framed by six questions:

• *What's the presenting problem?* Terry's lack of personal connection with students is producing a cold classroom environment.

• *What would be a good outcome?* Terry connects with students and creates a positive classroom climate.

• *What specifically would that look like?* Terry smiles at students, makes eye contact, laughs with them, kneels to be on the same level as students when checking in with groups, shares appropriate details about her life outside school, comments on students' sports and plays, attends school events, asks students about their backgrounds and uses some of that information in lessons, connects content to students' lives, and acknowledges feelings.

• *What knowledge, skills, or dispositions are needed?* This requires walking in Terry's moccasins and anticipating obstacles. Does Terry see herself only as a content provider? Does she understand the role of emotional climate in learning? Is pressure from above preventing her from being herself in class? Does she need icebreaker activities? Advice on how to share more about herself? Insights about nonverbal behavior and how it affects climate?

• *What strategies might promote the outcome?* A workshop on creating a positive classroom climate? A list of prompts to build relationships? Videotaping a lesson and watching it? A sociogram of classroom interactions? Observing a colleague who is strong in this area?

• *What supports does the coach need?* Perhaps funding to attend a workshop on positive classroom climate, a video camera, and a list of teachers to observe.

With this outcome map in mind, here's how the coach proceeded with Terry: "I noticed you didn't smile much in class, and you didn't bring up next week's homecoming events. The kids may feel you're a little disconnected. They might want a little more 'you' to come through in your teaching. Can you see how they might feel that way?" Terry sighed and said, "With so much content to cover, I just don't have time to bond with students."

The coach acknowledged the pressure but suggested that connecting with students needn't take much time. "Are you open to a quick suggestion or two?" she asked. Terry shrugged and said, "Sure." The coach made several suggestions and Terry added a couple more. The next day, she finished her board work early and chatted with students before the bell. At the start of the class, she smiled, looked at the class, and said enthusiastically, "Hello 2nd period!" and the students responded in unison with her name. Terry was on her way.

"Planning Productive Talk" by Jennifer Abrams in *Educational Leadership*, October 2011 (Vol. 69, #2), summarized in Marshall Memo 471.

7 Coaching with an Eye to Student Learning

In this article in *Educational Leadership*, Dwayne Chism (Omaha Public Schools) cautions against judging teachers' effectiveness based solely on their actions during a lesson and students' apparent energy level. "Student learning is the most meaningful measure of all instructional practices," says Chism, "and must remain the litmus test, or gateway, to determining future teacher practice."

How can administrators, instructional coaches, and other classroom observers know how much students are learning? Chism suggests ascertaining the lesson objective and then asking several students two questions as they work independently. Here are some responses to those questions in a third-grade class on prefixes:

Question 1: What are you learning?

- *I don't know.*
- *I am circling prefixes that I find in sentences.*
- *I am learning what a prefix is and how words change.*
- *We are looking at root words and how they change.*
- *We are learning to find prefixes and to know how they give new meaning to words and to use them in sentences to help us be better writers.*

Question 2: How do you know you are doing a good job?

- *When my teacher tells me I am doing a good job.*
- *If I am doing my best work and complete my assignment.*
- *If I have read each sentence to find prefixes and can show my teacher how I use them in a sentence.*
- *When I have identified the new meaning of the root words and share my answers with a partner.*
- *When I have found the prefixes in the sentences and know the new meaning of each word. If I can use a prefix in a sentence and can share the meaning of my word with a friend.*

These comments are a good starting point for a conversation with the teacher afterward, along with reviewing samples of students' work. In this lesson, students were asked to select a prefix they learned, combine it with one root word, and use the new word correctly in a sentence. Two responses:

- *The thunder recaused my dog to bark.*
- *I was unhappy with my brother when he disappeared with the last cookie.*

This post-observation conversation would help the teacher follow up with students who weren't successful, as well as improving the lesson next time—especially checking for understanding to catch some of these problems in real time.

"Excavating the Artifacts of Student Learning" by Dwayne Chism in *Educational Leadership*, February 2018 (Vol. 75, #5), summarized in Marshall Memo 724.

Peer Observation and Video

8 The Value of Peer Observations, Done Right

In this article in *Tools for Learning Schools*, Kathleen Sheehy (LearningAI) and Leslie Hirsh Ceballos (an assistant principal in Allen, Texas) list five potential benefits of teachers visiting each other's classrooms: another pair of eyes on classroom practices; low-stakes feedback that's less stressful than a supervisor's evaluative comments; helpful discussions about teaching and learning among peers; capitalizing on the instructional expertise within a school; and modeling for students that teachers are learners too.

That said, Sheehy and Ceballos believe peer observers need to think through several issues to ensure success. "It's important," they say, "that educators teaming up for this practice have open and honest communication about what their expectations are—what they hope to get out of the observations, in addition to anything they don't want to happen." Schedules need to be aligned or coverage arranged; each teacher should be observed the same number of times; there needs to be agreement on how long each observation will last and when the debrief will take place (ideally soon after the class); the lesson plan should be available and specific look-fors or a focus area agreed on (e.g., wait time, checking for understanding); thoughts about which student work products will be shared afterward; and perhaps discussion of the best note-taking approach and where in the classroom the visitor will sit or stand.

During each classroom visit, Sheehy and Ceballos suggest that the observer get close enough to students to see and hear what they are doing without being intrusive; ask questions of students while they're working (but not while the teacher is addressing the class); take detailed notes on what the teacher and students say and do; and focus on what the teacher asked for feedback on. Some no-nos: taking copious notes on details that aren't important; writing down only things that fit a preconceived idea; trying to fix the lesson in real time; and leaping to judgments and conclusions.

"Any debrief is more helpful with careful planning," say Sheehy and Ceballos. Prior to a face-to-face post-observation conversation, the observer needs to analyze the notes taken, highlight everything that worked well in the lesson, and decide on the most important growth area. Some possible prompts as the observer reflects: What questions will be most helpful for the teacher to answer during the debrief? Which suggestion could have the biggest impact on the teaching and learning? What is the teacher most likely to change based on my feedback? What is the ideal takeaway for my colleague?

The debrief conversation is where the most important work gets done. "Powerful questions offer many benefits," say Sheehy and Ceballos. "They lead to open dialogue and conversation, invite the observee to do the thinking, are open-ended to allow for many possible answers, create a culture of deep thinking about practice, and require the observee to examine events from multiple perspectives." Some possible questions:

- *In what ways did the lesson go as you planned?*
- *How well do you think students accomplished your instructional goal?*
- *Given the focus area we agreed on, what was successful and why?*
- *What happened that you didn't expect?*
- *What alternative strategies could you try?*
- *Can we look at student work?*
- *What might you change before you try this again? Possible resources?*
- *How can I be helpful?*

From these options, Sheehy and Ceballos suggest deciding on a couple of questions to launch the conversation, and then adding questions or comments depending on the teacher's responses—always trying to keep the conversation from becoming too emotional. Being direct and specific about what was observed, they say, increases the ease with which the teacher can understand, accept, and act upon the feedback.

"The Expert Next Door: Lesson Observations and Peer Feedback" by Kathleen Sheehy and Leslie Hirsh Ceballos in *Tools for Learning Schools*, Summer 2018 (Vol. 21, #3, pp. 1–3), summarized in Marshall Memo 757.

9 Video as a Coaching Tool

"To the untrained eye, classroom instruction often looks better than it really is," say Bradley Ermeling (a writer/consultant based in Shanghai), Ronald Gallimore (University of California/Los Angeles), and James Hiebert (University of Delaware/Newark) in this article in *Phi Delta Kappan*. An affable teacher, engaged students, and smoothly orchestrated activities may give the illusion of effective instruction, but there may not be much deep learning going on. The authors say classroom observers need to "bracket off the more superficial aspects of instruction" and answer these questions:

- *How does the instruction facilitate or fail to facilitate productive learning opportunities?*
- *What evidence is there that students achieve the intended learning goals?*
- *How can instruction be revised to provide stronger opportunities for students to achieve the learning goals?*

Ermeling, Gallimore, and Hiebert give an example of a well-planned, well-orchestrated math lesson for fifth graders:

The teacher's goal is for students to understand why fractions need a common denominator when they're added together. She reviews adding fractions with the same denominator and then presents this problem: 2/3 + 1/4 = ? She challenges students to come up with their own solutions. They can use color-coded fraction cut-outs from previous lessons, and the only rule is that answers need to make sense. Students work alone for five minutes and then compare ideas with their partners while the teacher circulates, jotting notes on the different methods being explored and asking questions: "Can you check to make sure your answer makes sense to you?" "Is there another way you can think of to add these fractions?"

The teacher then has students share their methods, strategically waiting till the end to call on students with the most-advanced solutions. After each presentation, she asks the class to discuss why that method did or did not make sense. Different approaches are floated—adding both numerator and denominator, combining the one-third and one-fourth colored pieces to make "a little less than one," finding a one-twelfth fraction piece that fits into the remaining space and concluding that the answer is eleven twelfths, and others. The class considers each method and the teacher prods them, finally asking, "Why did some groups choose twelfths? Would sixths work?" She then asks students to solve 1/3 + 1/2 = ? to see if the best method would work with new numbers.

Ermeling, Gallimore, and Hiebert love this lesson. "Asking students to work out their own methods for adding fractions encouraged them to notice that if pieces of different sizes are added, it can be difficult to determine the exact size of the total," they say. "This is the key concept needed to achieve the learning goal, and the teacher created opportunities for students to develop this concept by asking them first to grapple with this idea and then to participate in a class discussion about why some methods worked better than others. If the teacher had moved directly to showing students how to find common denominators and then asked them to practice this method, the opportunity to understand why such a method is needed would have been lost."

Observing and discussing a lesson like this is difficult—unless it's captured on video. That's why video is such an effective way of helping teachers and supervisors focus on the finer points of an effective lesson—and less-than-stellar lessons—and hone their observational skills. "Better and cheaper video technologies have opened the doors of classrooms," say the authors, "putting an end to the old joke about how teaching is the second most private act. Ordinary classroom teaching can easily be recorded, observed, analyzed, and—thanks to the Internet—shared and compiled into video libraries of instruction."

There are challenges with video—having a single viewpoint (often the back of the classroom), not being able to see the instructional task, and not hearing overlapping conversations and following the learning pathways of multiple groups of students. But the advantages of video far outweigh its limitations. It's a lot easier to record lessons than to organize live observations, and far more detailed and more helpful discussions can take place. Groups of educators can watch the same lesson together, replay particular segments, and actively debate ideas as they watch. "Ordinary, everyday teaching offers as many opportunities as ideal teaching to practice seeing learning opportunities in the midst of the typical, unscripted, sometimes untidy nature of classrooms," say Ermeling, Gallimore, and Hiebert. "Lessons need not to be taught by acknowledged teaching stars; lessons taught by colleagues provide as many opportunities to learn critical observation skills."

There are three considerations for getting the most out of classroom videos: high-quality audio (the teacher should wear a lavaliere microphone); moving the camera around the classroom to capture different students at work and show what they're working on; and viewers having access to unit and lesson plans and broader learning objectives.

"Rather than investing large amounts of time, effort, and money in formulaic methods of evaluating teachers," conclude Ermeling, Gallimore, and Hiebert, "school systems should invest in helping teachers learn to analyze learning opportunities carefully and integrate focused observation into their ongoing professional routines." The authors are especially critical of superficial, checklist-driven evaluation visits to classrooms, since there isn't one right way to teach. "Very different teaching behaviors can lead to equally powerful learning outcomes," they say, "and the same teaching behavior can be effective in one context but not in another. In the end, what matters most isn't the specific set of moves a teacher employs but the learning that occurs among the given students. To 'see' such opportunities requires careful analysis of lesson features that cannot be anticipated and reduced to a checklist. Meaningful data come from looking at what unfolds in a lesson, not from counting the number of times a teacher makes one move or another."

"Making Teaching Visible Through Learning Opportunities" by Bradley Ermeling, Ronald Gallimore, and James Hiebert in *Phi Delta Kappan*, May 2017 (Vol. 98, #8, pp. 54–58), summarized in Marshall Memo 687.

Principals as Coaches

10   Good Cop, Bad Cop: Can Principals Be Coaches and Evaluators?

"Coaching has quickly become one of the most popular forms of professional development in North American schools," say Jim Knight (University of Kansas), Christian van Nieuwerburgh (University of East London), John Campbell (Growth Coaching International), and Sharon Thomas (The Instructional Coaching Group) in this article in *Principal Leadership*. They believe it's possible for principals, busy as they are, to engage in nonevaluative, nondirective coaching that improves teaching and learning. Here's how:

• *Treat teachers as partners.* "Telling others what to do, especially professionals, is rarely a good strategy for change," say the authors. In coaching conversations, leaders should resist the urge to give advice and instead treat teachers as thoughtful decision-makers who have considerable knowledge and experience and most of the time know what they're doing.

• *Listen.* When principals are in coach mode, they should tune in to teachers' world, say Knight, van Nieuwerburgh, Campbell, and Thomas: "Listening, then, is not a trick to manipulate people into doing what the principal wants; rather, listening is an action grounded in a genuine desire to hear the teacher's perspective." That means:

- letting the teacher do most of the talking,
- pausing and affirming,
- not interrupting,
- refraining from being judgmental,
- asking for clarification when something isn't clear,
- confirming by paraphrasing.

In short, getting to the deeper meaning behind the teacher's words and body language.

• *Ask good questions.* Queries should stem from genuine curiosity and not be manipulative, leading, looking-for-one-right-answer, or advice disguised as a question.

• *Use dialogue versus the feedback sandwich.* With the latter, teachers wait for the criticism and often feel defensive because suggestions are simplistic and don't account for classroom complexities. "Furthermore," say the authors, "constructive feedback sets up the principal as the giver and the teacher as the receiver, with teachers infrequently having the chance to share what they know about their students and their strengths as a teacher." Better to look together at student work, data, or a video and discuss impressions and implications.

• *Focus on a positive future.* Discussing problems and causes "can decrease motivation and energy," say Knight, van Nieuwerburgh, Campbell, and Thomas, "and when we spend too much time thinking about problems, we lose hope." Questions like these are more effective:

- If a miracle happened tonight while you were sleeping and this problem completely disappeared, how would you know tomorrow that the miracle had happened? What would your students be doing? What would you be doing? How would your students feel? How would you feel? What else would be different?

- On a scale of one to ten (ten is best), how close was this lesson to your ideal class? Why did you give it that number? What would have to change to make it closer to ten?

This approach can increase energy, hope, and positive outcomes.

• *Set measurable goals.* The authors prefer the PEERS acronym to the more common SMART goals:

- Powerful—achieving the goal will make a significant difference to children's lives,
- Emotional—compelling to the teacher,
- Easy—the simplest and clearest way to achieve the outcome,
- Reachable—measurable via an identified strategy,
- Student-focused—framed as "students will____" versus "the teacher will____."

Having set goals, teachers are more open to support from the principal or another coach.

• *Identify resources.* Measurable goals beg the question of how they will be carried out, but principals should ask questions and give choices rather than making suggestions, say the authors—for example:

- What do you already have in place that can help you reach your goal?
- What have you tried so far that's working?
- What people or resources could you use?

"Coaching is about empowering others to solve their own problems rather than solving the problems for them," conclude the authors.

"Seven Ways Principals Can Improve Professional Conversations" by Jim Knight, Christian van Nieuwerburgh, John Campbell, and Sharon Thomas in *Principal Leadership*, January 2019 (Vol. 19, #5, pp. 10–13), summarized in Marshall Memo 768.

---

11 Can Principals Be Instructional Coaches?

"I believe changing practice starts with getting into classrooms and having conversations with teachers," says author/consultant Justin Baeder in this *Principal Center* article. "Office-based activities like analyzing data and planning professional development are important, but they're no substitute for actually seeing teachers at work, and talking to them about their work." He believes school leaders should make short, frequent, unannounced classroom visits every day (aiming to see each teacher about twice a month), and observe with an open mind (no checklists).

However, short classroom visits may not provide enough information for high-quality feedback, which is why it's important not to jump to evaluative conclusions. Teachers can become resistant to administrators' comments and suggestions, creating a psychological barrier for both teachers and administrators. Because of this dynamic, says Baeder, many principals end up doing the absolute minimum of required formal evaluation visits, and consequently are out of touch with the daily classroom realities.

The solution is simple: always have an informal face-to-face conversation with teachers after each classroom visit, and use the talks to get the bigger picture of what's going on in each classroom, build relationships and trust, and improve teaching and learning.

Of course, it's not as simple as popping into classrooms and chatting with teachers. In the same way that a good physician builds trust with patients, those supervising K–12 teachers need to draw on specific leadership tools:
- Expertise – Knowing curriculum and instruction;
- Firsthand knowledge – Knowing about individual teachers and what's going on in their classrooms;
- Listening – Post-visit conversations can't be a one-way street. "Listening is at the heart of strong relationships," says Baeder.

From his years as a teacher, principal, researcher, and consultant, Baeder has found that post-observation interactions fall into three categories, depending on what was observed in the classroom: boss-oriented directive feedback; coach-oriented reflective feedback; and leader-oriented reflexive feedback:

• *Directive feedback* – This usually involves telling a teacher who is using an ineffective practice that it needs to change—for example, *You must not raise your voice or yell at students. Instead, use a consistent signal to get everyone's attention, then give directions in a normal speaking voice.* "Even when we're working with teachers who are making serious and obvious mistakes," says Baeder, "—like failing to plan lessons or screaming at students—we need to have expertise, gain firsthand knowledge, and listen." It's helpful to give the rationale behind the directive, so the teacher sees it's a problem common to all teachers and not personal. For example, the principal might say, "In this school, we don't yell at our kids, and I want you to understand what happens when you do. When you're yelling, you can't hear students, so they can talk even more, and they're also losing respect for you."

Of course, teachers sometimes resist directives, as happened when Baeder told a teacher that it was unacceptable not to plan his math lessons. The teacher insisted that it was fine to wing it every day, and told Baeder to stop coming to his classroom, go back to his office, and do his job. Fortunately, Baeder got back-up from his boss and from the union representative—and the teacher started planning.

• *Reflective feedback* – This often involves asking questions after a visit – for example, *What are some ways you could get students to start asking higher-order questions, so they can take more leadership in directing class discussions?* "Because teaching is complex professional work, we can't make teachers' decisions for them," says Baeder. "By asking the right questions at the right time, we can prompt the kinds of thinking that can help teachers improve their practice …. The sweet spot for most instructional leaders is helping teachers understand the impact their instruction is having on students. In other words, our greatest opportunity is in helping teachers move from performance-aware to impact-aware."

Questions are also an opportunity for school leaders to show humility. When he moved from teaching middle-school science to being an elementary principal, Baeder knew very little about literacy and math instruction in the lower grades. Chatting with teachers after classroom visits, he found himself asking softball questions: *Tell me more about when you did___, What were your goals for the lesson? What are you thinking you'll do next?* Baeder realized that post-visit conversations were falling into what he calls the "fake feedback game":

- The administrator pretends to provide feedback.
- The teacher pretends to appreciate it—"Oh yeah, great point, Justin! I will definitely work on that and let you know how it goes. OK? Bye."
- Both pretend teacher practice has changed as a result of the conversation.

In addition to the emptiness of these conversations, Baeder wasn't learning anything about elementary literacy and math or getting insights into what was really going on in teachers' heads.

"It was through these conversations that I discovered the true reason it's so hard to change teacher practice," he says. "Teacher behavior is like the tip of the iceberg, and teacher thinking is what's beneath the surface." He learned that asking *Why* questions tended to make teachers defensive. *How* questions were more likely to get teachers to engage in nondefensive reflection.

Over time, he began asking questions that probed context (what happened before and after a visit); different perceptions and interpretations of the same events; the thinking behind decisions teachers made; adjustments they made to deal with unexpected events; alignment with curriculum expectations; and, most important, impact on student learning.

• *Reflexive feedback* – There are situations, says Baeder, when neither the "boss" nor the "coach" approach is appropriate. Here's an example. At one point in his principalship, Baeder noticed that kindergarten teachers weren't implementing a schoolwide antibullying curriculum. Asked why, the teachers said they were trying but there simply wasn't enough time in the schedule. This could have been taken as excuse-making and complaining, but Baeder investigated and concluded that the teachers were absolutely right; the way recess was scheduled didn't allow a big enough block to teach the antibullying lessons. He modified the schedule, and the problem was solved.

"We must see the whole iceberg of practice," says Baeder, "—what's above and below the surface—but *the current the iceberg is floating in* matters even more." The system within which teachers and school leaders are working can have an outsize impact on what happens in classrooms. *Reflexive* conversations are those in which teachers have a voice and know that the principal will take what they say seriously. "As a result," he says, "they're much more willing to invest effort in making changes in their practice—because they believe they'll get the support they need."

Over time, listening carefully to teachers talking about what was going on in the whole system helped Baeder make better decisions on professional development: whom to hire for existing and newly created positions; where to allocate funds; and where he could most productively focus his time and attention.

"How Instructional Leaders Change Teacher Practice" by Justin Baeder in *The Principal Center*, July 6, 2018, summarized in Marshall Memo 744.

Professional Learning Suggestions for Chapter Five Coaching Teachers

How to Improve Instructional Coaching

Coaching provides teachers with some of the best professional development they receive. Kim and Jenn's experiences have confirmed what the research says about coaching. Unlike one-shot workshops on unrelated topics, instructional coaching is ongoing, tailored to a teacher's particular needs, and clearly focused on instruction. There are three sets of activities below. The first two will help your instructional coaches (including you!) identify the attributes of successful coaching and improve coaching practice. The final section includes ideas for how the principal can support instructional coaching.

I. What Do Effective Coaches Do?

This first set of exercises gets your instructional coaches to read and think about what it is that effective coaches do that make them effective.

A. Discuss an engaging article about coaching.
While it may be obvious to you, it is worth having a discussion about the benefits of coaching with your instructional coaches.

• Have coaches read the Gawande article (it's a pleasure!) from the chapter or available online in its entirety: http://www.newyorker.com/reporting/2011/10/03/111003fa_fact_gawande. Ask everyone to underline a passage that resonates with them and take note of any implications of this article for the field of education.

• In groups of five, have people go around and share the following about the article:
  - Share a passage that resonated with you and explain why.
  - What do you think are the implications for coaches?
  - What do you think are the implications for those being coached?

B. Identify components of successful coaching.

The articles in this chapter provide a number of useful suggestions for effective coaching. Have your instructional coaches read this chapter and pull out and compile the suggestions they find using the chart below. Note that some suggestions are spelled out and others are implied. Either have your coaches do this individually or in pairs. If there is not enough time for everyone to read all of the articles, use the jigsaw method to divide up the articles and share findings at the end.

Article	Suggestions for Successful Coaching
1. Gawande, "Why Athletes, Doctors, and Teachers Need Coaches"	• •
3. Finkelstein, "Building Teacher Trust in Coaching Relationships"	• •
4. Bambrick-Santoyo, "Building Key Skills in a Teacher's First 90 Days on the Job"	• •
5. Aguilar, "Exercising Restraint as a Coach"	• •
6. Abrams, "Preparing to Coach a Resistant Teacher"	• •
7. Chism, "Coaching with an Eye to Student Learning"	• •
8. Sheehy and Ceballos, "The Value of Peer Observations Done Right"	• •
9. Ermeling, Gallimore, and Hiebert, "Video as a Coaching Tool"	• •
10. Knight and colleagues, "Good Cop, Bad Cop: Can Principals be Coaches and Evaluators?"	• •
11. Baeder, "Can Principals Be Instructional Coaches?"	• •

C. Discuss components of successful coaching and choose the most important ones.

Now that everyone has a list of suggestions to make coaching more successful, conduct a discussion about these approaches. Next, have coaches rank the suggestions that they believe are most important or that they personally believe should be a part of their coaching repertoire. They can simply put check marks by their highest-ranking choices or number them from 1 (the top) to the bottom of their list. Next, have them highlight the **top five** components of successful coaching on their list; they will use these to write a theory of action in the activities that follow. Note that everyone's **top five** list will be different because coaching styles differ and coaches need to choose the strategies that will work for them.

D. Write a theory of action for how best to coach teachers.
What is a theory of action? It is basically a set of underlying assumptions you make that shapes *how* you will approach the desired change you want in your school. A theory of action links cause and effect, "If we [take a particular action], … *then* we will see [the following change] …."

Have your instructional coaches take a look at the theories of action that are explicitly or implicitly suggested by the authors in this chapter when it comes to *what they believe* about effective coaching. If coaches don't have experience with writing a theory of action, have them practice writing one for several of these authors in the chart on the next page:

Author's Ideas	Possible Theory of Action for Coaching Teachers
Elena Aguilar describes the "belief that your role as a coach is not to fill someone else's head with ideas, advice, or direction. Your role is to facilitate reflection."	*If* I do the following as coach.… *then* the teachers will…
Justin Baeder suggests that he believes it's more important to focus on changing teacher *thinking* than teacher *behavior*, "I discovered the true reason it's so hard to change teacher practice.… Teacher behavior is like the tip of the iceberg, and teacher thinking is what's beneath the surface."	*If* I do the following as coach.… *then* the teachers will…
Carla Finkelstein believes that trust is essential in changing teacher practice, "Unless the coach successfully does this [mitigates teacher resistance], many teachers never sincerely engage in the learning process."	*If* I do the following as coach.… *then* the teachers will…
Paul Bambrick-Santoyo believes that teachers do best when you give them just a few pieces of feedback (often by co-observing a video of the teacher), provide them with a chance to think through what happened in the classroom, and then plan or practice to do better. "The mistake many principals make is pushing rookie teachers to master every element of teaching from Day One. A much better strategy is to focus on coaching a small number of building-block skills …"	*If* I do the following as coach.… *then* the teachers will…

Now it's time to have your instructional coaches discuss and really grapple with what *they* believe about the way teachers make actual changes to their practice. Have them review the **top five** components of successful teaching that they chose earlier, and discuss what these reflect about their own *beliefs* about teacher change. Some key questions you might explore in order to surface their beliefs include:

• Do they believe teachers need to come to their own conclusions about what to improve?

• Do they believe time is scarce and spending time "checking in" will detract from needed feedback about improving teaching?

• Do they believe feedback is more effective when it is "directive," "reflective," or "reflexive," as Baeder puts it?

• Do they believe teachers should "drive the process" (as Finkelstein describes) when it comes to a coaching conversation?

• Do they believe there is no point in discussing improvements in teaching without also addressing student learning?

• Do they believe it is most effective to withhold judgment and have teachers examine videos of themselves and the coach's low-inference notes in order to come to their own conclusions? Or, do they feel that is what the coach's expertise is there for—to share their professional observations and conclusions?

There are *a lot of assumptions* that influence how we coach teachers. It is useful to get these out into the open and grapple with them as a team of instructional leaders. Then have coaches write their own theories of action:

My own theory of action about improving teacher practice

If...

then...

E. Discuss coaching strengths and set a coaching goal

Have everyone pull out the **top five** components of successful coaching that they chose. Again, these lists will be different. After some individual reflection time on the following questions, have coaches discuss in pairs:

- Where are your strengths in these five aspects of coaching?
- What would you most like to improve this year (and you don't need to start with your area of greatest weakness—sometimes it helps to start by improving a strength)?
- What do you anticipate will be your greatest challenge in improving in this area?

> My goal for improving coaching this year (including a sentence explaining how you will address your greatest challenge):

II. Improving Coaching Skills

The following activities aim to help coaches improve their coaching skills. These are best done with a group of those who provide instructional coaching at your school.

A. Analyze a video of a coaching conversation.
If you have access to a sample video of a principal or coach giving feedback to a teacher, feel free to use that. If not, here is a sample coaching conversation. It is an ELA coach coaching a new English teacher (it is seventeen minutes, so choose an excerpt). Have coaches watch this sample video or one you have found and take notes on the top five elements they identified (above) for a successful coaching conversation: https://www.teachingchannel.org/video/complex-text-syntax-high-school

After the video, conduct a discussion with the coaches:
- What did the coach do well in the video? What examples of successful coaching strategies (from above) did you see in the video?
- How do you think the coaching conversation you saw could be improved based on the five elements you think are most important for successful coaching?

B. Plan, plan, plan—create a template for a coaching conversation.
Now that coaches have identified the five elements they believe should be part of a successful coaching conversation and have seen at least one video of a coach in action,

This template might include:

Opening, closing, sharing low-inference notes/evidence, questions to ask, one to two pieces of feedback or suggested strategies, trust-building, action steps to follow, learning the context of the lesson, lesson aim, notes about student learning, evidence of student learning, goal of the conversation, support the coach might offer, video clips (of the teacher or a model teaching segment) to discuss, space for notes on the conversation, etc.

Note that the template should *not* be a checklist, because this is a tool for a *conversation*, not for evaluation. It can be a simple set of questions (the Abrams, Article 6, lists six questions you can use to guide a coaching conversation), or it can include as many of the elements as you wish listed in the box above. Just keep in mind the amount of time you will have for these coaching conversations (keep it simple!). Your coaches can also look online for sample "coaching conversation" templates if they need ideas. Have coaches design a template like the one below:

Teacher's name: _____   Instructional leader: _____

Date and time observed: _____

Check in:

Questions to ask:

Key low-inference notes to share:

Evidence of student learning to share:

One to two action steps to implement:

C. Observe a fifteen-minute teaching segment and plan, plan, plan your coaching conversation.
School leaders often put a lot more time into planning PD sessions than they put into planning debriefing conversations with teachers. However, if they come to understand that these coaching sessions provide some of the best professional learning for teachers, they may be willing to put more effort into planning these meetings. This activity will help those who coach at your school plan for a mock coaching session:

• Have everyone who coaches at your school watch a segment of a teaching video. This can be a real video of one of the teachers at your school or you can find one online. Just make sure everyone watches the *same* video so they can share reflections and plans. Below are two samples: the first is an elementary classroom and the second is a middle-school ELA classroom.

    1. https://www.youtube.com/watch?v=tAz7TD02ytU

    2. https://www.youtube.com/watch?v=P4rWZrgyCbs

• After watching the video, ask everyone to take out the template they designed and plan for a mock coaching conversation they would have with the teacher in the video. Before they do this, have them do the activity below about planning *questions*.

A special note on questions—flow from your theory of action

In the same way that teachers often wing the questions they ask in class, as leaders, we often neglect to plan out questions to ask teachers in feedback conversations. The questions we ask teachers are crucial in every way: the tone, the focus, whether they generate teacher thinking, whether they are action-oriented, and whether the teacher is likely to follow through. Note that a coach's questions should *flow from his or her theory of action* (above). For this reason, it is vital that you ask your coaches to plan out their questions for the coaching conversation.

• Have coaches review the questions in the Aguilar (Article 5), the "powerful questions" in the Sheehy and Ceballos (Article 8), and the three types of feedback in Baeder (Article 11). Next have them review their own theory of action (completed above).

• Now have coaches think about the teaching segment they just observed and plan out three to five questions they would ask in the coaching conversation. Have them enter these questions on their coaching template.

D. Fishbowl a mock coaching conversation—now it's your turn.

Now that all instructional leaders have their templates filled out, they are ready to conduct a mock coaching conversation! Ask for a volunteer to act as the teacher from the video, and you (or another instructional coach) will act as the coach.

Have the "coach" and "teacher" act out a mock coaching conversation with the "coach" using his or her coaching template notes to guide the conversation. The other instructional leaders should observe and take notes. After the conversation, ask the group to discuss what went well and what could be improved. Be sure to let the person who served as the "coach" report back on how effective s/he felt the coaching template was and whether it needs to be revised.

Do the fishbowl activity again with different coaches getting the opportunity to play the "coach."

III. Principal's Role in Supporting Instructional Coaching

The role of the principal is crucial to the success of any coaching effort at a school. Use the following activities as a way for you, as the principal, to reflect and plan for how you will ensure coaching is a success.

A. Prepare your teachers.

1. Set up school-wide coaching expectations.
Coaching often gets derailed because of a lack of clear expectations. Take some time now to re-read the Sheehy and Ceballos (Article 8) and think through the questions below to start. Compile your answers into a document: *Schoolwide Expectations for Coaching at MS 123*. Plan for how you will share these expectations and be sure to allow time for teachers to ask additional questions:
- How long will observations last?
- Will short observations "count" toward a final evaluation?
- When leaders are observing and coaching, will they be interacting with students?
- If coaches are not evaluators, who will they share their observations with—just the teacher, or administrators, too?
- Is it optional to have a coach?
- When and how frequently will coaching conversations occur? How long will these meetings be?
- Will there be any "real-time" feedback during teaching?
- Will videos of lessons be used in coaching conversations?
- Will student results/work/learning be a part of coaching conversations?
- Will there be opportunities for peer coaching? Will this be voluntary?
- What are the expectations for following up on coaching conversation suggestions?

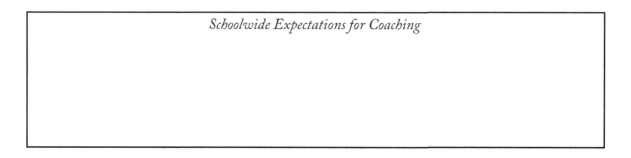

Schoolwide Expectations for Coaching

2. Prepare your teachers to receive feedback.

This is an activity from the next chapter (Chapter Six: Critical Feedback and Difficult Conversations), but which applies equally here. It will be helpful to emphasize just how important the teacher, as feedback *receiver*, is in making feedback work for *him/herself*. After all, it is the *receiver* who controls whether the feedback is even acted upon.

To help teachers take a deep dive into how important *their* roles as feedback receivers are, have them read the Heen and Stone article, "Find the Coaching in Criticism" (either the summary in the following chapter or the entire article here: https://hbr.org/2014/01/find-the-coaching-in-criticism) and see the activity at the end of the next chapter.

B. Prepare and support your coaches.

Another reason coaching fails is that the school leader does not support the program or the coaches themselves. Despite the fact that Knight's research has shown that coaching leads to teachers implementing new practices 90 percent of the time, the Kane and Rosenquist (Article 2) mentions that principals often see district-hired coaches as marginal to the school's improvement. How, as principal, can you support the instructional coaches who work with your teachers?

1. Reflect on and create a plan for support.
- How will you create time in the schedule for coaches to observe and provide feedback?
- How will you create a school culture that values and utilizes feedback?
- How will you ensure that you don't add too many noncoaching responsibilities to your coaches' plates?

2. Plan regular meetings with all of the instructional coaches together.

To provide ongoing support for your coaches in their coaching skills, plan to meet with them regularly. Even if schedules prevent you from doing this often, put at least a few whole-group instructional coach team meetings in the calendar. Two robust activities you can consider for these meetings include:

• Have one or a few coaches present a challenge they are experiencing with coaching a teacher and have the group brainstorm ideas to help. You can use the School Reform Initiative's Consultancy Protocol to structure this conversation: https://www.schoolreforminitiative.org/download/consultancy/

• Have one or a few coaches video themselves coaching a teacher and then have them share this video and ask the group for feedback.

Chapter Six: Critical Feedback and Difficult Conversations

The person getting the feedback has the power to decide whether it's on target, fair, or helpful, and to decide whether to use the feedback or dismiss it.
—Douglas Stone and Jenn David-Lang

Giving criticism and having difficult conversations is, well, difficult, so it's not surprising that many school leaders avoid, put off, and are flummoxed in such situations. Unfortunately, the result may be that students continue to get mediocre or ineffective teaching and adult interactions continue to poison school climate. The articles in this chapter fall into four categories: why it's so important to confront problematic behavior; the psychology of giving feedback; dealing with toxic people; and specific pointers for conducting difficult conversations.

Stepping Up to the Plate – Gary Pisano says that to be effective, leaders must balance collaboration with accountability, experimentation with rigorous discipline, and have zero tolerance for incompetence. Liana Loewus lists the reasons principals don't give negative evaluations to underperforming teachers, including burdensome paperwork, not wanting to undermine staff morale, and cowardice. Douglas Stone and Jenn David-Lang suggest separating coaching from the formal evaluation process and caution that if criticism isn't presented thoughtfully and strategically, nothing will change.

The Psychology of Feedback – Marcus Buckingham and Ashley Goodall say that telling people how they should improve actually hinders learning; it's better to get their perception of the situation, talk about how their actions affect others, and build on their strengths. Jennifer Gonzalez suggests that when addressing a colleague's negativity, it's helpful to paraphrase the upsetting comment, acknowledge the emotion behind it, and communicate that we understand where it's coming from. Adam Grant argues the time-honored "feedback sandwich" (praise/criticism/praise) is ineffective and suggests several ways to be more direct and enlist people in solving performance problems. Sheila Heen and Douglas Stone offer advice on how to *receive* criticism, including recognizing the internal reactions it often triggers.

Dealing with Toxic People – John Eller and Sheila Eller suggest strategies for working with eight types of difficult and resistant colleagues, including underminers, contrarians, and whiners. Corey Mitchell points to ways that principals can deal decisively and effectively with behaviors that undermine the mission, morale, and success of a school.

Pointers for Difficult Conversations – Thomas Hoerr has specific guidelines for conducting difficult conversations, including choice of location, timeliness, specificity, clarity, and body language. Deborah Grayson Riegel offers advice on helping colleagues who are defensive about criticism recognize problems with the way they receive feedback. Dolores Bernardo describes ways to handle the aftermath of a difficult conversation, including dealing with the emotions involved and increasing the chances of long-term gains. And Kim Marshall shares some worries about "real-time coaching" (giving teachers critical feedback as they're teaching) and suggests a better approach.

Questions to Consider

- How can leaders overcome the tendency to avoid giving tough feedback?
- What makes difficult conversations so difficult?
- What skills and structures make these conversations less fraught and more productive?

Stepping Up to the Plate

1 Balancing an Innovative Culture with Tough Love

In this *Harvard Business Review* article, Gary Pisano (Harvard Business School) says it's commonly believed that for an organization to be innovative, the culture must encourage experimentation and speaking up, tolerate failure, and be collaborative and non-hierarchical. However, says Pisano, these "easy-to-like behaviors that get so much attention are only one side of the coin. They must be counterbalanced by some tougher and frankly less-fun behaviors." Specifically:

• *Tolerance for failure must be balanced by zero tolerance for incompetence.* "The truth is that a tolerance for failure requires having extremely competent people," he says "Exploring risky ideas that ultimately fail is fine, but mediocre technical skills, sloppy thinking, bad work habits, and poor management are not. People who don't meet expectations are either let go or moved into roles that better fit their abilities." Of course, it's important for leaders to clearly articulate standards of performance and explain the difference between productive and unproductive failures.

• *A willingness to experiment requires rigorous discipline.* It doesn't mean "working like some third-rate abstract painter who randomly throws paint at a canvas," says Pisano. "Discipline-oriented cultures select experiments carefully on the basis of their potential learning value, and they design them rigorously to yield as much information as possible relative to their costs …. Being more disciplined about killing losing projects makes it less risky to try new things."

• *Psychological safety requires comfort with brutal candor.* When people feel they can speak truthfully and openly without fear of reprisal, learning is fostered and major problems are prevented. But psychological safety "is a two-way street," says Pisano. "If it is safe for me to criticize your ideas, it must also be safe for you to criticize mine—whether you're higher or lower in the organization than I am. Unvarnished candor is critical to innovation because it is the means by which ideas evolve and improve." Leaders need to model being candid in a respectful manner.

• *Collaboration must be balanced with individual accountability.* Working well together can be confused with consensus, says Pisano, and waiting for consensus can bog down decision-making. Good managers listen to input from collaborative colleagues, but in the end the leader must act and take responsibility.

• *Flatness requires strong leadership.* "In culturally flat organizations, people are given wide latitude to take actions, make decisions, and voice their opinions," says Pisano. Flat organizations tend to generate more ideas than hierarchical ones, and they respond more quickly to changing circumstances. But flat cultures can become chaotic and unproductive if there isn't strong, visionary, detail-oriented leadership carried out with "a deft hand."

Each of these is a balancing act, concludes Pisano, and any one of them can get out of whack. "There is a difference between being candid and just plain nasty," he says. "Leaders need to be on the lookout for excessive tendencies, particularly in themselves. If you want your organization to strike the delicate balance required, then you as a leader must demonstrate the ability to strike that balance yourself."

"The Hard Truth About Innovative Cultures" by Gary Pisano in *Harvard Business Review*, January/February 2019 (Vol. 97, #1, pp. 62–71), summarized in Marshall Memo 767.

2 Why Principals Avoid Difficult Conversations

In this *Education Week* article, Liana Loewus reports on a new study of one hundred principals in Miami-Dade revealing that many are pulling their punches when it comes to giving less-than-effective teachers honest evaluations. Asked confidentially for an assessment of their teachers, principals gave much more critical ratings than they did in the official process; for the record, almost all teachers were scored Effective or Very Effective. Another study confirmed this pattern, and also found wide variation among the states on the percentage of teachers receiving mediocre or unsatisfactory ratings. Hawaii is at one end of the spectrum with almost no teachers receiving negative ratings—New Mexico is at the other end with about a quarter of teachers getting dinged.

What's going on here? Wasn't there a big push in recent years to tighten up the process of teacher evaluation? There was, but here are seven reasons for the persistence of grade inflation:

• *Just too demanding* – "It's very, very time-consuming to document poor performance," says Marilyn Boerke of the Camas school district in Washington state. "At the end of the year, if you haven't repeatedly gone into the classroom and given the teacher suggestions for improvements, it's not really fair to give a poor evaluation."

• *Finding the time* – Harried principals find it difficult to carve out the time needed to write up critical evaluations. "We're spread so thin as administrators," said Boerke. "When all's said and done and it's June and you're responsible for submitting thirty-two evaluations, you'd err on the side of effective if you didn't have the documentation to prove ineffective."

• *Documentation* – Teaching is complex, and writing a fair and tenable critique based on relatively few classroom visits is challenging.

• *Being merciful* – "Somebody's job is in your hands," says Jennifer Nauman, a Delaware principal. "The rubric is very subjective."

• *Keeping the troops happy* – Principals need to maintain positive relationships with their colleagues, and low ratings on performance evaluations can wreak havoc. "We have to take seriously the fact that teacher evaluation is a relational enterprise," says Allison Gilmour, coauthor of the multi-state study.

• *The devil you know…* – If a teacher is dismissed or transfers to another school as a result of a negative rating, the replacement might be even less effective.

• *Cowardice* – Many principals find it hard to confront a teacher with negative information. "The most difficult part of the job is probably to deliver those difficult messages," says a veteran principal, "and not everyone is capable of that."

"Principals Are Loath to Give Teachers Bad Ratings" by Liana Loewus in *Education Week*, July 13, 2017, summarized in Marshall Memo 695.

3 Giving and Receiving Feedback with Grace and Skill

"Feedback is fraught and complex because human relationships are fraught and complex," say Douglas Stone (Triad Consulting, Harvard Law School) and Jenn David-Lang (*The Main Idea*) in this *Educational Leadership* article. Here are their ideas on making feedback less threatening and more productive:

• *Separate coaching from evaluation.* Teachers need evaluations to know where they stand, and principals are required to evaluate for compliance and decisions about tenure, promotions, and dismissals. But when an evaluation is shared in the same meeting as coaching, judgments hijack teachers' attention: *What will my evaluation score be? Will it be fair? Does the principal know what I've been contributing? What if I don't get the evaluation I deserve? What will I say to my spouse?* The coaching feedback goes in one ear and out the other.

The solution to this perennial problem is to separate formal evaluation meetings (conducted once or twice a year) from coaching (much more frequent). "Coaching sessions should include no rubric scoring or other evaluations," say Stone and David-Lang.

• *Be thoughtful about receiving criticism.* "The person getting the feedback has the power to decide whether it's on target, fair, or helpful," say the authors, "and to decide whether to use the feedback or dismiss it." This inconvenient truth challenges feedback-givers to tune in to the recipient's responses and know that if the interaction isn't handled skillfully, it's going to waste both people's time.

When a principal is the recipient of critical feedback—for example, the superintendent e-mails, expressing concern about a decline in math scores—the immediate reaction may be to discount the feedback: "This superintendent has no idea of the extraordinary efforts we're been making on this front now that the Algebra 2 test has become Common Core-aligned. He was an English teacher with little background in math, and he should respect the efforts the math teachers have made." This is an understandable reaction, say Stone and David-Lang, but it's important to look at what might be right about the feedback, pull in an assessment expert, and compose a thoughtful response to the boss.

When feedback rubs us the wrong way, it's also important to dig deeper to understand what's really going on. For example, a principal expresses displeasure with the way an assistant principal is supervising grade-level teams. The AP needs to find out if the principal observed something that was amiss in a team meeting, if it's an issue of supervisory style, or it's another problem. Time for a quick face-to-face meeting to unpack the principal's concern.

"For school leaders, becoming good at giving and receiving feedback comes with an added benefit," say Stone and David-Lang: "There is no training you can offer, no teaching you can provide, that will improve the quality of feedback at your school as much as your own example …. Be noisy about the importance of improving your school's feedback culture—for students, for teachers, for parents, and for yourself."

"Stop Sabotaging Feedback" by Douglas Stone and Jenn David-Lang in *Educational Leadership*, May 2017 (Vol. 74, #8, pp. 47–50), summarized in Marshall Memo 686.

The Psychology of Feedback

4 Three Ways Feedback Can Be Ineffective—and How to Do Better

"Telling people what we think of their performance doesn't help them thrive and excel, and telling people how we think they should improve actually *hinders* learning," say Marcus Buckingham (ADP Research Institute) and Ashley Goodall (Cisco Systems) in this *Harvard Business Review* article. Why? Because feedback is often based on three fallacies.

• *Fallacy 1. The source of truth:* "Our evaluations are deeply colored by our own understanding of what we're rating others on," say Buckingham and Goodall, "our own sense of what good looks like for a particular competency, our harshness or leniency as raters, and our own inherent and unconscious biases … Recipients have to struggle through this forest of distortion in search of something that they recognize as themselves." And the errors supervisors make in giving feedback to employees are systematic and can't be corrected by averaging multiple ratings, any more than a color-blind person's perception of the redness of a rose can be corrected by looking at the flower several times, or by averaging the ratings of a number of other color-blind people.

The solution: Ask for the other person's perception of the situation. In a hospital room, this means the doctor asking the patient, "On a scale of one to ten, with ten being high, how would you rate your pain?" What matters is the patient's subjective assessment, and the doctor can't second-guess that. "Just as your doctor doesn't know the truth of your pain, we don't know the truth about our colleagues, at least not in any objective way," say Buckingham and Goodall. "All we can do—and it's not nothing—is share our own feelings and experiences, our own reactions. Thus, we can tell someone whether his voice grates *on us*; whether he's persuasive *to us*; whether his presentation is boring *to us*. We may not be able to tell him where he stands, but we can tell him where he stands *with us*. Those are our truths, not his. This is a humbler claim, but at least it's accurate."

• *Fallacy 2. The theory of learning:* We believe that our feedback is "the magic ingredient that will accelerate someone's learning," say the authors. "Again, the research points in the opposite direction. Learning is less a function of adding something that isn't there than it is of recognizing, reinforcing, and refining what already is …. According to brain science, people grow far more neurons and synaptic connections where they already have the most neurons and synaptic connections. In other words, each brain grows most where it's already strongest …. Focusing people on their shortcomings or gaps doesn't enable learning. It impairs it …. Learning rests on our grasp of what we're doing well, not on what we're doing poorly, and certainly not on someone else's sense of what we're doing poorly …. We learn most when someone else pays attention to what's working within us and asks us to cultivate it intelligently."

• *Fallacy 3. The theory of excellence:* Good performance is highly personal and idiosyncratic, say Buckingham and Goodall; there isn't a single prefabricated description, whether for basketball, stand-up comedy, or teaching: "Show a new teacher when her students lost interest and tell her what to do to fix this," say the authors, "and while you may now have a teacher whose students don't fall asleep in class, you won't have one whose students necessarily learn anymore." Another thing: excellence isn't the mirror image of failure, so we don't get insights on success by looking at poor performance or doing exit interviews.

But for an individual, moving toward excellence is relatively straightforward: appreciate what's good and cultivate it through specific guidance tuned to that person's unique experiences and style, with the end in sight. This is how coach Tom Landry turned around the Dallas Cowboys: rather than focusing on missed tackles and bungled plays, he combed through films of previous games and compiled for each player a highlight reel of effective performance. "His instincts told him that each person would improve his performance most if he could see, in slow motion, what his own personal version of excellence looked like," say Buckingham and Goodall. "You can do the same. Whenever you see one of your people do something that worked for you, that rocked your world just a little, stop for a minute and highlight it …. 'That! Yes, that! … Did you see what you did there?'" and describe why it worked. This helps the person anchor it, be better able to recreate it, and subsequently refine it.

The authors share some additional pointers on how to give feedback in a way that fosters excellence:

- Instead of, "Can I give you some feedback?" say "Here's my reaction."
- Instead of, "Good job!" say "Here are three things that really worked for me. What was going through your mind when you did them?"
- Instead of, "Here's what you should do," say "Here's what I would do."
- Instead of, "Here's what you need to improve," say "Here's what worked best for me, and here's why."
- Instead of, "That didn't really work," say "When you did x, I felt y or I didn't get that."
- Instead of, "You need to improve your communication skills," say "Here's exactly where you started to lose me."
- Instead of, "You need to be more responsive," say "When I don't hear from you, I worry that we're not on the same page."
- Instead of, "You lack strategic thinking," say "I'm struggling to understand your plan."

- Instead of, "You should do x [in response to a request for advice]," say "What do you feel you're struggling with, and what have you done in the past that's worked in a similar situation?"

"The Feedback Fallacy" by Marcus Buckingham and Ashley Goodall in *Harvard Business Review*, March/April 2019 (Vol. 97, #2, pp. 92–101), summarized in Marshall Memo 776.

5 The Importance of Validation

"Validation is the act of recognizing and affirming the feelings or perspective of another person," says Jennifer Gonzalez in this *Cult of Pedagogy* article. "It's acknowledging that these thoughts and feelings are *true for that person*. It's a very simple, astoundingly fast way to make progress in a conversation; it eases tension, builds trust, and gets you and the other person to a solution more quickly."

But validation doesn't come naturally; more commonly, people respond to negative comments by:
- arguing with the person's viewpoint,
- dismissing their feelings,
- ignoring the concern,
- being snide or getting *ad hominem*.

"In all of these cases," says Gonzalez, "the other person has not learned anything new, you have not come to any new understandings or solved any problems, and you have very likely created new negative feelings. Keep repeating this cycle and you have the makings of a problem relationship."

Gonzalez suggests a three-step process when negativity from a colleague makes our gorge rise:

• Paraphrase the main thing the person is saying to make sure you heard it right. Doing this lets people know you're listening, are interested (even curious), and aren't judging. It can be helpful to use stems like *Let me see if I'm understanding you right*, or *In other words*.

• Acknowledge the emotion. The other person will feel "heard" if you can correctly identify what's going on under the surface: *That sounds frustrating*, or *So you felt confused?*

• Communicate acceptance. "You may not feel the same way, and their feelings might create problems for you, but they are what they are," says Gonzalez. Letting the person know that you accept their feelings without necessarily agreeing with them is important: *I can see why you'd feel that way*, or *It can be upsetting when that happens.*

The conversation might continue or it might end there; either way, the other person is likely to feel heard and accepted. Or you could do some additional prompting: *Can you tell me more about that?*

Gonzalez acknowledges that we might be reluctant to engage in this kind of validating dialogue. Why?

- The person's opinion is wrong, so why validate it?
- The person's position isn't valid, so why encourage it?
- This touchy-feely stuff isn't for me.
- I have better ways to spend my time.

Gonzalez pushes back: "If you make reflective listening and validation a regular part of your way of dealing with people, you will ultimately save yourself a TON of time." Any conversation is a fork in the road: one path is often more drawn-out, full of arguments, put-downs, and opinions not changing at all—while the other, if it starts with validation and calmer discourse, is more likely to produce an amicable resolution—and be much shorter.

_____

"The Magic of Validation" by Jennifer Gonzalez in *The Cult of Pedagogy*, December 18, 2017, summarized in Marshall Memo 721.

_____

6 Improving on the "Feedback Sandwich"

In this online article, Wharton professor Adam Grant says the standard way that many leaders, coaches, parents, and teachers share criticism is with a slice of praise on the top and bottom with the bad news in the middle. If someone taking this approach were completely honest, the opening statement would be: "I have some negative feedback to give you. I'll start with some positive feedback to relax you, and then give you the negative feedback, which is the real purpose of our meeting. I'll end with more positive feedback so you won't be disappointed or angry at me when you leave my office." Put this way, it's obvious why the feedback sandwich is usually ineffective—and annoying. Grant believes there are two common outcomes:

- The positives fall on deaf ears. "When people hear praise during a feedback conversation," he says, "they brace themselves. They're waiting for the other shoe to drop, and it makes the opening compliment seem insincere."
- The positives drown out the negatives. If the praise comes across as genuine and meaningful, and if the second slice of praise is the last thing the recipient hears, it can lead him or her to ignore the criticism.

"Giving a compliment sandwich might make the giver feel good," says Grant, "but it doesn't help the receiver." In its place, he suggests this four-step process:

• *Be explicit about the positive purpose of the feedback.* This might be a statement up front, such as "I'm giving you these comments because I have very high expectations and I know that you can reach them." People are open to suggestions and criticism as long as they know they're basically okay, the supervisor cares about them, and the purpose is to help them get better. One study found that a statement like this made feedback 40 percent more effective.

• *Take yourself off the pedestal.* "Negative feedback can make people feel inferior," says Grant. "If you level the playing field, it's a lot less threatening." Statements like these are helpful:

- *I've benefited a lot from people giving me feedback, and I'm trying to pay that forward.*
- *I've been studying great managers, and I've noticed that they spend a lot of time giving feedback. I'm working on doing more of that.*
- *Now that we've been working together for a while, I think it would be great if we gave each other suggestions for how we can be more effective.*

"All of these messages send a clear signal," says Grant: "I'm not perfect. I'm trying to get better too."

• *Ask if the person wants feedback.* An opening question might be, "I've noticed a couple of things and wondered if you're interested in some feedback." Grant says he's used this approach many times and no one has ever responded by saying no. "Once people take ownership over the decision to receive feedback, they're less defensive about it," he says.

• *Have a transparent dialogue, not a manipulative monologue.* Here's a suggested opening statement by a manager: "The presentation you gave to the leadership team this morning may have created confusion about our strategy. Let me tell you how I'd like to approach this meeting and see if it works for you. I want to start by describing what I saw that raised my concerns and see if you saw the same things. After we agree on what happened, I want to say more about my concerns and see if you share them. Then we can decide what, if anything, we need to do going forward. I'm open to the possibility that I may be missing things or that I contributed to the concerns I'm raising. How does that work for you?"

"Stop Serving the Feedback Sandwich" by Adam Grant on his website, May 4, 2016, summarized in Marshall Memo 646.

---

7 Defensive Reactions to Negative Feedback

In this *Harvard Business Review* article, Sheila Heen and Douglas Stone (Harvard Law School/Triad Consulting Group) say that in the corporate world, performance evaluations aren't working very well, especially when they contain critical feedback. They cite some recent survey results:

- Only 36 percent of managers complete appraisals thoroughly and on time.
- Fifty-five percent of employees said their most recent performance review was unfair or inaccurate.
- Twenty-five percent said they dread evaluations more than anything else in their working lives.
- Human resources leaders said their biggest challenge was managers' unwillingness to deliver negative feedback.
- There's relatively little helpful coaching and mentoring going on.

It's obvious that many managers need to get better at delivering criticism, say Heen and Stone: "But improving the skills of the feedback giver won't accomplish much if the receiver isn't able to absorb what is said. It is the receiver who controls whether feedback is let in or kept out, who has to make sense of what he or she is hearing, and who decides whether or not to change."

Heen and Stone believe feedback givers and receivers need to be in touch with the three ways criticism can activate psychological triggers.

- Truth triggers: The criticism seems untrue, off base, or unhelpful—making us feel wronged, indignant, exasperated.
- Relationship triggers: Something about this person makes it difficult to accept feedback that might be palatable coming from someone else. ("After all I've done for you, I get this petty criticism!")
- Identity triggers: The criticism attacks our core sense of who we are, causing us to feel defensive, off balance, perhaps overwhelmed.

These are natural reactions, say Heen and Stone: "The solution isn't to pretend you don't have them. It's to recognize what's happening and learn how to derive benefit from feedback, even when it sets off one or more of our triggers. Taking feedback well is a process of sorting and filtering." Once we've done that, we can figure out if the feedback is potentially helpful or genuinely worthless. Here are their suggestions:

• *Know your tendencies.* Over time, many of us establish patterns in the way we respond to criticism, for example:

- "This is plain wrong!"
- "You're doing this by *e-mail*?"
- "You of all people!"

Or:

- smiling on the outside but seething inside,
- getting teary,
- being filled with righteous indignation,
- rejecting feedback in the moment but considering it over time,
- accepting it right away but later deciding it's baloney,
- agreeing intellectually but having trouble changing your behavior.

If we are aware of our patterns, we can make better choices on how to process criticism—for example, "Usually after I sleep on it, I'm in a better place to figure out whether there's something I can learn."

• *Disentangle the* what *from the* who. "If the feedback is on target and the advice is wise, it shouldn't matter who delivers it," say Heen and Stone, "… but it does." We need to recognize when a relationship trigger has been activated, step back, and make an objective analysis of the validity of the criticism.

• *Hear the coaching side of criticism.* Most feedback has an evaluative component and a coaching component. We tend to be more attuned to the first, hearing it as an attack on how we've been doing things—even our professional competence (our identity trigger has been pulled). "Work to hear feedback as potentially valuable advice from a fresh perspective rather than as an indictment of how you've done things in the past," advise Heen and Douglas.

• *Unpack the feedback.* For example, a woman is told by a male colleague that she should "be more assertive." She might make a snap judgment and reject the suggestion ("I think I'm pretty assertive already") or acquiesce ("I really do need to step it up"), but what does this guy really mean?

- Does he think she should speak up more often?
- Should she speak with greater conviction?
- Should she smile less? More?
- Should she have the confidence to admit she doesn't know something?
- Or the confidence to pretend she does?

Before doing anything, it's important to find out what prompted the suggestion, what her colleague saw her do or fail to do, how he defines assertiveness, what he's worried about, and what he expects. In other words, they need to talk! Only then can she decide if the suggestion is worth acting on.

• *Ask for lots of mini-feedback.* "Feedback is less likely to set off your emotional triggers if you request it and direct it," say Heen and Stone. "Soliciting constructive criticism communicates humility, respect, passion for excellence, and confidence, all in one go." So don't wait for the annual performance review; during the year request bite-size advice. And don't ask global questions like "Do you have any feedback for me?" Rather, ask "What's one thing you see me doing (or failing to do) that holds me back?" Bosses and colleagues are usually happy to respond, and specific coaching tidbits are often very helpful.

• *Engage in small experiments.* "When someone gives you advice, test it out," suggest Heen and Stone. "If it works, great. If it doesn't, tweak your approach, or decide to end the experiment."

"Find the Coaching in Criticism: The Right Ways to Receive Feedback" by Sheila Heen and Douglas Stone in *Harvard Business Review*, January/February 2014 (Vol. 92, #1–2), summarized in Marshall Memo 518.

Dealing with Toxic People

8 Stepping Up with Teachers Who Need Critical Feedback

In this article in *Principal*, John Eller (St. Cloud State University) and Sheila Eller (a Minnesota elementary principal) suggest strategies for working with negative staff members who, even if they are small in number, can have a major impact on morale and school effectiveness. The authors suggest analyzing why a person might be resistant to change (Are they losing something important? Have they had negative experiences with change in the past?) and choosing which venue is best for addressing their resistance to change. If it's a face-to-face "difficult conversation," Eller and Eller have these pointers: set a serious tone, clearly describe the problem with specific examples, tell the person exactly what needs to be changed or addressed, and describe how you will follow up. "The most successful difficult conversations," they say, "are well planned, clear, and let the employee know that the principal means business."

Eller and Eller describe eight types of difficult and resistant colleagues and suggest possible strategies with each one.

• *Underminers*—Characteristics: They say they will comply when they're with you, then criticize and fail to implement behind your back. Strategies: Give everyone a chance to share concerns in private and public; check on implementation in their classrooms; confront noncompliance in a frank conversation.

• *Contrarians*—Characteristics: They believe that if they don't speak up, no one else will, and ignore other perspectives. Strategies: Structure pro-and-con discussions with all staff about new ideas; ask that an idea or strategy be discussed with respect to its impact on teaching and learning; confront the behavior in a difficult conversation.

• *Recruiters*—Characteristics: They try to win over others to their point of view, dropping the names of those who, they say, agree with them. Strategies: Help others develop the strength to resist being recruited; challenge recruiters to be specific about those who supposedly agree with them; confront the behavior in a personal conversation.

• *The Challenged*—Characteristics: They believe they're doing a good job and don't need to change, and cover up their lack of knowledge. Strategies: Ask them specific questions to see if they truly understand what's being proposed; determine what information is missing; and provide opportunities for them to learn the required skills, which might include coaching, peer modeling, and conferencing.

• *Retired on the Job*—Characteristics: They're open about not being motivated to change or improve. Strategies: Say you understand their situation but state your expectations about the work required; follow up with classroom visits.

• *Resident Experts*— Characteristics: They broadcast their knowledge about every issue. When they make mistakes, they blame others or outside circumstances, and they make excuses when you want to observe them implementing new ideas or techniques. Strategies: Privately ask them specific questions to assess their knowledge; hold them accountable when they make errors; and confront the behavior one-on-one.

• *Unelected Representatives*—Characteristics: They claim to represent a group or viewpoint without others' permission. Strategies: Ask the colleagues they claim to represent if they are in agreement; conduct open conversations about the issues in which everyone has a chance to speak.

• *Whiners and complainers*—Characteristics: They find fault with everything, fail to take responsibility for issues in their classrooms or professional practice, and go overboard in talking about issues and problems. Strategies: Hold pro-and-con conversations in which positive ideas as well as concerns are aired; confront in a difficult conversation; don't accept irrational explanations; ask them to reframe the situation and reduce the melodrama.

"Working Productively with Difficult and Resistant Staff" by John Eller and Sheila Eller in *Principal*, September/October 2012 (Vol. 92, #1, pp. 28–31), summarized in Marshall Memo 453.

9 Dealing with Colleagues Who Undermine the Mission

In this *Education Week* article, Corey Mitchell reports on veteran administrators' experience with colleagues who undermine and disrupt a school's mission. "On the surface, perhaps some of these troublemakers don't seem like the most horrible things in the world," says Virginia leader Diane Watkins. "But because they slowly erode the morale of your building, they can be." John Eller (St. Cloud State University) has catalogued some common problem behaviors and tactics.

- *Justifying actions based on the way things were done before* ("The last principal didn't have a problem with that." – Response: Reaffirm that you are a different principal with different expectations.

- *Oblivious about how the behavior affects others* – Response: Provide clear feedback to help the person understand the impact.

174

- *Denying, refuses to acknowledge the problem* – Response: Directly address the problematic behavior, leaving no room for misinterpretation.
- *Blaming others* – Response: Steer the conversation toward problem-solving.
- *Stalling, hoping to last you out* – Response: Make it clear that you want to solve the problem for the good of the staff and students.
- *Making excuses, spending more time justifying and rationalizing than it would take to change the behavior* – Response: Avoid getting pulled down that rabbit hole. Discuss how this response doesn't further your long-range goals.
- *Recruiting colleagues, parents, or community members to resist initiatives* – Response: Clarify with colleagues what you want to change and why, and while input is appreciated, you are the captain of the ship.
- *Passive-aggressive undermining by not completing assignments or giving 100 percent* – Response: Make sure people assigned to a task have appropriate training and a clear idea of what is intended.

A common mistake, says former principal Todd Whitaker, is ignoring troubling behaviors in hopes that they, or the perpetrators, will go away. Another mistake is addressing the whole staff rather than talking with the malefactor face-to-face. "Dealing with negative people is never easy," he says. "It's never fun. But if you don't do it, nothing about your job is fun."

Four additional pieces of advice from Mitchell's interviewees: address problems early rather than letting them fester; use a light touch at first, increasing the odds of a no-big-deal change in behavior; during difficult conversations, make it about the behavior, not the person; and listen to the other person's perspective because there may be something you're missing.

A proactive strategy, veteran principals told Mitchell, is to be in classrooms every day, complimenting effective practices and building relationships and rapport with colleagues. That way, when difficult conversations become necessary, they've been preceded by others that are more positive.

"Unfortunately," says Watkins, "sometimes the most difficult person in the building is the principal." Whitaker adds that an insensitive and ineffective leader can corrupt an entire school. One way to tune in on one's own shortcomings is conducting a regular staff survey and looking objectively at critical feedback.

"How Principals Can Banish Toxic Adult Behavior from Their Schools" by Corey Mitchell in *Education Week*, October 17, 2018 (Vol. 38, #9, pp. 18–20), summarized in Marshall Memo 759.

Pointers for Difficult Conversations

10 Giving Negative Feedback That's Heard

In this article in *Principal*, former St. Louis principal Thomas Hoerr has these suggestions for giving teachers and others critical feedback in a way that changes behavior:

• *Don't e-mail criticism.* This is not an appropriate forum for difficult conversations, which require face-to-face contact and an opportunity for clarification and interaction.

• *Pick the time and place carefully.* A good feedback session should not be spur-of-the-moment; it requires privacy and enough time to do justice to what's being said.

• *Be timely.* Don't wait a long time after you identify the problem. On the other hand, if you're still emotional, wait until you're calm and collected.

• *Be specific.* Vague generalities will not help the teacher. Details matter—for example, your reasons for believing the lesson was paced too slowly; evidence that a lesson wasn't well planned or that students were bored; what was problematic in the way a parent's complaint was handled. The more specific you are, the more pushback there may be (especially if you're off base!), but also the more chance there is for real learning and change on the teacher's part.

• *Watch your body language.* Nonverbal cues can communicate as much as words. "You need to be sure that your eyes, face, and body are giving the same message as your words." For a particularly difficult conversation, it may help to role-play with someone you trust.

• *Provide a rationale.* The teacher needs to understand why this incident is important to you, and its implications and the context of your thinking. This may be obvious, or it may need careful explaining.

• *Let the teacher know you've been there too.* It's disarming and helpful for you to acknowledge that you've made your share of mistakes and understand their feelings.

• *Allow for a response.* No drive-by feedback! If you want to change behavior, you need a two-way conversation. The teacher must have time to absorb what you have said and respond to it, making meaning of your criticism. It sometimes helps to ask, "Does this make sense to you?" or "Can you see why I'm disappointed?" If the teacher is at a loss for words, you might say, "Why don't you sit on this for a day or so, and then let's talk."

• *Clarify what you said.* Rephrasing the message at the end can help: "Let me be sure that I was clear in what I said ...." Alternatively, you might want to follow up with a memo outlining your key points so there will be no misunderstanding.

• *Praise more than you criticize.* Over the course of the school year, a 5:1 ratio is ideal, frequently making "deposits" in the "interpersonal bank account," which makes criticism easier to accept.

"Negative Feedback: Making Yourself Heard" by Thomas Hoerr, *Principal*, March/April 2004 (Vol. 82, #4, pp. 63–64), summarized in Marshall Memo 26.

11 Giving Feedback to Someone Who Can't Take Feedback

In this *Harvard Business Review* online article, Deborah Grayson Riegel (Wharton School and The Boda Group) has suggestions for managers who get pushback when they have difficult conversations with colleagues—defensiveness, shutting down, yessing them to death and not following through on promises, or calling in sick on the day of a performance review. "My advice to leaders in these situations is to take a break from giving other performance-related feedback," says Riegel. "Instead, start giving feedback on how the employee receives feedback …. It should be its own topic of conversation, addressed when you have enough evidence to assume a pattern and when both you and your colleague have adequate time and energy to tackle it." Here are her tips for these talks:

• *Make the case.* Say that it's important for everyone to be able to receive critical feedback seriously and professionally – and that resistance isn't helpful to the team, the organization, or the person's professional reputation.

• *Be curious.* The person may not see his or her behavior the way you do. Ask an open-ended question about how the person sees the supervisory dynamic.

• *Use neutral language.* "Want to make someone defensive?" asks Riegel. "Tell him he's being defensive!" Avoid blaming words and language with a negative connotation. Try something like, "When I give you feedback, I notice that you look at the floor. I'm curious to know what's going on for you."

• *Ask for feedback.* It's possible that your communication style is too direct, the timing of your critical conversations was bad, or that you've sent mixed messages by pairing negative feedback with praise. Perhaps ask, "How am I contributing to this problem?" and model how to receive critical feedback.

• *Eat humble pie.* Talk about a time you messed up, were criticized, and didn't take it well—and what you learned from that.

• *Secure a commitment.* Here's a possible opening statement: "So moving forward, here's what I'd like to see happen: I'll give you some feedback and if you feel like you disagree, have a different perspective on it, or that I am not getting the whole picture, you'll tell me that *in the meeting*. I'll agree to really listen to your take on the situation, and we'll come up with a plan together. Does that work for you?"

• *Acknowledge positive change.* After the feedback-on-feedback talk, start looking for evidence of improvement and immediately reinforce it.

"When Your Employee Doesn't Take Feedback" by Deborah Grayson Riegel in *Harvard Business Review*, November 6, 2015, summarized in Marshall Memo 613.

12 What to Do in the Aftermath of a Difficult Conversation

In this *Harvard Business Review* article, consultant Dolores Bernardo feels the pain of anyone who has been through a workplace confrontation—a clash of opinions, strong emotions, voices raised, a lot at stake, your stomach in knots. Afterward, we're likely to feel, "Glad that's over. I never want to have to have that conversation again." But what happens after one of these dramas is crucial, says Bernardo. "What specifically should you do and say to make things less awkward and to move forward, while also making sure that you're actually making some progress on the points that were discussed?" Here are her suggestions:

• *Acknowledge that the conversation happened.* Putting it out of mind is a mistake because it leaves you powerless and also may leave the other person guessing what to do next. Better to thank your colleague for being willing to engage with a big issue and get it out in the open, acknowledge that the conversation was tough, and focus on the positive.

• *Find ways to take next steps.* Send a follow-up e-mail to summarize the substance and the outcomes you both want. "Clear communication around next steps proactively moves the conversation forward," says Bernardo. "A written record also tracks any differences in perspectives, memory, or understanding, and prioritizes accuracy. Also, importantly, new information almost always comes to light. That 'new' information might actually be the true hidden sticking point that had stalled progress or created conflict in the first place. This step creates a path forward, out of the conflict zone, and builds a shared understanding of the issue."

• *Focus on building the long-term relationship.* Put the past on hold and focus on how to positively shape the working relationship going forward. What are the outcomes you both seek? What constraints do you both have to put up with? What's important to you that your colleague might not be aware of? What does success look like in your partnership? A casual dinner after work, a one-on-one walk, or sharing time at an event can help you connect as human beings and keep the common enterprise in mind. As former U.S. Army general Stanley McChrystal says, "It's not enough to be great; you have to be great together."

"You Just Had a Difficult Conversation at Work. Here's What to Do Next" by Dolores Bernardo in *Harvard Business Review*, May 29, 2017, summarized in Marshall Memo 693.

13 Should Principals Give Critical Feedback While Observing a Class?

In this article in *Phi Delta Kappan*, Kim Marshall explores the appropriateness of supervisors jumping in with redirection or contributions during short, informal classroom visits (versus observing and talking later). Here's when administrators are tempted to intervene during a lesson:

- If the teacher is missing an opportunity to make an important point;
- If some students seem confused, and the teacher isn't noticing;
- If the teacher makes a consequential error (like mixing up perimeter and area);
- If a student's behavior is seriously disrupting instruction;
- To contribute an idea in a discussion.

An example: A history teacher finishes explaining a point and asks, "Is everyone with me?" A student says yes, and the teacher starts to move on, but the principal at the back of the room senses that many students don't understand and asks, "Do you mind if I ask your students a couple of questions?" The teacher nods, the principal interacts with students for a couple of minutes, and when the teacher proceeds, student mastery is much improved—and she does a better job teaching the remaining classes that day.

Proponents of "real-time coaching" believe it's one of the best ways to get feedback to stick in teachers' minds, especially with rookies struggling with pedagogy and classroom management. But there are concerns that real-time coaching will undermine teachers' authority with students; throw teachers off their stride; distract students from curriculum content as they observe possibly tense adult interactions; change the dynamic being observed, resulting in a less-accurate picture of the teacher's work; and encourage teachers to game the system by nimbly showcasing what observers are looking for (e.g., turn-and-talk, checking for understanding) but not changing their practices the rest of the time. One former administrator had this reaction: "Improving adult practice is complex and requires lots of trust, time, and care. I fear advocates of real-time coaching are looking for a silver bullet, an easy way."

Those who believe in during-class interventions disagree. *Seize the moment!* they say. Waiting for the post-observation conference risks losing the immediacy of the classroom context and won't have nearly the same impact. Besides, supervisor/teacher conferences are often bogged down in compliance checklists and rubrics, and people are so busy that they often don't get around to having them. One New York City educator said that critics of in-class interventions should be less concerned with teachers' feelings and more concerned with students whose education is being compromised by mediocre and ineffective practices.

Marshall hears the arguments in favor of real-time coaching and wonders what the research will ultimately find about its effectiveness. For the present, he recommends starting with some basic questions: What is the ultimate goal of teacher supervision and evaluation? *Getting effective teaching in more classrooms more of the time.* What is the best way to accomplish that? "Since even the most energetic supervisors observe teachers only about 0.1 percent of their teaching time," says Marshall, "we need to create intrinsic motivation in teachers to use effective practices the other 99.9 percent of the time." And how can school leaders get struggling teachers to internalize effective teaching practices, bring their A-game every day, and adopt a continuous-improvement mindset? By judicious hiring, teacher teamwork, instructional coaching, peer observations, PD, and formal evaluations.

"Why is teacher evaluation ranked last?" Marshall asks. "Because research tells us that, with rare exceptions, traditional evaluations have not played an important role in improving teaching and learning. Alas, administrators' time is often consumed by documentation, evaluation, and compliance—and the myriad other things they need to do to keep their schools running smoothly. Real-time coaching is a well-intentioned attempt to improve this dismal record." And because of the crushing time-management challenges school administrators face, it's very appealing to be able to take care of coaching during an observation.

However, is it possible that real-time coaching is a false efficiency, asks Marshall. Here are some reasons to doubt its usefulness as a supervisory tool:

• *Difficulty level* – "Scoping out what's going on in a classroom during a short visit is complex and demanding work," he says, "and coming up with wise and helpful feedback on the spot is a high bar." Supervisors enter with background knowledge about the teacher and the curriculum but need to watch and listen carefully, look over students' shoulders at the instructional task, check in with one or two students ("What are you working on today?"), see what's on the board or screen, and listen to the teacher. "Shooting from the hip during the class seriously risks getting it wrong and undermining the kind of trust that's essential for teachers to be receptive to the input," says Marshall.

• *Superficiality* – The tendency with during-class interventions is to focus on classroom management and teachers' tactical moves rather than deeper curriculum and pedagogical issues, he says: "During short classroom observations, visitors can only guess at what occurred before and after the visit and may not understand the broad curriculum goals or a teacher's on-the-fly adaptations." The best way to get that information is a few minutes of face-to-face conversation with the teacher, but that's not possible during a lesson.

• *Power trip* – Teachers might hear this implicit message: "Not only can I walk into your classroom any time, but I will interrupt your teaching when I feel like it." To many teachers, this may come across as disrespectful—and 99 percent about administrative convenience. One educator told Marshall that if a supervisor had acted this way early in his teaching career, it would have driven him out of the profession.

• *Stress* – If there's always the possibility of being interrupted, teachers may find supervisory visits much more fraught. "Administrators are never going to be invisible during classroom visits," says Marshall; "—students and teachers are well aware of their presence—but the dynamic is heightened if supervisors frequently jump in."

• *Competence* – "Finally," he says, "let's be frank, some principals, assistant principals, and department heads don't have a good eye for instruction, lack an understanding of the essentials of good pedagogy, are opinionated about one best way to teach, and lack the skillset needed to have helpful feedback conversations with teachers. In the hands of supervisors like these, real-time coaching can do serious damage to teaching and learning, not to mention faculty morale." Of course, it's the job of superintendents and their designees to deal with competence issues, and that's best done by co-observing lessons with their building administrators on a regular basis, improving ineffective practices, and removing those who can't or won't get better.

Proponents of real-time coaching push back. These problems can be solved, they say, if administrators are competent, teachers know the process up front, there are trusting relationships, and students see all adults in the school as learners. With all this in place, they contend, on-the-spot feedback is much more powerful than traditional teacher supervision and evaluation. And there are kinder and gentler ways for supervisors to intervene during a lesson—for example, whispering in the teacher's ear while students do group work; texting or slipping the teacher a note; gesturing toward a student who seems confused; or giving a misbehaving student "the look." In some schools and teacher-training programs, supervisors equip teachers with a Bluetooth earpiece and use a cell phone to talk quietly into their ear from the back of the room.

Marshall agrees that the time-honored, four-hour process (pre-observation conference, full-lesson observation, analysis and write-up, and post-conference) is largely a waste of time, but argues that short classroom visits followed promptly by five- to ten-minute feedback chats can have significant impact. "Coaching suggestions are much more likely to be heard and acted on if the teacher has a chance to explain the context and the bigger picture in a face-to-face conversation," he says. "These conversations may include strong redirection (*I didn't hear a single higher-order thinking question while I was in there*), and supervisors can learn a great deal from how teachers react to criticisms and reflect on their work.

In short, high-quality debriefs are golden opportunities to get inside teachers' heads and strengthen instruction." Key factors, of course, are a manageable caseload of teachers and being liberated from the ineffective traditional evaluation process. Then supervisors can focus on two-to-three short observations and conversations a day, followed by brief narrative documentation.

"When it comes to affirming and improving teaching," Marshall concludes, "there are no shortcuts. With real-time coaching, the skill threshold is too demanding, the risks of being superficial or getting it wrong too high, the probability of upsetting and alienating teachers too great, and the chances of not having deeper conversations about teaching and learning too real. The good news is that supervisors can avoid these pitfalls by taking a little more time, reflecting a little more carefully, and engaging teachers in face-to-face coaching after each observation. Fitting in these conversations is challenging, and they are sometimes stressful on both sides, but this is the core work of school leaders. Doing it well will result in more effective teaching in more classrooms more of the time."

"Should Supervisors Intervene During Classroom Visits?" by Kim Marshall in *Phi Delta Kappan*, October 2015 (Vol. 97, #2, pp. 8–13), summarized in Marshall Memo 606.

Professional Learning Suggestions for Chapter Six
Critical Feedback and Difficult Conversations

Ameliorating Those Difficult Conversations

Arguably, one of the most challenging jobs as a school leader is having (and not avoiding!) difficult conversations. All of the activities in this section are designed to help you learn to deal with those difficult conversations. You can complete most of the activities on your own (not the role-play) or with your leadership team or cabinet. There is one professional learning activity to do with your teachers.

1. Identify what makes difficult teachers difficult.

While it won't help for leaders to go around putting staff members into boxes, *naming* what is difficult about certain teachers can be a useful first step in understanding why they may be exhibiting difficult behaviors and how you can better communicate with them. The following chart (from Eller and Eller, Article 8) is useful in helping to understand what makes difficult teachers difficult.

• Think about a few staff members who exhibit challenging behavior. Take a few minutes to write about what is challenging about each person's behavior and if they might fit into one of the eight categories below.

The Underminers	*Characteristics*: Say they will comply when they're with you, then criticize and fail to implement behind your back.
	Strategies: Give them a chance to share concerns in private and public; check on implementation in their classrooms; confront noncompliance in a difficult conversation.
The Contrarians	*Characteristics*: Believe that if they don't speak up, no one else will; ignore other perspectives.
	Strategies: Structure pro-and-con discussions with all staff about new ideas; ask that an idea or strategy be discussed with respect to its impact on teaching and learning; confront the behavior in a difficult conversation.
The Recruiters	*Characteristics*: Try to win over others to their point of view; drop the names of those they say agree with them.
	Strategies: Help others develop the strength to resist being recruited; challenge recruiters to be specific about those who supposedly agree with them; confront the behavior in a difficult conversation.
The Challenged	*Characteristics*: Believe they're doing a good job and don't need to change; cover up their lack of knowledge.
	Strategies: Ask questions to see if they understand what's being proposed; determine what information is missing; and provide opportunities for them to learn required skills through coaching, peer modeling, and conferencing.
The On-the-Job Retirees	*Characteristics*: Are open about not being motivated to change or improve.
	Strategies: Say you understand their situation; state expectations; follow up with classroom visits.
The Resident Experts	*Characteristics*: Broadcast their knowledge about every issue; when they make mistakes, blame others or outside circumstances; make excuses when you want to observe them implementing new ideas or techniques.
	Strategies: Privately ask them specific questions to assess their knowledge; hold them accountable when they make errors; confront the behavior in a difficult conversation.
The Unelected Representatives	*Characteristics*: Claim to represent a group or viewpoint without others' permission.
	Strategies: Ask the colleagues they claim to represent if they are in agreement; confront the behavior in a difficult conversation; conduct open conversations about the issues in which everyone has a chance to speak.
The Whiners and Complainers	*Characteristics*: Find fault with everything; fail to take responsibility for issues in their classrooms or professional practice; go overboard in talking about issues and problems.
	Strategies: Hold pro-and-con conversations in which positive ideas as well as concerns are aired; confront in a difficult conversation; don't accept irrational explanations; ask them to reframe the situation and reduce melodrama.

- With someone else on the leadership team, take turns discussing the behaviors of a few people on each of your lists and the category you each feel they fit into best. The goal is to better understand the behaviors, not to complain or gossip.

- For the first person on your list, look at the suggested strategies in the chart above and share:
    - Have you honestly tried any of these strategies? If so, how did it go?
    - Take ownership. Is there anything you've done to reinforce or condone these behaviors?
    - Brainstorm together how you might implement the suggested strategies. Continue for others on your list.

- Think together about whether there are any strategies or routines your school might put in place to *prevent* the difficult behaviors above. (To begin, think about communication, planning for new initiatives, and establishing norms for staff behavior.)

2. Learn some tips for difficult conversations.
Below are some tips you can glean from several of the articles (and one video) to help you better conduct difficult conversations.

- Think of a time when you have been on the giving or receiving end of the "feedback sandwich"—a positive comment, an area to improve, and then one more positive comment. Adam Grant (Article 6) claims that this approach to giving feedback is essentially saying: "I have some negative feedback to give you. I'll start with some positive feedback to relax you, and then give you the negative feedback, which is the real purpose of our meeting. I'll end with more positive feedback so you won't be disappointed or angry at me when you leave my office." Has this been your experience? Share your response.

- Reread the articles by Grant (Article 6), Hoerr (Article 10), and Gonzalez (Article 5). These articles contain a number of tips for how to best deliver critical feedback. Pull out the tips that most resonate with you and compile them in the box that follows. Once you are done, have everyone on the leadership team share the items they picked and the reasons they believe these are the most important tips to keep in mind.

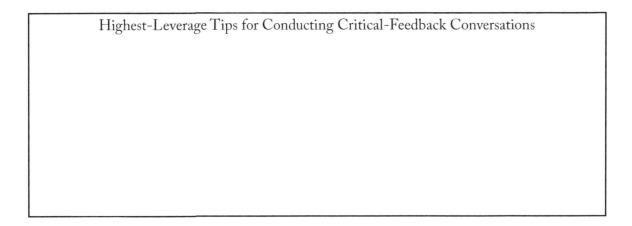

Highest-Leverage Tips for Conducting Critical-Feedback Conversations

• Find a video of a principal conducting a critical-feedback conversation with a teacher from your own school or district, or use this video of a mock conversation between a principal and teacher who received a low rating (1) on her value-added scores from the previous year: https://www.youtube.com/watch?v=FSvzgGzCu88. (Note that this is a mock conversation, so it is portrayed as a particularly smooth meeting!) Watch the video as a team, and look for any of the tips in the three articles you just reviewed:

- Which of the tips did the principal seem to follow?
- Which tips were missing?
- If you had an opportunity to conduct this difficult conversation differently, what would you have done as the principal?

3. Use case studies to plan a feedback conversation.
Now that you have explored some helpful tips for successful critical conversations, it's time to plan out one of those conversations. It's useful to outline ideas for a difficult conversation rather than simply winging it, at least until you get the hang of these types of conversations.

Have everyone on your leadership team (or you can do this alone), choose one of the two scenarios in the boxes that follow (or choose a real scenario from your own school)."

John is thirty years old and has been teaching history for six years. You observed his class and found that due to the structure of his class—mostly students taking notes on his PowerPoint presentations—there was little student engagement. You already had a debriefing meeting with him in which you presented several options for improving student engagement. He accepted the feedback and even thanked you for it. However, the next few times you walked by the window of his class or popped in you saw that he continued to lecture from his PowerPoint.

One teacher on a teacher team reports to you that Stella, the most veteran teacher on the team, rarely completes the tasks that everyone has agreed to complete in between meetings. The teacher says that Stella grumbles about having lost her prep time in order to attend this mandatory weekly meeting and openly states that she does not feel compelled to engage in the team's work.

Next, write notes or an outline (using the box that follows) for the meeting you would have with the teacher.

- An outline of the *structure* for the meeting like Grant's four-step process (Article 6) or Gonzalez's three-step process (Article 5);
- The *conditions* or tips you plan to follow, such as holding the meeting in the teacher's room or being specific (from Hoerr, Article 10);
- *Sentence starters* from the articles that you want to incorporate, such as, "I'm giving you these comments because I have very high expectations and I know that you can reach them." (Grant, Article 6)
- An *entire script* of what you plan to say during the meeting

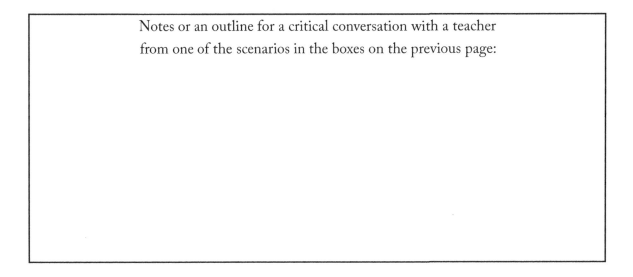

Notes or an outline for a critical conversation with a teacher from one of the scenarios in the boxes on the previous page:

4. Role-play a conversation with one of the teachers in the scenarios above.

Now that you've *planned* for a difficult conversation, it's time to role-play *conducting* it. Divide your leadership team into pairs and let everyone take turns acting as the principal and the teacher. After each mock conversation, both participants should debrief: What went well and what should be changed for next time?

5. Appeal to the feedback receivers—the teachers.

This activity is the one activity in this section to conduct with your *teachers*. The articles by Stone and David-Lang (Article 2), Heen and Stone (Article 7), and Riegel (Article 11) make it clear just how important the feedback *receiver* (that is, the teacher) is to the effectiveness of the feedback. It is the *receiver* who controls whether the feedback is even acted upon at all. Review these articles before conducting this activity with your teachers.

It is important to have an honest conversation with teachers about why the feedback receiver is so important and how they can take charge of making feedback work for them. To help teachers take a deep dive into how important *their* role as feedback receiver is, have them read the Heen and Stone article, "Find the Coaching in Criticism" (either the summary in the chapter or the entire article here: https://hbr.org/2014/01/find-the-coaching-in-criticism) and engage in small-group discussions of the article using the modified protocol as follows:

A modified version of: "Three Levels of Text Protocol" from the School Reform Initiative
http://schoolreforminitiative.org/doc/3_levels_text.pdf

Goal: To help teachers understand the text and the implications for them as *receivers* of feedback by reading the article on three levels: literal level, interpretation level, and implication level.

1. Teachers read the article or the summary of the article in the chapter and identify passages that resonate with them as *receivers* of feedback.

2. Do one to three rounds (five minutes for each round). Each round consists of:
   • One person shares the following (for up to three minutes total):
      Level 1: Read aloud the passage s/he has selected and what it means (a passage no one has shared yet).
      Level 2: Say what s/he thinks about the passage (interpretation, connections to own experience with receiving feedback).
      Level 3: Say what s/he sees as the implications for receiving feedback in the future.
   • The group responds to what has been said (for up to two minutes total).

While teachers are still in their small groups, ask if anyone would like to share a time when receiving feedback was challenging and if they now can identify whether any of the triggers introduced in the article were present:

Truth triggers – The criticism seems untrue, off base, or unhelpful—making us feel wronged, indignant, exasperated.

Relationship triggers – Something about this person makes it difficult to accept feedback that might be palatable coming from someone else. ("After all I've done for you, I get this petty criticism!")

Identity triggers – The criticism attacks our core sense of who we are, causing us to feel defensive, off balance, and perhaps overwhelmed.

Don't leave it up to teachers alone to be honest about their reactions to feedback. Make some type of commitment to the teachers, going forward, like the one that follows from Riegel (Article 11):

"So, moving forward, here's what I'd like to see happen: I'll give you some feedback and if you feel like you disagree, have a different perspective on it, or that I am not getting the whole picture, you'll tell me that *in the meeting*. I'll agree to really listen to your take on the situation, and we'll come up with a plan together."

6. Walk the walk—plan to model receiving feedback gracefully.

Stone and David-Lang (Article 2) write, "There is no training you can offer, no teaching you can provide, that will improve the quality of feedback at your school as much as your own example …. Be noisy about the importance of improving your school's feedback culture—for students, for teachers, for parents, and for yourself."

- Discuss what they might mean by a "feedback culture."
- Brainstorm (alone or with others) ways you can serve as a feedback-receiving model and commit to 3:

1. I plan to solicit feedback by:

2. I plan to put the following structure in place to regularly receive feedback by:

3. I plan to demonstrate to teachers that I have listened to and incorporated their feedback by:

Chapter Seven: Teacher Evaluation

For some teachers, a low rating may motivate them to invest in their own professional growth or pressure them to work harder. For others, it may raise their defenses, causing them to be less receptive to feedback on how to improve.
—MATTHEW KRAFT AND ALLISON GILMOUR

The traditional evaluation process is widely disliked because it's time-consuming, compliance-oriented, and rarely has any effect on teaching and learning. The articles in this chapter examine design flaws in the traditional system, present some new approaches, look at ways to measure classroom performance, and explore the controversial idea of using student learning as part of the process.

Problems with Teacher Evaluation – Julie Cohen and Dan Goldhaber list the multiple challenges involved in accurately capturing what's happening day-to-day in teachers' classrooms. Matthew Kraft and Allison Gilmour analyze a number of school-level factors that result in principals not giving honest evaluation ratings to underperforming teachers. Paul Murphy describes some ill-informed and unfair criticisms his principal e-mailed him after a classroom visit. And Shanyce Campbell and Matthew Ronfeldt report that certain teachers, including African Americans and Hispanics, consistently get lower observation ratings.

Rethinking Teacher Evaluation Systems – Kim Marshall suggests changes that superintendents, school board members, and union leaders should demand in their teacher-evaluation systems. Paul Bambrick-Santoyo argues for frequent, short, unannounced classroom visits followed by face-to-face debriefs focusing on one or two "leverage points." Madeline Hunter says the time-honored pre-observation conference is not a good use of teachers' or administrators' time.

And Ron Ferguson says that when students answer anonymous survey questions on their teachers, they paint a remarkably accurate and helpful picture of classroom practices.

Measuring Teachers' Performance – Rachel Garrett and Matthew Steinberg argue that while teachers' ratings on the Danielson framework correlate with student achievement, those ratings should not be used for high-stakes evaluations; rather, the framework should be used as originally intended: to initiate coaching conversations with teachers. Joseph Johnson, Cynthia Uline, and Lynne Perez say that during classroom visits effective principals tune in to student engagement, classroom climate, and a few other key factors. Rob Jenkins names eight important characteristics that can't be captured in teacher-evaluation rubrics, including sense of humor and creativity.

Using Student Learning as Part of Teacher Evaluation – Linda Darling-Hammond highlights serious methodological problems with using value-added test-score data to evaluate teachers. Douglas Reeves and Kim Marshall argue that student learning can be an effective part of the teacher supervision and evaluation process if done with medium stakes. And Nicholas Morgan and Daniel Schiff analyze the arguments for teacher performance pay and pose five challenging questions.

Questions to Consider

- How can teacher evaluations go beyond compliance and documentation?
- What should supervisors look for during classroom observations?
- Can student learning be part of teachers' evaluations?

Problems with Teacher Evaluation

1   Why Evaluating Teachers Is So Challenging

"Improving teacher evaluation is one of the most pressing but also contested areas of educational policy," say Julie Cohen (University of Virginia Curry School of Education) and Dan Goldhaber (American Institutes for Research) in this article in *Educational Researcher*. The challenge, they say, is designing classroom observations that provide valid data on what's happening day-to-day in classrooms; make meaningful distinctions among teachers; provide teachers with useful feedback; and support helpful, high-quality professional development. To accomplish these important goals, seven challenges need to be addressed:
- quality assurance of supervisors' observation and coaching skills,
- achieving a reasonable degree of inter-rater reliability among supervisors,
- a rubric with research-based criteria for classroom instruction,
- addressing the difficulty of capturing complex classroom dynamics in a rating instrument,
- getting an accurate sampling of each teacher's work,
- giving fair evaluations to teachers working with different types of students in different types of school cultures (so as not to create disincentives for working in challenging classrooms),
- addressing the tendency of principals to "go easy" on some teachers to keep the peace and/ or avoid the hard work of following up on critical evaluations.

To ensure that teacher evaluations are fair, valid, and helpful, Cohen and Goldhaber suggest that researchers, policymakers, and school leaders focus on these key questions:

• *Theory of action* – Is the primary purpose of classroom observations to give teachers formative feedback to help them get better, or is it to get an accurate sense of the very different levels of teacher performance that inevitably exist within every school?

• *Evaluator quality* – Who is best positioned to conduct classroom visits and provide accurate and helpful feedback and summative assessments (principals, department heads, instructional coaches, peers, master evaluators)? And what is the best training and support for people in these roles?

• *Accurately sampling instruction* – How many visits—of what length and of what type—are needed to form a reliable assessment of a teacher's performance?

• *The quality of teacher-evaluation rubrics* – "We need to develop greater conceptual clarity around the features of instructional quality that we want to capture in consequential evaluation systems," say Cohen and Goldhaber, "and make clear for teachers why and how we think such practices are essential in supporting a range of more and less readily assessable student outcomes .... Are there particular practices that teachers can more readily improve upon and that are also valuable to student learning, broadly defined? How does the composition of practices in observation instruments influence implementation and effectiveness of teacher evaluation?"

• *Student results* – Researchers need to answer the question of how well data from supervisors' classroom observations correlate with the most important long-term student outcomes—and whether observations can be an effective lever for improving those outcomes.

"Building a More Complete Understanding of Teacher Evaluation Using Classroom Observations" by Julie Cohen and Dan Goldhaber in *Educational Researcher*, August/ September 2016 (Vol. 45, #6, pp. 378–387), summarized in Marshall Memo 652.

2   Perennial Problems with How Teachers Are Evaluated

In this article in *Educational Researcher*, Matthew Kraft (Brown University) and Allison Gilmour (Vanderbilt University) revisit The New Teacher Project's widely read 2009 "Widget Effect" study. TNTP reported that teacher evaluation systems didn't accurately distinguish among teachers at varying levels of proficiency, failed to identify most of the teachers with serious performance problems, and were unhelpful in guiding professional development. Less than 1 percent of teachers were rated unsatisfactory, despite the fact that 81 percent of administrators and 57 percent of teachers could name a teacher in their school who was ineffective. The Widget Effect study concluded that "school districts must begin to distinguish great from good, good from fair, and fair from poor."

Has this situation changed as a result of a nationwide push to improve teacher evaluation? Looking at data from nineteen states and an in-depth analysis of one urban district, Kraft and Gilmour found:

- On average, only 2.7 percent of teachers were rated below Proficient/Exemplary on a 4- or 5-point scale.
- The range went from 1 percent below Proficient in Hawaii to 26.2 percent below Proficient in New Mexico.
- On average, principals estimated that 27.8 percent of teachers in their schools were performing below Proficient.
- Only New Mexico had ratings that were close to administrators' perceived distribution of performance, and that state's system was facing a series of legal challenges.

- The percentage of teachers given the top rating ranged from 73 percent in Tennessee to 8 percent in Massachusetts and 3 percent in Georgia.
- Many districts were drawing important distinctions between good and excellent teaching, but there was less differentiation among good, fair, and poor performance.

In short, although some states reported greater differences in teacher ratings than others, the general picture was very similar to the 2009 TNTP findings.

Why do so few teachers receive below-proficient ratings, despite the fact that school administrators estimate that more than a quarter of their teachers aren't up to par? From interviews with principals, Kraft and Gilmour identified the following factors:

• *The daunting workload involved in giving low ratings* – This includes the observational evidence needed to justify an unsatisfactory or marginal rating, the required corrective action plan, and the extensive support often needed to help an underperforming teacher improve—not to mention the legal wrangles involved in dismissing an ineffective teacher. Principals with a number of underperforming teachers often took a triage approach, focusing on only one or two.

• *Being merciful* – Some principals said they were hesitant to give low ratings to rookie teachers out of kindness and a desire not to discourage (or lose) a teacher who had potential for growth. "Assigning a Proficient rating was seen as a way to recognize teachers' efforts to improve," say Kraft and Gilmour. To cushion the blow, some principals addressed their concerns outside the formal evaluation process—an informal "word to the wise." Principals saw this as furthering the greater good of improving their teacher workforce. In addition, say the authors, "Assigning low ratings can undercut relational trust that is essential for mobilizing collective effort."

• *Personal discomfort* – "For some teachers, a low rating may motivate them to invest in their own professional growth or pressure them to work harder," say Kraft and Gilmour. "For others, it may raise their defenses, causing them to be less receptive to feedback on how to improve." One principal said, "The most difficult part of the job is probably to deliver those difficult messages, and not everyone is capable of that." Principals knew that teachers could lose their jobs as a result of a low rating, and were upset when teachers cried. A principal said, "The last thing I think I wanna do as a human being is to watch another human being walk out with their head down, dejected, because they just lost their job because they couldn't do it. This is something they wanted to do. That's a little bit harsh, you know?"

• *Other reasons* – These include racial concerns (for example, a disproportionate number of teachers of color receiving low ratings); burdensome dismissal procedures; principals making deals in which teachers agreed to leave the school in exchange for a higher rating; and concern about ineffective replacement teachers. A principal had this justification for rehiring a problematic teacher:

"He's a problem, but he's my problem, and he's one that I can really work with. Relative to the problems that were ringing my doorbell, I thought, 'I haven't begun to see how low it can go.'"

Kraft and Gilmour conclude that the continued failure of most teacher-evaluation systems to accurately report differences in teacher performance "is a product of conscious choices by evaluators as they navigate implementation challenges, competing interests, unintended consequences, and perverse incentives .... Policies are ultimately made by the 'street-level bureaucrats' who implement them rather than the policymakers who design them."

"Revisiting the Widget Effect: Teacher Evaluation Reforms and the Distribution of Teacher Effectiveness" by Matthew Kraft and Allison Gilmour, *Educational Researcher*, June/July 2017 (Volume 46, #5, pp. 234–249), summarized in Marshall Memo 637.

---

3. An Unfair Critique of a Teacher's Classroom

In this article in *Education Update*, Michigan third-grade teacher Paul Murphy lists the critical feedback his principal sent him after a five-minute "walkthrough":

- Sarah had her head down as the teacher addressed the class, and he didn't correct her.
- Patel went to the bathroom without permission.
- Joseph sat by himself at the front of the room.

Murphy understands how challenging the principal's job is, and how hard it is to get into classrooms frequently enough. But he wishes his principal had checked in with him before giving him these negative comments. Here's what he imagines saying to his boss: "You don't know that Sarah complained all morning about not feeling well and that she got only three hours of sleep because of her new baby sister. You don't know that the reason she's not 'engaged' is because her body won't allow her to be, and that five minutes before you walked in, I told her to put her head down. You don't know that Patel's mom e-mailed me at the start of the week to tell me that his dad is about to come home from prison after three years, and that Patel's anxiety over the change has manifested as a nervous bladder. You don't know that Patel and I have a deal to prevent a mortifying accident for which he'll be remembered for the rest of his life: don't ask, just go. You don't know that I've tried everything with Joseph for the past five months, but the kid just can't sit near anyone without bothering them all day. You also don't know that his seating location is a sign of tremendous progress, that he finally acknowledged his problem and asked to sit by himself so that he can focus better. He's not separated from his classmates because I gave up on him or I'm trying to shame him. He sits there because he *wants* to sit there."

When a principal doesn't follow up classroom visits with face-to-face conversations, says Murphy, teachers are in an awkward position. If they push back, giving some background to what the principal observed, they come across as whiny and defensive, which can be seen as "a tacit admission of error." But if they keep their mouths shut, they risk getting an unfair negative evaluation in their file. The clear implication for principals: always talk with teachers after observations to get the back story and allow the teacher (and the observer) to engage in nondefensive reflection about teaching and learning.

Oregon principal Rachael George echoes Murphy's concerns and says she tries to visit every classroom every day and engage in ongoing dialogues with teachers.

"The Why and When of Walkthroughs" by Paul Murphy and Rachael George in *Education Update*, September 2018 (Vol. 60, #9, pp. 2–3), summarized in Marshall Memo 754.

4. Equity Issues with Principals' Classroom Ratings

In this *American Educational Research Journal* article, Shanyce Campbell (University of California/Irvine) and Matthew Ronfeldt (University of Michigan) report on their analysis of teacher-observation data from the Measures of Effective Teaching (MET) study. They looked at teachers with similar instructional proficiency and found that certain teachers were consistently given lower classroom observation ratings by outside evaluators:

- male teachers;
- African American and Hispanic teachers;
- teachers working with students of color, male students, and low-performing students.

Campbell and Ronfeldt explored some possible reasons for these discrepancies. Are evaluators biased against certain teachers? Do less-proficient teachers tend to be assigned to more-challenging classes? Do teachers teach better or worse, depending on the kinds of students in their classrooms? Are evaluators judging teachers more or less favorably based not on the teacher's performance but on the kinds of students in their classrooms?

The researchers weren't able to come to a definitive conclusion, but they lean toward the last two explanations; it seems that teaching more-challenging groups of students is associated with lower evaluator ratings, regardless of teachers' instructional skills. There's an obvious problem with this: it creates a disincentive to teach students who have the greatest need for effective teaching.

"The implication," conclude Campbell and Ronfeldt, "is not to do away with observation ratings. To the contrary, observation ratings can provide teachers with formative feedback that has been shown to improve instructional quality. Rather, these results suggest that educational leaders, policymakers, and scholars should pay careful attention to possible unintended consequences of these evaluation systems and then make necessary adjustments to ensure they are fair and equitable."

"Observational Evaluation of Teachers: Measuring More Than We Bargained For?" by Shanyce Campbell and Matthew Ronfeldt in *American Educational Research Journal*, December 2018 (Vol. 55, #6, pp. 1233–1267), summarized in Marshall Memo 763.

Rethinking Teacher Evaluation Systems

5   A Better Way to Observe, Appreciate, and Evaluate Teachers

In this *Education Gadfly* article, Kim Marshall says that when he visits classrooms with the principals he coaches, he sees lots of effective teaching (Level 3 and 4 on a rating scale), very little that's really bad (Level 1), but some mediocre practices (Level 2)—for example, low-rigor worksheets, teachers calling only on students who raise their hands, and failing to answer students' unspoken question: *Why are we learning this?*

Every school has a range of teaching effectiveness, and a bell-shaped curve might seem inevitable. But Marshall argues that variation produces inequitable results: "Effective practices are especially beneficial to students who walk into school with any kind of disadvantages," he says, "and these same students are disproportionately harmed by mediocre and ineffective practices – kids who don't raise their hands when the teacher asks, 'Any questions?'; who haven't yet learned how to work around their disabilities; who are dealing with a family breakup or other trauma; who are openly defiant or sit in sullen silence. Truly bad teaching obviously needs to be addressed immediately, but so do mediocre practices, which all too often fly under the radar, and are *not okay.*"

But how can busy principals improve suboptimal classroom performance and bend the curve toward effectiveness? Certainly not by once-a-year announced observations with long evidence write-ups; not by superficial walk-throughs with checklists; not by correcting teachers in front of students; not by using student surveys as a high-stakes cudgel; and not by evaluating teachers on student test scores and value-added data (now thoroughly discredited). "We shouldn't be surprised that these and other practices driven by distrust and compliance have never shown up in the research on effective schools," says Marshall. "That dog hasn't barked."

The questions that school board members, superintendents, and union leaders should be asking about their teacher-evaluation system are: How often are teachers observed each year, and by whom? Are visits announced or unannounced (in other words, are observers seeing what students experience day by day)? How long do observers stay, and what are they looking for? Do they chat with students and look at their work? Afterward, is there a conversation with the teacher? How time-consuming is documentation? Are supervisors supervised, not only on their observation skills, but also on how well they orchestrate teacher teamwork (another key driver of instructional improvement)? And what goes in each teacher's file at the end of each school year?

Pondering these questions, Marshall and others have come up with a more effective way of supervising, coaching, and evaluating teachers:

- Short, frequent, unannounced classroom visits replacing traditional formal evaluations;
- A humble, curious, low-tech approach to visits—checking in with students ("What are you working on?"), looking for student outcomes, and jotting a few quick notes;
- A face-to-face conversation shortly after each visit;
- The observer sharing appropriate appreciation and one "leverage point";
- Afterward, a brief narrative summary sent electronically to the teacher (one software program limits the observer to one thousand characters);
- Administrators making brief visits to teacher teams as they plan curriculum units and look at student work;
- Rubric used only three times a year: in September for teacher self-assessment and goal-setting, mid-year to compare teacher's detailed self-assessment with the supervisor's and discussing any disagreements, repeating that at year's end.

"This approach takes about the same number of educator hours as traditional evaluations," says Marshall, "but is vastly more authentic and effective at understanding and improving teaching and learning."

But will teachers feel safe with unannounced visits to their classrooms? Marshall's experience is that they will if:

- Observers visit at least once a month;
- They stay long enough—ten to fifteen minutes gives a meaningful snapshot;
- Visits are randomized to capture different days of the week, subjects, student groups, time of day—and beginning, middle, and end of lessons;
- There's agreement on key look-fors;
- Observers have a good eye for instruction and aren't intrusive;
- There's *always* a face-to-face chat after each visit;
- There are other points of contact—team meetings, parent interactions, other activities;
- Teachers have input on rubric scoring;
- Observers are supervised and coached;
- Everyone knows the process is about improving teaching and learning, not a "gotcha."

Who should be doing these classroom visits? That will vary from school to school, says Marshall, and should involve as many administrators, instructional coaches, and peer observers as possible to get the best teacher-observer ratio and maximize visits and conversations.

Can this system be implemented skillfully in schools? Marshall argues that in most cases the answer is yes, because mini-observations avoid bureaucratic nonsense and liberate (and develop) the skills that administrators, instructional coaches, and peer observers already have. Here's how:

- Informal classroom visits, unshackled from copious note-taking, make people better observers and bring out their natural curiosity.
- A lot happens in ten to fifteen minutes, providing plenty of talking points (sometimes addressing mediocre practices).
- Teachers are less defensive in face-to-face conversations, especially if they take place in their classrooms when students aren't there.
- Focusing on one leverage point per visit makes feedback conversations less fraught.
- Conversations give teachers a chance to educate their observers.
- Observers have multiple at-bats, giving them a chance to continuously improve their feedback skills and get a meaningful sampling of teachers' work.

"For educators who are new to this approach," says Marshall, "there will be a learning curve. But the good news is that mini-observation and feedback skills are eminently coachable by superintendents or their designees through the use of co-observations and discussions of case studies and write-ups in leadership meetings …. The result: more good teaching in more classrooms more of the time. And that is the key to raising the next generation of well-educated Americans and closing our social-class and racial-achievement gaps."

"Rethinking the Way We Coach, Evaluate, and Appreciate Teachers" by Kim Marshall in *The Education Gadfly*, February 20, 2019 (Vol. 19, #8), summarized in Marshall Memo 775.

6 The Best Use of Rubrics

In this *Educational Leadership* article, New Jersey educator/author Paul Bambrick-Santoyo questions the efficacy of using rubrics for classroom observations. First, he says, most rubrics have so many criteria that it's difficult for a teacher to absorb and implement the feedback. Second, rubric-based evaluations are usually based on one or two lessons a year—lessons that may not be representative of a teacher's daily work. And third, evaluations usually take place toward the end of the school year—too late for teachers to make important changes.

Bambrick-Santoyo calls this the "scoreboard" approach to evaluation. In the real world of classrooms, he says, using a "theoretically complete framework of effective performance" is not what drives improved performance. In the high-performing Newark, New Jersey schools he manages, principals focus on *skillful coaching* of their teachers. Here are the key elements:

• *Frequent, short classroom visits.* Teachers get weekly, unannounced fifteen-minute visits, followed every time by a face-to-face feedback conversation. When administrators are in classrooms, they don't use a long checklist; instead, they jot notes on one or two "change levers" that will help each teacher become a little more effective with students.

Are weekly classroom visits feasible? Bambrick-Santoyo says they are if administrators and other support personnel divide up the faculty so no one supervises more than fifteen teachers, visit classrooms physically close to one another in blocks (for example, four in an hour), and lock in a schedule of weekly check-in meetings with teachers. "Routine coaching using this approach still takes significant time," he says. "But if your goal is to coach and drive teacher development, this time must be spent."

• *Focus and practice.* In feedback conversations, supervisors zero in on one or two specific, bite-size, attainable goals—for example, how an elementary teacher might get every single student participating in choral responses—and then role-play with the teacher to hone the skill. "This focus on key action steps cuts through the confusion that an elaborate rubric might have created and provides a clear path," says Bambrick-Santoyo. "Feedback and evaluation won't change real classrooms unless teachers build the skills needed to make a change."

• *Coach for growth, not for scores.* Instead of rubric ratings, teachers walk away from each meeting with a specific goal, knowing the administrator will be back soon to see how it's going.

• *Use rubrics for summative evaluations.* Principals pull together their impressions from the weekly visits and conversations and evaluate each teacher twice a year using a detailed rubric. Teachers self-assess and compare their ratings with the administrator's, agreeing on final scores and goals for the remainder of the year or the next year.

"To improve the team, you don't study the scoreboard; you go out and practice," concludes Bambrick-Santoyo. "When teachers see the concrete steps they must take to improve their practice, and when they can continually practice skills connected to those steps, transformational success comes within reach."

"Beyond the Scorecard" by Paul Bambrick-Santoyo in *Educational Leadership*, November 2012 (Vol. 70, #3, pp. 26–30), summarized in Marshall Memo 459.

---

7 Is the Pre-Observation Conference a Good Use of Time?

"The pre-observation conference is a vestigial organ remaining from the days when observation of teaching was a 'fuzzy' activity, depending on the intuition or bias of the supervisor," says instructional guru Madeline Hunter in this article in *Educational Leadership*. "Today, with our knowledge of cause-effect relationships between teaching and learning and of the way formative evaluation increases teaching effectiveness, it is time to discard the time-consuming pre-observation conference." Here is Hunter's rationale for doing away with a longstanding part of the teacher-evaluation process:

• Teachers should know at the beginning of the year the agreed-upon criteria for effective teaching.

• The pre-observation conference builds bias in both teacher and observer. "Having already told the observer the plan," said Hunter, "the teacher may proceed to develop it even when data emerging from the class indicate a change should be made."

• The time required for the pre-conference reduces by one-third the time available for observation and post-conferences.

• An observation requires interpretation of each part of a lesson in relation to what came before and after. "Viewed in isolation, no technique can be interpreted as productive or destructive," said Hunter. "There are no absolutes in teaching."

• Trust and support result from what happens in the post-observation conference. "The observer who shows empathy for the teacher," said Hunter, "by understanding the tremendous complexity of successful teaching, seeking the teacher's reasons for actions rather than proceeding on unfounded assumptions, appreciating and identifying productive teaching skills, refraining from imposing his or her own style on the teacher, and enabling the teacher to continue to grow in teaching effectiveness—will be welcomed back to that teacher's classroom."

Hunter believed that *planning* lessons with teachers is a good use of administrators' time. The teacher gets the benefit of collaborative planning, and the administrator "accepts part of the teacher's daily responsibility for planning, teaching, and evaluating countless lessons and experiences, and the fact that 'it ain't all that easy.'"

"Let's Eliminate the Pre-Observation Conference" by Madeline Hunter (1916-1994) in *Educational Leadership*, March 1986 (Vol. 43, pp. 69–70), summarized in Marshall Memo 464.

8 Student Input on Teachers' Evaluations

In this article in *Phi Delta Kappan*, Ronald Ferguson (Harvard University) describes a scenario in which a principal peeks into a classroom and likes what she sees (students are busy and well-behaved) and students' test-score results are good (they're almost always above average). But the students, if asked, would have told a very different story: lessons are uninteresting, assignments emphasize memorization more than understanding, and the teacher seems indifferent to their feelings and opinions. In short, it's not a happy place, and there's no love of learning.

Universities routinely survey students on how professors are performing, but until recently, K–12 students have not been given the chance to evaluate their teachers. This is because, although elementary and secondary school students spend hundreds more hours in classrooms than any administrator, people doubt that students can provide valid, reliable, and stable responses about the quality of teaching.

But recent research, including studies conducted by Ferguson and his colleagues, have found that K–12 students provide remarkably accurate information on their teachers' performance. "Students know good instruction when they experience it, as well as when they do not," says Ferguson. Over more than a decade, almost a million K–12 students have filled out Ferguson's anonymous Tripod surveys on their teachers, and the questions have been refined to the point where they pass muster with other researchers.

The survey questions are grouped under Ferguson's seven Cs—Care, Control, Clarify, Challenge, Captivate, Confer, Consolidate—and students respond by rating their agreement or disagreement with each statement on a 5-4-3-2-1 scale. Here are sample questions in each area:
- *Care – My teacher really tries to understand how students feel about things.*
- *Control – Our class stays busy and doesn't waste time.*
- *Clarify – My teacher has several good ways to explain each topic that we cover in this class.*
- *Challenge – My teacher wants us to use our thinking skills, not just memorize things.*
- *Captivate – I often feel like this class has nothing to do with real life outside school.*
- *Confer – My teacher gives us time to explain our ideas.*
- *Consolidate – My teacher takes the time to summarize what we learn each day.*

Ferguson notes that five of these areas (Care, Clarify, Captivate, Confer, and Consolidate) measure teachers' support of students, and two (Control and Challenge) measure what's sometimes called "press."

What have the survey results revealed about teachers? Even lower-elementary students make clear distinctions among teachers, with greater variation within than between schools. Overall, studies have found that Tripod survey results are valid and reliable predictors of student learning in math and ELA—in fact, more reliable than administrators' classroom observations. Students whose teachers scored in the top quarter on Tripod questions learned the equivalent of four to five months more per year than students whose teachers scored in the bottom quarter. The differences in ELA were about half as large as in math.

However, not all the Seven C items are equally predictive of student achievement. When Ferguson asks audiences which of the Seven C's they think are most important to student achievement, most pick Care. But that's not what studies show. Here are the seven survey questions that correlate most strongly with achievement gains:

- *Students in this class treat the teacher with respect.*
- *My classmates behave the way my teacher wants them to.*
- *Our class stays busy and doesn't waste time.*
- *In this class, we learn a lot every day.*
- *In this class, we learn to correct our mistakes.*
- *My teacher explains difficult things clearly.*

However, the difference between these and other Tripod items is not large, says Ferguson: "Educators should keep all of them in mind as they seek ways to improve teaching and learning."

What about student outcomes beyond test-score gains? "We also want attentiveness and good behavior, happiness, effort, and efficacy," says Ferguson. The good news is that he and his colleagues have found "the same teaching behaviors that predict better behavior, greater happiness, more effort, and stronger efficacy also predict great value-added achievement gains." It's not either-or; it's both—and student survey results, used wisely, can help give teachers and administrators valuable data to improve teaching and learning.

These findings notwithstanding, Ferguson offers two caveats about using student survey results to evaluate teachers:

- Any method of assessing teacher effectiveness is prone to measurement error.
- Teachers may temporarily alter their behaviors to improve their survey results, especially if students' opinions have high stakes.

These concerns lead Ferguson to say, "No one survey instrument or observational protocol should have high stakes for teachers if used alone or for only a single deployment." He supports the idea of student surveys being one of *several* measures used to evaluate teachers.

"Can Student Surveys Measure Teaching Quality?" by Ronald Ferguson in *Phi Delta Kappan*, November 2012 (Vol. 94, #3, pp. 24–28), summarized in Marshall Memo 461.

Measuring Teachers' Performance

The Most Effective Use of Rubrics

9

In this article in *Educational Evaluation and Policy Analysis*, Rachel Garrett (American Institutes for Research) and Matthew Steinberg (University of Pennsylvania) report on their analysis of teacher effectiveness data from the Measures of Effective Teaching (MET) study. They reached four conclusions:

First, there is a strong correlation between teacher ratings on Charlotte Danielson's Framework for Teaching (FFT) and student test scores. "On average," say Garrett and Steinberg, "student achievement is higher among teachers who receive higher FFT ratings."

Second, there are problems with using this correlation for high-stakes personnel decisions on individual teachers (e.g., tenure, performance pay, or dismissal). That's because "relying heavily on FFT measures ignores one of the key drivers of this relationship," say Garrett and Steinberg, "—the systematic sorting of students to teachers. We find consistent patterns of noncompliance with randomization that moves students to teachers with higher FFT scores. Such nonrandom sorting limits the ability of teacher performance measures to provide a valid estimate of a teacher's contribution to student learning, thereby constraining policymakers' and school leaders' ability to identify truly effective teachers."

Third, Garrett and Steinberg conclude that Danielson rubric data, while an interesting marker of teacher effectiveness, is less useful as an intervention to improve teaching. "Implicit in this distinction," they say, "is the impossibility of either fully capturing or randomly assigning instructional quality. While better teachers, on average, may receive higher FFT ratings, there are likely other aspects of teacher quality that are salient to student learning but not measured by the FFT .... Disentangling the effect of quality instruction on student achievement is further complicated by the fact that instruction undoubtedly interacts with numerous factors, including the composition of students in a given class. The mix of students on observed and unobserved dimensions will vary both across teachers within a school, as well as across classes taught by the same teacher." That's why individual teachers' Danielson ratings fluctuate from year to year.

Finally, Garrett and Steinberg note that the Danielson framework was originally created to coach teachers, encourage self-reflection, and inform professional development, but the MET study and their own analysis of MET data used it only to measure correlations between teacher effectiveness and student achievement. In other words, teachers in these studies were analyzed in a way that didn't capture the feedback conversations with principals and the subsequent professional development that Danielson envisioned—which any good school implements on a routine basis.

Therefore, conclude Garrett and Steinberg, "this study does not speak to either the potential impacts on student and teacher performance when the FFT protocol is fully implemented, or how performance can be shaped over time. Indeed, this potential for professional development embedded within the complete FFT protocol is one of the compelling reasons for its use, as compared with value-added scores, which provide little guidance for teachers on how to improve their practice."

"Examining Teacher Effectiveness Using Classroom Observation Scores: Evidence from the Randomization of Teachers to Students" by Rachel Garrett and Matthew Steinberg in *Educational Evaluation and Policy Analysis*, June 2015 (Vol. 37, #2, pp. 224–242), summarized in Marshall Memo 589.

10 What the Best Principals Look for In Classrooms

In this article in *JESPAR*, Joseph Johnson, Cynthia Uline, and Lynne Perez (San Diego State University) report on their study of what principals in fourteen of the nation's highest-performing, non-selective urban schools looked for during formal and informal classroom visits. Principals focused on three areas:

• *Student engagement, learning, and understanding* – "In every interview, principals spoke first and most passionately about noticing the extent to which students were participating, learning, thinking, making sense, and understanding the concepts and skills being taught," report the authors. "Principals discussed the importance of seeing students talking about lesson content, discussing concepts, asking questions, explaining complex ideas, and solving problems."

One principal explained, "When I watch, I look first for *all* students, and I look around the class to make sure that they're all participating. I also walk around and ask kids. I'll take three kids at different areas of the room and if they're doing partner-share, I listen to what they are saying. Is the conversation that they are having related to what the teacher is asking them to participate in? When they're doing independent work, I look at what they're doing and I ask them, 'How do you know how to do this? What are you doing? What are you working on?'"

Principals looked not only for lesson objectives but also the level of rigor and cognitive complexity being asked of students as they pursued the objective, and how many were understanding the lesson. "I want to see students thinking, grappling, writing, articulating their thoughts," said one principal. "If all the children are able to answer all of the questions, there is something wrong," said another. "They're not learning new information .... I want to see them inquisitive. I want them to be eager. I want to see some eagerness to learn."

All the principals said they looked for whether students were responding to teachers' questions and were talking to each other, both as evidence of students' engagement and understanding and also as on-the-spot assessments that helped teachers adjust the lesson content, pacing, and rigor.

• *Climate, tone, and atmosphere* – In the interviews, principals used a number of adjectives to describe the "feel" they expected in classrooms: *warm, nurturing, calm, relaxed, respectful, stimulating, flexible, organized, neat.* They sought evidence of routines that helped students feel the classroom was predictable and safe. "I look at how they are sitting, how they're reacting, their body language, the feel of the classroom," said one principal. "Is there light laughter? Are there smiles?" Principals also wanted to see high-quality materials and displays of recent student work.

• *Effective teacher actions* – "I look to see if the teacher has been pretty clear about what the intended learning is and how it ties in with [student] interest," said one principal. "Students will engage if the teacher has been clear about where the lesson is going and what the students need to learn and why." Another principal said, "I want to see teachers asking lots of questions and keeping track of who is answering." Others emphasized getting students to explain their thinking, probing, listening carefully to what students say, assessing their understanding, and adjusting questions and instruction accordingly.

"I'm also looking for modeling in the lesson," said another principal. "And that's a critical piece. There's a difference between explaining and actually modeling the thinking. If that's going really well, that makes it a really strong lesson." Another principal looked for thinking maps and students brainstorming their thinking before they were asked to write.

Johnson, Uline, and Perez say their findings dovetail nicely with what teachers say they admire in effective principals: these leaders hold up a mirror to classroom practices and provide another set of eyes, sharing detailed and specific feedback aimed at solving problems—all in an atmosphere of trust and respect.

What are the implications of this study? The authors contrast their findings with the training and advice many principals receive on formal and informal classroom visits. For example, Carolyn Downey et al. (in *The Three-Minute Classroom Walk-Through*, Corwin, 2004) say that principals should see if "students appear to be attending when you first walk into the room .... The goal of this step is to notice whether students appear to be oriented to the work .... This is just a quick look to see if attending behavior seems to be in place" (p. 21).

The principals in the Johnson, Uline, and Perez study were not satisfied with this level of student attention. "They believed that it was essential for teachers to obtain evidence that students understood the concepts and skills being taught," say the authors. "They did not want teachers to assume that a student's fixed gaze was evidence that the student understood the vocabulary, internalized the relationships, or acquired the skills. They refused to equate attending behavior with learning behavior."

Furthermore, say the authors, "Downey and colleagues encouraged principals to notice safety and health issues, offering little or no attention to issues of relationships between teachers and students or among students"—or to student learning.

"The distinctions may not be huge," conclude Johnson, Uline, and Perez. "However, might these nuances influence the success of urban principals in promoting excellent and equitable learning? Are principal training programs driving attention and focus to the issues that are most likely to influence the academic success of black, Latino, and low-income students, or are they oversimplifying the complexities of instructional leadership?"

Intriguingly, during the five years that Johnson, Uline, and Perez observed the fourteen schools in their study, they found "substantial congruity between the issues principals claimed to notice and the attributes of classrooms in their schools .... So, if 'what principals see' somehow influences 'what principals get,' it may be worthwhile to learn more about what principals of high-performing schools notice and how they use this knowledge to influence improvements in teaching and learning."

"Expert Noticing and Principals in High-Performing Urban Schools" by Joseph Johnson, Cynthia Uline, and Lynne Perez in *Journal of Education for Students Placed at Risk*, April-June 2011 (Vol. 16, #2, pp. 122–136), summarized in Marshall Memo 389.

11 | The Ineffable Qualities of Great Teachers

In this *Chronicle of Higher Education* article, Rob Jenkins (Perimeter College of Georgia State University) reflects on the specific characteristics of the best teachers he's had from kindergarten through graduate school—not necessarily the teachers and professors he liked the most but those who had the greatest influence on him. Jenkins describes his most memorable teachers as:

• *Good-natured* – By that, he means approachable and easy to get along with. A grouchy, misanthropic, short-tempered curmudgeon can be effective—or at least prepare students for bosses who are like that—but the opposite qualities are more likely to make a teacher effective (as long as you pay attention in class and do the work).

• *Professional without being aloof* – "My best teachers always seemed to effortlessly walk that fine line between being an authority figure and being someone I felt I could talk to," says Jenkins. "I didn't even understand what they were doing—or how difficult it was—until I had to do it myself years later."

• *A good sense of humor* – "Funny how an ounce of humor can sometimes help students grasp the material better than a pound of gravitas," he says. The teachers who had the biggest impact didn't take themselves or their subject too seriously and sometimes made jokes at their own expense.

• *Enjoy what they do* – They clearly like teaching and get a kick out of associating with students every day. The opposite extreme is teachers who whine about the workload, don't seem to like students, and make kids feel like a nuisance.

• *Demanding without being unkind* – Most students appreciate high expectations and don't mind working hard as long as the demands aren't mean-spirited.

• *Comfortable in their own skin* – "The best teachers are confident without being arrogant, authoritative without being condescending," says Jenkins. They like themselves without being in love with the sound of their own voices.

• *Tremendously creative* – "My best teachers … were truly innovative," says Jenkins, "coming up with creative ways—sometimes on the spur of the moment—to help us understand, internalize, and remember what they were trying to teach. What made them innovative was not tools or technology but their minds."

• *Make teaching look easy* – "Great teachers are like great athletes, dancers, or musicians," says Jenkins. "We may know, cognitively, that what they do isn't easy, but they seem to do it so effortlessly that we're lulled into thinking it's no big deal—until we try it ourselves."

Are these characteristics innate or can they be developed? A bit of both, concludes Jenkins, but "simply by recognizing those traits as desirable, by acknowledging that we don't possess them to the degree we would like, and by committing ourselves to working on them—we can become more approachable, creative, and yes, funnier than we would be otherwise. It's the journey of self-improvement that makes the difference."

"What Makes a Good Teacher?" by Rob Jenkins in *The Chronicle of Higher Education*, June 24, 2016 (Vol. LXII, #39, p. A26), summarized in Marshall Memo 643.

Using Student Learning as Part of Teacher Evaluation

12 Problems with Value-Added Measures (VAM)

"The notion of using VAMs to evaluate educators and schools is intuitively appealing," says Linda Darling-Hammond (Stanford University) in this article in *Educational Researcher*. She was initially enthusiastic about their possibilities, especially given long-standing problems with the way many districts evaluate teachers. But the key question, Darling-Hammond realized, is whether value-added measures "can accurately identify individual teachers' contributions to student learning and hence offer a credible measure of teacher 'effectiveness.'" For this to occur, she says, three conditions need to be in place:

- The right assessments – Individual students' actual achievement must be measured by tests that reflect valuable learning on a vertical scale with equal-interval units.
- Random student assignment – Classroom conditions and group traits can't vary substantially from one classroom to another.
- Ability to measure what each educator has contributed to student learning – Teachers' individual value-add needs to be isolated from other factors that affect student learning.

"Of course, none of these assumptions holds," says Darling-Hammond, "and the degree of error in measuring learning gains and attributing them to a specific teacher depends on the extent to which they are violated, as well as the extent to which statistical methods can remedy these problems. Unfortunately, in the United States, at this moment in history, the violations of these assumptions are considerable." Specifically:

• *Assessments* – Many standardized tests focus mainly on basic skills and, because they are grade-specific, don't accurately measure the achievement of students working above or below grade level. This means that VAMs are especially inaccurate for teachers working with low- and high-achieving students, English language learners, and students with special needs. The new PARCC and Smarter Balanced tests have vertical scales, but because they are grade-specific, they have the same problems as the previous generation of state tests.

• *Random student assignment* – Darling-Hammond says U.S. schools have "extraordinarily high rates of childhood poverty, homelessness, and food insecurity" and these are not randomly distributed across schools. Teachers working in low-income communities have far more students with educational, psychological, health, and social needs. Add to that the prevalence of tracking and other inequities in the way students are assigned to teachers and "it is clear that the assumption of equivalence among classrooms is far from reality."

• *Isolating teachers' contributions* – Darling-Hammond lists some of the factors affecting student achievement beyond the efforts of individual teachers:

- Class size;
- Curriculum choices;
- Instructional time;
- Other educators working with students;
- Availability of specialists, tutors, books, computers, science labs, and other resources;
- The quality of prior teaching and school experiences;
- Opportunities for professional learning and collaborative planning with colleagues;
- Peer culture and achievement;
- Differential summer learning experiences;
- Home factors, including parents' ability to help with homework, food and housing security, physical and mental support, or abuse;
- Individual student needs, health, and attendance.

"Given all of these influences on learning," says Darling-Hammond, "it is not surprising that variation among teachers accounts for only a tiny share of variation in achievement, typically estimated at under 10 percent."

All these factors, she says, "pose considerable challenges to deriving accurate estimates of teacher effects" and explain why VAM data are so unstable. In one study, of the teachers who scored in the bottom 20 percent one year, only a quarter were still there the following year, while 50 percent scored in the top half. About half of teachers who scored in the top half of the distribution one year moved to the bottom half the next.

Teachers' VAM ratings also fluctuate based on the formula used: 40–55 percent of Los Angeles teachers got noticeably different scores when researchers used a different model. Ratings also depend on the tests students took: 20–30 percent of teachers who ranked in the top quartile on one state test ranked in the bottom half when students were given a different test. In New York City's VAM ratings several years ago, the error range was such that a teacher ranked in the 43rd percentile could be scoring anywhere from the 15th to the 71st percentile.

"These are not small differentials," says Darling-Hammond, "and in current high-stakes contexts can mean the difference between a teacher being rewarded with a bonus or being fired." All this, she says, points to the profound difficulties with attaching high stakes to measures that are so volatile and so often inaccurate. Efforts are being made to improve the validity and reliability of VAM measures, but, says Darling-Hammond, "Trying to fix VAMs is rather like pushing on a balloon: The effort to correct one problem often creates another one that pops up somewhere else ….There is reason to be skeptical that the current prescriptions for using VAMs can ever succeed in measuring teaching contributions well." Darling-Hammond quotes her Stanford colleague, Edward Haertel: "No statistical manipulation can assure fair comparisons of teachers working in very different schools, with very different students, under very different conditions."

Advocates insist that VAM measures will motivate teachers to improve and rid the profession of "incompetent deadwood." But Darling-Hammond believes their high-stakes use may create disincentives to collaborating with colleagues, discourage teachers from working with high-need students and working at certain grade levels, lead some teachers to "cook" their rosters, demoralize teachers and drive away high-performers, and dissuade talented individuals from going into education. These possibilities are especially likely if principals are unable to explain VAM errors and fluctuations—but are asked to square classroom observation data with inscrutable VAM scores or rank-order teachers and dismiss those who score low.

What is to be done? Darling-Hammond has a "modest proposal": policymakers need to acknowledge the serious limitations of VAMs, stop using them for high-stakes personnel decisions, and allow educators "to develop more thoughtful approaches to examining student learning in teacher evaluation"—for example, "a collection of evidence about their students' learning that is appropriate for the curriculum and students being taught and targeted to goals the teacher is pursuing for improvement …."This might consist of beginning- and end-of-year rubric scores on student essays assigned by a grade-level team and scored collectively. Other possibilities: gains in Developmental Reading Assessment (DRA) levels, English language proficiency tests, and pre- and post-tests in AP Calculus.

"Evaluation ratings," in Darling-Hammond's scheme, "would combine the evidence from multiple sources in a judgment model, as Massachusetts' plan does, using a matrix to combine and evaluate several pieces of student learning data, and then integrate that rating with those from observations and professional contributions. Teachers receive low or high ratings when multiple indicators point in the same direction …. This approach would identify teachers who warrant intervention while enabling pedagogical discussion among teachers and evaluators based on evidence that connects what teachers do with how their students learn. A number of studies suggest that teachers become more effective as they receive feedback from standards-based observations and as they develop ways to evaluate their students' learning in relation to their practice."

"Can Value-Added Add Value to Teacher Evaluation?" by Linda Darling-Hammond in *Educational Researcher*, March 2015 (Vol. 44, #2, pp. 132–137), summarized in Marshall Memo 581.

13 Using Student Learning as Part of the Evaluation Process

In this *Edutopia* article, Douglas Reeves and Kim Marshall say there was good reason for the pushback on using student test scores, value-added measures (VAM), and student learning objectives (SLOs) as part of teacher evaluation. Among the problems, say Marshall and Reeves: "This year's A teacher can be next year's F teacher because of random variations that have nothing to do with teaching quality," and test scores give few clues on how classroom instruction can be improved. These and other design flaws have contributed to the widespread consensus that the United States needs a different approach to teacher accountability. Fortunately, the 2016 Every Student Succeeds Act (ESSA) opens the door for states to make better choices.

Two key questions should be at the center of accountability, say Marshall and Reeves: *Are students learning?* and *How will educators respond when some students aren't successful?* But is it possible to put student results at the center of teacher assessment without using test scores? Yes, say the authors: by "dialing back the pressure and using lower-key measures of student learning throughout the year." Here's when and how:

• *During frequent classroom visits* – Dropping into each classroom for short, unannounced visits at least ten times a year, principals and other supervisors can look over students' shoulders or sit down next to them and ask, "What are you learning today?" and "How will you know when you're successful?" Insights from these informal conversations can be part of helpful teacher-administrator conversations afterward.

• *Looking at student work* – Chatting in the teacher's classroom when students aren't there is an ideal time to look at student writing, creations, and exit tickets in a nonthreatening and highly productive way.

• *During curriculum planning meetings* – As teacher teams create curriculum units and assessments, administrators can make suggestions on ways to check for understanding during lessons, in paper-and-pencil tests, and through performance tasks—a proactive way of focusing on student learning. "Without high-quality assessments," say Marshall and Reeves, "analysis of student learning will be unproductive."

• *During collaborative data meetings* – When teams discuss the results of common assessments, administrators can join in and help make these meetings the engine for instructional improvement (which is not always the case). Again, the conversation is about student learning without high stakes, embedded in an ongoing conversation about helping students who aren't yet successful and talking about the most successful teaching strategies.

• *In teams' value-added reports* – Same-grade/same-subject teacher teams can set goals (for example, 100 percent of second graders reading at least on grade level by June) and at the end of the year report to the principal on student progress from the September baseline. The principal then notes the team's accomplishments in each teacher's individual performance evaluation.

This last item is the basic idea behind SLOs, conclude Marshall and Reeves, "but done at the team level with medium-stakes, school-based accountability. By reporting before-and-after data within the same school year with the same teachers, there's a much better chance that teams will set ambitious goals, use rigorous measures they respect, *care* about the results, use during-the-year data to improve instruction, spur each other on (focusing especially on team members who aren't pulling their weight), and at the end of the year take real pride and satisfaction in their collective gains in student learning. This fundamentally transforms accountability from a threatening and mysterious process into a credible reflection of the impact of teachers on their kids."

"Using Student Learning in Teacher Assessment" by Douglas Reeves and Kim Marshall in *Edutopia*, April 30, 2018, summarized in Marshall Memo 734.

14 Thinking Through Merit Pay for Teachers

In this *District Management Journal* article, Nicholas Morgan and Daniel Schiff provide a systematic analysis of performance pay for teachers. They begin with three theories of action for why performance pay might improve instruction and student achievement.

- Incentive to work harder: Clear recognition and rewards will motivate teachers to put in extra effort, improve classroom instruction, and thereby improve student achievement.
- Incentive to work smarter: Increased transparency of goals and outcomes (tied to rewards) will motivate teachers to get the best training, upgrade their professional skills, and use more effective classroom strategies, which will improve student achievement.
- A way to improve the faculty: Clear rewards for top performers will attract and retain more-effective teachers, create a culture in which less-effective teachers self-select out, thereby improving instruction and student achievement.

Morgan and Schiff report that there have been some promising pilot programs, mostly abroad, but so far there's no definitive research on which of these theories is most valid. In addition, there are concerns that test results aren't accurate enough for high-stakes pay decisions.

The authors pose five questions that need to be answered to design a fair and equitable performance-pay system:

• *What is measured?* Should teachers be rewarded for classroom performance (judged by observations), for their students' achievement, or for a combination? The big advantage of including classroom observation is that teachers in non-tested grades (who constitute well over half the teaching force) can be eligible.

• *What is rewarded?* If student achievement is the criterion, should teachers be rewarded for absolute test scores or value-added data? There are simple-fairness advantages to the value-added approach—but serious technical issues in getting valid data in a timely fashion. Using test scores alone raises concerns about narrowing the curriculum and teaching to the test.

• *Who gets rewarded?* Should merit pay go to individual teachers, teacher teams, or the school staff? If the latter, should all campus personnel be eligible, only certified staff, or only core-subject teachers? Rewarding individuals can undermine teacher teamwork, but group rewards can create a "freeloader" problem (team members who don't contribute but still get rewarded), which can demotivate top performers.

• *Are there limits on rewards?* Should merit pay go to all who meet the criteria, or only to a fixed number? The first option seems fairer, but it's financially risky since if many teachers do well, awards might exceed the budget. A fixed number of recipients, on the other hand, could create unhealthy competition among teachers, undercutting collaboration and a common sense of mission.

• *How big a reward?* A number of districts believe that paying teachers in the vicinity of $1,000 extra a year isn't that enticing. Houston came to the conclusion that teachers needed the chance to earn up to 20 percent above their base salaries for the program to make a difference, but most plans are nowhere near that generous. The problem is that substantial rewards might be unaffordable and/or unsustainable over time. To launch a performance-pay program, districts need to tap into district funds, state grants and appropriations, federal grants, and philanthropic and corporate support—none of which are guaranteed over time.

Morgan and Schiff say the jury is still out on which of these approaches is most effective at improving teaching and learning. Here are their recommendations for districts and schools thinking about setting up a performance-pay system:

- Think through each of the design questions above and come up with a good overall rationale and plan.
- Align the program design with the strategic objectives and local context.
- Simplify the program as much as possible to promote broad understanding.
- Use performance indicators that are objective and measurable.
- Create enough flexibility to respond to new challenges.

- Offer rewards large enough to motivate employees to excel.
- Ensure that the program has sufficient funding and is sustainable over time.

"Pay-for-Performance Programs: Strategies, Structures, and Funding" by Nicholas Morgan and Daniel Schiff in *District Management Journal*, Spring 2010 (Vol. 4, #1, pp. 29–36, 41–44), summarized in Marshall Memo 342.

Professional Learning Suggestions for Chapter Seven
Teacher Evaluation

Improving Teacher Evaluation

Despite a number of changes to teacher evaluation systems across the country, there are still challenges to ensuring that the evaluation of teachers is fair, valid, and useful. Kim has spent a lot of his career thinking about and working on this issue, and his approach to teacher evaluation along with his rubrics are used in schools throughout the country. The exercises in the first section below are for principals to reflect on alone, or with a group of leaders at the school or district level, regarding what *is* and what is *not* working with teacher evaluation. The second section includes exercises to help schools improve the implementation of their teacher evaluation system.

I. Examine the Current Teacher Evaluation System (How Fair, Valid, and Useful is It?)

Before moving to action, the exercises below help school leaders think through what *is* and *is not* working with their current approach to teacher evaluation.

A. Discuss the challenges of the current teacher evaluation system.
A number of the articles in this chapter point to concerns in teacher evaluation structures and practices. Take some time to review the articles by Cohen and Goldhaber (Article 1), Kraft and Gilmour (Article 2), Murphy (Article 3), Campbell and Ronfeldt (Article 4), Hunter (Article 7), Garrett and Steinberg (Article 9), Jenkins (Article 11), and Darling-Hammond (Article 12), and Morgan and Schiff (Article 14). Compile a list of the concerns about teacher evaluation that are introduced in these articles using the following chart:

Concerns about teacher evaluation systems			
Cohen and Goldhaber (1)	Kraft and Gilmour (2)	Murphy (3)	Campbell and Ronfeldt (4)
Hunter (7)	Garrett and Steinberg (9)	Jenkins (11)	Darling-Hammond (12)
Morgan and Schiff (14)	Concerns About *Our* System		

As a group, discuss the concerns listed in the articles.

Next, think about the concerns you have with the current teacher evaluation system in your school or district. List these in the last box in the table above. As a group, discuss: What do you think are some of the biggest problems with *our* teacher evaluation system in terms of fairness, validity, usefulness, and more? Are there any items *not* included in the articles? Of the items you've listed above, which are the most concerning problems?

B. *Identify the hallmarks of fair, valid, and useful evaluations.*

Either explicitly stated, or implicit in the articles in this chapter, is a set of indicators of components of an *effective* teacher evaluation system. Go back to the articles and list the factors (in the chart below) that would lead to a more fair, valid, and useful teacher evaluation system. Next, brainstorm a list of the strengths of your current teacher evaluation system and enter those in the last box of the table below.

Components of an *effective* teacher evaluation system			
Cohen and Goldhaber (1)	Kraft and Gilmour (2)	Marshall (5)	Bambrick-Santoyo (6)
Hunter (7)	Ferguson (8)	Garrett and Steinberg (9)	Johnson, Uline, and Perez (10)
Darling-Hammond (12)	Marshall and Reeves (13)	Morgan and Schiff (14)	Strengths of *Our* System

C. *Conduct a self-assessment of your own role as supervisor and evaluator.*

Now that you have had time to discuss some challenges in the current teacher evaluation process and examine the hallmarks of what would make for a better system, it's time to look inward at what you, as the principal, are doing to evaluate your teachers. Below is a sample self-assessment you can complete, or you can create your own with the elements you believe to be part of an effective evaluation system. Have every leader who evaluates teachers at your school complete the self-assessment. Give yourself a rating of 1 (novice) to 4 (expert) in the following areas:

Self-Assessment of the Principal's Role as Evaluator and Supervisor

(1 to 4)

_____ Principal has strong observation and coaching skills.

_____ Principal accurately captures nuances of teaching in his/her notes.

_____ Principal gets an accurate sampling of each teacher's work through frequent visits.

_____ Principal gives fair evaluations to teachers working with different types of students in different settings.

_____ Principal does not "go easy" on some teachers to keep the peace. End-of-year ratings reflect performance.

_____ Principal uses end-of-year rubric to accurately distinguish teachers who are great, good, fair, and poor.

_____ Principal makes sure teachers are clear about agreed-upon criteria to be used in evaluations.

_____ Principal relies on measures other than classroom observations as part of teacher evaluation (student work, curriculum planning, participation in team meetings, etc.).

_____ Principal only gives feedback on a few criteria after each visit.

_____ Principal follows observations with brief face-to-face visits.

_____ Principal does not focus feedback conversations on scores—rather, on growth.

Once you complete the self-assessment, take some time to reflect on the scores. Choose a few areas to work on and incorporate these into professional goals you have for yourself for the year.

II. How Might We Improve Our Teacher Evaluation System?

While you may feel that your teacher evaluation system is set in stone and there is nothing you can do, this is not the case. The exercises below help leaders improve the way they evaluate teachers in a number of ways, such as honing their observation skills, clarifying teacher evaluation criteria for teachers, involving teachers in the process, and more.

A. It's your Robert Frost moment; choose your teacher evaluation path.

Help the leaders in your school or district consider the ultimate purpose of teacher evaluation. Alone, or with a team of leaders, reflect on and discuss the following:

- Look at the image below of the fork in the road that shows two paths schools and districts could take for teacher evaluation. Where is your school in this graphic? Where would you like to be? What might you have to do to alter the way teacher evaluation is conducted to reflect your priorities?

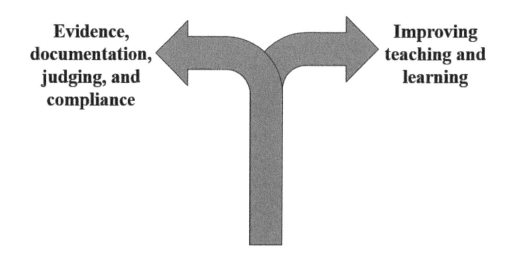

B. Hone supervisor observation skills.

Several articles (such as Marshall, Article 5; Bambrick-Santoyo, Article 6; and Marshall and Reeves, Article 13) emphasize the importance of brief, frequent observations followed by face-to-face feedback. The challenging part of brief visits is knowing which one or two comments would provide the highest-leverage pieces of feedback for the teacher.

To practice identifying what is most important in a ten- to fifteen-minute observation, gather the administrators who observe teachers and together have them:

1. Observe a fifteen-minute segment of a class (either during a walkthrough or by watching a video of a class).
2. Individually choose one to two pieces of feedback they would give the teacher.
3. Compare individual findings with the team and note commonalities and differences.
4. With the team, discuss: What would you want to ask this teacher? What information would you need to find out to understand the context? Of all of the areas you might focus on with the teacher, which ones would provide the highest-leverage feedback to the teacher?

Discuss scoring individual observations with a rubric.

Note that the exercise above focuses on finding the best feedback to give the teacher, *not* how to score the observation of a single lesson on a teacher-evaluation rubric. Discuss with the leadership team why this practice has flaws (even though it is done in some schools). After the discussion, share the following slide, which Kim frequently includes in his own presentations, about teacher evaluation:

Nine Reasons Not to Rubric-Score Minis

- Rubrics are not suited for lesson feedback, no research.
- The supervisor is seeing only a small part of a lesson.
- Distracts the supervisor from being a good observer.
- Top-down, evaluative, bureaucratic tone.
- Too many feedback points overwhelm the teacher.
- "The moment it becomes part of your rating, it stops being meaningful."
- Spurs defensiveness, discourages risk-taking and creativity.
- Scores are averaged; growth isn't reflected.
- Time-consuming "evidence" and "artifacts."

C. Help teachers fully understand the criteria in the teacher evaluation rubric.

After honing the school leadership team's observation skills above, it is an excellent idea to go through the same process with your teachers. This will not only help them better understand the elements of the teacher evaluation rubric, but it will help teachers understand the difference between the various performance levels (for example, how do *Ineffective, Developing, Effective,* and *Highly Effective* look different?). At a staff meeting, show a fifteen-minute segment of a teaching video (of a teacher *not* from your school), and then divide teachers into groups of five to do the following:

1. Individually choose one to two aspects of the lesson they think need the most help. Which part of the teacher evaluation rubric might these areas fit under?

2. Next, compare individual observations with the team and note commonalities and differences.

3. With the group, list *all* of the areas this teacher needs to work on.

4. Now discuss, of all of these areas, what might be one or two important areas to work on first? Where in the teacher evaluation rubric do these areas fit? In order for the teacher to become *Effective* or *Highly Effective* in these areas, what might s/he have to do? What would that look like?

D. Get input from teachers on the teacher evaluation and coaching process.

One idea to improve your teacher evaluation system is to get input from teachers on the evaluation or coaching process. This would be particularly useful to avoid the types of criticisms that teacher Paul Murphy (Article 3) describes after his principal's recent inaccurate observation. As a leadership team, consider implementing the following:

- Create a survey to ask teachers about their experience with the teacher evaluation process. You might ask about the frequency of observations, their accuracy, whether there was any written or face-to-face follow-up, the usefulness of the feedback, and if any support or professional development was provided as a result.
- An anonymous survey would yield the most accurate feedback.
- To maximize the benefits of the survey, be sure to compile and share results publicly and make it clear what two to three changes to the evaluation system you plan to put into place as a result of this survey.

E. Brainstorm ways to involve students in developing teaching skills (not high-stakes evaluation).

Article 4 in this chapter mentions the MET (the Measures of Effective Teaching study). While the results of this study remain controversial, without a doubt, students spend significantly more hours observing teachers than we do. Given that teachers certainly have something to learn from student observations of teaching, it's time to think about how to make use of students' views of their teachers.

At a staff meeting, share the simple survey that follows on the seven Cs of effective teaching with your teachers. Ask teachers to brainstorm ways to use this survey. Possible ideas include giving it to students to fill out anonymously for each class, having teachers self-assess using the criteria that predict teacher performance below, find ways to plan PD to improve teachers' skill with the seven Cs below, etc.

Student Survey on Teacher Performance		
Dimensions	**Example Items**	Rate from 1 (strongly disagree) to 6 (strongly agree)
Care	My teacher really tries to understand how students feel about things.	
Control	Students in this class treat the teacher with respect. Our class stays busy and doesn't waste time.	
Clarify	My teacher has several good ways of explaining topics in class and explains difficult things clearly.	
Challenge	In this class, my teacher accepts nothing less than our full effort and wants us to think, not just memorize.	
Captivate	My teacher makes lessons interesting. I like the ways in which we learn in this class.	
Confer	My teacher gives us time to explain and share our ideas.	
Consolidate	My teacher checks to make sure that we understand when s/he is teaching us and summarizes what we learn.	

F. Improve end-of-year teacher evaluation write-ups.

Many school leaders must write a narrative as part of the teacher evaluation process. Regardless of what you think of this process, it's worth it to do it in as efficient and effective a way as possible. Gather the leaders in your school or district who write these evaluations and do the following:

- Ask the school leaders to bring a few sample teacher evaluations they have written.
- As a group, discuss: What considerations are important in successfully writing these evaluations? (Examples might include: specificity, accuracy, tone, length, time put into the writing, etc.).
- Have school leaders pair off, trade, and read the sample teacher evaluations they brought with them.
- Ask each leader to choose one to two aspects of the evaluation they just read that are effective and one to two things that might improve the evaluation.
- As a group, discuss strategies and tips leaders have found to write these evaluations more *efficiently*.

C. STRUCTURES FOR STUDENT SUCCESS

Chapter Eight: Positive Classroom Discipline

Effective teaching and learning can take place only in a harmonious learning environment.
—Matthew Kraft

As rookie teachers, almost all of us had discipline problems, but we gradually figured out or borrowed strategies to create safe and productive classrooms. The articles in this chapter address classroom discipline from four angles: ways to predict and prevent problems; a systems approach to student misbehavior; effective discipline tools; and schoolwide systems, mediation, and restorative justice.

Heading Off Discipline Problems at the Pass – Timothy Landrum, Amy Lingo, and Terrance Scott say that if teachers put their minds to it, they can predict and prevent most student behavior problems. Justin Minkel believes some behavioral demands are unreasonable and even disruptive, such as having students sit for long periods of time and pass silently in the hallways. Eric Toshalis names five teacher actions that can provoke student misbehavior, and suggests alternatives. Lee Ann Jung and Dominique Smith criticize the use of behavior charts, advocating instead systems that teach self-regulation and set students up for long-term success.

A Systems Approach to Discipline – Ross Greene says the key to solving discipline issues is understanding challenging behavior, communicating effectively with children, and solving problems collaboratively. Nathan Levenson presents a way to work successfully with students who come to school with serious social, emotional, and behavioral problems.

Discipline Tools – Matthew Kraft describes how teachers can move from "discipline ringmaster" to "learning conductor." Margaret Metzger shares the hard lessons she learned in her early months as a high-school English teacher. Fred Jones suggests strategies for dealing with "nasty backtalk."

Schoolwide Systems, Mediation, and Restorative Justice – George Sugai describes a three-tier discipline system for elementary and middle schools and suggests steps for successful implementation. Ondine Gross describes how a confrontation in a high-school biology class was successfully mediated. Katherine Evans and Jessica Lester present the seven key principles of restorative justice and how this approach might be rolled out in schools.

Questions to Consider

- How can schools address the root causes of student misbehavior?
- Which discipline problems can be prevented, and how?
- How can educators build the skills to effectively handle classroom discipline?

Heading Off Discipline Problems at the Pass

1	**Predicting and Preventing Classroom Problems**

In this article in *Phi Delta Kappan*, Timothy Landrum, Amy Lingo, and Terrance Scott (University of Louisville) assert that classroom misbehavior is predictable and preventable. Their insights:

• *Seeing it coming* – How students respond to environmental cues is highly predictable through observation and trial and error, say the authors. If teachers were offered $1 million to predict when a certain student would display his typical problem behavior, most will do so with pinpoint accuracy. For example, he'll act up during whole-class instruction, when questions are asked orally in front of the class, or during independent work in the science lab. Academic deficits in reading, writing, and math are linked to problem behaviors in a chicken-and-egg relationship: "No matter which came first," say the authors, "students identified as having challenging behaviors or academic deficits in the classroom are more likely to experience negative or punitive interactions with teachers, regardless of their behavior; less likely to receive time engaged in instruction with their teachers; and more likely to be subjected to reduced demands and lowered expectations."

• *Preventing problem behavior* – Accurate prediction is the first step. Now imagine that a teacher who's made a precise prediction about disruptive behavior is offered $1 million to ensure that the student is successful at that moment rather than disruptive. The teacher would probably do two things: create physical and instructional routines and environments that help the student succeed, and teach specific skills that would help the student deal more effectively with the trigger situation.

• *Engaging through pedagogy* – "What teachers do during instruction is often simply a matter of what's most comfortable or familiar to the teacher," say Landrum, Ling, and Scott, "often with little attention to evidence-based strategies." The research points to several factors that improve instruction and behavior:

- Clarity,
- Modeling,
- Guided practice,
- Relevant and engaging opportunities for students to respond,
- Teacher feedback on students' efforts.

Feedback on academics and behavior is particularly important, say the authors: "If we asked a student to solve a math problem and then refused to let him or her know whether the problem was solved correctly, we wouldn't have taught anything, nor would we have changed the probability of the student's success or failure in the future .... As a general rule, what makes instruction effective in the academic realm applies equally to teaching social behavior."

"Classroom Misbehavior is Predictable and Preventable" by Timothy Landrum, Amy Lingo, and Terrance Scott in *Phi Delta Kappan*, October 2011 (Vol. 93, #2, pp. 30–34), summarized in Marshall Memo 406.

2 | Not Making Unreasonable Behavioral Demands on Students

"Children aren't just smaller versions of adults," says Arkansas teacher Justin Minkel in this article in *Education Week Teacher*. "They are their own kind of being. They need to move, talk, question, and explore more than we do, because they're in the midst of that mind-boggling explosion of cognitive, physical, and social-emotional growth that marks childhood in our species." Because of this, he believes there are four things teachers should not ask students to do:

• *Silent passing* – Some schools have a no-talking rule when students walk through the hallways, ostensibly to avoid disturbing work in other classrooms. But students may wonder why it's okay for teachers to chat with colleagues as they walk around the school and may have noticed that what's truly distracting is teachers loudly reprimanding students outside classrooms.

• *Sitting still for a long time* – Teachers who shadow students for a day are often struck by how uncomfortable, even exhausting, it is to be sedentary for an entire class period. It's even worse when students are listening passively to "teacher talk." Minkel suggests a guideline for the length of teachers' lectures: students' age—such as five minutes for kindergarten, fifteen minutes for high-school sophomores. In addition, students need to get up and move, which can take the form of organized movement breaks (see the following article) or class rules that allow students to get up to sharpen a pencil or get a book.

• *Forced apologies* – "I've definitely been guilty of this one," says Minkel, but he's come to realize that when an angry child is told to say, "I'm sorry," the apology isn't sincere and won't be received as such. "Turbulent emotions take a long time to settle," he says. "We need to give kids time."

• *Zero tolerance for forgetfulness* – Adults forget as well, says Minkel, and we need to take a deep breath and cut students some slack.

"4 Things Teachers Shouldn't Be Asking Their Students to Do" by Justin Minkel in *Education Week Teacher*, April 8, 2019, summarized in Marshall Memo 782.

3

When Educators Act in Ways That Increase Student Misbehavior

"Misbehavior is a form of communication," says consultant Eric Toshalis in this article in *Educational Leadership*. "When we feel vulnerable, misunderstood, humiliated, or betrayed, we're inclined to act out. Families do it at the dinner table, educators do it in faculty meetings, and students do it in classrooms."

So when students misbehave, Toshalis argues, we need to consider the *context*. Remembering his mistakes as a teacher, he believes "we need to admit the possibility that we sometimes create circumstances in our classrooms that provoke student misbehavior. Admitting this doesn't absolve students of responsibility for their actions, nor does it make us bad educators if we make a mistake here or there. Rather, acknowledging that we sometimes inadvertently provoke student misbehavior helps us recognize that we're all part of complex relationships in complicated institutions, both of which don't always function optimally for everyone." He addresses five ways students may be set off by adults' actions:

• *Highlighting ability differences* – Teachers may draw attention to hierarchies: grouping students based on "ability"; using competition, which inevitably produces losers; not asking higher-order questions of low-achieving students; never posting those students' work; cold-calling students to embarrass them and produce compliance; emphasizing scores and class rank versus learning and growth; and praising students for intelligence rather than effort. "All these approaches broadcast to students that some are smart, whereas others are—well, not," says Toshalis. "They compel students to look for ways to avoid situations where they might be labeled 'the dumb one' .... Research has shown that when educators reduce or eliminate experiences that highlight ability differences, student misbehavior tends to decrease." He believes classrooms should be de-tracked, challenging all students with lots of differentiated support.

• *Promoting a performance-goal orientation* – Grading homework and classroom assignments attaches high stakes to practice work with which students will naturally have some difficulty. Teachers' well-intentioned goal is to assess progress and motivate students to work hard, but the message is that it's about performance, not learning. This produces anxiety and focuses students on how they compare to classmates and what it takes to get an A. "Because it's the answer that matters, not the learning, they will often ask to be spoon-fed the answer rather than try to figure something out on their own," says Toshalis. "They may be reticent to collaborate with others because helping a peer reduces one's own chance to be the best. They may ridicule classmates' mistakes because instigating insecurity in others is one way of staying on top." The solution is formative assessments for practice work and proficiency-based grading that fosters a mastery-goal orientation.

• *Establishing vague norms* – BE RESPECTFUL is a common rule/admonition posted on classroom walls. "Unfortunately, that's as ambiguous as it is succinct," says Toshalis. "The ambiguity of an expectation like 'be respectful,' coupled with its inevitable arbitrary enforcement, will often provoke misbehavior in students …." That's because a student's definition of "respect" and good behavior may be very different from a teacher's. It's a little like visiting a country where cars drive on the opposite side of the street. Crossing a street and driving become much more demanding, and an admonition to "drive respectfully" will not be very helpful. "Likewise, in our classrooms, we tend to establish norms as though they were self-explanatory," says Toshalis, "and we expect a diverse range of students to adhere to them." Schools need to involve students and families in defining what is meant by respectful, caring, kind, polite, appropriate, and mindful; generate examples and counter-examples; and frequently revisit and revise behavioral norms as the year progresses. "This invites students into a democratic process that will inspire more expansive ways of taking care of one another," says Toshalis, "It will also make students want to adhere to the norms rather than subvert them."

• *Letting students choose their seats* – The rationale is that it empowers students and helps them feel less dominated. "But students experience open seating not as freedom but as a form of abandonment," says Toshalis. "The tiny uptick in self-rule a student might experience when choosing a desk is quickly eclipsed when that student must search for the least dangerous seat amid adversaries, bullies, cliques, and even crushes that are always operating in our classrooms." Open seating opens the floodgates to peer segregation, off-task chatting, and, inevitably, the need to move disruptive students. The "in crowd" loudly advocates for choosing seats, but teachers should see their classroom from the vantage point of the marginalized. *Assign seats!* Toshalis advises, guaranteeing students a place that is always theirs, and then mix things up quarterly to foster heterogeneity and intercultural collaboration.

• *Using tired, old scripts* – When we say: *Do as I say, not as I do—Rules are rules—Because I said so—*and *Well, life is unfair,* Toshalis believes we're telling students "that their experience of school (or of us) is invalid, that their insights or critiques are unwelcome, and that their resistance is pointless." This, too, provokes misbehavior.

"5 Practices That Provoke Misbehavior" by Eric Toshalis in *Educational Leadership*, October 2015 (Vol. 73, #2, pp. 34–40), summarized in Marshall Memo 605.

4   The Case Against Behavior Charts

In this article in *Educational Leadership*, Lee Ann Jung (San Diego State University and Lead Inclusion) and Dominque Smith (Health Sciences High and Middle College, San Diego) launch a frontal attack on behavior charts. They believe that telling misbehaving students to go up and move their clip from green to yellow or red amounts to public shaming, harms vulnerable children, and fails to teach self-regulation. Shaming doesn't work, they say, and has the most destructive impact on children with disadvantages, propelling them to more serious behavior problems down the road. "Instead of using charts," say Jung and Smith, "we could just as effectively reduce undesirable behaviors by dumping ice water on a student or inflicting corporal punishment. … Behavior charts are a way to excuse ourselves from the hard work of meeting a student's self-regulation and behavior needs. The fact of the matter is, when we use behavior charts, we are sacrificing student dignity in favor of teacher convenience."

Behavior charts teach students that they will be punished if they don't comply with directions or rules, say Jung and Smith. This may work in the short run, but compliance is not the ultimate goal in classrooms. We're not in the business of creating what William Deresiewicz, in his 2015 book, calls "excellent sheep." Rather, we should be teaching the habits of mind—among them persistence, managing impulsivity, listening to others with empathy—that will prepare students for successful and productive lives. Jung and Smith suggest three alternatives to behavior charts:

• *"Take ten" for each learner.* The teacher spends ten minutes each day sitting with a student talking about his or her personal interests, passions, fears, hobbies, family. Having these mini-conferences with each student over several weeks builds relationships and trust and prevents many classroom problems.

• *Keep it off-stage.* "Students tend to react negatively when they're called out in front of others," say Jung and Smith. "Instead, when a student's inappropriate behavior needs to be addressed, have a one-on-one conversation with the student, staying calm but firm." Ideally these talks occur after class and without an angry summons, and should conclude by making sure students understand that although you are unhappy with the behavior, you care about them and are there to support their growth. Of course, there are situations where a student has to be removed from class immediately to prevent injury or disruption.

• *Hear students out.* "Generally, students prefer to have a conversation *with* a teacher rather than having a teacher conversation happen *to* them," say Jung and Smith. "Students often have a hard time knowing why they acted in a certain way. It's only once their emotion has calmed—and through a guided analysis—that they can identify the reason." Then they can think about alternatives for next time and discuss consequences.

"Tear Down Your Behavior Chart!" by Lee Ann Jung and Dominque Smith in *Educational Leadership*, September 2018 (Vol. 76, # 1, p. 18), summarized in Marshall Memo 751.

A Systems Approach to Discipline

5 Collaborative Problem Solving

In this article in *Phi Delta Kappan*, Harvard Medical School psychiatry professor Ross Greene says we need to stop blaming poor parenting and move past giving students diagnostic labels like "oppositional defiant disorder." Greene believes it's much more helpful to describe the specific skill deficits that prevent some students from doing the right thing in school, for example:

- *He finds it very hard to understand the effect of his behavior on others.*
- *She has difficulty handling unpredictability, ambiguity, uncertainty, and novelty.*

Statements like these, says Greene, "provide a far more informative, compassionate, productive set of lenses than do diagnoses."

When educators discern the specific skills students lack, it becomes clear that challenging students aren't challenging all the time. Their skill deficits become problematic only in situations that demand those skills—for example, when the girl who can't handle transitions is confronted with a transition. This means that almost all challenging behavior is highly predictable.

Greene has pioneered an approach called Collaborative Problem Solving in which schools work to understand challenging behavior, communicate effectively with children, and work together to solve the behavior problems. Greene's program, which claims significant results in schools, is built on these propositions:

• *Children do well if they can.* If they don't do well, it's because they can't—that is, they lack certain skills. So the crucial task for adults is to identify those lagging skills.

• *Doing well is preferable to not doing well.* Children want to succeed, and if they don't, adults shouldn't attribute the failure to kids' attention-seeking, manipulation, coercion, limit-testing, and button-pushing. The problem is skill deficits.

• *Challenging behavior doesn't exist in a vacuum.* Adults need to change their lens, says Greene, and view misbehavior in the context of the child's development.

• *Behind every challenging behavior is a demand for the missing skill.* But that "demand" is rarely articulated by the child; it's up to adults to figure out how lagging skills are colliding with the demands of the environment. "In schools," says Greene, "common unsolved problems include: getting started on an assignment; completing an assignment; participating appropriately in circle time; behaving adaptively in the hallway, on the school bus, at recess, and/or at lunch; getting along with a peer; and interactions with a teacher."

• *Problems should be solved proactively rather than in the heat of the moment.* "Because unsolved problems are highly predictable," says Greene, "solving problems before they occur is far preferable and more productive."

• *Problems should be solved collaboratively.* Unilateral problem-solving by adults (which Greene calls Plan A, very common in schools) often increases the chances of challenging behavior. "That's because having someone else's expectations imposed on you requires skills to handle well," he says, "and those are skills that challenging students are lacking. Better to involve the student in the process."

Plan A is counterproductive, says Greene. Plan B (his program) has three steps: [Plan C is deferring a non-critical problem so people don't get overloaded.]

• *Empathy – The adult gathers information from the student and gets a clear picture of the problem and the lagging skills.* For example, Shawn was sent to the assistant principal because he rudely told his math teacher that her help didn't help. The assistant principal questions Shawn and learns that he doesn't understand fractions, is fatalistic about failing math, and is embarrassed when the teacher offers to help him in front of his peers—hence his rude remark. Other than math, Shawn is doing well in school.

• *Define the problem – The adult states his or her concern or perspective about the unsolved problem.* The assistant principal says that Shawn's frequent trips to the office during math class need to stop and arranges a meeting with Shawn, the math teacher, and herself. It becomes clear that Shawn needs help with fractions but will continue to react inappropriately if the teacher tries to help him in class. He's willing to stay after school for help, but has formed a negative view of the teacher's ability to help him, mostly because he's embarrassed by her attempts to help him in class—plus, he's concerned that his friends might find out he's staying after school for help in math.

• *Invitation – The student and adult brainstorm realistic and mutually satisfactory solutions.* The assistant principal tries to find a time during the school day when the math teacher can help Shawn with fractions. Third period doesn't work but lunchtime is a possibility as long as Shawn's friends don't know what's going on. He and the teacher agree to give it a try, and the teacher rises to the challenge of being a better explainer of fractions.

"Collaborative Problem Solving Can Transform School Discipline" by Ross Greene in *Phi Delta Kappan*, October 2011 (Vol. 93, #2, pp. 25–29), summarized in Marshall Memo 406.

6 Macro Strategies for Social, Emotional, and Behavioral Issues

In this article in *District Management Journal*, Nathan Levenson says principals and teachers he works with are reporting an increase in the number of students coming to school with significant social, emotional, and behavioral problems. When these needs are not addressed, they create disruptions in classrooms, undermine learning, put great stress on educators, and contribute to teacher and administrator attrition.

Districts across the country are investing in curriculum, programs, and additional staff to solve these problems, and some are getting a much bigger bang for their buck than others. What's the difference? Levenson and his colleagues conducted a thorough investigation and came up with ten practices that maximize the impact of existing staff, focus on prevention, and get the most from outside expertise:

Make best use of the talent, expertise, and time of current staff.
Before investing in additional staff, says Levenson, "schools and districts can first take steps to ensure that teachers, psychologists, social workers, behaviorists, counselors, and others are able to effectively use their talents and time to do the most good for the most children." The biggest challenges are paperwork and meetings. Here's what the most successful schools do:

• *Streamline meetings and paperwork to increase time with students.* The average social worker is with students for 32 percent of the school week, but some manage to spend 66 percent of their time with students. Similarly, most school psychologists spend 14 percent of their time counseling students, but some spend more than 30 percent. It can take three-and-a-half days to complete a special-education evaluation, but some psychologists need only one-and-a-half days.

Levenson and his colleagues have analyzed every step that educators take creating an IEP and attending meetings. The most efficient schools use these strategies to boost student contact time and reduce nonstudent hours:

- Pre-meetings of teams are not necessary for students with simpler diagnoses.
- Sharing reports in advance is not always necessary.
- Certain psychological assessments aren't needed for every IEP.
- Psychologists don't have to attend every IEP, RTI, and staff meeting.
- The same is true for other service providers' attendance at IEP and staff meetings.

All this significantly increases time with students without pushing paperwork into evenings and weekends. Streamlining can save as much as two hours of professional time a week.

• *Assign roles based on strengths, not titles.* In one school, a psychologist was assigned to coordinate the PBIS program, despite having no formal training in behavior management. People assumed she was "good at everything" and didn't ask about specific strengths. Levenson recommends that service providers be surveyed to identify the areas in which they have the most training and experience, including:

-   academics (reading, English, math),
-   supporting students with challenging behaviors,
-   counseling,
-   substance abuse and addiction work,
-   case management,
-   IEP assessments,
-   scheduling paraprofessionals and other staff,
-   managing outside partners.

"While many staff have multiple strengths," says Levenson, "it is unrealistic to think all staff are equally skilled in all of these areas. When administrators allow staff to identify their areas of expertise and then match job responsibilities to their skills, both students and staff can benefit."

• *Strengthen teamwork through common planning time.* In many schools, there are very few opportunities for administrators, guidance counselors, school psychologists, social workers, special-education teachers, behaviorists, classroom teachers, and paraprofessionals to discuss students they're working with. Yet this kind of cross-disciplinary meeting is essential to share insights, monitor progress, and serve students effectively. Levenson recommends that schools build their schedules around "sacrosanct" times once or twice a week when it's possible to convene staff working with particular students.

• *Provide behavior management support to teachers in their classrooms.* Too much is being asked of front-line teachers with behaviorally challenging students, says Levenson: "What classroom teachers want, deserve, and need is in-the-classroom support from staff skilled in behavior management. Such support includes hours-long observation of students; leading conversations with students to help identify triggers; observations of the student, class, and teacher after the behavior strategies have been set; and acting as a parent liaison at times as well."

Focus on prevention.

• *Identify and manage behavioral triggers.* Levenson tells the story of a first grader in a suburban school who periodically screamed ugly insults at his teacher, threw scissors and other objects, and ran out of the classroom. The boy's teacher and principal had disciplined the boy numerous times, had worked with his parents, and had reached their limit. They demanded that this student be removed from the school and sent to an out-of-district placement. But then the superintendent brought in a behavioral specialist who observed the boy and noticed that he exploded when he felt embarrassed—even when the embarrassment was subtle, like being given a hint to answer a question. Once the teacher understood the trigger and adjusted her approach, the boy improved dramatically and was able to be successful in the school.

• *Increase access to staff with expertise in behavior management.* "Some teachers and special educators may have a knack for identifying triggers," says Levenson, "but few have formal training." It's important for schools to have access to educators with this highly specialized and valuable skill. Districts should be on the lookout for opportunities to bring such people on board when vacancies occur. Effective behavior specialists will reduce severe problems and make it possible to economize on one-on-one paraprofessionals, shifting those funds to specialists and other resources. Levenson also recommends having a small, highly skilled district-wide team to do initial planning for the most challenging students and share insights and support across schools.

• *Don't let discipline policies create more discipline problems.* A fair and comprehensive discipline code has these basic provisions:

- It ensures student and teacher safety.
- It has consistent expectations from classroom to classroom.
- Suspensions are used as a last resort and not for nonviolent infractions.
- It minimizes loss of learning time.
- It mitigates for unconscious bias.
- It is applied similarly regardless of race, gender, or school.

But a discipline code should not be so rigid that it can't account for individual prevention efforts and behavior management plans—for example, a student walking to a time-out space without a pass being disciplined by an overly rigid assistant principal.

• *Stay focused on academic achievement.* "Too many 'behavior programs' seem to undervalue the importance of academic learning and student achievement," says Levenson. Behaviorally challenged students are often academically able, and if they sense that teachers believe they're not, that can be a trigger. The key is figuring out and addressing behavioral issues as quickly and effectively as possible and then providing rigorous academic instruction with general education teachers.

Seek and support outside expertise.

• *Nurture partnerships.* Local mental health agencies, nonprofit counseling services, and universities can often provide social and emotional services at little or no cost, waiving co-pays and deductibles and billing students' insurance for services. Levenson cites a five-thousand-student district that was able to leverage over $1 million in counseling services a year for almost no cost. In addition, outside agencies might address areas in which the district doesn't have in-house expertise—body image issues, alcohol and substance abuse, dealing with trauma, summer and school vacation coverage, and coaching district staff on best practices.

• *Support and coordinate local partnerships.* Small problems can become deal-breakers with external partners, says Levenson—for example, a counselor showing up at a school and finding that someone else is in the room he was scheduled to use. To get the most out of partnerships, says Levenson, schools need a single point of contact—"a dedicated point person who has time to manage, communicate, and smooth over the inevitable bumps in the road." Responsibilities would include:

- Providing counseling space inside schools;
- Providing an online room calendar to avoid double-booking;
- Scheduling services on a five-day cycle, even if the school's master schedule isn't on that cycle;
- Placing services into student schedules;
- Introducing outside partners to all school-based staff;
- Inviting partners to faculty, department, and other key meetings;
- Checking in weekly by phone, and monthly in person, with each provider.

"Improving and Expanding Social, Emotional, and Behavioral Supports: 10 Best Practices" by Nathan Levenson in *District Management Journal*, Fall 2017 (Vol. 22, pp. 10–27), summarized in Marshall Memo 710.

Discipline Tools

7 | Classroom and Behavior Management 101

"No amount of dedication, lesson planning, or content knowledge is sufficient to compensate for ineffective classroom and behavior management techniques that result in discordant learning environments," says former teacher and school founder Matthew Kraft in this article in *Phi Delta Kappan*. "Effective teaching and learning can take place only in a harmonious learning environment." To help move from discipline ringmaster to learning conductor, Kraft has these suggestions on classroom and behavior management.

Classroom management:

• *Engaging curriculum* – "There's no substitute for teaching a rigorous curriculum that's relevant to students' lives and actively engages students in their own learning," says Kraft. "Despite common assumptions about the immature and impulsive nature of students, more often than not, they're making very calculated, rational choices to act inappropriately. Students are off-task when they don't perceive any benefit from on-task behavior."

• *Nonnegotiable rules* – Kraft believes that a short list of classroom rules should be laid down unilaterally by the teacher. In his own classroom, there were two rules: (a) Don't interrupt the speaker, and (b) Don't use inappropriate language.

• *Clear expectations* – Students are often flummoxed as they move from one teacher's expectations to another. "Students might be rewarded for interjecting ideas during history class while they're reprimanded in math for speaking without being called on," says Kraft. "They may be encouraged to get out of their seats in art class while they're prohibited from leaving their seats in English." Kraft believes there are three basic types of classroom activity, each with its own expectations:

- Direct instruction – Students stay at their desks, pay attention to the teacher, raise their hands before speaking, and speak one at a time.
- Working time – Students can talk about the collective work, collaborate with classmates, and leave their seats as needed.
- Individual silent time – Students remain in their seats, direct their attention to their own work, and may not speak out.

Kraft suggests telling students explicitly at the beginning of each lesson segment which mode they're in and what the expectations are.

• *Smooth transitions* – Shifts from one activity to another can be ragged and lead to problems. They are best managed by "Do Now" assignments at the beginning of each class, clear routines, and assigning students jobs.

• *Getting attention* – "One of the simplest but most commonly cited frustrations among teachers is that they can't get their classes to quiet down," says Kraft. He suggests three techniques: (a) ask for students' attention and wait—in other words, don't talk while students are talking; (b) use a zero-noise device like a rain stick or chime; and (c) if things are out of control, raise your voice with a serious tone. "If you rarely shout, this is extremely effective because it startles students," says Kraft. "But be careful not to abuse it, or it loses its impact."

Behavior management:

"Fundamentally," says Kraft, "all behavior is a form of communication. Students are often unable to communicate or are uncomfortable expressing their feelings, so they act out." Some remedies:

• *Behavior modification systems* – This is the teacher's way of communicating to students when their behavior is inappropriate. Kraft's system was to give a citizenship grade, with all student's grade reset to an A at the beginning of each class. He would then lower individual grades if a student used profanity, socialized during silent time, talked over someone, etc. Citizenship grades were factored into students' overall grades.

• *Avoiding public confrontations* – "Students will go to great lengths to avoid being embarrassed in front of their peers," says Kraft. "When students are publicly reprimanded, they often feel disrespected and respond by drawing teachers into arguments to bolster their image." Kraft suggests reprimanding students in silent or low-key ways, including physical proximity, hand signals, facial expressions, or indirect prompts such as, "Do you need anything to get started?"

• *Private conversations* – Inevitably, some students will challenge the teacher, and Kraft says the best strategy is to talk to the student away from his or her peers. In these conversations, it's important to listen to the student first and make sure, if there is a reprimand, that the student understands the logic behind it, signing a contract if necessary.

• *Overcome the discipline myth* – Some students believe that teachers love to get them in trouble. "Remind students daily that you're a teacher because you want to help them achieve their goals," says Kraft, "not because you want to police them in the classroom."

• *Communicating about moods* – Students should feel able to give a heads-up if they are feeling poorly, and the teacher can model this by disclosing occasionally about feeling tired or frustrated. "When students learn to communicate about their moods, they're offering precious information that teachers can use to prevent conflicts," says Kraft. "Allowing an irritated student to work individually instead of in a group or to skip a turn at reading aloud is far better than forcing them into a situation that will likely cause them to act out."

"From Ringmaster to Conductor" by Matthew Kraft in *Phi Delta Kappan*, April 2010 (Vol. 91, #7, pp. 44–47), summarized in Marshall Memo 332.

---

8   A Massachusetts Teacher on Discipline Lessons She's Learned

In this article in *Phi Delta Kappan*, veteran high-school teacher Margaret Metzger shares her wisdom on classroom discipline. "No one is born knowing how to control 125 adolescents for five hours a day and teach the curriculum at the same time," she says. "Learning to discipline takes years. Mostly it's trial and error. Nothing works all the time, and what works well in one class has no effect on another. However, over time, our repertoire of responses grows; we learn what we can tolerate; we gain a sense of timing; we make alliances within a school. Trust me, you will improve."

Metzger describes the mistakes she made as a rookie teacher. "I hated disciplining adolescents," she writes. "Kids attacked my most vulnerable character flaws, and they could undo my self-esteem in a matter of minutes .... I ricocheted between being a drill sergeant and Mary Poppins .... One critical comment could haunt me for days .... I kept making the same mistakes over and over .... I thought everything was my fault."

Metzger's mother, an accomplished teacher, told her to quit wallowing in failure and learn from classes that went badly. "You need a theory for each problem," her mother said. "Why is it a problem? What do you bring to the situation? What could you have done differently? What other lens could you use to understand the situation? What does the student think happened?" She urged Metzger to keep track of the number of classes a week that were true meltdowns, and sure enough, the number was smaller than Metzger imagined. Having righted the ship, Metzger began to internalize a few beginning "anchoring principles."

Early lessons—

• *Don't escalate, de-escalate.* Metzger realized that she was making bad situations worse with knee-jerk, self-righteous anger. "I never liked this trait in myself," she says, "and the kids ridiculed it." She found that if she consciously de-escalated her annoyance with students' foolishness, she could deal with the behavior. She emulated calm teachers, even if she didn't feel calm. "Teachers, like parents, need to use a light touch," she says. "Let go of some infractions. Whisper instead of yell. Use humor. Change locations. Divide and conquer. Talk to students privately. Make a tiny hand movement. Call kids by name. Smile a lot. Listen. Listen. Listen."

• *Let students save face.* Metzger discovered that certain lines allowed her to deftly avoid no-win confrontations.

- "It's a good thing I like you."
- "Here's the deal: I'll pretend I didn't see that, and you never do it again."
- "That's inappropriate."
- "Consider yourself scolded."
- "Can you solve that? Or do you need me to intervene?"
- "Am I driving you over the edge?"

These allowed her to keep the lesson going, and gave malefactors a chance to back down without embarrassment.

• *Insist on the right to sanity.* "It took two years before I completely understood that, as an occupant of the room, I had rights too," says Metzger. She made a long list of "awful behaviors" and rank-ordered them by how much they bothered her: Cheating, ridiculing, shouting, insults, backtalk, eye rolling, throwing things, gum chewing, tardiness, etc. Then she started working her way down the list, knowing that if she didn't solve the ones at the top, she would leave teaching. Unlike other teachers she admired, Metzger found she couldn't start classes crisply and was therefore less concerned with students being a minute or two late. "On the other hand," she says, "when I ask for student attention, I expect it within three seconds."

• *Reach out.* "For the first several years, I felt too humiliated by my failures to ask for help," says Metzger. "By the second year, I began to make alliances. I learned which guidance counselors really helped, which administrators trusted my judgment, and whether to trust the truant officer. I learned which teachers made good witnesses in difficult meetings. I began to feel not so alone."

• *Get out of the limelight.* "Stand-up teaching made me an easy target," she writes. Plus, beginning teachers "don't have the energy, resources, or ideas that would enable you to teach actively all the time." So Metzger got students doing most of the work—student presentations, seatwork, in-class reading, critiques of movies, quizzes, and group work.

More-mature lessons—

After a few years, Metzger felt calmer and more confident, and her discipline methods were closely linked to how she taught. Some principles from this era:

• *Ask questions.* Teachers sometimes assume they have all the information they need, but if they ask students questions, they learn more. Throughout one year, Metzger lost sleep over a class that seemed perpetually angry and blamed herself for the problem. On the last day of school, she asked students what was up. "Four people here have parents getting divorced this semester," came the reply, "so when we came in and yelled at you, we were really yelling at them." It would have been nice to know this earlier in the year.

• *Suck it up.* "Sometimes you feel you have already spent too much time on the disruptive students," says Metzger. "Frankly, you don't want to talk to them. Too bad. Do it. Not during class time, and not always in the hall. If you don't trust yourself or them in a conversation, use notes."

• *Give adult feedback.* Students need feedback, sometimes on sensitive cultural and interpersonal issues, but too often, educators withhold that information. Here are some examples of things Metzger said to students.

- "In the United States, it's considered a sign of disrespect not to look someone in the eyes when they're speaking to you. So, when I speak to you, you should look directly at me. If you don't, I'll point to the bridge of my nose to remind you."

- "I know that in your culture, modesty is the highest value. But in school you need to assert yourself. I'll try to help you."

- "Your posture, your mumbling under your breath, and your tardiness all show disrespect. If you hate this class, you should talk to me about it. If you like this class, you should know that you are giving misleading signals."

- "You have complained about everything we have done for the past two months. I now see you as a constant whiner. You probably don't want to give this impression, and it's getting on my nerves. So, for the next two months, let's have a moratorium on complaining. You can start whining again in January. Does this seem fair?"

• *Respect the rights of the whole class.* "Some students take much more than their fair share of the psychic space in the room," says Metzger. "Try not to focus only on the difficult students; quiet, earnest students are waiting for your attention too."

• *Ask the students to do more.* "If the work seems authentic and interesting, students usually behave well," she writes. "If I up the intellectual ante, if I make the work more compelling, if I focus more on how students learn than on how I teach, I do not need to coerce them."

• *Remember which rules are important.* Metzger tells how her own son, when he was in ninth grade, carefully hatched an elaborate plan to cut a class so he could get the autograph of his favorite author. He figured out which class he could afford to miss and when he would be back, but when he asked his mother to sign him out, she loudly refused. "Oh yeah," he said sarcastically, "I forgot the rule—take responsibility for what you do." Metzger ruefully thought, "That *was* the real rule. No cutting was a minor rule." She says she admires the way her school breaks minor rules to help students stay in school. Teachers have to decide all the time which rules they will enforce and which they are willing to break for a greater good.

• *Bypass or solve perennial problems.* Teachers go nuts when students don't bring pencils or pens to class or keep forgetting their books. We can get ulcers fighting these battles day after day, says Metzger, or we can keep a supply of pencils and a few extra copies of key books. With books, though, it's important to demand collateral, since students who forget their own book often fail to return a borrowed book. "Ask for something students won't leave the classroom without," she advises: "a watch, an earring, a shoe. Some days I have a collection of shoes and watches on my desk, but every student has a book."

The bigger picture—

Metzger concludes by noting that bad discipline situations are composed of what students bring to the table, but also the school context and adults' baggage. We tend to focus only on what students bring, forgetting the other two. Her pointers:

• *The school context* – "When discipline deteriorates in a classroom," she writes, "we need to remember to ask questions of the whole institution."

- Do we explain the school culture and expectations adequately?
- Did a student get assigned to the wrong class to keep class sizes equal?
- Should certain students be getting help from a specialist?
- Should the supervisor be giving more help to the teacher?
- Do we support new teachers adequately?
- Do new teachers have a chance to watch experienced teachers in action?
- Are administrators being asked to do so much that they can't provide timely help?

And the biggest question: Are teachers, parents, and administrators all working together efficiently and sanely to produce the results we want?

• *The personal context* – The hardest part of classroom discipline is coming to grips with what *we* bring to the situation, says Metzger. Here are some questions she asks herself.

- Am I tired, grouchy, or distracted?
- What else is going on in my life?
- Has the student hit a raw nerve in me?
- Does this interaction remind me of another one?
- What from my background is being triggered?
- Why am I threatened by this behavior?

- Why do I lack resilience on this matter?
- Does race or gender influence my response?
- Is this problem mine or the student's?
- Am I being inflexible? Am I being authoritative or authoritarian?
- Who is watching?

Metzger remembers some truly productive disciplinary meetings in which everyone benefited: the student, the teacher, and the school. That's a triple-win, she says.

"Learning to Discipline" by Margaret Metzger in *Phi Delta Kappan*, September 2002 (Vol. 84, #1, pp. 77–84), summarized in Marshall Memo 247.

---

9 Dealing with Nasty Backtalk from a Student

In this *Tools for Teaching* article, classroom discipline guru Fred Jones shares his advice on how to respond to nasty backtalk from students. "If we can think of discipline management as a poker game in which the student raises the dealer (you) with increasing levels of provocation," says Jones, "then nasty backtalk is going 'all in.' The student is risking it all for the sake of power and control. What separates nasty backtalk from whiny backtalk is not so much the words, but rather, the fact that it is personal. The backtalker is probing for a nerve ending."

The key, says Jones, is never taking anything a student says personally. If you do, you'll probably feel wounded and respond emotionally, in which case the student has won.

The first kind of backtalk is an insult. Students have a limited number of options, all of which have been used through the years.

- Dress:
  - *Say, where did you get that tie, Mr. Jones? Goodwill?*
  - *Hey, Mr. Mickelson, is that the only sport coat you own?*
- Grooming:
  - *Hey, Mr. Gibson, you have hairs growing out of your nose. Did you know that?*
  - *Whoa, Mrs. Wilson. You have dark roots! I didn't know you bleached your hair. Ha!*
- Hygiene:
  - *Hey, don't get so close. You smell like garlic.*
  - *Hey, Mrs. Phillips, your breath is worse than my dog's!*

"Take two relaxing breaths," says Jones. "When the sniggering dies down, the kid is still on the hook." The key is staying rational, not getting angry, not showing that you're upset. Remember, *Calm is power, upset is weakness.*

The second kind of nasty backtalk is profanity. The words students use are all-too familiar to you—some low-grade and some "biggies." Jones says the underlying agenda with student profanity is power. Power boils down who controls the classroom. And that boils down to who controls you. "Can a four-letter monosyllable control you and determine your emotions and your behavior?" Jones asks. "If so, then the student possesses a great deal of power packaged in the form of a single word." If kids see the impact of these words on you, they will use the tactic repeatedly.

So what to do? Jones advises thinking of the response to nasty backtalk in two time-frames:

• *Short-term response* – Take two relaxing breaths, stay calm, and give the student "the look"—calm, almost bored, totally unruffled, while thinking of an appropriate long-term response. "Your lack of an immediate response is very powerful body language," says Jones. "It tells the student, among other things, that you are no rookie. You have heard it all a thousand times. If the student runs out of gas and takes refuge in getting back to work, count your blessings, and consider getting on with the lesson." How about what the other students think? They've just seen the backtalker try "the big one" and fail—and they saw you handle it with cool professionalism, and learned that profanity won't work in this classroom.

• *Long-term response* – Talk to the student after class. It's quite possible that the student's outburst was related to something that happened outside your classroom. In that case, delivering a consequence might make the situation worse. You might start off like this: "Vanessa, what you said in class today was not at all like you. Tell me, what is really going on?" You've opened the door and really don't know what the student will say. Be patient. "Silence is truly golden since young people have a very low tolerance for it," says Jones. "If you wait calmly, the whole story will probably come spilling out. Do not be surprised if the lip starts to quiver. Have some tissues handy." Vanessa might need a pass to visit the nurse and pull herself together before going to her next class. And make sure she knows you're available to talk more. This might be the turning point in a year-long relationship.

A student who backtalks may very well be in an abusive situation at home, and lashing out at a teacher is a way of testing to see if you are as uncaring as other adults in his or her life and if you will respond as expected—with anger and another trip to the office. "What does surprise students in this situation," says Jones, "is to find a teacher who says, 'I can see that you are hurting. Tell me about it.' It catches them off guard. Sometimes their defenses crumble because they are so unaccustomed to anybody caring about whether or not they hurt. Sometimes, healing is mediated by simply taking the time to ask and to listen. Without going that far out on a limb, you can answer the defining question in your relationship with the child, 'Do you even care?'"

"Our calmness and skill," Jones concludes, "allow us to say 'no' to backtalk while potentially strengthening the fabric of our relationship with the student rather than tearing it." The more emotionally intense an interaction is, the more possibilities there are. "A student's crisis in class, therefore, presents us with a rare opportunity .... These heart-to-heart talks are some of the most precious moments between adult and child. They teach important lessons within a context that says that being 'bad,' while it leads to real consequences, cannot threaten the bond of caring."

"Nasty Backtalk" by Fred Jones in *Tools for Teaching*, December 16, 2016, summarized in Marshall Memo 670.

Schoolwide Systems, Mediation, and Restorative Justice

10 **A Three-Tier Program for Student Behavior**

In this *Harvard Education Letter* interview conducted by Mitch Bogen, University of Connecticut professor George Sugai describes the key features of Schoolwide Positive Behavioral Supports (PBS), a program that has been adopted by about seventy-five hundred U.S. schools and has, according to Sugai, a solid research track record for improving student behavior and school climate in elementary and middle schools. Some highlights:

• Schoolwide PBS has three tiers.

a. All students are exposed to a formal social-skills curriculum that supports the academic mission of the school and is implemented in classrooms, public spaces, cafeteria, and buses; this gets about 70–80 percent of students on the right track;

b. Students who are not reached by the first tier (have difficulty following directions, don't participate appropriately in classrooms, need to be reminded over and over again to follow procedures, and repeatedly break rules) get additional, intensive social-skills instruction, cognitive-behavioral counseling, and conflict management—often in small groups;

c. Students who are still misbehaving get high levels of individualized contact and monitoring—for example, meeting one-on-one with a counselor or special education teacher; getting frequent positive reinforcement, reminders, and prompts around desired behavior; or meeting with a mental health specialist who works with the student, family, and school staff.

Students in all three tiers are helped with conflict management, bullying prevention, respect, and cooperative learning.

• Sugai cautions against labeling students (*She's third-tier*). Instead, he suggests statements like this: "Timothy needs Tier Two supports because of noncompliant behavior." The key is being descriptive and diagnostic—for example, a student might be doing well overall but have problems responding aggressively to teasing.

• Sugai says that most schools try to be proactive but end up spending inordinate amounts of time reacting to negative behaviors (*Stop that! You're not following my directions! Why aren't you listening to me?*) and hardly any time teaching positive behaviors. Adults' anger escalates and eventually the offending student is removed from the classroom or the school. Most schools realize that removal isn't effective. "We've suspended him twelve times and there's no change," they say.

• Zero tolerance policies and making the discipline code stricter (*One more time and you're gone!*) are not the solution, says Sugai—although, of course, the school needs to set limits and be safe. "The code of conduct is for students who have learned the rules and expectations and are basically doing OK socially," he explains. "We argue that the code of conduct is really a screening tool for knowing which students need more than what is typically available." Noncompliant students who are having trouble getting along with adults are highly resistant to threats from adults. "Being sent to the office is actually a way to get more peer and adult attention or get out of class," says Sugai. "Suspension gives them 'permission' to go home to be with friends, watch TV, or play computer games."

• To implement Schoolwide PBS successfully, Sugai recommends a systematic approach.

- Set up a leadership team with the principal, grade-level staff, specialists, non-classroom staff (e.g., a bus driver and cafeteria worker), and a parent.

- Come up with a common purpose statement and articulate a short list of values, skills, and expectations for everyone (e.g., respect, responsibility, safety, cooperation, and problem solving).

- Teach these positive behaviors as seriously as reading, math, or music; elementary students need role-playing, middle-school students need practice, and high-school students need discussion.

- Publicly recognize students who are behaving well, which might include making "positive office referrals."

- Publicize a continuum of consequences for rule violations in a discipline handbook.

- Monitor discipline referral rates to see if they go down as the new policy is implemented. It's also helpful to gather survey data to see how students, staff, and parents perceive the policy.

"Beyond the Discipline Handbook—A Conversation with George Sugai" by Mitch Bogen in *Harvard Education Letter*, May/June 2009 (Vol. 25, #3, pp. 8, 6), summarized in Marshall Memo 285.

11 Teacher-Student Mediation in Action

In this article in *Roots of Action*, school psychologist Ondine Gross describes a confrontation in a high-school biology class:

- The teacher asks a student to open her book and stop talking.

- The student, angry about the reprimand because other students were also talking, yells, "Leave me the f--- alone!"
- The teacher sends the student to the office.
- The student gets an in-school suspension, and a parent is called.
- When the student reenters the class a day later, the teacher has moved on to a new topic and the student realizes she missed an exam and her grade has dropped.
- The student refuses to approach the teacher to make arrangements to do a make-up test.

Incidents like this happen with great regularity, and although many schools have tiered systems of positive behavioral supports and interventions, as many as 20 percent of students don't respond well to them.

Gross believes the way to handle this kind of conflict is a structured, fifty-minute meeting led by a trained, impartial adult mediator. "Mediation provides teacher and student with ways to listen and understand each other's perspectives, restore goodwill, and develop positive plans to move forward," she says. "The process boosts social, problem-solving and communication skills—all of which are important for students' resourcefulness should problems arise in the future." Here's how a mediation might play out in the scenario above:

• The mediator asks the teacher to speak first. She says how frustrated she was that the student was disruptive in class and is failing the course. The teacher says she can feel the girl's anger and wishes to better understand what's going on. She acknowledges that she sometimes removes a student from class to restore order even though other students were also misbehaving. Asked about the student's strengths, the teacher says she did great work at the beginning of the semester and recalls an insightful comment she made about mitosis. The teacher says she is discouraged that the girl isn't interacting with her anymore and genuinely wants to help her get back on track and raise her grade.

• The mediator turns to the student, who says she is touched that the teacher came to the meeting and wants to help her do better. The student seems surprised by the teacher's sincerity, especially that she remembered the mitosis comment, and begins to let down her guard. She confesses that it's hard to keep up in biology since most of her time after school is taken up helping around the house, adding that her home environment isn't conducive to studying. She says that when the teacher moved her seat away from the front of the class, it was more difficult to pay attention. In addition, by fourth period she is hungry and that makes her cranky. She says the teacher is a good instructor who explains things well. She expresses a desire to improve her grade.

• The mediator then asks the teacher and student to speak directly to each other. The student looks the teacher in the eye and says, "I'm really sorry for the way I've been acting. You are a good teacher and you didn't deserve that." The teacher responds warmly and says she wants to help the girl do better. They discuss moving her seat up to the front of the class, allowing a snack if she is hungry, and getting help after school with missed homework and tests. Both teacher and student leave the meeting smiling, relieved that a positive plan is in place and the relationship has been mended.

Gross concludes with data from a pilot of teacher-student mediation in a diverse high school in the Midwest:

- Eighty-two percent of students who participated in mediation had no further discipline referrals from the teacher in question.
- More than 70 percent of mediations were conducted with African American students and white teachers, showing that mediation can bridge the racial divide.
- Eighty-seven percent of participating teachers said mediation improved student behavior and learning.
- Administrators unanimously said mediation was the single most effective Tier II intervention they had used.
- Parents and guardians were grateful that the school was building students' skills rather than using disciplinary interventions that took students out of class.

"Schools are social institutions and their effectiveness is based on the quality of the relationships between people," concludes Gross. "When classroom management strategies include teacher-student mediation, those involved become more self-aware and resourceful. Relationships improve. Learning is enriched."

"Classroom Management Begins with Respect" by Ondine Gross in *Roots of Action*, August 15, 2016, summarized in Marshall Memo 651.

---

12 Restorative Justice

In this *Middle School Journal* article, Katherine Evans (Eastern Mennonite University) and Jessica Lester (Washington State University) say that "zero tolerance" discipline policies have failed to make schools safer. They point to a growing body of research suggesting that restorative justice, implemented in some schools in Australia, New Zealand, England, Scotland, South Africa, Canada, and the US, is a better approach. Its purpose is to "hold offenders accountable, repair harm to the victims, and provide support and assistance to offenders to encourage their reintegration into the community." Restorative justice can be seen as "a response to misbehavior and as a way to facilitate healthy school climates." Evans and Lester explain its key principles:

• *Meeting needs* – An underlying assumption of restorative justice is that humans have three basic requirements: autonomy, order, and relatedness. "When these needs are not met, students may go to great extremes to meet their needs," say Evans and Lester. The result is misbehavior, conflict, and sometimes violence.

• *Providing accountability and support* – "While zero tolerance policies promote accountability, they often do so without compassion," say Evans and Lester. Restorative justice "promotes accountability within a supportive and compassionate learning community." If it's clear that a child's actions were wrong and resulted in harm, the perpetrator must accept responsibility.

• *Making things right* – A bad deed is defined "not as an offense against the institution (i.e., the school) but as an offense against the members of the institution (i.e., the students' school community)." Restorative justice is different from restitution, which can be seen as another form of punishment. Rather, restorative justice should serve the needs of the victim, "restoring the relationship between the victim and the offender," say Evans and Lester. "Further, the effectiveness of a restitution plan is contingent on the offender developing and being responsible for the plan, rather than having that plan imposed on them by an authority figure. In this way, the restitution becomes not only a way of repairing harm but also an opportunity to learn."

• *Viewing conflict as a learning opportunity* – Externally imposed sanctions deprive students of the chance to problem-solve, learn, and grow, say Evans and Lester, and "teach students that only those in power are able to make decisions and solve problems …. Restorative models of school discipline open conversations between victims and offenders, allowing them a space to share perspectives, listen to one another, and work collaboratively to design solutions that bring about healing and restoration."

• *Building healthy learning communities* – Restorative justice "defines school violence as a breakdown of social relationships and implements specific processes to rebuild those relationships," say Evans and Lester. "Strengthening school community and enhancing student-student, student-teacher, teacher-teacher, and school-community relationships is viewed as the most effective way to prevent misbehavior and school-based violence."

• *Restoring relationships* – Conflict and violence are a violation of relationships more than a violation of rules, say the authors. Restorative justice "seeks an understanding of what has occurred, the needs of those affected—including students, teachers, parents, and anyone else involved in the conflict—and ways to address the harm that was done." Restorative justice "works *with* students and teachers rather than doing things *to* them or *for* them."

• *Addressing power imbalances* – Restorative justice goes beyond students' behavior and looks at the harm that can be done by institutional practices—for example, long out-of-school suspensions.

Evans and Lester say that, despite research pointing to the efficacy of restorative justice, schools have been slow to adopt it. Why? Three possible reasons: restorative practices require a lot of time and resources, proponents haven't provided enough conceptual clarity, and the philosophy clashes with existing punitive models of school discipline.

Ideally, restorative justice has three tiers. The first is schoolwide instruction in social and emotional skills to build school community. The second involves repairing relationships when conflict happens, mostly in small-group conferences or peer mediation. The third deals with situations where harm has been done, providing mediation and victim-offender conferences.

Evans and Lester suggest the following steps for gradually introducing restorative justice in a school:

- Combine top-down leadership with bottom-up energy. "This approach helps to gradually develop a critical mass within a school," they say.
- Start where you are. There may already be elements of restorative justice within the school and staff members who support the idea.
- Start with voluntary participation. Staff buy-in is important, and the restorative process shouldn't begin until offenders have admitted guilt and begun to take responsibility for their actions.
- Shift the paradigm from punishment and control. To implement restorative justice, schools need to move from managing students' behavior to collaboration, mutual respect, accountability, and growth.

"Restorative Justice in Education: What We Know So Far" by Katherine Evans and Jessica Lester in *Middle School Journal*, May 2013 (Vol. 44, #5, pp. 57–63); summarized in Marshall Memo 489.

Professional Learning Suggestions for Chapter Eight Positive Classroom Discipline

Improving Our Approach to Discipline

Unfortunately, during school visits, Kim and Jenn have seen too many classrooms that were focused on addressing discipline issues *after they occurred* that could have been prevented with some planning and assistance. For this reason, the articles in this chapter focus heavily on *prevention* as the key to addressing discipline issues. They focus on four major areas that are important if you want to act proactively: (1) creating a climate that is conducive to good behavior, (2) teaching the behavioral and social-emotional skills for students to manage themselves, (3) avoiding the types of triggers that lead to most discipline problems, and (4) ensuring that academics are taught in a clear and engaging way. This may seem like a lot of work, but as Sugai points out, schools that *don't* put the time into prevention spend inordinate amounts of time reacting to negative behaviors.

Below are three sets of activities to do with your teachers to think preventatively about discipline, to set up school-wide systems to deal with discipline issues, and to put a plan in place to address misbehavior when it does (inevitably) occur.

I. How Effective Are We at Preventing Discipline Problems in the First Place?

Although you can examine your school's approach to discipline with your leadership team, we highly recommend that you involve teachers as well. Teachers have the most in-the-trenches awareness of what happens when a school does *not* have enough preventative discipline measures in place. These first activities get teachers to think through what exactly in their classrooms and in the school might be inadvertently causing discipline problems.

A. Assess current preventive discipline measures.
Before a meeting, have teachers and/or a leadership team individually and anonymously fill out the self-assessment survey that follows about factors that lead to discipline problems. Find the average rating for each item. Then at the meeting, discuss which areas the school seems to be strong in and which areas need improvement.

Rate each of the following elements from 1 (poor) to 10 (excellent) in the column to the right	
1. We create a class and school climate conducive to good behavior.	
Expectations and rules for behavior are consistent across the school.	
Implementation of disciplinary measures are consistent across the school. We know which issues should be handled inside the classroom versus sent to the office/counselor/specialist.	
Expectations and norms are specific (not vague, like "Be respectful").	
Our staff generally believe that students behave well if they can. They do not *want* to be disruptive.	
We highlight and reinforce positive behavior.	
We have a team that ensures a systematic and effective approach to discipline at our school.	
2. We teach appropriate behavioral and social-emotional skills.	
Teachers have regular classroom routines (collecting work, starting class, transitions) and actively teach these to students.	
Students have opportunities to learn and practice social-emotional learning either in class, in advisory, with specialists, with counselors, or by some other means (how to manage selves, manage relationships with others, and make decisions).	
When a discipline incident occurs, we involve students in solving it (through mediation, collaborative problem solving, or some other structure) so they can learn from the incident.	
We have several tiers—so that we provide the right supports for the right students at the right time.	
3. We avoid triggers that often lead to disciplinary issues.	
We don't highlight ability differences (through competition, emphasizing class rank, reserving higher order work for higher-achieving students).	
We focus on learning rather than grades (formative over summative assessment).	
We avoid zero tolerance policies and allow for some flexibility in rules.	
We avoid public confrontations and instead speak with students privately about concerns.	
We know our students well enough to know individual student triggers (*She has trouble with transitions*) so we can carefully handle those specific triggers for those students.	
4. We ensure classes are academically engaging.	
We have a strong curriculum that is rigorous, relevant, and engaging.	
Classes are student-centered rather than teacher-centered.	
Students have opportunities for autonomy, choice, and working collaboratively.	
Lessons are clear and include modeling, guided practice, opportunities for students to respond, and teacher feedback.	

B. Conduct a peoplegraph and discuss.

From the completed self-assessments (on the previous page), choose five of the items that had wide disagreement among participants. Then read those sentences out loud and have staff physically stand to represent their agreement or disagreement along a continuum.

For example, you might read out loud, "We don't highlight ability differences" and assign one wall to those who completely AGREE, the opposite wall to those who DISAGREE. Then those who are in the middle stand in the appropriate space between the two walls (closer to the AGREE wall if they agree more than disagree). Once everyone is positioned along this physical continuum, discuss why people stood where they did.

Alternatively, you can have staff discuss the following quotations from the articles in this chapter:

"Misbehavior is a form of communication." (Toshalis, Article 3)

"We sometimes create circumstances in our classrooms that provoke student misbehavior." (Toshalis, Article 3)

"Effective teaching and learning can take place only in a harmonious learning environment." (Kraft, Article 7)

C. Think of students who struggle with behavioral issues.

Have teachers write down the names of a few students who struggle with discipline issues.

Then share this line from Ross Greene (Article 5), "When educators discern the specific skills students lack, it becomes clear that challenging students aren't challenging all the time." Discuss Greene's idea as a group and then ask teachers if they can identify *when* the students on their list seem to struggle.

For example, the following two statements show that teachers know *when* these students struggle. Share these examples with the teachers and have them write sentences describing *when* their own students struggle:

"He finds it very hard to understand the effect of his behavior on others."

"She has difficulty handling unpredictability and ambiguity."

Next, in pairs, have them discuss what they might do to *prevent* these students from disrupting class.

D. Have teachers assess their own classroom management.

To help individual teachers pinpoint aspects of their own classroom management that could be tightened up to better prevent discipline problems, have teachers use Kim Marshall's Classroom Management rubric on the next page. Either they can video their own classes and self-assess, or they can team up with a partner, visit each other's classes, and assess their partner using the rubric.

Classroom Management

The teacher:	4 Highly Effective	3 Effective	2 Improvement Necessary	1 Does Not Meet Standards
a. **Expectations**	Is direct, specific, consistent, and tenacious in communicating and enforcing very high expectations.	Clearly communicates and consistently enforces high standards for student behavior.	Announces and posts classroom rules and consequences.	Comes up with *ad hoc* rules and consequences as events unfold during the year.
b. **Relationships**	Shows warmth, caring, respect, and fairness for all students and builds strong relationships.	Is fair and respectful toward students and builds positive relationships.	Is fair and respectful toward most students and builds positive relationships with some.	Is sometimes harsh, unfair, and disrespectful with students and/or plays favorites.
c. **Respect**	Creates a climate of respect and buy-in such that disruption of learning is virtually unthinkable.	Wins almost all students' respect and discipline problems are few and far between.	Wins the respect of some students but there are regular disruptions in the classroom.	Is not respected by students and the classroom is frequently chaotic and sometimes dangerous.
d. **Social-emotional**	Implements a program that successfully develops positive interactions and social-emotional skills.	Fosters positive interactions among students and teaches useful social skills.	Often lectures students on the need for good behavior, and makes an example of "bad" students.	Publicly berates "bad" students, blaming them for their poor behavior.
e. **Routines**	Successfully inculcates class routines up front so that students maintain them throughout the year.	Teaches routines and has students maintain them all year.	Tries to train students in class routines but many of the routines are not maintained.	Does not teach routines and is constantly nagging, threatening, and punishing students.
f. **Responsibility**	Gets virtually all students to be self-disciplined, take responsibility for their actions, and have a strong sense of efficacy.	Develops students' self-discipline and teaches them to take responsibility for their own actions.	Tries to get students to be responsible for their actions, but many lack self-discipline.	Is unsuccessful in fostering self-discipline in students; they are dependent on the teacher to behave.
g. **Repertoire**	Has a highly effective discipline repertoire and can capture and hold students' attention any time.	Has a repertoire of discipline "moves" and can capture and maintain students' attention.	Has a limited disciplinary repertoire and some students are not paying attention.	Has few discipline skills and constantly struggles to get students' attention.
h. **Efficiency**	Skillfully uses coherence, momentum, and transitions so that almost every minute of classroom time produces learning.	Maximizes academic learning time through coherence, lesson momentum, and smooth transitions.	Sometimes loses teaching time due to lack of clarity, interruptions, inefficient transitions, and off-task teacher behavior.	Loses a great deal of instructional time because of confusion, interruptions, ragged transitions, and off-task teacher behavior.
i. **Prevention**	Is alert, poised, dynamic, and self-assured and nips virtually all discipline problems in the bud.	Has a confident, dynamic presence and nips most discipline problems in the bud.	Tries to prevent discipline problems but sometimes little things escalate into big problems.	Is unsuccessful at spotting and preventing discipline problems, and they frequently escalate.
j. **Incentives**	Gets students to buy into a highly effective system of incentives linked to intrinsic rewards.	Uses incentives wisely to encourage and reinforce student cooperation.	Uses extrinsic rewards in an attempt to get students to cooperate and comply.	Gives out extrinsic rewards (e.g., free time) without using them as a lever to improve behavior.

II. Setting Up Schoolwide Systems to Address Discipline

In many schools, a large problem is that discipline is addressed differently in different classrooms. Below are some activities to begin to help schools move toward a schoolwide approach to discipline. Some activities are for a team charged with improving discipline and some are for the principal alone.

A. Set up a team to follow up from self-assessment survey above.

On your own or with a leadership team, follow up from the results of the survey above to address gaps in your preventative approach to discipline. Choose one of the four areas to work on (these are the four subheadings in the self-assessment survey in the activity I.A., the first activity in this section) and outline *TWO* action items to complete. Below you will find one sample action item for each of the four areas in the survey:

For #1: Although most schools have long student handbooks and lists of rules, it's hard for people to remember them and know which are most important. Outline three key rules to set expectations for behavior across the school and then *communicate* these often—in meetings, conversations, on posters, etc.

For #2: Reread Bogen (Article 10) and consider ways to strengthen your tiered behavioral system—perhaps by putting a leadership team in place to oversee and monitor it.

For #3: Look at those triggers over which you, as school leader, have the most control (those *outside* of the classroom). For example, do your AP classes end up tracking the entire schedule? Can your zero tolerance policies be modified? Can you de-emphasize the importance of state tests over learning? Do a little investigation into which of these schoolwide triggers you can address.

For #4: Have the team do some walkthroughs in classrooms to look for the five areas Landrum, Lingo, and Scott (Article 1) outline that contribute to an engaging classroom: clarity, modeling, guided practice, opportunities for students to respond, and feedback. Have the team give feedback to observed teachers *only* on these areas and explain the connection between these five and improved behavior.

Our two action items to improve our preventative approach to discipline:
1. _____
2. _____

B. Five things you, as the principal, can do unilaterally right now.
Not everything needs to wait for consensus. If you want to dig into discipline issues right now, below are some unilateral actions from Levenson (Article 6) that you can attack right now:

1. Streamline meetings and paperwork. Your psychologists and counselors will be more effective if they have more face time with students. Meet with them to implement some of the five suggestions from the article to streamline paperwork and meetings.

2. Assign roles based on strengths. Maximize the strengths of those who can help with behavioral issues by distributing a survey to your psychologists, social workers, counselors, special education coordinators, and other service providers—asking them about their skills and strengths and then assigning them to work on areas of their greatest strengths.

3. Provide common planning time. Look for time in the schedule or give up some all-school meeting time so service providers and teachers can have time to discuss the most challenging students.

4. Nurture partnerships. Engage someone on staff to research local organizations that provide counseling and social and emotional services for little or no cost. Look for agencies that provide expertise the school lacks—in body image issues, drug and alcohol abuse, summer and vacation coverage, etc.

5. Ensure someone is coordinating local partnerships. When you successfully forge partnerships with these outside agencies, give the job of coordinating their school visits to *one* person on staff.

C. Determine which behaviors should be handled in and out of the classroom.
With teachers or leaders, create a school-wide set of expectations for which behaviors should be handled *in* and *out* of the classroom. One high school, the Centennial High School, divides up *who* should handle which type of discipline problem as outlined in the following chart. (Ondine Gross, *Restore the Respect: How to Mediate School Conflicts and Keep Students Learning* [Baltimore: Paul H. Brookes Publishing Company, 2016], 51).

Handled by teachers:	Referred to administrators:
Excessive talking	Insubordination
Being off task	Fighting
Chewing gum/eating	Vandalism
Drinking non-alcoholic	Verbal or physical intimidation
Missing homework	Carrying a weapon
Unprepared for class	Making threats
PDA	Gang representation
Backtalk to adults	Cutting class, repeated tardies
Cheating, plagiarism	Theft
Sleeping	Drug/alcohol violations
Shutting down	Directed profanity
Noncompliance	Harassment, including sexual
Minor disobedience, disruptive behavior	Security threat/breach
Minor vandalism	Passing lewd notes
Electronic device	Repeated backtalk
	Repeated PDA
	Dress code violations
	Creating a fake pass

Share the above chart with everyone, let them review it, and then brainstorm and agree upon which issues you would like handled *inside* and *outside* the classroom at your own school using the blank table below:

Issues to Manage INSIDE the Classroom	*Issues to Manage OUTSIDE the Classroom*
(Examples: excessive talking, being off task)	(Examples: fighting, theft, dress code violation)

III. Addressing Misbehavior When It Does Occur

Even with a wide repertoire of preventative measures in place, misbehavior will occur. We are dealing with large numbers of students in one location over many hours each week; it's inevitable. Below are two simple role-play activities staff can use to practice addressing misbehavior.

A. Practice a problem-solving approach to misbehavior.
Two of the articles introduce ways to engage students in addressing their misbehavior: Ondine Gross introduces mediation in Article 11 and Ross Greene introduces his Collaborative Problem Solving in Article 5. Reread these articles (or, both authors have books you can read). Introduce the one approach you think would work best in your school.

Divide leaders, teachers, and specialists into groups of four to role-play (one as the student, one as the teacher involved in the incident, one as the facilitator, and one as an outside observer to take notes).

Choose your own age-appropriate incident, or use the one from the Gross article:

The teacher asks a student to open her book and stop talking.

The student, angry about the reprimand because others were talking yells, "Leave me the f--- alone!"

The teacher sends the student to the office.

The student gets an in-school suspension and a parent is called.

When the student returns to class a day later, the teacher has moved to a new topic, and the student realizes she missed an exam and her grade has dropped.

The student refuses to approach the teacher to make arrangements to do a make-up test.

Project the steps you want the groups to follow on a screen so everyone can see them. For example:

Collaborative Problem Solving:

Step 1. Understand – Use empathy to gather information about what the problem is from the student's perspective.

Step 2. Communicate – After the student has articulated her concern, it's the adult's turn to define the problem.

Step 3. Work together – Invite both parties to come together to find a solution.

After the groups role-play addressing the incident with this approach, have them debrief, looking at the observer's notes, to figure out what they did well and what they could improve. Repeat as necessary.

B. Practice the Fred Jones response to nasty backtalk.

Have teachers pair up and choose who will role-play the teacher and who will role-play the student who engages in nasty backtalk. Next, choose one of the instigating comments students make described by Fred Jones (Article 9), such as "Hey, Mr. Gibson, you have hairs growing out of your nose. Did you know that?" or, "Hey, Mrs. Phillips, your breath is worse than my dog's!" Give the teacher role-playing the student a moment to think of a back story for why he or she is speaking to the teacher like this.

Now have the pair role-play the student making the nasty comment and the teacher responding using Fred Jones's two-step response:

1. Take two relaxing breaths, stay calm, and give the student "the look"—calm, almost bored, totally unruffled.
2. Talk to the student after class (assume it is now after class). You might start off like this, "Vanessa, what you said in class today was not at all like you. Tell me, what is really going on?"

After the role-play, have the two teachers debrief. What did the teacher do well and what might she or he do differently next time?

Chapter Nine: Planning Units and Lessons

Teaching is a means to an end, and planning precedes teaching. The most successful teaching begins with clarity about desired learning outcomes and about the evidence that will show that learning has occurred.
—GRANT WIGGINS AND JAY MCTIGHE

All the theory and research on elementary and second education come down to what students actually do when they walk into a classroom. This might be listening to a lecture, taking part in a discussion, asking and responding to questions, reading texts, taking notes, exploring online, doing worksheets, conducting experiments. Ideally, every classroom activity is part of a larger plan to engage students and produce college- and career-prepared graduates. For that to be true, there needs to be careful planning—and artful improvisation—at the teacher, team, school, and district level. The articles in this chapter look at macro curriculum planning, unit and lesson planning, and structuring instruction so all students learn.

Macro Curriculum Planning – Mike Schmoker says it's essential that schools ensure a coherent, content-rich curriculum that gets students reading, writing, and discussing in every subject area. Terry Heick suggests a way to prioritize curriculum content: ask what we want students to remember for the next forty days, forty months, and forty years. Nancy Frey, Douglas Fisher, and Heather Anderson show how a California high school posed schoolwide essential questions and used them to spark deeper inquiry and thinking across the disciplines. And Seth Weitzman describes how the capstone projects completed by his school's eighth graders demonstrate key middle-school learning and skills in engaging and dramatic ways.

Unit Planning – Laura Varlas lists five traps teachers can fall into as they plan lessons—entertaining students, coverage, overloading, and the curse of knowledge—and suggests backwards unit planning as the solution. Grant Wiggins says that if students are going to apply what they learn in new and unfamiliar situations, transfer must be built into unit and lesson plans and assessments. Jon Saphier presents a fifteen-minute discussion protocol to help teachers think through the big ideas and student learning outcomes of a curriculum unit. And Karen Engels describes a fourth-grade unit on "Our Changing Nation" that integrates science and social studies standards, immersing students deeply in answering essential questions.

Lesson Planning – Norman Eng argues that lesson plans should be very short and focus on three basic questions: What will students learn? How will they learn it? and Why does this matter? Jay McTighe describes the ingredients that should be included in a well-designed lesson plan. And Rachel Curtis shares the detailed lesson desiderata of the Achievement First charter schools.

Structuring Lessons So All Students Learn – Brian Sztabnik suggests ways to plan the launch and closing minutes of a lesson to maximize student learning. Cathy Seeley upends the typical I-We-You lesson plan, arguing that students should engage in productive struggle at the outset. Spencer Salend and Catharine Whittaker describe the key components of a Universal Design for Learning (UDL) lesson that makes lesson content accessible to all students. And Katie Novak shows how a conventionally taught second-grade and high-school lesson can be improved by applying UDL principles.

Questions to Consider

- What is the problem to which unit planning is the solution?
- What can a lesson plan add to a good unit plan?
- What evidence of curriculum planning should a supervisor see in a classroom?

Macro Curriculum Planning

1 Building a Coherent Curriculum

In this article in *Phi Delta Kappan*, author/consultant Mike Schmoker says the single most important factor in highly effective schools is "a coherent, content-rich curriculum that abounds in opportunities for reading, writing, and discussion in every subject area." This, he says, is what improves students' reading skills, higher-order comprehension, test scores, and success in college and careers. *How* the curriculum is taught matters, says Schmoker. "But even the best pedagogy can't overcome the negative effects of incoherent curriculum, just as the best exercise regimen can't overcome the damage done by a diet of fast food."

The problem, says Schmoker, is that very few schools have the kind of content he describes. "Many schools implement a test-prep curriculum that is nothing but a content-poor corruption of real curriculum," he writes. "The actual taught curriculum continues to depend, more than anything, on which teacher a student happens to get."

The Common Core State Standards are a good start, says Schmoker, but he agrees with two Common Core authors that there are still too many English Language Arts standards and we should "focus on the cornerstones"—specifically:
- a carefully selected sequence of increasingly complex texts within and across each course and grade level—books, essays, speeches, opinion pieces, newspaper and magazine articles, poems, and textbook pages;
- high-quality questions on those texts;
- abundant opportunities for students to closely read, discuss, and write about the texts in response to the questions;
- assigning writing that takes the form of arguments supporting claims with evidence as students analyze, explain, and research the topics they're studying;
- devoting at least one week per grading period to helping students write a short research paper.

"Only this will ensure that they're college and career ready," says Schmoker. For schools that don't already have this kind of curriculum, he believes, nothing is more important than putting it in place. Some immediate steps:
- Have teacher teams reduce and identify the most essential content standards and topics for each course.

- Organize those topics by grading period.
- Choose interesting, content-rich texts for the content in each grading period.
- Continuously share the best work and texts with other teams and other schools.
- Don't worry about having a "perfect" curriculum. "Even rough, conscientious efforts here will result in more coherence and an invaluable selection of quality texts for most courses."

"First Things First: Curriculum NOW" by Mike Schmoker in *Phi Delta Kappan*, November 2011 (Vol. 93, #3, pp. 70–71), summarized in Marshall Memo 411.

| 2 | **The Ultimate Power Standard: What Kids Will Remember in Forty Years** |

In this article in *TeachThought*, Terry Heick suggests a way to prioritize curriculum content: Ask whether this is something we want students to remember and understand...

- For the next forty days?
- The next forty months?
- The next forty years?

"As you can see," says Heick, "this is a powerful way to think about academic content… It occurred to me that it was more about contextualizing the child in the midst of the content, rather than simply unpacking and arranging the standards." It's about enduring value beyond the classroom—one of the criteria for framing an Understanding by Design Big Idea—the kind of lifelong learning teachers dream about instilling in their students. Here are Heick's suggestions for implementing *the 40/40/40 rule*:

• *Work solo at first.* Before discussing the layers with colleagues, she believes it's wise to analyze standards by yourself, "rather than simply being polite and nodding your head a lot."

• *Discuss with colleagues.* Share your take on the 40/40/40 layers and debate different opinions.

• *Keep it simple.* Heick suggests using concentric circles or a simple three-column chart to start separating the wheat from the chaff.

• *Be flexible.* "You're going to have a different sense of priority about the standards than your colleagues," she says. "These are different personal philosophies about life, teaching, and your content area emerging. As long as these differences aren't drastic, this is normal."

• *Know that children aren't little adults.* What's the focus now, and how will it play out in the future? "Rarely is a child going to be able to survey an array of media, synthesize themes, and create new experiences for readers without being able to use a verb correctly," says Heick.

• *Tackle the big ideas first.* Heick suggests a way to push key concepts to the fore: "If they learn nothing else this year, they're going to know *this* and *that*." You can't control everything kids will know and be able to do down the pike, "no matter how great the lesson, assessment design, use of data, pacing guide, or curriculum map," he says. "But if you can accept that—and start backwards" from the down-the-road big picture, you'll have a good road map for forty years and beyond.

"Which Content Is Most Important? The 40/40/40 Rule" by Terry Heick in *TeachThought*, March 17, 2016, summarized in Marshall Memo 694.

3 A California High School Crafts Schoolwide Essential Questions

In this article in *Principal Leadership*, Nancy Frey and Douglas Fisher (San Diego State University) and Heather Anderson (Health Science High School) draw a distinction between essential questions that are course-specific (for example, *how do fractions, decimals, and percentages allow us to describe the world?*) and schoolwide essential questions. Frey, Fisher, and Anderson describe how Health Science High School has used a set of schoolwide essential questions each year to provoke high-level discourse and improve student achievement. In developing its questions, the school used the definition developed by Grant Wiggins and Jay McTighe (2013):

- Essential questions are worthy of inquiry, calling for higher-order thinking—analysis, inference, evaluation, and prediction.
- They are thought-provoking and intellectually engaging—sparking discussion and debate, giving students the tools and a forum to wrestle with important ideas.
- They are open-ended—that is, there isn't a single, final, correct answer.
- They require support and justification, not just the answer.
- They produce a humbling acceptance that some matters are never truly settled, but at the same time a desire to think about such questions.
- They point toward important, transferable ideas within and across disciplines.
- They raise additional questions, spark further inquiry, and need to be revisited over time.

Each year the school collects possible questions, screens them using the Wiggins/McTighe criteria (plus one more—questions involve two or more academic disciplines), asks students to vote on them, and decides on the best sequence (one question for each academic quarter). Here are some of the school's essential questions from recent years:

- If we can, should we?

- Does age matter?
- How do people approach their health?
- What is race, and does it matter?
- What sustains us?
- Can you buy your way to happiness?
- Who am I? Why do I matter?
- What is beauty and/or what is beautiful?
- Does gender matter?
- Who are your heroes and role models?
- What's worth fighting or even dying for?
- What will you, or won't you, do for love?
- What is normal, anyway?
- How does your world influence you?
- Is there a limit to tolerance?
- What makes you "you"?
- Which is worse, failing or never trying?
- You exist, but do you live?
- If you could have a superpower, what would it be and why?
- Are humans naturally good or evil?
- Is freedom ever free?
- Do looks matter?

Each year's questions are displayed in public areas of the school and sent home to parents, and visitors are given the opportunity to comment in a response log.

Teachers start the year by thinking about how to integrate the chosen questions into their own course content and, if possible, make cross-disciplinary links. For example, a 2010–11 schoolwide question about the nature and importance of beauty led English teachers to have students read *The Metamorphosis* by Franz Kafka, *The Birthmark* by Nathaniel Hawthorne, *Body Rituals Among the Nacirema* by Horace Miner, "Ain't I a Woman" by Sojourner Truth, and "Ode to a Grecian Urn" by John Keats. A tenth-grade world history teacher addressed the issue through a study of philosophers of the Enlightenment, and a geometry teacher looked at the concept of the golden mean in architecture and design.

When the school first started using schoolwide questions, students were asked to write about them in a single discipline. "Over time, we began to understand that complex interdisciplinary thinking requires that students participate in discussion and debate before writing," say Frey,

Fisher, and Anderson. "Teachers now devote a portion of one class period each week to a Socratic circle on the question of the quarter." The location of these discussions rotates among the four core academic classes so students think about the questions from every possible angle. Student responses can come in a variety of formats—formal research papers, Facebook postings, 3-D sculptures, animations, and more.

"Using Schoolwide Essential Questions to Drive Learning" by Nancy Frey, Douglas Fisher, and Heather Anderson in *Principal Leadership*, February 2014 (Vol. 14, #6, pp. 52–55), summarized in Marshall Memo 525.

4 Capstone Projects for About-to-Graduate Eighth Graders

In this article in *AMLE Magazine*, veteran middle-school principal Seth Weitzman sings the praises of capstone projects, which aim to sum up the inquiry skills and other key qualities students have acquired over their middle-school years. A good capstone project has several characteristics: it sparks intense curiosity and passion; there's a meaningful purpose to what's presented that's obvious to an outside audience; and the project's conclusions must be justified by evidence. Some sample projects from the Mamaroneck, New York school where Weitzman was principal:

- redesigning football helmets to prevent concussions;
- Japanese Americans' internment: Could something like this happen again?
- social justice topics, for example—Asian American stereotypes, racism in the judicial system, and animal rights;
- proposed amendments to the Patriot Act to better balance civil rights and national security;
- addressing concerns with the school's homework guidelines (*Is homework helpful or harmful?*);
- the impact of divorce on children;
- the desirability of a therapy dog for the school;
- chronicling a week-long "social media cleanse";
- the growing popularity of food trucks;
- how color choices influence marketing decisions;
- what makes something funny?
- turning a violin into an electronic instrument and performing a musical composition.

Teachers, counselors, and administrators at Weitzman's school set the guidelines and then acted as "inquiry guides" as eighth graders shaped their projects (the adult-to-student ratio was 1:7).

In May and June, with most state testing finished, the school trimmed six minutes from each period in the schedule and created a forty-eight-minute Capstone Period each day over four weeks for students to work on their projects, either with their cohort or individually in the library or a hallway. The school followed the Stripling Model of Inquiry—

- *Wonder*: Develop questions, make predictions and hypotheses.
- *Investigate*: Find and evaluate information to answer questions and test hypotheses; think about information to illuminate new questions and hypotheses.
- *Construct*: Build new understandings connected to previous knowledge; draw conclusions about questions and hypotheses. *What does all this mean?*
- *Express*: Apply understandings to a new context or situation; express new ideas to share learning with others.
- *Reflect*: Think about what's been learned and ask new questions.
- *Connect*: See links to self and previous knowledge; gain background and context.

One addition the school made to this inquiry model was a requirement for field study: interviewing an expert; conducting a survey; or visiting a museum, historic site, laboratory, or business.

The culmination of all this work took place on two mornings in June, with presentations made in classrooms—to seventh graders on the first day and to eighth-grade parents on the second. Students used PowerPoint slide shows, tri-fold poster boards, models, and simulations—one boy cooked three varieties of pancakes. Capstone projects were assessed with a rubric on four dimensions: evidence of quality research and sources, originality, organization and preparedness, and works cited.

Before the advent of capstone projects, says Weitzman, the last few weeks of school were consumed with preparing for and taking final exams. "In contrast," he says, "our students now finish middle school practicing inquiry, a lifelong learning skill, and making learning their own … putting together the most important lessons we've taught them the previous three years."

"Capstone Projects" by Seth Weitzman in *AMLE Magazine*, August 2018 (Vol. 6, #3, pp. 6–9), summarized in Marshall Memo 747.

Unit Planning

5 | Solving Lesson-Planning Challenges with Backwards Unit Design

In this *Education Update* article, Laura Varlas addresses five challenges teachers face as they plan lessons:

• *Coverage* – Getting through the curriculum is an imperative, but if that's the main focus, teachers may lose sight of deeper goals. In an English class, says *Understanding by Design* author Grant Wiggins, planning shouldn't be about what book is being read but "how students are different when they're finished reading it." UbD coauthor Jay McTighe agrees: "Just like a coach plans with the game in mind, teach individual skills and knowledge with the performance in mind, not as ends in themselves."

• *The fun trap* – Many teachers plan cool, engaging activities that don't necessarily push toward understanding. "Activity-oriented lessons can be fun in the short run, but they're cotton candy," says McTighe. "They don't have any deep nourishment." Wiggins: "It's possible to build a model of a working roller coaster but not learn any physics." Visiting classrooms, he likes to ask students:

- What are you doing?
- Why are you doing it?
- What's it helping you learn?

The key: deciding on lesson strategies *after* formulating learning outcomes and how they'll be assessed. Activities should be a series of steps leading students to being able to perform the objective and explain what they're doing.

• *Information overload* – "The wealth of free online lesson-planning resources can become tempting distractions as teachers sit down to design learning," says Varlas. The same is true of digital planning software that links a unit to standards and spits out forty objectives. Teachers need to take a deep breath and (ideally with colleagues) think through the content and what students should learn, focusing on the new standards being taught.

• *Educator egocentrism* – It's important for teachers to step out of their own mastery of the material and imagine how students will experience it—in particular, what misconceptions they may have and what rough spots they'll hit. This means working through the material in advance and preparing during-lesson questions that probe for deeper understanding—and then responding nimbly to students' partial answers and errors.

• *Lesson plans* – Wiggins and McTighe believe the smallest unit of curriculum planning should be the unit plan. "I'm not saying 'stop planning,'" says instructional coach Mike Fisher. "I'm saying, 'stop planning for the isolated moment.'" Varlas adds: "Moving away from the potential myopia of daily plans requires schools to shift from isolated teacher planning to collaborative, integrative teams. It also begs principals to question the merit of requiring teachers to submit daily plans. Instead, look for a coherent unit plan with rich, well-aligned assessment tasks built into it." McTighe sums up: "Don't micromanage day-to-day teaching. Manage results on things that matter."

"Writing a Master Plan" by Laura Varlas in *Education Update*, April 2016 (Vol. 57, #4, pp. 1, 4–5), summarized in Marshall Memo 584.

6 Teaching So Students Will Transfer What They Learn

In this *Perspectives* article, "backwards-design" author Grant Wiggins tells the story of a college professor who used the following problem in his physics class: *A ball weighing three kilograms is dropped from a one-hundred-meter tower. How many seconds does it take to reach the ground?* At the end of the semester, the professor included a variation of this question in the final exam: *There is a one-hundred-meter hole in the ground. A ball weighing three kilograms is rolled off the side of the hole. How long does it take to reach the bottom?* A number of students were stumped by this question, and one complained to the professor afterwards, "I think this exam is unfair. We never had a hole problem!"

Difficulty transferring what's been learned to a new situation is "depressingly common," says Wiggins. "Students will typically not cue themselves to use all their prior learning or recognize how the 'new' situation reflects prior learning …. Transfer doesn't just happen as a result of a typical regimen of teaching and testing, no matter how rigorous the course of study. Transfer happens only when we aggressively teach and test for understandings that are applied in situations."

Some teachers say they don't have time to teach for transfer because they're under so much pressure to get their students ready for standardized tests. Wrong! says Wiggins. Secure state tests, by their very nature, contain questions that students have never seen before, so every high-stakes test is an exercise in applying learning to a new situation. "Transfer," he argues, "must be every teacher's goal."

But how are teachers going to pull this off? By systematically training students to use, adapt, extend, and understand the basics of what they have learned in novel, "messy" situations. And the best way to do that is to build in transfer from the very beginning of the backwards-design process. "What we need to see more clearly," Wiggins says, "is that the common learner failure to transfer is not a student weakness or a teaching deficit but a mistake in planning. You have to design backward from the goal of transfer if you want to achieve it ....Too often, though, teachers merely teach, then ask in their tests: Did you learn my lesson?"

To improve students' performance at transferring learning, Wiggins continues, teachers need to skillfully orchestrate three steps:

• *Giving formative performance tasks or tests that demand transfer.* Students must get used to being thrown "curve balls" that involve more than just regurgitating what they have been taught.

• *Explicitly teaching students how to transfer with plenty of feedback.* Initially, says Wiggins, "we simplify and scaffold the performance, giving cues and techniques... But gradually, we must remove the scaffolds and cues ... [and introduce] a steady increase in the demand on learners to judge for themselves, based on learned 'moves' of how to assess each new situation effectively and act appropriately." Some students need fewer hints and support than others; just asking "can you think of something you did earlier that might be relevant?" is enough for them. Others may need more explicit prompts. Wiggins suggests using the following rubric in the classroom so students can assess themselves (4 and 3 are an A, 2 is a B) and see that the ultimate goal is to be able to do it on their own:

4 – Could do with no prompting entirely on one's own,

3 – Required only one minor hint in which the general problem type was referred to,

2 – Required two or more hints about the general problem type,

1 – Required a prompt in which the specific knowledge/skill was cited,

0 – Could not do the problem, even with prompting.

• *Designing summative tests so they require transfer* and giving students no prompts, so it's clear that the objective is to be able to transfer independently.

Wiggins sums up all the steps needed to prevent the "we never had a hole problem" syndrome:

- Establish clear and explicit transfer goals with students—i.e., in terms of assessment and grading.

- Use "essential questions" as part of teaching, review, and assessing to suggest the kinds of connections students will have to make all year.

- Have students practice the ultimate transfer, not just the discrete elements, as part of instruction and homework.

- Change the situation/setup so students realize that any real challenge or problem involving prior learning comes in many guises, sometimes unfamiliar ones.

- Have students practice autonomous self-cueing and knowledge retrieval on their own, without grade penalty.
- Require students to constantly reword/rephrase/re-present what they learn.
- Include in instruction, generalizing from specific cases and connecting discrete lessons via the same idea.
- Simplify the ultimate transfer and require (easier) transfer early and often.
- Make sure that any tool or technique is seen as one of many for meeting a more general transfer goal.
- Provide many examples of think-alouds in transfer situations, and practice such think-alouds as part of instruction.
- Shift perspective so that all key content is viewed from multiple points of view.
- Require self-assessment and self-adjustment related to transfer as part of all major assessments.

"Transfer as the Goal of Education" by Grant Wiggins in *Perspectives*, September 2006 (originally published in Big Ideas, Authentic Education), summarized in Marshall Memo 154.

7 Focusing a Curriculum Unit on Intended Outcomes

In this *Journal of Staff Development* article, author/consultant Jon Saphier suggests a fifteen-minute protocol to be used in face-to-face meetings with teachers to focus on the deeper purposes of a curriculum unit. The key, says Saphier, is to analyze the *content* students are meant to understand before getting into the activities, materials, student groupings, and behavior management. By digging deeply into the content, the teacher can reflect on the big ideas, the sequence, hierarchy, and relationships among them, the prior knowledge required to do the tasks assigned, what will be difficult for students, and what the big takeaways should be for students. Here are some guiding questions:

- What content will you be focusing on?
- What are the most important things you want students to understand?
- Can you explain them in kid-friendly language?
- What would students need to know from their own experience in order to be ready to move forward?
- How would you break down this concept into parts?

- Which part of this concept do you think students need to understand first?
- How will you present the objectives to the class?
- Say it out loud just as if you were talking to the class.
- How will you present the content information? On the board? Smartboard?
- How will you know if students understand? Will you have an assessment?
- If you were to go around and interview students at the end of the unit, what would you want them to say to show they really understand?
- Okay, now what are you going to have students *do*?

"When practiced in 15-minute conversations with peers, coaches, or administrators," says Saphier, "content analysis quickly becomes a habit of mind that individual teachers internalize. The reward is intellectual satisfaction as well as better student learning."

Here's what this protocol produced for a middle-school unit plan on the human respiratory system.

The big ideas:
- Every cell in the body, not just the muscles, needs oxygen. That includes bone marrow, hair, everything.
- When oxygen arrives at a cell, the chemical reactions within the cell release energy. In other words, oxygen is absolutely necessary for all cells to grow and for muscles to move.
- The bloodstream is the highway that carries oxygen to the cells.
- We also have to get rid of the carbon dioxide that is produced by this release of energy. If we didn't, we'd die.
- Respiration is a process for getting oxygen into the body so the oxygen can do its work as well as get rid of waste products. It's a lot more than what we call "breathing."

Students will be able to:
- Describe the mechanism by which oxygen enters the body and the pathways it follows,
- Explain the magic moment when oxygen crosses cell membranes (the alveoli) into capillaries and thus is transported through the bloodstream/circulatory system,
- Explain the process by which oxygen does its work in the body,
- Explain how the respiratory system expels items the body needs to get rid of (carbon dioxide and water).

"15 Minutes to a Transformed Lesson" by Jon Saphier in *Journal of Staff Development*, August 2013 (Vol. 34, #4, pp. 56–59), summarized in Marshall Memo 497.

8 Teachers as Curriculum Designers versus Curriculum Implementers

In this *Educational Leadership* article, Massachusetts teacher Karen Engels worries that the proliferation of curriculum standards in different content areas won't produce students who are active and engaged participants in our democratic society. "With so many bits and pieces of content," she says, "it can be hard to organize instruction into lessons that *matter*, that connect students to larger questions about themselves and the world." Implementing new standards can feel like "a frantic forced march from one topic to the next or a collection of isolated facts."

Driven by these concerns, Engels and colleagues in two local schools met with central-office officials and won permission to teach an interdisciplinary, project-based curriculum integrating the fourth-grade science and social studies standards. In a series of retreats, teachers, instructional coaches, and central-office directors crafted "Our Changing Nation," narrating how people in five U.S. regions fought for a better life from the 1830s to the 1930s. The unit's essential questions:

- How has the land affected the people in our nation?
- How have the people in our nation affected the land?
- When should we consider change to be progress?
- How can we evaluate the benefits and costs of change?
- How can we be supporters of positive change in our nation?

The goal was for students to absorb important content knowledge and gain a sense of empowerment by learning how people fought against oppression, adversity, and injustice.

During the first quarter of the year, students studied the science of changes in the earth's surface and the topography and geography of each U.S. region, along with the experiences of Native Americans prior to the Europeans' arrival. Over the remainder of the year they worked with seven case studies:

- the Lowell Mill Girls campaigning for a ten-hour workday during the 1840s,
- enslaved African Americans and abolitionists during the 1850s,
- European and African American pioneers moving west after the 1862 Homestead Act,
- the Navajo during the Long Walk of 1864,
- Chinese immigrants building the Transcontinental Railroad and going on strike in 1867,
- the Lakota fighting the United States government during the 1870s,
- the Dust Bowl and the Great Depression in the 1930s.

For each case study, students worked with primary sources, read-aloud texts, historical fiction, documentary footage, paintings, field trips, hands-on projects, and other resources. They looked at the scientific principles behind new technology (including waterwheels in early factories), and wrote about connections to contemporary issues, culminating in April by creating nonfiction picture books with text, illustrations, diagrams, glossaries, and the works cited. In the final weeks of the year, students chose whether to (a) perform a play bringing together their historical writings, (b) serve as a curator for an interactive science museum, or (c) present their nonfiction books. All this was shared with other classes, families, and community members over two days in June.

"Our teaching team ended the year feeling exhausted but exuberant," says Engels. Students had been immersed all year in meaty content and higher-level thinking, and the excitement and engagement markedly improved their writing skills. "For meaningful teaching and learning to flourish," she concludes, "students must *care* about what they're learning; they need to know why it matters. Students care when their learning experiences are part of an interconnected narrative and when these experiences spark their innate interest in big, authentic questions about people and the world we live in."

"The Story of Us" by Karen Engels in *Educational Leadership*, November 2017 (Vol. 75, #3, pp. 38–42), summarized in Marshall Memo 712.

Lesson Planning

9   Lesson Plans Focused on Three Key Questions

In this *Cult of Pedagogy* article, Norman Eng says he was once required to write full lesson plans in advance for the whole week. "There's no way to know what'll happen Friday when so much changes on Monday," he says. And who has *time* to write all those lesson plans in advance? After a while, he defaulted to jotting notes on what he wanted to teach each day of the week and amending his daily lesson plans as needed.

But that was less than ideal. Eventually, he hit upon the idea of formulating lesson plans focused on three big ideas:

• *The What* – What do I want my students to know (or do) by the end of class? What is the content knowledge or skill to be learned?—for example, evaluating the credibility of online sources.

• *The How* – What method, strategy, tool, or activity will ensure they reach the goal? Often it will be a hands-on activity—for example, students will evaluate the credibility of online sources by working in groups to triangulate and address critical questions such as, *Does the author cite or provide links to research?*

• *The Why* – Who cares? What is the ultimate purpose for learning this content or skill? What's in it for students? How will they benefit? Well, students need to be proficient at evaluating the credibility of online sources so they can make better decisions down the road. The *WHY* question also helps formulate a good lesson opening or hook—for example, *With so much out there, how do you decide what information to trust online?*

Eng likes to boil all this down to a one-sentence lesson plan—for example, *Students will be able to evaluate the credibility of online sources by working in groups to address a critical question so that they will be prepared to make better decisions as they explore the Internet*. Here's how this would play out in one lesson's details.

- Opening: Ask students about their experiences searching for information online.
- Mini-lesson: Ask them to think about better ways to find information and teach them how to triangulate.
- Guided practice: Model your "think-aloud" process for triangulating information by searching online for the question, *Is climate change real?*
- Activity: Students apply the same triangulating strategy to another topic—for example, *Do vaccines cause autism?*

- Closing/assessment: Why is good judgment so important in the information age?

Eng addresses some likely questions about this super-short lesson planning format:

• *What if I'm required to write and submit full lesson plans?* The one-sentence What/How/Why is the lesson objective. "Once established," says Eng, "it's fairly straightforward to flesh out …. Remember to bookend your lesson with the WHY."

• *Isn't the one-sentence lesson plan really just a lesson objective?* Ideally, lesson objectives would include the What, How, and Why—but they often don't. The How and Why push us to think from the students' perspective and make it easier to plan the lesson opening, activities, and closing.

• *What if I'm required to write lesson plans based on standards?* "Then your WHAT is already done," says Eng. If there's a Common Core or other standard for the lesson, turn it into a one-sentence lesson plan.

• *What if I'm having trouble figuring out the WHY?* Asking this question spurs us to think about the underlying theme or Big Idea. For example, what's at the heart of just-in-time operations management? *Efficiency.* What's behind the 1989 Tiananmen Square protest? *Injustice.* Why does oxidation matter? *Certain foods go bad (a half-eaten apple turning brown) and there are ways to avoid that.* If you're really stuck with the WHY, says Eng, just Google it.

"Introducing the One-Sentence Lesson Plan" by Norman Eng in *The Cult of Pedagogy*, October 15, 2017, summarized in Marshall Memo 708.

---

10 Lesson Plans: Suggested Elements

Jay McTighe, coauthor (with Grant Wiggins) of the backwards-design classic *Understanding by Design*, is frequently asked what he thinks a good lesson plan should contain. McTighe says that a single lesson is too narrow a slice of instruction to encompass a curriculum unit's big ideas, enduring understandings, essential questions, and performance tasks. These need to be thought through for the unit (for example, the five-week unit on the Civil War, the six-week unit on poetry). But individual lessons are how all that content is delivered to students day by day, so lesson plans are a vital extension of unit planning. Here are McTighe's recommendations on what a lesson plan should contain.

• *Objectives that flow logically from the overall unit plan:* the essential questions, previous activities, and unit assessments;

• *Materials and resources:* a list of what is needed by the teacher and students;

• *An anticipatory set:* a "hook" that is linked to the essential questions, previous and future activities, and assessments;

• *Key learning activities and strategies:* listed in sequence with the approximate time that each one will take; (For example—Students will explore two contradictory primary source documents and discuss the different points of view expressed – forty-five minutes. The teacher will use "concept attainment" to help students distinguish fact from opinion – thirty minutes.)

• *Checking for understanding:* a planned approach to assessing whether all students are learning what's being taught;

• *Closure:* some kind of synthesis, review, and reflection, with foreshadowing of the next lesson. (Some lessons may need to begin with a diagnostic assessment, although this is probably more suitable at the beginning of the curriculum unit.)

How detailed should lesson plans be? McTighe recommends including enough information so that a teacher who is familiar with the content and grade level can follow the plan without further explanation.

"Understanding by Design and Lesson Plans" by Jay McTighe, an unpublished paper circulated to the UbD Cadre, January 20, 2006, summarized in Marshall Memo 120.

11 What Makes an Effective Lesson?

In this Aspen Institute white paper, teacher evaluation expert Rachel Curtis describes the performance management system used by Achievement First charter schools. Of particular interest are Achievement First's *Essentials of Effective Instruction*, which are used by administrators and coaches when they observe classrooms and plan professional development and support. Note that there are a number of references to techniques from Doug Lemov's book, *Teach Like a Champion 2.0* (Jossey-Bass, second edition: 2015).

• *Great aims*: Rigorous, bite-sized, measurable, standards-based lesson goals are written on the board and reviewed with students. The aims clearly drive activities, not vice-versa.

• *Assessment of student mastery of the aims*:

- There is a systematic way at the end of class to assess every student's mastery of the aim(s) and to diagnose areas of student misunderstanding. Most of the time, assessment is through an exit ticket.

- The goal is for at least 85 percent of students to master the aim.

- *The most effective and efficient strategies to reach the aim*:
  - Content knowledge/right strategy – The teacher demonstrates strong knowledge of the relevant standards and concepts and uses the most effective and efficient strategy to guide students to mastery.
  - Pacing and urgency – The teacher moves students briskly from one part of the agenda to the next; there is a palpable sense of urgency and purpose in the room. Time is held sacred; the teacher spends the appropriate amount of time on each activity and maximizes each minute spent. The teacher sets clear guidelines for how long activities should take and uses timers, time reminders, and countdowns effectively. The class is set up to maximize efficiency, and the teacher is fully prepared to maximize each moment.
- *Modeling/guided practice* (I/WE or WE):
  - Mini-lesson – The lesson includes a clear "think aloud," explicit modeling, heavily guided practice, or other form of clear mini-lesson; examples and step-by-step processes are thoughtfully planned and tightly delivered.
  - The teacher may sometimes start a lesson with a YOU-activity: short discovery activity, activation of prior knowledge, or some other strategy to lay a conceptual foundation.
  - Guided practice/declining scaffolding and guidance – The teacher then leads students through guided practice with gradually reduced scaffolding/guidance so that students can eventually provide both the answers and the thought process.
  - Visual anchor – The mini-lesson is captured (on a whiteboard, butcher paper, overhead, and/or scaffolded notes) so that students can reference it during independent practice.
  - Check for understanding – The teacher regularly assesses learning during guided practice so that students transition to independent practice when they are ready. A small number of students may need more guided support during independent practice, and this should not hold up the entire class.
- *Sustained, successful independent practice* (YOU—at least fifteen to twenty minutes):
  - Many successful "at bats" – Students have ample, successful opportunities for active learning so that they get to practice the aim independently. The YOU-activity should be at the same difficulty level as the WE-activity so that complexity doesn't increase while support decreases. The teacher moves around the classroom constantly during independent practice to assess mastery and provide individual help.
  - Read, baby, read! In reading classes, teachers make sure that "nose in text" time is very high and that independent work time has at least a 7:2 ratio of reading to activity/ writing/ discussing.

- *Classroom culture*:
  - High expectations, clear routines – The teacher sets (with clear What-To-Do statements) and reinforces clear expectations and routines for high standards of behavior. With a Strong Voice, the teacher "sweats the small stuff," including no call-outs, no laughing at other students' mistakes, and insists students Do It Again if not great.
  - The J factor – The class is a fun, joyful place where kids are enthusiastic and excited about learning.
  - Positive-corrective ratio – The teacher uses Positive Framing to correct behavior and narrate class activity; there is a high ratio of positive to corrective comments. The classroom feels like a place where students want to be. Students are nice and respectful to each other, and the teacher is nice and respectful to the students.
  - Students own it – Students are given the responsibility, tools, and strategies to fix problems they have or created. The teacher resists the temptation to be the sole problem-solver; students who make mistakes must own and fix them.
  - Teachable character moments – The teacher uses key moments in class to explicitly talk about, celebrate, and reinforce character skills; these moments flow naturally from the lesson and are quick and high-impact; the teacher strategically picks examples, texts, and activities that, when appropriate, reinforce the key messages (e.g., going to college).

- *Student engagement*:
  - One hundred percent – The teacher insists on 100% of students on task with hands consistently in the air; students are either asking or answering questions.
  - Engagement strategies – The teacher uses high-engagement strategies (e.g., cold-calling, rapid-fire call-and-response, mini-whiteboards, frequent choral responses, and/or "everyone writes") to ensure that all students are accountable for engagement. The teacher makes it impossible for students to be desk potatoes and simply copy from the board. The teacher limits use of round-robin reading or questioning strategies that engage only one student at a time.

- *Academic rigor*:
  - Teacher-talk-to-student-work – There is a high ratio of student work to teacher talk with students taking on most of the "heavy lifting," doing the work and explaining their thinking.
  - Planned, rigorous questioning – The teacher plans his/her key questions in advance with a range of questioning, both lower-level knowledge (recall and basic comprehension), and higher-level (application, analysis, synthesis, and evaluation). The teacher regularly uses the Stretch-It technique—Why? What does that relate to? How would you apply it?

- Top-quality oral responses – The teacher knows that Right Is Right and refuses to accept low-quality student responses. That means insisting on correct grammar, complete sentences, use of appropriate vocabulary and sufficient detail/rationale and not settling for so-so. The teacher is a No Opt Out champion—no student is allowed to opt out because the teacher cycles back to students who didn't answer.

- Top-quality student work – The teacher sets clear expectations and has an accountability mechanism for ensuring all students complete top-quality work. Examples of this kind of work are posted for reference and to celebrate great student work.

• *Cumulative review:* As a part of the lesson and homework routine, students get fast, fun opportunities to systematically and successfully review and practice skills that they have already mastered. Standards included in cumulative review are truly review, and the teacher has a clear method of using data to inform which standards to review.

• *Differentiation:* The teacher works to ensure that the needs of every student are met. Especially during independent practice, the teacher can work with some students to provide extra support or enrichment and/or can otherwise vary the volume, rate, or complexity of work that students are asked to complete. In classes that are grouped homogeneously by skill level, pronounced differentiation may be less necessary.

"Achievement First: Developing a Teacher Performance Management System That Recognizes Excellence" by Rachel Curtis, March 2011, The Aspen Institute Education and Society Program, summarized in Marshall Memo 382.

Structuring Lessons So All Students Learn

12 Beginning and Ending Lessons Effectively

In this *Edutopia* article, English teacher Brian Sztabnik says that lesson planning should follow the time-honored maxims of good writing: start with the end in mind, plan effective beginnings and endings, and grab students' attention. "That is the crux of lesson planning right there," he says, "endings and beginnings. If we fail to engage students at the start, we may never get them back. If we don't know the end result, we risk moving haphazardly from one activity to the next. Every moment in a lesson plan should tell." Sztabnik suggests four key elements for lesson launches and four for wrapping up.

Lesson beginnings:

• *Use video clips.* Well-chosen YouTube nuggets are a great way to create an anticipatory set. For example, Sztabnik asked students to draw comparisons between Carl Sandburg's poem "Chicago" and a Chrysler Super Bowl commercial featuring Eminem.

• *Start with good news.* "If you want to create a safe space for students to take risks, you won't get there with a pry bar," says Sztabnik. One alternative is spending the first two minutes of class having students share positive thoughts.

• *Forge links to other subject areas.* "Integrating other disciplines teaches students that ideas and concepts do not stand alone but rather exist within a wider web of knowledge," he says. For example, have math students measure the angles of a Picasso painting, play a song that makes a classical allusion in a unit on mythology, or toss a football around the class before teaching the physics of a quarterback's spiral.

• *Write for five.* Students need to write a lot if they are to improve and build stamina—five times more than the teacher can grade, says Sztabnik. One idea is to have students spend the first five minutes of class writing in response to an essential question.

Lesson endings:

• *Level up.* Emulate this compelling feature of video games by having students chart their own progress toward mastery of standards, perhaps challenging them to move from Beginner to Heroic to Legendary to Mythic.

• *Use exit tickets.* These can provide on-the-spot assessment information, ask students to analyze their own performance, give the teacher feedback on the lesson, and provide a channel for communication. "However they are used," says Sztabnik, "they provide quick and comprehensive bits of data and feedback."

• *Harness social media.* Twitter, Pinterest, and Instagram can be used in positive ways in the classroom, especially for wrapping up lessons—for example, challenging students to compose a tweet or find an image that best captures what they just learned.

• *Make peer learning visible.* Sztabnik suggests that a few minutes before the closing bell, students should write one thing they learned from someone else in the class on a sticky note and put it on the board—then start the next lesson by reading the notes aloud.

"The 8 Minutes That Matter Most" by Brian Sztabnik in *Edutopia,* January 5, 2015, summarized in Marshall Memo 572.

13 Structuring Lessons So Students Engage in Productive Struggle

In this *Educational Leadership* article, math educator and writer Cathy Seeley remembers the logical, straightforward way she was trained to teach math: explain the concept, guide students as they work with examples, and then have them apply what they've learned as they work independently. The problem with this pedagogy is that it "may set students up for frustration and failure," says Seeley, "especially when they're faced with challenging problems they haven't been taught how to solve."

The alternative is what Seeley calls *upside-down teaching*—teacher-structured but with students doing most of the work. Here's what it looks like: the teacher presents a problem that students don't already know how to solve, provides support as they wrestle with it, and then joins with them to connect their solutions to the mathematical goal. As students work, the teacher circulates, asks questions to clarify students' thinking, and makes strategic decisions about which students should share their work, and in what sequence. The upside-down lesson reverses the conventional I-We-You sequence to:

- *You* tackle a problem.
- *We* talk together about your thinking and your work.
- *I* help connect the discussion to the lesson goal.

"The focus is on students coming up with ideas, solutions, approaches, and models," says Seeley, "even as the teacher facilitates the discussion …." It's important to create a climate where it's okay to make mistakes, students listen to each other's contributions, and the ultimate solution is a group endeavor.

What makes this approach effective? Because, says Seeley, "constructively struggling with mathematical ideas can engage students' thinking and help them learn to persevere in problem solving." In addition, upside-down teaching also helps students develop a growth mindset—the belief that they can get smarter through effort, strategy, and persistence.

The key to launching such lessons is a "low-floor, high-ceiling task" with multiple entry points so all students can access the task at some level—and also plenty of depth. As students work, the teacher circulates and might say:

- How did you decide to divide by seven?
- Can you draw a picture of what you just said?
- Let me know when you've decided between your three different models.

When the class comes back together, students present their findings and the teacher asks clarifying questions, facilitates the discussion, makes good use of errors and misconceptions, and finally makes explicit the connections between students' work and the mathematical goal of the lesson. Seeley describes four examples of upside-down lessons:

• Second graders watch a video of the Cookie Monster grabbing an unopened package of cookies, eating several, and putting the package back on a kitchen counter. "What did you notice about the video?" asks the teacher. "What did you wonder?" The question: How many cookies were eaten? Students work in pairs, the class reconvenes, and the teacher highlights different approaches and summarizes with a subtraction equation.

• A sixth-grade teacher shows students she can achieve the perfect shade of purple paint by mixing two cups of blue paint with three cups of red paint. Students are challenged to figure out and model with colored cubes and drawings—how many cups of red and blue paint would be needed to make twenty cups of perfect purple paint.

• A 12th-grade teacher has students examine a tire from her car, noting its dimensions and characteristics, and then asks what would happen if someone replaced her tires with bigger ones. How would the car's speed, gas mileage, odometer accuracy, and the space the car would take up on the road or in a parking space be affected?

• A pre-calculus teacher draws a graph on the board with coordinates labeled in two different colors and tells students there might be an error in the coordinates shown in red.

"Turning Teaching Upside Down" by Cathy Seeley in *Educational Leadership*, October 2017 (Vol. 75, #2, pp. 32–36), summarized in Marshall Memo 707.

14 Universal Design for Learning in Action

In this *Educational Leadership* article, Spencer Salend and Catharine Whittaker (State University of New York/New Paltz) deconstruct Universal Design for Learning. UDL makes instruction accessible to all students in the same way that a ramp makes a sidewalk accessible to wheelchairs, strollers, bicycles, skateboards, and delivery carts. When UDL is executed skillfully, it meets the needs of a wide range of students by providing multiple means of—

- Representation: Content is presented in a variety of ways.
- Action and expression: Students can respond and show their learning in several modes;
- Engagement: Teachers use a range of practices to boost student motivation.

Salend and Whittaker suggest seven steps for optimal implementation of UDL:

• *Understand students' learning differences.* Before designing a unit and its component lessons, teachers need to get a handle on students' cultural and linguistic backgrounds and their academic, behavioral, and social interests, strengths, preferences, and challenges.

• *Conduct an ecological assessment.* This includes curriculum expectations, assessments, technology, class size, classroom layout, support personnel, collaboration with colleagues, and how students are accustomed to working with each other.

• *Customize learning goals and objectives.* "Learning objectives may vary," say Salend and Whittaker, "in the amount of content to be learned, the level of difficulty of that content, the pace at which students are expected to learn, and the ways in which students are expected to demonstrate their learning."

• *Identify possible barriers to student success.* Certain ways of presenting content may cause problems; there might be limits on how students are allowed to respond; and certain approaches might not motivate students.

• *Select UDL solutions.* Taking into account the barriers, teachers need to find the best ways to present material, engage all students, and get them responding. For example, a teacher might use color, graphic organizers, and enlarged type size to highlight important information; incorporate animals to spur interest in particular students; use manipulatives; and get students working in small groups.

• *Ensure that UDL solutions are well-implemented.* This means monitoring timing, materials, technology, groupings, and implementation.

• *Assess results.* The bottom line: how did the UDL plan affect student learning, behavior, and socialization? This might be based on teacher observations, student interviews, student work, tests, performance tasks, and self-reflection.

"UDL: A Blueprint for Learning Success" by Spencer Salend and Catharine Whittaker in *Educational Leadership*, April 2017 (Vol. 74, #7, pp. 59–63), summarized in Marshall Memo 681.

15 What UDL Looks Like in Two Classrooms

In this article in *School Administrator*, Massachusetts district administrator Katie Novak describes two lessons:

-   Third graders sit on the floor as the teacher reads Chapter Two of *Charlotte's Web*. Then each student quietly writes a paragraph about Fern's feelings about Wilbur.
-   In a high-school United States History class, students read John Locke's 1690 *Two Treatises of Civil Government* and respond to a document-based question on their Chromebooks. The teacher circulates and conferences with individual students.

In both cases, students are reading an appropriately rigorous text and the lesson is aligned to standards, but the teachers' one-size-fits-all assignments don't meet the needs of their diverse groups of students. Novak suggests how each lesson could be improved by applying Universal Design for Learning (UDL) principles:

• In the third-grade class, students choose where to sit (beanbag chairs, a couch, chairs, the rug) and the way in which they read the chapter: an audiobook, reading aloud to a group of peers, or reading the book silently to themselves. The teacher has listed vocabulary words (apple blossom, woodshed, brook) on a whiteboard, paired with photos. When students have finished the chapter, they choose how they will show their understanding of Fern's feelings toward Wilbur: writing a letter from Fern to Wilbur; using purple gel pens to craft a poem or song about Fern's feelings; or forming a group and creating a skit. All students set goals for their work and have access to appropriate graphic organizers and rubrics, and the teacher circulates, providing support where needed. Toward the end of the lesson, students reflect on their learning; write, type, or dictate a self-assessment; and then share their products with classmates.

• In the United States History class, one group of students participates in a Socratic seminar in a corner of the room, using a template as they explore whether citizens have a right to dissolve their government. Other students design John Locke's Facebook page and interpret the book through a series of status updates. A third group sits with the teacher, reviewing strategies for closely reading a primary-source document and responding to a document-based AP question.

"A Scene Shifter: Personalization Under UDL" by Katie Novak in *School Administrator*, November 2015 (Vol. 72, #10, p. 34), summarized in Marshall Memo 612.

Professional Learning Suggestions for Chapter Nine Planning Units and Lessons

Instructional Planning for Impact

Helping your teachers improve their skills in curriculum, unit, and lesson planning provides enormous dividends. Most of the professional learning activities in this section are geared toward improving teacher craft in instructional planning. But make sure to read through to the end to see an important section on expanding ideas of principal supervision and coaching to include more than just the classroom observation.

I. Schoolwide Curriculum Planning

This section contains activities you can do with teachers to help them think about the importance of schoolwide coherence in planning, choose priority standards for teaching, and develop schoolwide essential questions or unit plan templates.

A. Conduct a forced-choice activity about the importance of a coherent curriculum.
Mike Schmoker (Article 1) believes that the single most important factor in highly effective schools is "a coherent, content-rich curriculum that abounds in opportunities for reading, writing, and discussion in every subject area," and that "even the best pedagogy can't overcome the negative effects of incoherent curriculum."

Have your teachers make a forced choice. If they had to choose the *one* most important factor in highly effective schools, do they agree with Schmoker above that it would be a *coherent curriculum*:

Group 1. Those who agree go to one side of the room.

Group 2. Those who disagree (the *curriculum* is not the *most* important factor in highly effective schools) go to the other side of the room.

Teachers in Group 1 should discuss why they believe a coherent curriculum is so essential, and those in Group 2 should discuss why they think it is not the *top* factor in highly effective schools.

Back together as one large group, ask everyone why they think Mike Schmoker argues for this point.

B. Outline schoolwide priority standards.

Several articles (Schmoker, Article 1; and Heick, Article 2) mention the importance of honing in on a more limited number of standards, because it is difficult to give equal attention to all of the standards that need to be covered in each grade. Have your teachers work in teams—either by grade in the lower grades or by department in the upper grades—to choose priority or power standards.

Step One: Have each team take all of the standards for one subject for one year, and choose one of the following methods below (a. or b.) to identify which standards to prioritize.

a. Teams list all standards in the column to the left and then check off which standards meet the criteria for *endurance, leverage,* and *readiness.*

ALL STANDARDS	Endurance: will be important over a lifetime	Leverage: has cross-curricular implications	Readiness for the Next Level: is necessary to prepare students for the next level of learning

b. Teams review Heick (Article 2) and then use a blank copy of the concentric circles (on the next page) to divide up their standards into three groups: those we want students to remember in forty days, forty months, and forty years.

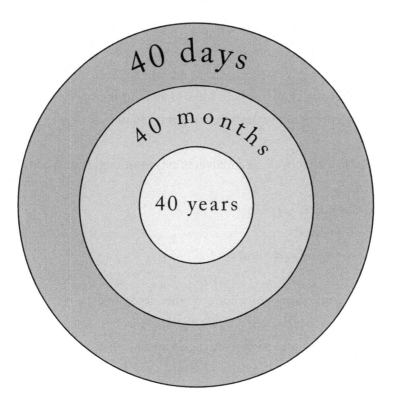

Step Two: Next, have each team discuss their reasoning for how they put their standards into the forty-year circle or for what made them give certain standards three check marks for meeting the endurance, leverage, and readiness criteria. These are their *priority* standards.

Step Three: Have teams post their graphic representations of priority standards on a wall and let everyone do a gallery walk to look for *vertical alignment, redundancies*, and *gaps*. Have teams engage in follow-up discussions to work out any of these three issues or others that arise.

Step Four: Have volunteers compile what has been decided so there is a clear document with school-wide, agreed upon, priority standards. Note that this does *not* mean that teachers do not teach the other standards; it just means they will emphasize those they agreed to prioritize.

C. Two ways to engage in schoolwide unit planning
Part of what leads to a coherent curriculum is consistency in schoolwide curricular planning. The articles point to some ways to build this consistency. Choose one of the following ways to build coherence in schoolwide curricular planning (either through: *1. Schoolwide essential questions for units*, or *2. Schoolwide unit templates*) and engage your teachers in the planning activities below.

1. Schoolwide essential questions for units:

Schoolwide essential questions are one way to bring some coherence across the curriculum. Below is an idea to *introduce* the concept of having schoolwide essential questions to your teachers. If this activity produces enough interest and engagement, have a committee work on developing schoolwide essential questions for your school.

• Introduce a few of the schoolwide essential questions from Frey, Fisher, and Anderson (Article 3):

> *Does age matter?*
>
> *Can you buy your way to happiness?*
>
> *What is normal, anyway?*
>
> *How does your world influence you?*

• Ask teachers to sit with colleagues who teach the same subject/grade and ask them to answer these questions as a group: *If each of the four essential questions (above) was the overarching question for a different unit this upcoming year, would you be able to integrate it into your own course content? Which of the four essential questions would work with your subject or grade? How might it work?*

• Now ask teachers to examine the four essential questions closely to discuss the following question in their groups: *Looking at these questions, what seem to be the characteristics of a schoolwide essential question?*

• Finally, have them brainstorm three other possible schoolwide essential questions your school might use. Give them the criteria of an essential question (in the chart below) from Frey, Fisher, and Anderson (Article 3) and ask them to check off how many of the criteria their three questions met in the following chart:

Criteria of an Essential Question (according to Wiggins and McTighe)	Question 1	Question 2	Question 3
Worthy of inquiry, calling for higher-order thinking			
Thought-provoking, engaging—sparks discussion and debate			
Open-ended—that is, there isn't a single, final, correct answer			
Requires support and justification, not just the answer			
Produces a humbling acceptance that some matters are never truly settled			
Points toward important, transferable ideas within and across disciplines			
Raises additional questions, sparks further inquiry, and needs to be revisited over time			

2. Schoolwide unit templates:

To help bring coherence to the *planning* of a curricular unit, have your teachers meet and collaboratively design a common schoolwide unit template, using the following steps.

• Have teachers bring their laptops to the meeting or use school computers. Alone or in pairs, have them search online for "unit planning templates" to get an idea of the variety of formats different schools use.

• Ask teachers individually to make a list of the elements they believe should be included in a unit plan (e.g., essential question, vocabulary, final assessment, formative assessments, etc.) Ask them to review Saphier (Article 7) to give them some ideas as well.

• Conduct a large-group brainstorm of all possible elements your school might include in a unit template. Post this list on a wall for everyone to see.

• Give everyone five dot stickers to vote for the top five elements they believe should be a part of any unit plan.

• Count the dot stickers and announce the top five to eight elements. Next, conduct a discussion with teachers about the importance of these top elements with the goal of arriving at agreement on which elements will appear in your schoolwide unit-planning template. You can use this reasonable definition of *consensus*: (1) all points of view have been heard, and (2) the will of the group is clear—even to those who oppose it. Find a way to ensure that all teachers who have something to say are heard.

• Charge a committee with putting these elements into a unit-planning template that is easy to use, clear, and simple. Now you have your *schoolwide unit template*!

II. Lesson Planning

As McTighe (Article 10) suggests, individual lesson plans are a vital extension of unit planning. Below is a suggestion for honing the lesson-planning skills of your teachers.

Write a collaborative lesson plan.
It is a fabulous professional learning activity to have a group of teachers who teach the same grade or subject come together to write a lesson plan. In fact, conducting a "lesson study" in Japan is a common form of professional development. However, sometimes there is a misconception that the goal of this activity is to craft the perfect plan. The real goal is the *learning* that happens when teachers come together to grapple with a lesson's aim, methods of checking for understanding, potential student misconceptions, and more.

Set aside one long block of professional learning time with nothing else on the agenda—this takes time! Tell teachers to arrive with a sample lesson plan they've written and go through the following steps. First, tell teachers that they will be conducting a *modified* version of Japanese lesson study. Tell them that by the end of today's session, they will have collaboratively written one single lesson plan. Make sure they know that the goal is to work collaboratively to create a lesson aim, activities, assessments, and more—as a way to see how others approach each part of the lesson plan and to improve everyone's lesson planning skills—*not* to craft the perfect lesson plan. You can show them an introductory video about lesson study, as long as teachers know they will not be following up with the other phases. Here is a two-minute overview: https://www.youtube.com/watch?v=MHHryuuohpM

Step One: Put teachers into groups with other teachers who teach the same subject or grade. If teachers do not know each other well, plan some icebreakers.

Step Two: Give teachers time to independently read the following articles: Eng (Article 9), McTighe (Article 10), Curtis (Article 11), Sztabnik (Article 12), Salend and Whittaker (Article 14), Novak (Article 15), and Seeley (Article 13) about lesson planning and jot down or underline what they believe to be the most crucial elements of a lesson plan.

Step Three: Ask teachers to look through their notes on effective lesson plan elements as well as their own lesson plan that they brought with them. Have each group choose a facilitator and conduct a discussion—*What makes a lesson plan effective?*

Step Four: As a team, decide which lesson plan elements they feel are most important to include in the one collaborative lesson plan they are about to write.

Step Five: Using the elements each group has decided to include in their plan, have them write a collaborative lesson plan. Tell them to make sure to think through what the students will be doing during each part of the lesson, include anticipated student responses in the plan (including incorrect ones), and how they will know if the lesson is successful.

Step Six: Have each group write out their lesson plan on large paper or project it on a screen. Let each of the teams walk around and observe each other's lesson plans.

Step Seven: Conduct a large group discussion around the following question: *What did you learn about lesson planning today?* Ask people to be as specific as possible. For example, *I learned that one way to make the lesson aim measurable is to...*

Note: Rather than bounce around and hear snippets of different groups' discussions, you and each of the instructional leaders should choose *one* teacher team to observe for the entire time. This will give you a more complete understanding of what this process looks like from soup to nuts and which aspects of lesson planning teachers still need to work on.

III. The Principal's Role in Supervising Curriculum and Lesson Planning

In this section, leaders are encouraged to think about ways to supervise and coach teachers in *lesson and unit planning*. Below is a graphic Kim often shows in his workshops to get leaders to think about the limited impact of limiting supervision to observing just one or a few classes. On average, teachers teach nine hundred classes a year. When you observe one class, the black dot represents the fraction of a teacher's classes you see.

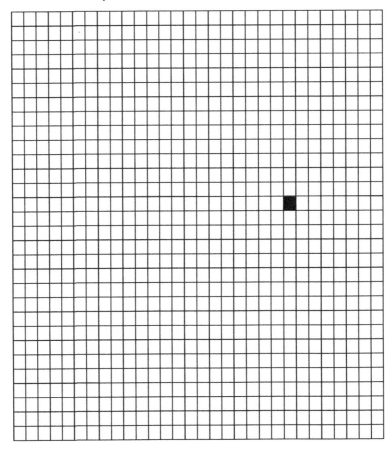

The vast majority of what happens in classrooms is out of sight. So how can principals have a larger impact on teaching and learning? One way is to expand our idea of what it means to "supervise" and "coach" teachers so that we think beyond pedagogy. Michael Fullan agrees. He argues that the role of the principal has become too narrowly focused on classroom instruction. (Michael Fullan, *The Principal: Three Keys to Maximizing Impact* [San Francisco: Jossey-Bass, 2014]). So, how might we expand the idea of "supervision" beyond the classroom observation?

Together with other school leaders, brainstorm ways you might supervise and coach teachers in *lesson and unit planning*. This may involve co-planning a lesson with a teacher face-to-face, reviewing unit plans, observing a team meeting in which curriculum planning is a topic, examining lesson plans when you observe teachers, structuring professional learning to focus on lesson and unit planning, and more. Each leader should commit to one way to expand his/her supervisory actions and a date to share the results with this team:

Name_____

In addition to observing classes, I plan to:

I will share what worked and what changes I need to make to this plan when we meet as a group on:

Chapter Ten: Assessment for Learning

The more you teach without finding out who understands the information and who doesn't, the greater the likelihood that only already-proficient students will succeed.
—GRANT WIGGINS

Research tells us that checking for understanding during instruction makes it possible to fix students' errors and misconceptions in real time and also provides insights that continuously improve teaching. Some teachers do this instinctively, but it's not happening in many classrooms. The articles in this chapter review the problems with traditional assessments, describe effective checking for understanding, look at low-tech and high-tech ways of assessing student learning, and describe the most effective follow-up with students.

Improving on Traditional Assessments – Paul Black and Dylan Wiliam report their widely read meta-analysis on assessments. Rick Stiggins lists the ineffective ways assessments are often used in many classrooms, including: vague learning goals, unhelpful feedback to students, and struggling students falling further and further behind. Dan Barrett describes how a Harvard physics professor figured out what was wrong with the time-honored lecture-and-test format dynamic in his classes.

Effective Checking for Understanding – Kim Marshall shows how assessments can improve learning in real time, keep the focus on learning targets, and shift the conversation to results. Craig Barton describes how he poses carefully formulated diagnostic questions at several points in his lessons and then uses students' correct and incorrect responses to decide on next instructional moves. Dylan Wiliam maps out the process of crafting "hinge-point" questions to measure student understanding midway through a lesson.

Low-Tech and High-Tech Tools – Sarah Nagro, Sara Hooks, Dawn Fraser, and Kyena Cornelius suggest three low-tech ways to check for understanding during lessons with particular benefits for students with disabilities. John Rich describes six ways audience response devices (clickers) can contribute to effective lessons.

Following Up with Students – Paul Black and colleagues follow up on the classic article summarized in Article 1 with further insights on how teachers can use assessments to improve teaching and learning. Dylan Wiliam gives three examples of teachers using on-the-spot assessment data to enhance understanding and get students to take responsibility for their own learning. And Brent Duckor, Carrie Holmberg, and Joanne Rossi Becker show how teachers can immediately follow up on formative assessment data.

Questions to Consider

- What is the problem to which formative assessments are the answer?
- How can we get more teachers checking for understanding as they teach?
- What kinds of assessments are most productive and why?

Improving on Traditional Assessments

How Classroom Assessments Can Change the Game

| 1 |

In this article in *Phi Delta Kappan*, British professors Paul Black and Dylan Wiliam discuss the evidence from 250 research studies on formative assessment and argue that when teachers use minute-by-minute, day-by-day assessments to check for understanding—and follow up by adapting instruction to clear up their students' confusions and misunderstandings—they are on the road to getting high achievement from all their students. In fact, argue Black and Wiliam, this is better than external programs as a way of raising standards and is the most powerful engine for closing the achievement gap.

Black and Wiliam don't think most school reformers pay enough attention to what goes on inside the classroom, treating it as a "black box" and assuming that the pressure of high-stakes tests will be enough to get teachers to improve learning. "It seems strange, even unfair," they argue, "to leave the most difficult piece of the standards-raising puzzle entirely to teachers. If there are ways in which policy makers and others can give direct help and support to the everyday classroom task of achieving better learning, then surely these ways ought to be pursued vigorously." Some key insights:

• *Formative assessments are a highly effective way to raise student achievement.* Black and Wiliam say the research supports this conclusion for students from kindergarten to college, in different subject areas, and in different countries. Effect sizes range from 0.4 to 0.7, which is higher than many other educational interventions. In addition, formative assessments have their most positive effect on low-achieving students and therefore narrow the achievement gap.

But it's not a simple matter to implement on-the-spot assessments. Research indicates that positive impact depends on teachers making significant changes in classroom practice, modifying instruction based on formative evidence, getting students actively involved in the process, and using these assessments—and students' self-assessments—to improve motivation and self-esteem.

• *Classroom assessments are often problematic.* Teachers have a strong tendency to teach, test, and move on with the curriculum, without using classroom data to adjust instruction or help struggling students. "Marking is usually conscientious but often fails to offer guidance on how work can be improved," said a UK inspection report. "Information about pupil performance received by the teacher is insufficiently used to inform subsequent work." There are several other problems with the way teachers use classroom assessments:

- Many classroom tests measure rote and superficial learning even when teachers are trying to develop understanding.
- Teachers seldom share their classroom assessments with colleagues; lacking critical scrutiny, tests may not be of the highest quality.
- "For primary teachers particularly," say Black and Wiliam, "there is a tendency to emphasize quantity and presentation of work and to neglect its quality in relation to learning."
- Some teachers use tests for social and managerial purposes, rather than to diagnose students' learning needs or give useful advice; when this happens, the impact on low-achieving students can be quite negative.
- Some teachers use classroom assessments to foster competition and compare students to one another; this can lead low-achieving students to believe that they lack ability and cannot learn.
- Some teachers use classroom tests to predict students' performance on external tests, rather than to diagnose their students' learning needs.
- Some teachers don't pay attention to the assessment records from students' previous teachers.

Black and Wiliam go on to list a number of ways that schools can improve the use of on-the-spot assessments:

• *Assessment feedback to students should be about the particular qualities of their work, accompanied by advice on how to improve it, and should not compare students to each other.* "When the classroom culture focuses on rewards, 'gold stars,' grades, or class ranking," they say, "then pupils look for ways to obtain the best marks rather than to improve their learning." This leads students to avoid difficult tasks for fear of not being successful and losing points. Students who don't do well come to believe that they lack innate ability and can't do anything about that. They tend to avoid investing effort in learning, are content to "get over," and build up their self-esteem in other arenas.

Effective use of formative assessments reverses this negative culture. The message to students is that their failures are temporary and can be fixed by effective effort. Classrooms that use assessments in this way have a culture of success, backed by a belief that all students can achieve. This dynamic is especially helpful for low-achieving students because the focus is on the specific problems they are having with their work and what they can do to improve.

• *Self-assessment by students is an essential component of formative assessment.* "When anyone is trying to learn," say Black and Wiliam, "feedback about effort has three elements: recognition of the *desired goal*; evidence about *present position*; and some understanding of a *way to close the gap* between the two. All three must be understood to some degree by anyone before he or she can take action to improve learning." First and foremost, students need to have a clear picture of what they are supposed to be learning. "Surprisingly and sadly," continue the authors, "many pupils do not have such a picture, and they appear to have become accustomed to receiving classroom teaching as an arbitrary sequence of exercises with no overarching rationale. To overcome this pattern of passive reception requires hard and sustained work. When pupils do acquire such an overview, they then become more committed and more effective as learners."

• *Teachers need to build in opportunities for students to communicate their evolving understanding as a unit unfolds—and give them adequate wait-time to respond.* Effective teachers plan open-ended questions, classroom tasks, and homework assignments that develop and assess student understanding of the big ideas and details of the unit in real time. Master teachers are also alert to unexpected student responses. Less-effective teachers tend to listen for the "right" answer and, quite unconsciously, respond in ways that signal that there's only one answer and the students' job is to figure it out and give it back. "Over time," say Black and Wiliam of this pattern, "the pupils get the message: they are not required to think out their own answers. The object of the exercise is to work out—or guess—what answer the teacher expects to see or hear."

When teachers ask questions and don't give students enough time to think through their answers (moving quickly on to another student or answering their own questions), two things happen: the questions often become low-level, with simple answers; and the classroom "dialogue" tends to take place between the teacher and a few students who are good at giving rapid-fire answers to a succession of questions. "So the teacher," say Black and Wiliam, "by lowering the level of questions and by accepting answers from a few, can keep the lesson going but is actually out of touch with the understanding of most of the class. The question/answer dialogue becomes a ritual, one in which thoughtful involvement suffers." Black and Wiliam suggest a number of ways to break out of this pattern:

- giving students time to think after a question is posed,
- asking students to discuss their thinking in pairs or small groups,
- giving students a choice between different possible answers and asking them to vote on the options,
- asking all students to write down an answer and then reading out a selected few.
- "What is essential," say Black and Wiliam, "is that any dialogue should evoke thoughtful reflection in which all pupils can be encouraged to take part, for only then can the formative process start to work."

• *Teachers need to get the most out of classroom tests.* Tests should be opportunities for learning, insist Black and Wiliam. "It is better to have frequent short tests than infrequent long ones. Any new learning should first be tested within about a week of a first encounter ...." Generating good test items that are relevant to the main learning aims and communicate clearly with students is difficult, say Black and Wiliam—which is a strong reason for teachers to collaborate and draw on outside sources.

Equally important is the quality of feedback that students get after a test. "Research studies have shown that, if pupils are given only marks or grades, they do not benefit from the feedback," say Black and Wiliam. "Feedback has been shown to improve learning when it gives each pupil specific guidance on strengths and weaknesses, preferably without any overall marks .... Pupils must be given the means and opportunities to work with evidence of their difficulties."

"The worst scenario," say Black and Wiliam, "is one in which some pupils who get low marks this time also got low marks last time and come to expect to get low marks next time. This cycle of repeated failure becomes part of a shared belief between such students and their teacher."

• *It's quite challenging for teachers to implement on-the-spot assessments well.* Some students will resist this change from the familiar classroom routine. Being asked to think for oneself and take responsibility for self-assessment is difficult. In addition, using formative assessments takes more classroom time at first. It's a leap of faith for many teachers to make these changes, but it will produce wider and deeper learning in the long run.

Teachers need to address two other issues if they are serious about using formative assessments. The first is their theory of action about how students learn. Teachers who believe their job is pouring information into students' brains won't see the point of continuously assessing student learning. Fortunately, most teachers have moved past the transmission model and know that teacher-student interaction is vital for learning to take place.

A second possible barrier is doubt about the potential of all their students to learn. There are two polarities:

- The "fixed intelligence" view—a belief that each student has a fixed intelligence that cannot be altered much by schooling.
- The "untapped potential" view—a belief that ability is a complex of skills that can be learned.

Formative assessments are most likely to be embraced by teachers who hold the second belief, say Black and Wiliam, who operate on the assumption that "all pupils can learn more effectively if one can clear away, by sensitive handling, the obstacles to learning—be they cognitive failures never diagnosed, or damage to personal confidence, or a combination of the two." The "untapped potential" approach helps all students learn better and has its most powerful impact on students who have previously struggled in school.

"Inside the Black Box: Raising Standards Through Classroom Assessment" by Paul Black and Dylan Wiliam in *Phi Delta Kappan*, October 1998 (Vol. 80 #2, pp. 139–148), summarized in Marshall Memo 146.

2 Common Problems with Classroom Assessments

In this *EDge Magazine* article, assessment expert Rick Stiggins paints a bleak picture of the way assessments have often been used:

- Learning goals are vague; criteria for good work are largely secret.
- Feedback to students is evaluative (grades), rather than helpfully descriptive.
- The amount of time available to learn is fixed: one year per grade.
- Students' learning varies greatly; some learn a lot, some much less.
- Students who do well in the early grades score well on assessments, build on success, come to believe they are capable learners, and are confident enough to risk striving for more success because they feel it is within their reach.
- These successful students' emotional reaction to assessments is often: "I know what to do next to learn more. I can handle this. I choose to keep trying."
- Students who do less well in the early grades score poorly on assessments, don't master essential learning skills, fall further and further behind, feel stupid, lose confidence, become discouraged, and give up. Chronic failure is hard to hide and becomes embarrassing, says Stiggins. "It's better not to try.
- These students' emotional reaction to assessments is often: "I don't know what these results mean for me. I have no idea what to do next. I can't handle this. I quit."
- The wide span of achievement, from superstars to dropouts, is regarded as an inevitable product of schooling. If a student does well, it's because the student is smart and worked hard. If a student does poorly, it's because the student is not smart and didn't work hard. In other words, it is the student's fault, not the school's fault.
- The basic mission of schools is to separate the sheep from the goats.

Stiggins believes this dynamic is highly destructive for students who are not doing well. Any school where it's still alive today must change it to reach today's ambitious goals.

For all students to learn at high levels, says Stiggins, our assessments must do more than churn out scores for administrators; they need to serve teachers and students and be used in a way that narrows, rather than widens, the achievement gap. We need to use frequent formative assessments—assessments *for* learning—in a skillful way. Specifically—

• Assessments need to give rich, descriptive information that is genuinely helpful to teachers and students and elicits productive reactions:

- "For the teacher," writes Stiggins, "the assessment is helpful if it reveals what comes next in the learning. The assessment is counterproductive when it leaves teachers with no idea of what to do next."

- For the student, "if assessments are to support improvements in student learning, their results must inform students how to do better the next time. This requires communicating results that transmit sufficient, understandable detail to guide the learner's actions."

• Assessments need to happen frequently enough (and be sensitive enough) so patterns of student learning will be revealed. "In this way," says Stiggins, "both the learner and the teacher will be able to discern not only the student's current level of achievement, but also how much the student's capabilities have improved, which is a powerful booster for confidence and motivation."

• Students need to be involved in the assessment process, using results to continuously assess themselves in ways that are encouraging, not overwhelming. "Students become partners in the self-assessment process," says Stiggins, "by, for example, collaborating with their teachers in creating and using assessments like those they will be held accountable for later. This reveals to them the secret to their own learning success while they are still learning. Students become partners in the accumulation of growth portfolios that reveal to them, their teachers, and their families the changes in their own achievement as it is happening …. This feedback builds progressively over time and thus helps students continue to believe that success is within reach if they keep trying."

• Students need to see a clear road map of where the curriculum is going and exactly what is required of them. This enables students to watch themselves grow and continuously reinforces their belief that success is within reach if they keep working hard.

"Assessment *For* Learning: A Key to Motivation and Achievement" by Rick Stiggins in *EDge Magazine*, November/December 2006 (Vol. 2, #2, pp. 3–19), summarized in Marshall Memo 163.

3 Why a College Professor Stopped Lecturing

In this *Chronicle of Higher Education* article, Dan Berrett describes the pride felt by young physics professor Eric Mazur when he got excellent student ratings at the beginning of his teaching career at Harvard. "The signals Mr. Mazur received as a young professor pointed to one conclusion," says Berrett: "He rocked. His lectures were clear and well received. His students could solve complex problems about rotational dynamics by calculating triple integrals."

But then Mazur gave his students the Force Concept Inventory, a test of their basic understanding of Newtonian physics, and was shocked by the results: more than half of the students did poorly, even though he'd covered the subject just a few weeks earlier. When students took the test again at the end of the course, they made only slight gains. Comparing answers on "plug and chug" and conceptual questions, Mazur found they did better on calculating, not deeper understanding. He realized that what he had been teaching his students was memorizing formulas.

Other data points suddenly jumped into focus: In his otherwise stellar student evaluations, a few students jotted that the subject was boring (one said, "Physics sucks"). What's more, young women's grades were lower than those of their male classmates. Mazur recalled some adults saying they'd aced physics in school but never really understood it. And he remembered what sparked his own love of science: designing and carrying out experiments in the lab, not classroom lectures. Mazur began to see the lecture method as ineffective, even unethical.

The turnaround came when Mazur followed up on one question on the Force Concept Inventory that only half his students had answered correctly: *Compare the forces in a collision between a car and a truck.* To Mazur, the answer seemed clear from Newton's third law: the forces were equal. But many students clung to misconceptions (*The truck is heavier!*) and weren't convinced by the equations Mazur was scribbling on the board. Frustrated, he told students to discuss the answer with the student sitting next to them.

"The tenor of the room changed," Berrett reports. "The students grew animated and the staid lecture hall began buzzing. Mr. Mazur realized he's developed an entire method around that experience." And he's never turned back. Here's his method:

- Students do most of the lower-level computational physics for homework and are accountable for mastering it.
- In class, Mazur gives brief lectures on core ideas, and then poses carefully framed conceptual questions to which all students must respond using clickers.
- He displays the results, and if 30–70 percent of students haven't answered a question correctly, he asks students to convince their neighbors.
- Mazur circulates, listening to what students are saying to each other.
- He poses the clicker question again and, almost always, there are significant learning gains; students are good at teaching each other.
- If necessary, Mazur follows up with a further explanation.

The results of this "peer instruction" approach have been dramatic. Three years after he changed his approach, students' scores on the Force Concept Inventory had doubled, and four years after that, they had tripled—the result of Mazur's increasing skill as a teacher and his students' steadily improving peer instruction. "I'd been fooling myself for many years thinking I was an effective professor," says Mazur. "But it was a house of cards …. Deep down, everybody realizes that there are huge failures in the system."

As Mazur has traveled the nation talking about this approach, there have been some spirited defenses of the lecture method:

- It's endured for centuries because it works.
- Lectures demand that students pay close attention, connect ideas, and understand how to build an argument; discarding them means acquiescing to the erosion of educational standards and letting students off the hook.
- A lecture is only as passive as the listener; students need to learn to think about what they're hearing and organize it into salient points. The responsibility for learning should be on the student, not the instructor.
- Lectures affirm the importance of expertise and let students see how a masterful thinker works through a problem.
- Lectures can be inspiring.

But Mazur pushes back on the pushback. "The lecture creates the perfect illusion," he says. Students and professors walk out of class convinced they've both gotten something out of the exchange, but research shows that students consistently overestimate how much they learn in a brilliant lecture, and professors are fooling themselves about their efficacy. "As a primary vehicle for teaching," says Mazur, "it's completely outmoded …. Learning is not a spectator sport." You don't learn how to dance by watching an expert dancer, nor do you learn how to drive by observing the instructor. You have to do it yourself.

"The Making of a Teaching Evangelist" by Dan Berrett in *The Chronicle of Higher Education*, June 10, 2016 (Vol. LXII, #38, pp. A20–A22), summarized in Marshall Memo 641.

Effective Checking for Understanding

4 Nine Ways to Use Assessments

In this article in *Phi Delta Kappan*, Kim Marshall says any assessment can be handled badly, but when they're used well, assessments play a critical role at three levels of effective instruction: providing feedback during each lesson, keeping educators and students focused on where they're going, and shifting instructional conversations to student results. Here's how.

Assessments to improve instruction during each lesson:

• *Fixing learning problems immediately* – On-the-spot checks for understanding have great potential (and a robust research track record) when they provide accurate information and teachers' follow-up. Students' facial expressions aren't a good gauge (too many "compliant pretenders"), and teachers asking, "Is everyone with me?" won't uncover embarrassed confusion, willful evasion, and daydreaming. But many teachers are now using a better repertoire of methods that truly reveal students' level of understanding.

• *Improving memory through the "retrieval effect"* – Many of us have forgotten where we parked a car in a large garage. That, like students' inability to remember the content of a textbook chapter they read and highlighted the night before, is a retrieval failure. Recent research by cognitive scientists has shown that strategically retrieving about-to-be-forgotten information—testing ourselves—is the best way to remember it. "Retrieving a fact is not like opening a computer file," says Henry Roediger III, one of the pioneers of this research. "It alters what we remember and changes how we subsequently organize that knowledge in our brain." This means the best way to study for a test is to read the textbook chapter, close the book, write down as much as we can remember, and then go back and restudy (and retest) the parts we thought we had mastered but in fact didn't. Retrieval practice works best when we're about to forget something; to commit important information to long-term memory, it needs to be repeated at widening intervals— a day later, a week later, a month later.

• *Leveraging peer instruction* – When a significant number of students answer a teacher's question incorrectly (as ascertained by audience response devices), an effective technique is to tell them to convince their neighbors and then poll the class again. Student understanding usually improves markedly, and then the teacher can follow up with further clarification.

Assessments to keep educators and students focused on where they're going:

• *Fostering a growth mindset* – Classroom tests often trigger fixed-mindset thinking in students: *I aced it, I'm a genius; I flunked, I'm dumb at math.* Carol Dweck and her colleagues have shown that students with a fixed mindset (negative *and* positive) tend to avoid challenges, give up easily, see effort as fruitless, ignore useful criticism, and feel threatened by the success of others. But if teachers (and parents) are sensitive to this cognitive trap and choose their words carefully, tests are an opportunity to foster a growth mindset. The key message for students: tests show how much you've learned, how hard you've worked, the strategies you've used, and the help you've solicited. Those are also the words adults should use to praise or, if things haven't gone well, to get students thinking about how they can improve their performance. When we succeed in getting students to shift to a growth mindset (sometimes one subject, sport, or activity at a time), they are more likely to embrace challenges, persist in the face of failure, see effort as the path to mastery, learn from setbacks and criticism, and find lessons and inspiration in the success of others.

• *Generating helpful graphic displays* – "Tests produce detailed information on student learning," says Marshall, "and data displays can help students, teachers, and school leaders track progress, identify weak areas in the curriculum and test items, diagnose learning problems, set goals, and celebrate success." While data from interim assessments may not be psychometrically precise, they can give helpful and timely feedback on performance and pedagogy.

• *Growing students' ability to monitor their own learning* – An important long-term goal in every school is getting students to take increasing responsibility for their learning. "Working with assessment results," says Marshall, "helps students think like assessors, measure progress toward goals, zero in on weak areas, recognize a fixed and growth mindset, and understand retrieval practice."

Assessments to shift the instructional conversation to student learning results:

• *Providing substance for teacher collaboration* – Data from common interim assessments and performance tasks are the ideal focus for same-grade/same-subject teacher team meetings. Key prerequisites are well-crafted assessments, enough time for substantive discussion, an adult culture of humility and trust (so one teacher can say to another, "Your kids did better on this item than mine. What did you do?"), and systematic follow-up with students who aren't yet successful. "The ideal dynamic," says Marshall, "is a balance of common curriculum goals and assessments, teacher autonomy and creativity around instructional methods, constant experimentation with new ideas in classrooms, and an ethos of seizing on the best ideas and spreading them to all teachers on the team."

• *Helping school leaders supervise with an eye to learning* – The idea of using student test scores as part of teachers' evaluations is now largely discredited, says Marshall, but advocates of test-based accountability do have a point: student learning should be part of the conversation: "The trick for school leaders is to turn down the accountability pressure and join with teachers in looking at assessment results with a curious, problem-solving frame of mind." School leaders and instructional coaches have plenty of opportunities to do just that—

- Checking in with students during classroom visits (*What are you learning today?*);
- Chatting with teachers after classroom visits about intended and actual outcomes;
- Looking with teachers at on-the-spot assessments and exit tickets;
- Sitting with teacher teams as they plan assessments for upcoming curriculum units;
- Observing teacher teams as they analyze student work and test results;
- Getting reports from teacher teams on before-and-after evidence of learning through the year.

"The best leaders," says accountability advocate Douglas Reeves (2018), "will use assessment results not as a hammer to embarrass teachers, but as a lever to prod even the best and most experienced to improve their practices."

• *Ensuring that all students learn the right stuff* – Marshall remembers the pedagogical freedom he had teaching Boston sixth graders in the 1970s and concludes that laissez-faire curriculum policies have a major problem: "Disadvantaged students emerge with lots of gaps in knowledge and skills while advantaged students pick up what's not taught in school in their homes and communities." The best approach is:

- A well-thought-out K–12 curriculum (the *what*);
- Lots of room for creativity at the school and classroom level (the *how to*);
- High-quality tests that don't consume too much time;
- Stakes attached to test results so everyone takes them seriously, but with sufficient time and support to reach the standards;
- Prompt and helpful data on students' progress;
- Frequent, structured opportunities for teachers to share effective practices.

This approach creates a sense of urgency (but not panic) at the school level, getting people on the same content and skill page while still allowing freedom to experiment with effective practices—always asking what's working and what isn't.

The bottom line, says Marshall: "The wise and effective use of assessments is essential to solving inequities within and among our schools .... Let's use assessments so that all students have the skills, knowledge, and habits of mind to enter adulthood as well-educated, responsible citizens—who can sit down with any challenging test and say, 'I've got this.'"

"In Praise of Assessment (Done Right)" by Kim Marshall in *Phi Delta Kappan*, March 2018 (Vol. 99, #6, pp. 54–59), summarized in Marshall Memo 726.

5 A Teacher Realizes What He Wasn't Doing

"For much of my career, I did not reflect on why I was doing the things I did," says British teacher/podcaster/author Craig Barton in this article in *American Educator*. "I was a relatively successful teacher whose students always got decent results and seemed to enjoy their lessons, and that was good enough for me." But when Barton started interviewing educators around the world and reading research, his "cozy little world began to crumble." A major realization was the importance of on-the-spot (a.k.a. formative) assessments. Barton now believes that "asking and responding to diagnostic questions is the single most important thing I do every lesson …. Teaching without formative assessment is like painting with your eyes closed." The best label for this approach, he believes, is "responsive teaching." This captures the core idea of checking for understanding in real time and improving teaching and learning before it's too late.

Once Barton had this revelation, the first classroom change he made was establishing a culture in which students weren't afraid to make mistakes. He told kids that the math questions they answered were not for grades but *for learning*—to inform students and their teacher how things were going. He also began to use an all-class response system that required all students to answer every question—no opt-out or "I don't know." This meant giving up the time-honored practice of calling on one or two confident volunteers, which, one researcher said, leads to "a small discussion group surrounded by many sleepy onlookers" and is a really ineffective way to see how well the class as a whole is doing.

Barton went through two other mindshifts: (a) changing the types of questions he asked students during class, and (b) planning for the fact that students get wrong answers for a variety of reasons. He used to shun "closed" questions—those with short responses—in favor of thought-provoking "open" questions like, *Why do we need to ensure that denominators are the same when adding two fractions?* and *How would you convince someone that 3/7 is bigger than 4/11?* Open questions are great for tests, extension activities, or homework, says Barton, but they're not good when the teacher's goal is to do a quick mid-lesson check for all-class understanding and decide whether to move on or spend more time on the concept.

However, not all closed questions lend themselves to on-the-spot assessing. For example, *Can a triangle have two right angles?* is a clever question with a yes/no answer, but it would be impossible for a teacher to know from a class's responses whether students who answered yes didn't understand the concept of a triangle's angles, didn't grasp the concept of a zero–degree angle, were confused about parallel lines meeting at infinity—or just guessed.

So what types of closed questions will help the teacher accurately and efficiently identify students' mistakes and misconceptions, illuminating all the possible reasons students answered incorrectly? Good diagnostic questions are difficult to write, says Barton. His ideal question has four multiple-choice options, one correct and each of the other three revealing a specific mistake or misconception. "If the question is designed well enough," he says, "then I should gain reliable evidence about my students' understanding without having to have further discussion." Barton has written around three thousand diagnostic questions (all available on his website, https://diagnosticquestions.com/Quizzes/Collections). His criteria for each question:

- It should test a single skill or concept. "The purpose of a diagnostic question," he says, "is to home in on the precise area that a student is struggling with and provide information about the precise nature of that struggle."
- It should be clear and unambiguous. The teacher should be able to accurately infer students' understanding from the answers.
- Students should be able to answer it in less than ten seconds.
- The teacher should learn something from each incorrect response without further explanation from the student. (That's because the teacher has chosen the incorrect answers very carefully.)
- It cannot be answered correctly while still holding a key misconception. This is the most important characteristic, and the one that makes formulating questions so difficult.
- What's the best way to collect students' responses to diagnostic questions? Barton has tried clickers, cell phones, and small dry-erase boards but has decided that too much can go wrong with those approaches (dead batteries, weak WiFi signal, etc.). His current system:
- Project the diagnostic question.
- Ask students to consider the question in silence.
- On the count of three, have students raise their hands high in the air, showing one finger for answer A, two fingers for B, three for C, four for D. This gives Barton a quick picture of the overall level of understanding.
- He then asks a student who chose answer A to explain his or her reasoning—then a student for answer B, then C, then D.
- He projects a different diagnostic question on the same skill and has students vote again.
- If some students are still struggling at this point, he helps them during the remainder of the lesson.

Barton says he always asks at least three questions per lesson, with each one taking about two minutes.

"I love good diagnostic questions," Barton concludes. "I know of no more accurate, efficient way of getting a sense of my students' understanding of a concept and then adjusting my teaching to meet their needs. ... In the past, I would often find myself on the receiving end of a completely unexpected answer, while standing in front of a sea of thirty confused faces all looking to me for help. I would be forced to think on the spot—attempting to diagnose the error and think of a way of helping resolve it, all while trying to juggle the hundreds of other considerations tumbling through a teacher's mind in the middle of a lesson. Now, I do not need to. By using diagnostic questions and studying the wrong answers in advance, I can plan for these errors, ensuring I have explanations, resources, and strategies ready to help. My thinking is done before the lesson, thus making me much more effective during the lesson."

"On Formative Assessment in Math: How Diagnostic Questions Can Help" by Craig Barton in *American Educator*, Summer 2018 (Vol. 42, #2, pp. 33–38, 43), summarized in Marshall Memo 742.

6 Crafting Good "Hinge" Questions

"Every teacher I've ever met knows that no lesson plan survives the first contact with real students," says assessment guru Dylan Wiliam (University College, London) in this *Educational Leadership* article. "And yet most teachers plan their lessons as though they're going to go perfectly. They plan them on the basis of assumptions they know to be false." The result is that learning problems arise during the lesson and the teacher finds out only when grading the papers that night. "And then," says Wiliam, "long after the students have left the classroom, you'll have to try to get their learning back on track, in writing, one student at a time."

The solution, he says, is to "build plan B into plan A" by designing lessons with a "hinge question" somewhere in the middle. The benefits of doing this are "huge," says Wiliam. "It means that you can find out what's going wrong with students' learning when they're right in front of you and that you can put the whole class's learning back on track right away." Of course, checking for understanding is nothing new, but writing hinge questions is harder than it appears; he's found that teachers typically take more than an hour to design a good one. Here are the key steps:

• *Design questions that elicit the right response for the right reason.* Students shouldn't be able to get the correct answer for the wrong reasons, or vice-versa. The key is plausible distractors that attract students with incomplete understanding. These can be written only by educators with good pedagogical content knowledge who have been working with students for some time. Another technique for making it more difficult for students to guess the right answer is to have multiple right answers and ask students to identify all of them.

• *Get responses from every student.* Calling on students who raise their hands is obviously inadequate, and choral responses are ineffective because it's impossible to tell who really knows and who's mouthing an imitation of others. Some kind of all-class response system is essential—fingers on chest, colored cards, dry-erase boards, Plickers, clickers, etc. The technology used is far less important than the quality of the question, says Wiliam.

• *Make the check for understanding quick.* All students should be able to respond within two minutes, and the teacher should be able to collect and interpret the responses within thirty seconds.

• *Based on students' responses, decide whether to go forward or reteach.* If few students have the right answer, going back is the obvious choice. If most have it correct, moving on makes sense, perhaps with a side conversation with those who are confused. If similar numbers of students get the answer right and wrong, the teacher can get students debating in pairs ("convince your neighbor") or have an all-class debate.

Assessment purists might argue that one question can't possibly assess mastery of a concept—for that you need up to thirty questions. But Wiliam says that this matters only if the teacher is using the question for high-stakes decisions. With hinge questions, the teacher is trying to make a quick, low-stakes decision for the whole group. "If the response of a student to a thirty-item test provides a reasonable basis for drawing conclusions about that student," he says, "then the responses of thirty students to a single question probably provide a reasonable basis for drawing conclusions about that class."

"Designing Great Hinge Questions" by Dylan Wiliam in *Educational Leadership*, September 2015 (Vol. 73, #1, pp. 40–44), summarized in Marshall Memo 602.

Low-Tech and High-Tech Tools

7 Simple Assessments That Involve All Students

"To be successfully included in general education settings, students with learning disabilities must have a sense of belonging," say Sarah Nagro (George Mason University), Sara Hooks (Towson University), Dawn Fraser (Kennedy Krieger Institute), and Kyena Cornelius (Minnesota State University/Mankato) in this article in *Teaching Exceptional Children*. Because of these students' challenges with organizational skills, higher-order thinking, working memory retention, and making connections—inclusion teachers need to make an extra effort to help them stay engaged and get better at self-assessing their level of comprehension. What's guaranteed *not* to work during whole-class instruction is the teacher asking a question and then calling on one (usually high-performing) student for the answer. Better to use strategies that elicit responses from all students and use the responses to make wise in-the-moment instructional decisions and monitor the learning of students with special needs. The authors recommend several approaches:

• *Hand-signals to check for comprehension* – Students can hold up four fingers to signify "I got it and can explain it to the class," three fingers for "I got it," two fingers for "I think I got it," and one finger for "I did not get it." This kind of whole-class check-in on a four-point scale is vastly superior to the frequent teacher question, "Does that make sense?" or "Do you understand?" If every student knows that he or she be will be asked to signal a specific level of comprehension, students are more likely to stay tuned in, feel accountable, and improve their ability to self-monitor. Teachers can also track 4-3-2-1 response data to help modify lessons and/or work with a special education coteacher and zero in on particular students who are having difficulty.

• *Hand signals to structure a discussion* – An alternative signaling strategy is for students to hold up one finger if they want to share a new idea or two fingers to add to the current idea, which enables the teacher to call on students strategically. Hence, the teacher can keep the discussion from veering off to another topic by calling on students who will take the conversation deeper in the current area, or can allow it to branch off into other areas. It's also a way to scaffold a discussion by helping students think about not only what they want to share, but also how their ideas fit into the topic.

• *Response cards* – Asking for choral responses to a question gets every student involved, but it's difficult for the teacher to know who really understands. In addition, students with learning issues can "hide in the crowd" and become passive learners. A better system is having students hold up response cards after a question or prompt. The cards can be True/False, colored for multiple-choice answers, or content-specific—for example: phone-me components, vocabulary words, parts of speech, story elements, or (for a math lesson) coins. "The purpose," say the authors, "is to create a positive learning community so all students, including students who would otherwise not participate, have frequent opportunities to respond and actively learn. Some students may require additional wait time or prompting to generate a correct response." The teacher might also ask students to think-pair-share to allow time to interact with peers.

• *Dry-erase boards, open-ended poll questions, surveys, and exit tickets* – These work best when the teacher wants to capture and make judgments about specific details of student learning. Questions can probe content knowledge, prompt students to take a stance on a topic, or have them explain their thinking, show their work, or reflect. Wait-time is always an issue when students are writing. "When asking for written responses beyond one sentence," suggest the authors, "consider including sentence starters or a mnemonic device such as POW (pick my ideas, organize my notes, write and say more), because students with learning disabilities require planning time and a way to organize their thoughts before writing." Again, the teacher can collect data on students' responses over time to track how well they are doing, intervene with individual students or small groups, and continuously improve instruction.

"Whole-Group Response Strategies to Promote Student Engagement in Inclusive Classrooms" by Sarah Nagro, Sara Hooks, Dawn Fraser, and Kyena Cornelius in *Teaching Exceptional Children*, May/June 2016 (Vol. 48, #5, pp. 243–249), summarized in Marshall Memo 640.

8. What Clickers Can Do for Teaching and Learning

In this article in *Edutopia*, John Rich (Delaware State University) gives six reasons for using audience response devices in classrooms, whether clickers or programs like Poll Everywhere and Plickers that allow students to use their phones as response devices.

• *Teachers can get a response from every student.* In all too many classrooms, only a few students engage in discussions and, says Rich, "The teacher has no idea what's brewing in the minds of the students." After asking a well-framed clicker question, the teacher can get immediate data on students' thinking and how well the content is getting across. Students can't hide.

• *Students are more active and engaged.* The fact that clicker questions are anonymous takes the risk out of getting a wrong answer, and the public display of the whole class's data increases students' curiosity about how their responses compare to those of classmates.

• *There's increased motivation to understand the material.* Students who want to do well will more readily grapple with questions because they'll get immediate feedback on where they stand. Students can also be encouraged to discuss questions in dyads or small groups.

• *Questions help students clarify their thinking.* Errors are powerful sources of information and nudge students to correct misconceptions and learning problems. Most important, the question-answer-feedback loop can prevent students from walking out of a class with incorrect information. As one student said: "The questions are either a confidence builder or a wake-up call."

• *Devices can be seen as part of the learning process.* In classrooms where having cell phones out is forbidden, being asked to use them as part of instruction can be exciting and motivating.

• *The process can do a lot for the teacher.* Formulating clicker questions up front focuses attention on essential content and skills and how best to assess mastery; seeing students' responses provides immediate feedback on what's understood and what's not; and clicker data guide mid-course corrections, important corrections and clarifications, and productive discussions.

"Polling Students to Check for Understanding" by John Rich in *Edutopia*, December 14, 2017, summarized in Marshall Memo 719.

Following Up with Students

9   Using Assessments to Improve Teaching and Learning

After the publication of the article summarized above, British researchers Paul Black, Christine Harrison, Clare Lee, Bethan Marshall, and Dylan Wiliam continued studying the impact of on-the-spot assessment with groups of secondary teachers and reported their results in this article in *Phi Delta Kappan*. The most important finding is that, when teachers make good use of formative assessment, students learn more *and* score higher on rigorous exams; in other words, teachers don't have to choose between teaching well and getting good test scores. The authors have five specific recommendations on effective use of day-by-day feedback on student learning.

• *Improve questioning.* "Many teachers do not plan and conduct classroom dialogue in ways that might help students to learn," they say. For example, it's very common for teachers not to give students enough wait-time after posing a question; a second or two after asking, most teachers move on to another student or answer the question themselves. This dynamic results in teachers using mostly questions that students can answer quickly from memory without much thought. Teachers find it difficult to break this habit, but when they do (usually with the help of colleagues or a coach), they find that the quality of student answers and the level of discourse improves markedly. These steps are helpful:

- Work at framing questions that are worth asking (big ideas, essential questions that students need to think about) versus questions requiring only recall.
- Increase wait-time to several seconds.
- Expect every student to have an answer and contribute to the discussion.
- Use every answer, right or wrong, to develop understanding. "The aim is thoughtful improvement rather than getting it right the first time."
- Use rich follow-up activities that create opportunities to extend understanding.

• *Use comments versus grades.* A striking research finding is that, for homework and assignments during a teaching unit, it is far more productive for teachers to give students written comments than to give scores or grades. This is because when students see a grade, they take it as a summative judgment on their work and shut down, ignoring any written comments. "We now believe," say the researchers, "that the effort that many teachers devote to grading homework may be misdirected. A numerical score or a grade does not tell students how to improve their work, so an opportunity to enhance their learning is lost."

But not all comments are helpful; some are brief and have no more value than a grade. To promote learning, comments must: (a) say specifically what the student has done well, (b) point out what needs to be improved, and (c) give guidance on how to make the improvement. Teachers also need to build in a mechanism to ensure that students actually *use* the comments. One teacher developed a two-column sheet, the left-hand side for his comments, the right-hand side for students to give evidence that they had put the comment to work (e.g., a page reference in their notebook). Some teachers found it particularly valuable to have students spend class time rewriting a piece of work integrating feedback in a supportive environment. They found that this changed students' expectations about class work and homework.

• *Use self-assessment and peer assessment.* Teachers need to be transparent about what is to be learned in a unit and how students' work will be evaluated. Giving rubrics and exemplars of proficient student work is an excellent way to make expectations clear and help students self-assess as they go along. But most students, especially low-achievers, need help evaluating their own work. Explaining rubrics to students is helpful. So is giving students "traffic light" icons with which they can signal how they're doing: green means they get it, yellow means partial understanding, red means they're lost. A teacher can ask the whole class to think about which light applies to them, then ask for a show of hands for red, yellow, and green, and then decide whether to re-teach, pull out a group of red/yellow-light students, or organize students into green/red pairings for peer tutoring.

Once the table is set for self-assessment, peer assessment is a valuable adjunct. Peer help works because (a) students often accept criticisms from peers that they wouldn't take seriously coming from a teacher, (b) students often understand the language that peers use better than a teacher's, and (c) a student who is confused is more likely to interrupt a peer for clarification.

• *Use summative tests formatively.* The English researchers believe summative tests should be part of the learning process, not just final judgments. Effective practices include: (a) having students "traffic light" the questions on a summative test, enabling the teacher to use the red/yellow/green data to organize peer tutoring, reteach, etc.; (b) in preparing for tests, an effective process is having students generate test questions themselves (and then answer them), which helps them think like assessors and get their heads inside the goals of the curriculum unit; and (c) after a test, having students self-assess (solo or with peers) how their work might be improved.

Black, Harrison, Lee, Marshall, Wiliam close with a series of suggestions for working with teachers on assessments:

• *Explore the psychology of learning.* Once teachers are thinking in terms of improving the learning results of all students, they are often eager to know more about how students learn. This leads them to take greater care selecting tasks, questions, and prompts to help move students along more effectively, and also makes them more attentive to the knowledge and misconceptions that students bring to the table. When teachers are constantly checking for understanding and being serious about real learning, students sometimes push back. One teacher was stunned when a student said, "Look, we've told you we don't understand this. Why are you going on to the next topic?"

• *Realize that each subject is different.* There is a spectrum of learning, from "closed" tasks with a single well-defined outcome to "open" tasks with a wide range of acceptable outcomes. Math tends to be fairly straightforward in terms of the questions a teacher asks. In science, the information being taught is straightforward, but many students bring misconceptions to the table (for example, that all heavy objects sink, or that the sun goes around the earth). The teacher's challenge, say the authors, is to "open up discussion of such ideas and provide feedback that challenges them by introducing new pieces of evidence and argument that support the scientific model." In language arts, peer assessment and self-assessment are particularly valuable because there are so many variables. Fortunately, the development of rubrics in recent years makes it possible to put students in the driver's seat of their own learning—although rubrics have limitations in subjects where creativity is at a premium.

• *Use feedback to motivate students.* "Students will invest effort in a task only if they believe that they can achieve something," say the researchers. "If a learning exercise is seen as a competition, then everyone is aware that there will be losers as well as winners, and those who have been losers in the past will see little point in trying."

• *Plan units carefully.* This includes thinking through "big ideas" and possible misconceptions and orchestrating lessons to maximize student thinking and understanding.

• *Realize that this isn't easy.* For teachers to effectively implement formative assessment, they need to unlearn and change deeply-ingrained practices. The researchers suggest starting small (for example, with one class or one subject area), working with a supportive group of colleagues, and constantly measuring results.

"Working Inside the Black Box: Assessment for Learning in the Classroom" by Paul Black, Christine Harrison, Clare Lee, Bethan Marshall, and Dylan Wiliam in *Phi Delta Kappan*, September 2004 (Vol. 86, #1, pp. 8–21), summarized in Marshall Memo 53.

---

10 Using Formative Assessment Well

In this article in *Voices from the Middle*, Dylan Wiliam says Albert Einstein had good advice for teachers making formative use of assessments: "Make things as simple as possible, but not too simple." Some examples:

• A seventh-grade English teacher gives a test under exam conditions and collects students' papers. After quickly reading them, the teacher decides not to grade them; rather, she gives them back the next day, has students sit in groups of four, and asks each group to write the best composite paper. Each group then reports out to the whole class and the merits of their collaborative work are discussed and debated. "What is interesting about the example," says Wiliam, "is that the assessment being used had been designed entirely for summative purposes, but the teacher had found a way of using it formatively."

• A fifth-grade teacher introduces students to five kinds of figurative language: alliteration, hyperbole, onomatopoeia, personification, and simile. Five minutes before the end of the lesson, she writes the five on the board and reads these sentences aloud.

- He was like a bull in a china shop.
- This backpack weighs a ton.
- The sweetly smiling sunshine warmed the grass.
- He honked his horn at the cyclist.
- He was as tall as a house.

Students "finger vote" which kind of figurative language they heard (one finger for alliteration, two for hyperbole, etc.).

Most students give correct responses to the first two, but the third sentence gets a mix of one finger and four fingers. The teacher notes that they are both right and wrong: the sentence has both alliteration and personification. Realizing that a sentence might contain more than one, most students get the last two correct (alliteration and onomatopoeia, and simile and hyperbole). In less than three minutes, this teacher used a formative assessment to check for understanding, grade, and take follow-up action.

• A sixth-grade class works on suspense stories, with these ground rules: (a) stories need to contain four phases: establishment, build-up, climax, and resolution; and (b) stories must contain at least two examples of figurative language. When students finish a first draft, they exchange papers with a classmate and everyone switches roles from "author" to "editor." Each editor marks up the story using four different colored pencils to mark the beginning of each phase and a fifth color to underline the two examples of figurative language. With the editor's approval, a story is submitted to the "chief editor" (the teacher). Because each editor is accountable for ensuring that the required elements are there, students take the role very seriously.

Wiliam concludes with a quote from researcher Roy Sadler (1989): "The indispensable conditions for improvement are that the student comes to hold a concept of quality roughly similar to that held by the teacher, is able to monitor continuously the quality of what is being produced during the act of production itself, and has a repertoire of alternative moves or strategies from which to draw at any given point."

"Assessment: The Bridge Between Teaching and Learning" by Dylan Wiliam in *Voices from the Middle*, December 2013 (Vol. 21, #2, pp. 15–20), summarized in Marshall Memo 766.

---

11 Putting On-the-Spot Assessment Data to Work in Math Classes

"Teaching must balance lesson planning with improvising," say Brent Duckor, Carrie Holmberg, and Joanne Rossi Becker (San José State University) in this article in *Mathematics Teaching in the Middle School*. They believe formative assessment in classrooms is more than calling for thumbs up/thumbs down, using clickers, giving quizzes, processing exit slips, and managing interim test data. It should also include real-time instructional adaptations, listening carefully to and making sense of students' unexpected responses (a "window" into their thinking), giving feedback on the fly, and interjecting "just-in-time moves that promote a conscious and strategic use of student thinking."

Duckor, Holmberg, and Becker suggest seven formative assessment moves that should be "fluid, flexible, and ubiquitous" during a lesson and "create opportunities for all students to interact productively and persistently with higher-order thinking."

• *Priming:* Preparing the groundwork, establishing norms, acting to acculturate students to learning publicly. For example, a teacher might say: "I'm so glad you asked that question because it seemed like maybe some other people had the same question."

• *Pausing:* Giving students adequate time to think and respond as individuals or as groups. The teacher poses a question to the whole class but doesn't call on students for a few seconds, putting hand to chin in a pose reminiscent of Rodin's Thinker and conveying the message, "We take our time to raise our hands. I am protecting individual student think time now."

• *Bouncing:* Sampling a variety of student responses intentionally and systematically to better map terrain of student thinking: "Take sixty seconds. Talk with your team" or "Anyone have anything to add to that?"

• *Probing:* Asking follow-up questions that use information from actual student responses: "Based on what you saw around the room, would you stick with that answer?"

• *Posing:* Asking questions that size up the learner's needs in the lesson and across the unit: "Why would the 3 x 2 x 4 box have less surface area than the 6 x 4 x 1 box?"

• *Binning:* Noticing patterns in student responses, categorizing them along learning trajectories, and using responses to inform next steps; the teacher displays several student solutions in correct and incorrect "bins" without disclosing an opinion and asks, "Which are correct?"

• *Tagging:* Publicly representing variation in student thinking by creating a snapshot or running record of a class's responses: "So let's come to an agreement as a group about terms."

Duckor, Holmberg, and Becker say these steps "amplify the voices and values of quieter students, particularly those English language learners in middle-school math classrooms who too often have been rushed past in the race to the top."

"Making Moves: Formative Assessment in Mathematics" by Brent Duckor, Carrie Holmberg, and Joanne Rossi Becker in *Mathematics Teaching in the Middle School*, February 2017 (Vol. 22, #6, pp. 334–342), summarized in Marshall Memo 675.

Professional Learning Suggestions for Chapter Ten Assessment for Learning

The Importance of Formative Assessments

Formative assessments have the potential to dramatically impact student learning. However, this is only if they are *implemented well*. Kim and Jenn have observed lots of teachers who go through the motions of using exit ticket or clickers, but then neglect to use the results to inform instruction. This is why it is so crucial for teachers to develop a deep understanding of just what formative assessments are and what is needed to implement them well.

The first two sets of exercises aim to help teachers make better sense of formative assessments and the final section is for school leaders—to help them plan ways to be more supportive of the use of formative assessments.

I. What Makes Assessments Formative?

The activities in this section can be used to help teachers develop a deeper understanding of what it means for an assessment to be "formative" and to assess their current use of formative assessments in their own classrooms.

A. Watch a video about formative assessments.
After having teachers read some of the articles in this chapter, show them this video of Rick Wormeli discussing formative assessments. (Note that he refers to the original Black and Wiliam Article 1, as well as several concepts in the chapter.): https://www.youtube.com/watch?v=rJxFXjfB_B4

B. Discuss formative assessments.
After reading the articles and watching the video, have a large group discussion about formative assessments:
- How are formative assessments different from summative assessments?
- Some of the authors use different terms. Why do these terms accurately describe formative assessment?
  > Stiggins (Article 2) calls formative assessments "assessments *for* learning." Why?
  > Barton (Article 5) calls formative assessments "responsive teaching." Why?

- Some authors discuss the *motivational* aspects of formative assessments (Stiggins) and others focus not on the assessment itself, but on how the results are *used*. Discuss these two aspects of formative assessments.

C. Write one sentence capturing the definition of formative assessment.

A great activity for any class or professional learning session is to ask participants to encapsulate the discussion or a concept in one to two sentences. For this activity, ask teachers to write a one- or two-sentence overview of their understanding of what formative assessments are. Below are some catchy ones from the chapter and elsewhere.

- Craig Barton (Article 5): "Teaching without formative assessment is like painting with your eyes closed."
- Robert Stake: "When the cook tastes the soup, that's formative; when the guests taste the soup, that's summative."
- Doug Reeves: The difference between a formative and a summative assessment is like the difference between a medical and a post-mortem.

D. Discuss the "testing-is-bad" movement.

In Article 4, Marshall suggests that the present "testing-is-bad" movement, as he describes it, makes it difficult to focus on formative assessments and maximize the benefits, as discussed above. Discuss whether this is a problem at your school (with a leadership team or with teachers themselves) and how to address it.

E. Assessing our use of formative assessments.

In the fourth article, Marshall outlines nine potential ways formative assessments can significantly impact learning. However, not everyone milks their formative assessments for all they are worth. Use the self-assessment chart that follows to rate yourself (individually or as a team) and then discuss: Which of these nine do we make good use of in our school or do I make good use of in my classroom?

Nine Ways Formative Assessments Improve Teaching and Learning	Rate this item on how much you maximize it: (0 = not at all, 5 = we maximize this benefit)
1. On-the-spot checks for understanding help teachers address confusions immediately.	
2. Self-testing during class helps students take advantage of the "retrieval effect" and improve their memory.	
3. When students struggle on a formative assessment and teachers engage peer instruction to address gaps, this boosts learning.	
4. Formative assessments foster a growth mindset.	
5. Formative assessments produce useful data for students, teachers, and leaders.	
6. When teachers involve students, formative assessments help students monitor their own learning.	
7. Formative assessments provide useful information for teacher team meetings.	
8. Formative assessments provide an opportunity for leaders to make student learning part of supervision.	
9. Formative assessments provide insight into curriculum implementation.	

II. What Are the Implications for Teaching and Learning?

The activities in this section help teachers think through what it means to implement formative assessment *well* and to improve their own ability to give effective feedback to students.

A. Make a web of aspects of teaching and learning that will be impacted by formative assessment.
Reading these articles makes you aware of how *many* aspects of teaching and learning are connected to formative assessment. The articles refer to everything from pedagogical implications (wait time, deeper questions) to implications for supervision (leaders discussing formative assessment results with teachers) to implications for culture (helping students feel comfortable making mistakes).

Take some time to review the articles and pull out all of the aspects of formative assessment that have the potential to affect teaching and learning. Write "formative assessment" in the middle circle in the web below and then fill in the ovals for larger areas (like pedagogy). Then draw even more branches from those ovals and draw in smaller ovals (for wait time, etc.) When you are done—with a partner, discuss how overarching formative assessment can be.

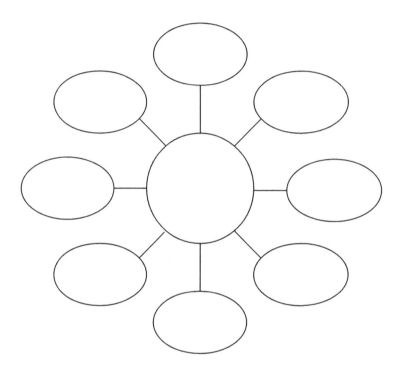

*B. Create a list of what we must do to implement formative assessments **well**.*
It is important to know that formative assessments are effective *if* implemented well. There are a number of extremely useful recommendations in the articles to help educators improve their implementation. To comb through the articles to find and compile these recommendations, do the following: First, divide up teachers into five groups and have each group read one article in the chapter. Have the groups discuss their article using the Three Levels of Text Protocol, found here: http://schoolreforminitiative.org/doc/3_levels_text.pdf

This protocol has individuals share a passage from the article, what they think about it, and implications for their work. In this case, teachers should share implications for what to *avoid* and what to *do* to implement formative assessments well in their classrooms.

Once the five groups have completed their discussions, have each group share the *implications* with the entire group and compile one large list of strategies to implement formative assessment.

C. Work on giving better feedback to students.
Several articles point to the importance of giving better feedback, so it is worth having your teachers spend some time on this topic.

1. First, give your teachers the following scenario: Students are given an assignment that they will have the opportunity to improve for a better grade. After teachers look at a first draft of the student work, which of the following will most likely improve the quality of it the *second* time they turn it in:
   a) Just a letter or number grade on the assignment
   b) Just narrative comments on the assignment
   c) A grade *and* comments

Have teachers raise one finger if they think it's a), two fingers for b), and three fingers for c). Share with them that the answer is b). Several of the articles point this out. Ask them *why* they believe this is the case.

2. Determine the criteria for effective feedback.
Have teachers review the first and fourth articles (Black and Wiliam and Marshall) and make a list of the criteria that will help them give better feedback. (They might include the following: clarify the learning goal, show the students' present position, and show them what to do to close the gap; give specific guidance on how to improve, preferably without any grades at all; ensure that students *use* the comments; and make sure that comments not be too brief so as to function like shorthand for a grade.)

3. Have teachers improve their own feedback.
Before the meeting, gather some examples of student work with written teacher feedback. Distribute these to teachers and give them an opportunity to use the criteria from above to take a stab at improving the written teacher feedback and describe what else they would do in their classrooms to help improve the sample student work (such as implementing the two-column sheet for teacher comments on one side and the student's evidence that s/he has made improvements on the other—or reviewing learning goals—or any other idea.)

D. Write a lesson plan for tomorrow that includes one type of formative assessment.

The articles provide a plethora of recommendations for integrating formative assessment techniques into the classroom. Have teachers bring in their lesson plans for the next day. After reviewing the articles in this chapter, have them choose one formative assessment method to integrate into the lesson plan they brought. Methods they might choose include: on-the-spot formative assessment methods such as dry-erase boards, clickers, Plickers, quick-writes, think-pair-share, cold calling, or exit tickets—or the planning of three diagnostic questions as introduced in Barton (Article 5).

III. How Can School Leader Actions Support the Effective Use of Formative Assessments?

This section encourages leaders to choose two practices to commit to that will support the use of formative assessments across the school.

Look at the six suggestions toward the end of Marshall (Article 4) for ideas for ways administrators can support formative assessment. As a leadership team, choose two of these practices to adopt for the year. Next, outline four criteria your team would use to know what to look for in these observations or conversations:

- During observations, check in with students about the learning (*What are you learning today?*).
- Chat with teachers after observations about *intended* versus *actual* outcomes.
- With teachers, examine formative assessment results (look at actual student responses as well as compiled data).
- Sit with teacher teams as they plan upcoming assessments.
- Observe teacher teams as they analyze student work and assessment results.
- Ask teacher teams for reports with *before* and *after* evidence of student learning.

Chapter Eleven: Grading Practices

Although measurement experts and professional developers may wish grades were unadulterated measures of what students have learned and are able to do, strong evidence indicates that they are not.
—SUSAN BROOKHART ET AL.

The ways in which we were graded as students, and the grading practices many of us have used in our own classrooms, have been around for decades. But recent research has highlighted a number of problems with those practices. The articles in this chapter describe some troublesome flaws, the characteristics of effective assessment of student work, and what some schools are doing to make things better.

Problems with Grades and Grading – Susan Brookhart and seven colleagues summarize a century of research on the importance and limitations of grades. Thomas Guskey tackles five mistaken beliefs, among them, that low grades will motivate students to work harder and that grades should be arrayed on a bell-shaped curve. Jennifer Gonzalez points to some additional problems with grading, including students not having advance notice of assessment criteria and the pesky issue of extra credit. Ross Kasun adds that variations in how homework is graded can distort students' grades and undermine motivation. And Amber Northern and Michael Petrilli point to the disconnect between students' report card grades (often inflated) and performance on rigorous, Common Core-aligned final exams and state tests.

Characteristics of Effective Grading – Thomas Guskey recommends giving students separate grades for three dimensions of their work: product (academic achievement), process (homework, attendance, class participation, etc.), and progress toward the goal. Ken O'Connor, Lee Ann Jung, and Douglas Reeves say that if grades are FAST (fair, accurate, specific, and timely), the process of assessment will advance the ultimate goal of providing information that improves teaching and learning.

Improving Grading Practices – Dick Corbett and Bruce Wilson describe the positive impact of schools refusing to accept incomplete or unsatisfactory work and not letting students give up until they have achieved mastery. Timothy Quinn suggests two ways of helping students look beyond the letter grades they get on assignments and focus on how they can improve specific parts of their work. Eric Anderman and Alison Koenka analyze why cheating occurs in schools and recommend steps that can reduce or eliminate it. And Thomas Buckmiller and Randal Peters allay parents', students', and educators' worries that colleges won't give a fair shake to students who submit non-traditional grades.

Questions to Consider

- How can we solve the problem of equally proficient students getting different grades?
- Is changing traditional grading practices worth it?
- Can grades *improve* students' learning as well as documenting their performance?

Problems with Grades and Grading

1 One Hundred Years of Research on Grading

In this *Review of Educational Research* article, Susan Brookhart (Duquesne University), Thomas Guskey (University of Kentucky), Alex Bowers (Columbia University), James McMillan (Virginia Commonwealth University), Jeffrey Smith and Lisa Smith (University of Otago), and Michael Stevens and Megan Welsh (University of California/Davis) review a century of research on grading practices. Some key conclusions:

• *Grades convey important information.* Over the years, grades have been maligned by researchers and psychometricians as subjective and unreliable measures of student achievement. Actually, grades are useful indicators of things that matter to students, teachers, parents, schools, and communities—and they're more accurate predictors of high-school completion and transition to college than standardized test scores. In addition, when grades are aggregated from individual pieces of student work to report card or course grades and GPA, their reliability increases. For example, the reliability of overall college grade-point averages is estimated at 0.93.

• *Grades are multidimensional.* They often include noncognitive information that teachers value, including: effort, motivation, improvement, work habits, attention, engagement, participation, and behavior. That's probably why grades are more accurate than test scores at predicting downstream success, since we now know that noncognitive factors play an important role. Teachers typically distinguish between noncognitive factors and academic ability on the one hand—and other factors they believe should *not* be factors in grading (gender, socioeconomic status, and personality)—on the other.

• *Grades have a subjective element.* Each teacher's values come into play, including a desire to help all students be successful and wanting to be fair—i.e., the feeling that kids who worked hard shouldn't fail, even if they haven't learned. "Although measurement experts and professional developers may wish grades were unadulterated measures of what students have learned and are able to do," say the authors, "strong evidence indicates that they are not." Over the years, researchers have attributed variations in teachers' grades to a number of factors: the rigor of the learning task, the actual quality of student work, the grading criteria, the grading scale, how strict or lenient the teacher was, and teacher error.

• *Transparency is important.* Problems arise when teachers aren't clear with students, parents, and colleagues about what goes into grades. When that happens, grades can convey inaccurate and misleading information.

• *Grading practices have improved.* Earlier research found fault with teachers for giving different grades to the same piece of student work. But teachers in these studies were often flying blind; they weren't given the grading criteria. Recent studies have shown that with clear rubrics and proper training, teachers can achieve an impressive level of inter-rater reliability.

• *Grades are only the tip of the iceberg.* There are several possible explanations for a student who worked hard not mastering the intended learning.

- The learning goals were developmentally inappropriate.
- The student lacked readiness or appropriate prior instruction to master the material.
- The teacher didn't make clear what students were expected to learn.
- The curriculum materials weren't appropriate.
- The teacher didn't instruct students in appropriate ways.
- The teacher didn't use on-the-spot assessments to catch learning problems and help struggling students in real time.

In other words, say the authors, "Research focusing solely on grades typically misses antecedent causes …. Investigating grading in the larger context of instruction and assessment will help focus research on important sources and causes of invalid or unreliable grading decisions."

"A Century of Grading Research: Meaning and Value in the Most Common Educational Measure" by Susan Brookhart, Thomas Guskey, Alex Bowers, James McMillan, Jeffrey Smith and Lisa Smith, Michael Stevens, and Megan Welsh in *Review of Educational Research*, December 2016 (Vol. 86, #4, pp. 803–848), summarized in Marshall Memo 667.

2 Misconceptions Get in the Way of Better Grading

"Educators seeking to reform grading must combat five long-held traditions that stand as formidable obstacles to change," says University of Kentucky professor Thomas Guskey in this *Educational Leadership* article. "Leaders who have the courage to challenge the traditional approach and the conviction to press for thoughtful, positive reforms are likely to see remarkable results." Here are the misconceptions.

• *Misconception 1: Grades should differentiate students on the basis of talent.* If it's true that naturally talented students should receive high grades and vice-versa, then schools are in the business of *selecting for* talent rather than *developing* it. If the goal is selection, then it follows that schools should maximize the achievement differences among students. One way of doing this is using assessments like the SAT and ACT, which eliminate questions on which most students score well. Another way to maximize student-achievement differences is to teach poorly; it works every time, says Guskey. But if the goal is developing talent, the school should be clear about learning outcomes and do everything possible to ensure that all students reach them. The result should be almost all students reaching high levels of achievement.

• *Misconception 2: Grade distributions should form a bell-shaped curve.* The logic here is that intelligence is distributed along a normal curve, and achievement is related to intelligence, so grades should look the same. The flaw in this logic is that bell-shaped curves represent human variation when nothing intervenes. When learning conditions are optimized, the relationship between intelligence and achievement approaches zero. With effective teaching, the curve should look much different. In fact, if there's a normal curve after teaching, it's a sign that instruction was ineffective.

• *Misconception 3: Grades should be based on students' standing compared to classmates.* This kind of grading means that a student who receives an A did better than others in the class, versus achieving success against an objective standard. The problem with norm-referenced grading is that it's possible for students to perform poorly and still get high grades compared to other students who are performing even worse. Comparative grading also cranks up competitiveness, which is seldom a productive dynamic in classrooms. "Students are discouraged from cooperating or helping one another because doing so might hurt the helper's chance of success," says Guskey. "Similarly, teachers may refrain from helping individual students because some students might construe this as showing favoritism and biasing the competition." In standards-based grading, on the other hand, grades are based on rigorous, challenging, and transparent learning outcomes and have much more meaning.

• *Misconception 4: When they get low grades, students try harder.* In fact, there's no research evidence that low grades are motivational. In fact, low grades often lead students to dismiss the importance of grades and stop trying. A much more effective strategy is giving students who don't achieve mastery an *I* for incomplete and requiring them to get help the same day (during lunch or after school) to reach mastery.

• *Misconception 5: Students should get a single grade for each subject or course.* There's plenty of evidence that combining achievement, attitude, effort, behavior, punctuality, and level of responsibility into one composite grade doesn't work, says Guskey. It's far more effective to give separate grades for three things: *product* (a summative assessment of student learning); *process* (how students got there); and *progress* (the value-added from the learning experience)—with separate marks and rubrics for homework, class participation, punctuality, effort, etc. Using this system, grade-point averages are based solely on the product grade.

"Five Obstacles to Grading Reform" by Thomas Guskey in *Educational Leadership*, November 2011 (Vol. 69, #3, pp. 16–21), summarized in Marshall Memo 409.

---

3 Pointed Questions About Grades

"Grades are inherently imperfect," says Jennifer Gonzalez in this *Cult of Pedagogy* article. "To truly assess our students' learning, we need to get to know them, observe them, and study a wide sampling of their work over time." But in the real world of classrooms, there's a strong tug to simplify achievement into grades, and that can introduce all manner of distortions—for example:

- a student who got a D on a thoughtful essay because it was messy and contained some errors,
- a student who earned extra credit by donating tissues and hand sanitizer to the class,
- a volcano-building project (with extra credit if the model erupted) where parental resources were a big factor,
- a student who got half credit for a project turned in a day late under the teacher's "no excuses" late policy.

"In all these cases," says Gonzalez, "the grade was not an accurate representation of what a student has learned. This is a problem of design." Parents, students, and teachers act as though grades have some absolute value, but they actually depend on lots of decisions that each teacher makes about assignments, assessment, and grading criteria.

Gonzalez acknowledges the challenge of making grades meaningful and poses questions that she, as a parent and an educator, believes need to be answered:

• *What learning does this task measure?* With her own children, Gonzalez is amazed at how often assignments "have no real connection to what the curriculum says students are learning"—for example, students making a relief map showing geographic features, when the objective is explaining how geography affects culture.

• *Are you teaching what you will measure?* "We often assign points for skills and qualities that students happen to bring with them, but are never taught in class," says Gonzalez. The skill of collaboration is an example: we grade on it, but is this something we're systematically teaching?

• *What will quality work look like on this task?* Sometimes teachers have a vague idea of what the end product should be, but don't know exactly until the work is turned in—too late for students to rise to expectations. "We'll get better work from students and judge it more fairly if we identify and communicate the criteria for success ahead of time," says Gonzalez.

• *How much of the grade depends on outside resources?* Parents' contributions of supplies, access to technology, transportation, and assistance vary from home to home.

• *Can all students do well on this task, regardless of how they learn best?* Assignments shouldn't be designed with only one kind of learner in mind. (The Universal Design for Learning framework is helpful in assigning work that is accessible to all students.)

• *Should this assignment be called "practice" instead?* Teachers may believe that students will apply themselves only if the work will be graded. But some activities should be practice for a task that will be graded subsequently. For example, students might practice long-division problems until they're proficient enough to take the real test. This approach also saves teachers a lot of grading.

• *How should we deal with late work?* "In classes where late work is penalized, a grade is a reflection of the student's time management, or of stress, or perfectionism, or dozens of other possible factors," says Gonzalez. "What it isn't is a reflection of learning."

• *What about extra credit?* Giving credit for work that doesn't directly reflect learning distorts grades, including giving a false impression of mastery. "Students who are doing so well on the regular class work that they finish early don't need extra credit," says Gonzalez; "they need differentiated assignments and more challenge. Students who do poorly on assignments don't need extra credit to make up the missing points; they need opportunities to re-do and improve the work."

• *And what about averaging grades?* Simply adding up grades and dividing by the number of assignments can give an inaccurate picture of what students are actually learning. An alternative is giving more weight to grades later in the learning progression so the final grade reflects students' improved level of mastery.

"How Accurate Are Your Grades?" by Jennifer Gonzalez in *The Cult of Pedagogy*, April 22, 2018, summarized in Marshall Memo 737.

---

4. A New Jersey District Deals with How Homework Is Graded

In this article in *School Leader*, Ross Kasun says that as a new superintendent he received a slew of parent calls about children who had straight As on their report cards but were assigned to remedial classes because they'd done poorly on New Jersey state tests. There were also students with the opposite problem: excellent scores on state tests but Cs and Ds on their report cards. The common factor? Homework was counted as a major portion of students' grades. Some low-performing students were able to get high grades by always doing their homework, and some high-performing students didn't do homework and were dinged on their report cards.

Kasun convened a group of colleagues, and they quickly concluded that "homework performance is not an accurate portrayal of final proficiency or mastery. It's the path to learning, so it's a formative assessment. We grade students against standards, not the routes by which they achieve them. Homework is practice and not a determination of mastery and grades are saved for declarations of mastery …. When students fail to complete homework, we tend to approach the problem more like a discipline problem than a learning issue." This led the group to question how much homework should count in students' grades.

The committee also looked into the disproportionate impact of giving zeroes to students for not doing homework or failing to turn in assignments. "Traditional practices of giving zeroes and not accepting late assignments allow students to escape accountability for learning," says Kasun. "Learning is not about compliance, and we do not teach responsibility with a stick and carrot …. We are faced with the irony that a policy that may be grounded in the belief of holding students accountable (giving zeroes) actually allows some students to escape accountability for learning."

Based on this analysis, the district rolled out a new policy: homework would count as only 5 percent of students' final grades; there would be no zeroes (the lowest grade was 50); there was a maximum number of minutes for homework at each grade level; and teachers would focus on giving high-quality assignments. As the new policies were implemented, there was pushback. Kasun lists the arguments and how he addressed them:

• *Students won't do homework if it isn't a big part of their grade.* In fact, he says, grades aren't the factor that determines who does homework and who doesn't; it's the *usefulness* of homework.

• *Giving students a 50 for doing nothing is wrong.* Kasun stressed the unfairness of giving zeroes on a 100-point scale (it's virtually impossible to recover from a zero), and pointed out that teachers' evaluations on the district's teacher-evaluation rubric were on a 4-point scale, with 1 being the lowest possible score.

• *Homework teaches responsibility and time management.* "This is also an incorrect idea," says Kasun, "as homework does not reinforce time management if adults have to coerce children into doing it; if children are coerced, they are not in charge of making decisions about the use of time."

"Busy Work or Home Learning? One District's Journey to Remake Homework for the 21st-Century" by Ross Kasun in *School Leader*, May/June 2015 (Vol. 45, #6), summarized in Marshall Memo 592.

5   Grade Inflation in High Schools

In this *Education Gadfly* article, Amber Northern and Michael Petrilli say that although state tests have become more demanding since the advent of the Common Core, student achievement hasn't kept pace and many parents are in a state of denial about their children's level of proficiency. According to a 2018 study by Learning Heroes, a parent information group:

- Ninety percent of parents believe their children are performing at or above grade level.
- Sixty-seven percent believe their children are "above average" in school.
- Eighty-five percent say their children are on track for academic success.
- Eight percent say their children are performing below average.

This despite the fact that only one-third of U.S. teens leave high school ready to pass credit-bearing college courses.

What's the disconnect? Northern and Petrilli believe it's that parents trust the grades their children bring home from school, but the grades teachers give aren't in synch with recently upgraded state standards. This conclusion comes from a Thomas B. Fordham Institute study of grade inflation in North Carolina high schools (see the link below). By looking at data on students taking Algebra I from 2004/5 to 2015/16, including course transcripts, statewide end-of-course exam scores, and ACT scores, the study found that:

- While many students get good grades from their teachers, few earn top marks on end-of-course exams.
- The Algebra I end-of-course exam scores predict math ACT scores much better than do teachers' course grades.
- There was more grade inflation in schools attended by more-affluent students than those attended by less-advantaged students.

Northern and Petrilli say teachers' grades convey important information, especially because they often include student behavior, class participation, and effort—important ingredients in college and life success. However, Parents aren't seeing the red flags fluttering when their children get low scores on state tests. The Learning Heroes study found that parents make excuses (*My child doesn't test well.*) and parents aren't aware that most of their children's peers are also bringing home As and Bs. "The sad fact," say Northern and Petrilli, "is that some will only become aware that their child is marching off a cliff with regard to college readiness—along with many others—after it's too late."

The solution? Rigorous end-of-course exams geared to national standards. "Having an external measure that is not developed or graded by the classroom teacher," say Northern and Petrilli, "can be an effective way to preserve high standards, and it also serves as an 'audit' of course grades and progress."

"How to Reverse Grade Inflation and Help Students Reach Their Potential" by Amber Northern and Michael Petrilli in *The Education Gadfly*, September 19, 2018 (Vol. 18, #37), summarized in Marshall Memo 754.

Characteristics of Effective Grading

6 The Shift to Standards-Based Grading

In this *Phi Delta Kappan* article, Thomas Guskey (University of Kentucky) says it's common for American high-school students with very different knowledge and skill levels to receive identical grades. This is because their schools' marking systems squeeze too much information into a single letter grade. Here are some of the factors that teachers use, to varying degrees, to decide what grades to give their students:

- Major exams or compositions
- Class quizzes
- Reports or projects
- Student portfolios
- Exhibits of student work
- Laboratory projects
- Student notebooks or journals
- Classroom observations
- Oral presentations
- Homework completion
- Homework quality
- Class participation
- Work habits and neatness
- Effort
- Attendance
- Punctuality submitting assignments
- Class behavior and attitude
- Progress made

Some teachers base their grades on two or three of these; others use evidence from as many as sixteen. When teachers try to combine multiple criteria into a single A or C or F, the result is what Guskey calls a "hodgepodge" grade that often does a poor job of communicating vital feedback to students, parents, and the community.

There are actually three different messages that most teachers want to send when they give students grades.

- Product: Telling students their summative achievement based on final exams, reports, projects, overall assessments, and other culminating demonstrations of learning.
- Process: Giving students feedback on how they worked in the class based on classroom quizzes, homework, punctuality handing in assignments, class participation, or attendance.
- Progress: Giving students feedback on how much they gained from the learning experience—the "value added" or improvement delta over a specified period of time.

Many teachers are loath to use only product criteria (tests, for example), believing this might damage some students' motivation, self-esteem, and peer relationships. Instead, teachers combine product, process, and progress criteria in an attempt to be fair to all students. The answer to the question "Why do we give grades?" is that teachers want to tell students how they are doing in all three areas. Teachers also want to hold higher-achieving students accountable for working hard (not coasting) and avoid discouraging low-achieving students from working hard.

But combining three types of message in one grade causes problems. How can parents, students, administrators, and community members make sense of such grades? "A grade of A, for example," says Guskey, "may mean that the student knew what was intended before instruction began (product), did not learn as well as expected but tried very hard (process), or simply made significant improvement (progress)." Clearly, the more teachers use process and progress criteria, the more subjective grades become. And yet there are good reasons for taking these two elements of student performance into account.

The solution, says Guskey, is to give three separate grades for product, process, and progress. This allows teachers to give explicit feedback on all three aspects of a student's work and not water down the all-important mark on academic achievement. Some high schools in the U.S. have begun to split apart their grades, and the practice is quite common in Canada. The usual approach is to mark academic achievement with a percent or letter grade:

A - advanced

B - proficient

C - basic

D - needs improvement

F - unsatisfactory

Grade-point averages and class rank are computed from these achievement or product grades, which are based on explicit learning goals for the course.

For process and progress grades, teachers most commonly use a 4-3-2-1 scale, backed up by a rubric. Some schools divide process grades into homework, class participation, punctuality of assignments, effort, learning progress, etc. Here's a sample rubric for homework grades:

4 - All homework assignments completed and turned in on time.

3 - Only one or two missing or incomplete homework assignments.

2 - Three to five missing or incomplete homework assignments.

1 - Numerous missing or incomplete homework assignments.

Teachers who have tried giving multiple grades report that it gives students much more explicit feedback—and actually saves time. The worry of estimating how to weight the different subcomponents for a single grade is gone, and everything is clear and explicit to students and parents. Teased-out grades also send more meaningful and helpful messages. For example, if a parent questions a C on achievement, the teacher can point to other grades and suggest that perhaps if the child did homework, showed up on time, and participated more in class discussions, the product grade might improve.

Split-apart grades also provide college admissions officers and prospective employers more-detailed information on students' work ethic and overall status. "The transcript thus becomes a more robust document," says Guskey, "presenting a better and more discerning portrait of students' high-school experiences." He also predicts that when schools present grades this way, there will be a much better correlation between letter grades and students' scores on state tests.

What's critical, concludes Guskey, is being explicit about the criteria for product, process, and progress grades. "Teachers must be able to describe exactly how they plan to evaluate students' achievement, attitude, effort, behavior, and progress," he says. "Then they must clearly communicate these criteria to students, parents, and others." No surprises, no excuses.

"Making High-School Grades Meaningful" by Thomas Guskey in *Phi Delta Kappan*, May 2006 (Vol. 83, #9, pp. 670–675), summarized in Marshall Memo 136.

7 Making Grades Fair, Accurate, Specific, and Timely

In this *Phi Delta Kappan* article, Ken O'Connor (an author and consultant), Lee Ann Jung (San Diego State University), and Douglas Reeves (Creative Leadership Solutions) advocate for grades that are FAST—*fair, accurate, specific, and timely*:

• *Fair* – Fairness involves communicating current achievement to everyone who has the need and right to know—especially students—and giving all students equal opportunity to learn and show what they know, understand, and can do. "This means, for example, that the time available on tests and exams must be flexible, not fixed," say O'Connor, Jung, and Reeves, "and that students should almost always have a variety of ways to demonstrate their knowledge, understanding, and skills."

• *Accurate* – A key element is separating students' grades on academic achievement from judgments on non-academic behaviors. The frequency of assessment is also important, say O'Connor, Jung, and Reeves; teachers need to find the Goldilocks amount of testing—sampling enough to get a good sense of how students are doing, giving them multiple opportunities to show their stuff but not burdening them with too many assessments (especially those of low quality). Teachers should factor in their own professional judgment when giving final grades; rather than relying on calculating the mean of a semester or year of grades, they should assess students' ultimate level of proficiency. The authors urge school leaders to forbid practices that produce inaccurate grades, such as: penalties for late work, academic dishonesty, absences, and inappropriate behavior; extra credit for behaviors that are unrelated to standards; group scores; grading on a curve; zeroes on the 101-point scale; students' level of English proficiency masking math proficiency; and grading homework.

• *Specific* – This means basing grades on standards and learning goals (not assessment methods) and clear descriptions of a limited number of levels (not points and percentages). The worst-case scenario, say O'Connor, Jung, and Reeves, is final grades representing "a mechanical and mindless calculation that reflects not the students' progress, but punishment for every missed homework assignment and wrong answer along the way." The best scenario is lots of specific error-correction and praise along the way, like the kind given by good music teachers and athletic coaches, and then a fair summation of progress and attainment at the end. A growing number of schools are joining the Mastery Transcript Consortium and working toward a radically different transcript that de-emphasizes grades and shows proficiencies developed over students' years in high school.

• *Timely* – This is a key pathway to the ultimate purpose of classroom assessment, say the authors: "to provide information that improves teaching and learning." The more promptly assessment results are communicated, the sooner teachers and students can do something about learning problems. Grades that are eleventh-hour predictions of failure don't help anyone. But timely feedback is challenging for middle- and high-school teachers with more than a hundred students and elementary teachers juggling multiple subjects. The big question is whether the teacher is measuring what matters. "If we have more checklists, quizzes, and assignments than we have time for," say O'Connor, Jung, and Reeves, "it may be best to reduce the quantity of assessments in order to increase the quality. Thoughtfully assessing students' performance on a single project that showcases their skills authentically across multiple standards may be a better choice than marking many quizzes that provide little fuel for reflection and improvement."

In conclusion, the authors caution against waiting for complete buy-in before making necessary changes in grading. Leaders need to challenge their colleagues to look at the evidence about better approaches and test hypotheses. "Effective change requires a sense of urgency, common ground, and action, but it doesn't necessarily require universal agreement," say O'Connor, Jung, and Reeves. "Change is best achieved through a judicious balance of pressure and support …. We must reject the 'pep rally' model that attempts to garner universal excitement for change. Rather, we can use what researchers have called the 'nudge' factor … to create circumstances where the FAST approach is more appealing and easier to implement …. Parents, communities, unions, and thought leaders may never agree on a specific grading procedure, but it's probable that they will agree on values, such as the desire to build personal responsibility and preparedness for the world beyond school …. Grading practices that have the potential to reduce failure, reduce dropouts, and improve school safety are, indeed, urgent."

"Gearing Up for FAST Grading and Reporting" by Ken O'Connor, Lee Ann Jung, and Douglas Reeves in *Phi Delta Kappan*, May 2018 (Vol. 99, #8, pp. 67–71), summarized in Marshall Memo 737.

Improving Grading Practices

Failure Is Not an Option

8

In this article in *Theory Into Practice*, researchers Dick Corbett and Bruce Wilson describe a five-year program in which several urban middle schools in Michigan experimented with not accepting failing performance from students. Following the mastery learning principles enunciated by Benjamin Bloom in the 1970s, students were required to make up failing assignments and keep trying until they achieved passing grades.

This approach is quite different from what Corbett and Wilson describe as the "*luck-based education*" most students experience: "That is, they have to be fortunate enough to be placed in classrooms where their teachers refuse to let them fail. The unlucky ones are left to endure the 'I already told you that,' 'I'm not going to keep repeating myself,' and 'You'll have to catch yourself up' statements that signal to students that their teachers are not very concerned whether they learn. Indeed, an all-too-prevalent pattern in schools is for teachers to settle for using good instructional practices and leaving it up to students to decide if they want to do their part. Tragically, in urban schools especially, many students—when given the choice to fail—do."

The four essential ingredients of the Michigan program (which Corbett and Wilson evaluated) were:

• *Educators bought into insisting on student success.* The philosophy behind the program (see links below) was that schools needed to use work completion as the primary academic lever to bring all students to mastery. Basically, teachers decided to take responsibility for students' success and not blame factors outside their control. Of course, having nothing but motivated students and involved parents would make life easier, but teachers faced the fact that they could control only what happened during school hours. *It's on us*, they concluded, knowing that if they ceded responsibility for success to students and parents, many students would fail and the achievement gap would widen.

• *Schools switched to a no-failure grading system.* They took all the *Ds*, *Es*, *Fs*, and zeroes out of the grading system. Placeholder grades were given for incomplete assignments: *I* for incomplete, *NY* for not yet finished, or *NQ* for not quality. The schools were basically saying that "every student could and would do quality work," explain Corbett and Wilson. "Some students might take longer than others, but no teacher would ever signal the end of an assignment with an *F* or zero." Students were expected to do every assignment, and students didn't receive grades until all their work was at an acceptable level of quality. This shone a bright spotlight on failing students. "We've made the invisible students visible," said one teacher.

• *Staff set up numerous interventions.* When students' work was unsatisfactory or incomplete, teachers knew there were two possible explanations: students didn't understand the assignments, or they weren't motivated to do them. For the first category of students, teachers led in-class re-teaching and enrichment sessions and used lunchtime makeup sessions, before- and after-school tutoring, Saturday school, and summer school. Even with the support, catching up was challenging for students. "They give us lots of chances to make up work," said one, "but teachers still give new assignments, which makes it hard to catch up." Some students who were doing well chafed at having to do assignments again, arguing that they had a passing average, but teachers still insisted. There were two types of interventions: (a) extra time and alternative tasks for students who didn't understand, and (b) "annoyances" like lunch study for students who were doing okay but chose to put off doing their work. "Giving good students the freedom to procrastinate—and watching them take advantage of it—was probably the most surprising and frustrating development, according to teachers," report Corbett and Wilson.

• *Teachers took a critical look at the assignments they gave students.* The no-failure policy raised immediate questions about whether some assignments were worth the battle. "Teachers realized … that if they were going to be instructionally stubborn and enforce the completion of all assignments, they needed to take a very careful look at what they were asking students to do and make sure that the work was worth doing in the first place," say Corbett and Wilson. "They realized that if students were going to have to go to summer school to finish certain tasks, then the assignment had better be pretty worthwhile to begin with." Teachers talked frequently in grade-level teams about what constituted a good assignment that merited grades and what was busywork or less important. They decided to give grades only for assignments that broke new ground or demonstrated proficiency. Homework, daily class work, and practice exercises didn't rise to that level, teachers reasoned, so they stopped giving grades for this type of work; if it was done well enough, proficiency would show up on culminating graded tests and assignments.

How did students respond to the no-failure regime? They appreciated—but also groused about—their teachers' unwavering insistence on doing assigned work at an acceptable level. "My teacher is mean, out of the kindness of her heart," said one student. "There is no way you can fail and get away with it," said another. "I hate it," said many, but equally common were comments like, "It makes you buckle down and finish things." Some students noticed improvements in pedagogy: "The program makes teachers give better assignments because they don't want to fight with us about stupid things," said one. And students liked having second chances. "If I fall behind, I can make it up and I won't just flunk because I didn't get it the first time," said another student. "I would rather do the work again than take a *D* or *F*. That way I will be better prepared for the next grade."

Did the no-failure policy make a positive difference? Corbett and Wilson report that teachers definitely had to work harder and regretted the fact that they often had to match wits with students and keep them from gaming the system. One insight was that they should have done more at the beginning of the program to enlist students and parents in the overall philosophy of no failure. "In light of what we have learned from students' reactions to a reform based on principles they valued in the first place (i.e., teachers who did not give up on them), just having adults work harder at putting a program in place will not be sufficient," say Corbett and Wilson. "Students need to be participants and not just beneficiaries of the reform."

But after five years, Corbett and Wilson report that student achievement was impressive and teachers in these middle schools "stridently reaffirmed that going back to blaming students and parents for poor performance and to failing scores of students each year was not what they wanted to do."

"Students' Reactions to a 'No Failure' Grading System and How They Informed Teacher Practice" by Dick Corbett and Bruce Wilson in *Theory Into Practice*, Summer 2009 (Vol. 48, #3, pp. 191–197), summarized in Marshall Memo 296.

9 How to Deal with Students Who Look Only at Their Grades

In this article in *Phi Delta Kappan*, high-school English teacher Timothy Quinn says that for many students, the grade they get on an assignment is the sole focus of their attention. This is driven by parents' intense interest in grades, which in turn is driven by the college admission process. The result is that few students look *beneath* the grade, get a sense of what they understood and didn't understand, and draw lessons for improvement.

And that's discouraging for teachers: "I have spent many a late night wondering why the heck I was writing comments on student essays that were never going to be read," says Quinn, "thinking why not just read it, put a letter on it, cut my grading time by 90 percent and get busy writing that great novel that all English teachers know they could write if they didn't have to spend so much time grading."

Quinn has two ideas for dealing with this problem. The teacher develops a rubric that deconstructs the content and skills students are asked to display in the assignment. Papers are graded and the teacher writes a rubric score for each domain on the papers, computes each student's overall grade, and writes it in your grade book but not on students' papers. Students have to figure out the overall grade themselves. When students get the papers back, rather than having a vague sense of having done "okay" with an overall B, they get a more nuanced understanding of their performance: "I got an A for organization so I must have organized my essay very well. I got a B for writing because there were a few too many errors, so next time I need to proofread better. But I got a C-minus for ideas, so I guess I'd better put some more thought into my next essay."

The second idea: the teacher writes comments on students' papers *without* rubric scores. Students are then asked to figure out their scores by reading the comments, then e-mail the teacher with an estimate of the grade they believe they earned. "If they make a good faith effort to do this," says Quinn, "you'll respond with their overall grade for the assignment. If not, they can wait for report cards to come out." Quinn believes this approach gets students to read comments, sparks better conversations (especially when the student's estimate of a grade differs from the teacher's), and fosters students' self-assessment skills.

"A Crash Course on Giving Grades" by Timothy Quinn in *Phi Delta Kappan*, December 2011/January 2012 (Vol. 93, #4, pp. 57–59), summarized in Marshall Memo 416.

10 Preventing Cheating by Shaping Classroom Motivational Climate

"Academic cheating occurs frequently in schools," say Eric Anderman and Alison Koenka (The Ohio State University) in this article in *Theory Into Practice*. "Cheating is a deliberative act, in that students make a conscious decision to engage in academic dishonesty." Why is there so much cheating (75 percent of students admit to it in high school or college) and what can be done about it? There are three questions students might ask themselves as they confront a situation where they might be tempted to cross the line:

• *What is my goal in this class?* Among the possibilities—Getting a good grade, really learning and understanding the material, doing better than my classmates, not looking dumb. The key variable is whether the teacher and students are more focused on *mastery* (really learning the material) or *performance* (for extrinsic or intrinsic rewards).

• *Can I do this?* This involves students' beliefs about their skillset and ability to complete the task, their expectations for success, and whether the teacher will evaluate the work fairly. Research has shown that low self-efficacy is a key factor when students cheat.

• *What are the costs of cheating?* Students consider the chances of being caught and punished, the effect of being a cheater on their self-concept, guilt, and whether they're willing to live with any or all of those outcomes.

Anderman and Koenka say that classrooms focused on mastery and intrinsic motivation have much less cheating: "If students are learning in an environment in which they (a) are encouraged to master the material, and (b) have the opportunity to work on various tasks, activities, and assessments until they reach a point of mastery, then cheating serves little purpose and results in minimal benefits… In contrast, when students learn in environments that are highly competitive and stress relative ability and exam performance (i.e., extrinsic or performance goals), cheating will be a more viable option for students." The same is true for situations where students are anxious to avoid appearing incompetent.

Anderman and Koenka have the following suggestions for principals and teachers who want to minimize cheating in classrooms:

• *Emphasize mastery.* One of the best ways is framing assessments as opportunities for students to improve understanding (through formative checks for understanding), enrich learning (through detailed feedback on attempts), and demonstrate proficiency (in summative tests). It's especially helpful to allow students to retake assessments until they demonstrate mastery. Teachers should also make parents aware of learning goals and assessments.

• *Orchestrate cooperative learning.* Handled well, this can foster a mastery orientation and discourage cheating. The key conditions are that students in cooperative learning groups are interdependent, have a common goal, are individually accountable for learning, build interpersonal skills, and have their eye on the bigger picture of the curriculum unit.

• *Don't stress students out about grades.* Rather than saying, "Friday's test is really big; if you fail it, you're sunk for the semester," say, "Friday's test covers concepts that are fundamental building blocks for your understanding of more advanced material."

• *Clearly communicate learning and assessment expectations.* When students don't know what will be covered on a test, aren't clear on the criteria for a successful essay, or believe grading policies are unfair (for example, grading on a curve), they're more likely to cheat.

• *Don't publicize students' grades.* Some teachers believe that displaying test results or hanging up A assignments is a motivator, but Anderman and Koenka say these practices convey a performance goal structure. Rather than public display of grades or papers, they recommend giving students private feedback on what's effective and what needs to be improved and not comparing work with that of other students. "In cases where providing exemplars is necessary," say the authors, "we recommend aiming to provide specific ones from every individual's or team's assessments (e.g., a particularly strong topic sentence from one team and an especially creative approach to solving a problem from another team).”

• *Talk explicitly about cheating.* Students and parents should be crystal clear on what constitutes cheating, the strong likelihood of being caught, and the serious consequences that will ensue. But the emphasis should be on how cheating undermines the real goal: mastering the material.

“The Relation Between Academic Motivation and Cheating” by Eric Anderman and Alison Koenka in *Theory Into Practice*, Spring 2017 (Vol. 56, #2, pp. 95–102), summarized in Marshall Memo 688.

---

11   Innovative Grading Systems Are Acceptable to Colleges

In this article in *School Administrator*, Thomas Buckmiller and Randal Peters (Drake University) address the concern voiced by some parents that students in schools using innovative grading practices won't get fair and equitable consideration from selective colleges. Buckmiller and Peters interviewed admissions officers at two large state universities, one midsized state university, and one midsized private university (all in the Midwest) and came away with the following insights:

• *Letter grades and transcripts based on standards are acceptable, even preferable.* For years, universities have been frustrated with high schools' grade inflation, inaccurate portrayals of student performance, grades that mush together academic and behavioral information, and the result—needing to provide remediation to significant numbers of admitted students. There's real appreciation for high schools that delineate standards and distinguish between different strands of information on students' achievement and conduct. The one caveat is that admissions officers prefer letter grades to any other grading metric.

• *Colleges are working to ensure equitable treatment for students with non-traditional grades.* They're already dealing with home-schooled students and an increasing number of students without class rankings. As more applicants submit non-traditional grades, colleges will adjust their formulas and try to be fair. They'll also give more weight to standardized test scores with these students. High schools' college counselors are key middlepeople in making sure colleges understand the grades and other information being submitted.

• *For college admissions personnel, efficiency and accuracy are key.* They're handling thousands of applications with limited staff and need concise, objective information that will tell them if each applicant can make it in their college. "The worst thing we can do," said one official, "is admit them when they don't have the skills to be successful. It's on our shoulders when they're … dropping out and walking away with debt." What's most helpful is accurate, non-inflated information on achievement and, separately, objective information on students' attendance, work ethic, and perseverance.

One high-school administrator summed it up well in a statement to students: "You will get into college, but that's not why we're here. We're here to make sure you get *through* college."

"Getting a Fair Shot?" by Thomas Buckmiller and Randal Peters in *School Administrator*, February 2018 (Vol. 75, #2, pp. 22–25), summarized in Marshall Memo 725.

Professional Learning Suggestions for Chapter Eleven
Grading Practices

Improving Grading and Homework Practices

Until recently, we thought grades were quite simple. When students didn't perform well, they received poor grades, when they did perform well, they received good grades. However, research has shown that a lot of what we had traditionally assumed about grading and homework is not accurate. Kim and Jenn have witnessed the inaccuracy of grades not only in their work with schools, but in the grades their own children have brought home from school, year after year.

The first set of professional learning activities below can be used to help teachers develop their understanding of how to make grading fairer and more accurate. The second set helps teachers and leaders rethink grading and homework policies and expectations across the entire school.

I. Understanding the Truth About Grading

Below are exercises to help teachers understand why some traditional grading practices are not effective.

A. Give teachers a True-False pretest about grading.
Have your teachers individually and privately take the True-False pretest about grading on the following page. Tell them no one is going to see the results. As the school leader, you may want to take it yourself before you do this with teachers! Do not yet discuss the answers to the quiz.

Enter T (true) or F (false) on the line after each statement:

1. When different students receive the same grade (say, a C) it means they have the same level of mastery. _____
2. Low grades do *not* encourage students to try harder. _____
3. The grades in an effective teacher's class should fall along a normal bell curve. _____
4. Grades are not as accurate as standardized tests in predicting high school completion and entrance into college. _____
5. Class grades typically reflect student achievement accurately. _____
6. Homework is *not* an effective way to determine student mastery of the material taught. _____
7. Less than 50 percent of high school students admit to cheating. _____

(Answers are: 1. F, 2. T, 3. F, 4. F, 5. F, 6. T, 7. F (It's about 75 percent.)

B. Discuss grading.

Before discussing the quiz, have your teachers discuss the following questions:

- If you had two very different students receive a C for their semester grade in a class, what might be some different factors that led to these grades (quizzes, homework completion, punctuality, etc.)? Brainstorm as complete a list as possible. Then discuss if it makes sense for them to receive the same grade.
- Why do we give grades? What do we hope to communicate through grades?

C. Find the answers to the True-False quiz.

Distribute Articles 1 (Brookhart et al.), 2 (Guskey), 4 (Kasun), 6 (Guskey), 7 (O'Connor, Jung, and Reeves), and 10 (Anderman and Koenka), and have teachers look through them to find answers to the True-False quiz above. To save time, different teachers could be assigned to read different articles. Next, have them discuss as a large group:

- What surprised you about the findings from these articles?
- Which problematic aspects of grading do you find exist at our school?
- Which findings will most impact your practice as a teacher?

D. Create a compiled list of lessons learned.

After taking the quiz, reading through the articles, and beginning to discuss grading practices, put teachers into groups to create a compiled list of lessons learned. Or, as the leader, you might want to do this on your own. The next page shows what a sample list might look like:

Lessons Learned about Grading Practices

⇒ Grades are more accurate predictors of high school completion and transition to college than standardized test scores.

⇒ Grades often include measures of *non*cognitive factors such as effort, motivation, and behavior.

⇒ Grades are subjective; they fall prey to teacher error.

⇒ We often do not clearly communicate what measures are included in grades.

⇒ Grades alone can't help us diagnose problems. There may be many factors that contribute to a poor grade—problems with the curriculum, instruction, materials, etc. Two students might receive a grade of C for entirely different reasons.

⇒ We often combine too many elements into one grade—product, process, and progress.

⇒ With effective teaching, there should *not* be a normal curve in grading. Grades should be criterion-referenced, not norm-referenced.

⇒ Getting low grades does *not* make students try harder.

⇒ For grades to be fair, students should have multiple ways to demonstrate mastery, and time given for tests must be flexible.

⇒ Homework is not an accurate portrayal of mastery.

⇒ Giving zeroes for homework is not a good way to hold students accountable.

⇒ 75 percent of students in high school and college admit to cheating.

II. Addressing Issues with Grading and Homework

It's not easy to change entrenched grading practices, but the activities below are designed to help teachers and leaders begin to take small steps to reform grading and homework practices deeply in need of a makeover.

A. Discuss the idea of splitting apart the components of grades.

Have teachers review the sixth article, in which Guskey proposes that, instead of giving one single grade for each subject, we break up grades into three components:

> *Product* – student performance on exams, reports, projects, assessments;
>
> *Process* – noncognitive student performance including how they work in class, punctuality in turning in assignments, participation, attendance, etc.;
>
> *Progress* – how much students have gained from their learning experience over a certain time.

Conduct a large-group discussion of the pros and cons of using this approach to grading.

B. Brainstorm and organize all of the factors that go into grades.

Next, have teachers look at all of the components of grades that they brainstormed in Section II / Activity B. above. Have them also look at the list of factors that go into grading that Guskey includes in his article (quizzes, homework completion, punctuality, etc.) Now have them individually list the components of *their own* grades that they currently include.

In grade teams or departments, have teachers share their lists and begin to compile a grade-wide list of what *should* go into grades. Now have them organize the factors their team wants to include in grades into these three categories:

Product   *Process*   *Progress*

C. Create rubrics for the Process and Progress components of grades.

Divide up each team into two groups: One will create a rubric for a *process* grade and one will create a rubric for a *progress* grade. For example, if "effort" is going to be a part of the Process grade, what would Levels 1, 2, 3, and 4 look like in your grade for effort? Groups should write these descriptions into the rubric.

Part of creating this rubric is *choosing* which components of process and progress they would want to include in a grade:

Process	Level 1	Level 2	Level 3	Level 4
Component of process:				
Component of process:				
Component of process:				
Component of process:				

Progress	Level 1	Level 2	Level 3	Level 4
Component of progress:				
Component of progress:				
Component of progress:				
Component of progress:				

D. Set school-wide homework and/or grading guidelines.

As the leader or as a leadership team, one way to address problems with grading and homework is to set school-wide homework and/or grading guidelines. Before creating this, do some of your own homework.

First, review the list of lessons learned above (in the first section) that you or the teachers created to begin to think about which lessons learned might translate into *guidelines.*

Second, informally survey teachers as you walk around the school by asking, "In your experience, when has homework you've assigned led to learning?" Jot down answers.

Third, to fully understand the problem with assigning zeroes for homework (or any assignment) that isn't turned in, do a little math: Find the average of the following grades for homework: 90, 90, 90, 90 and 0. Now ask yourself, is this average indicative of the student's mastery level?

Finally, review the three homework guidelines that the district put into place in Kasun (Article 4):
1. Homework should make up only 5 percent of a student's grade.
2. Do not assign zeroes—a 50 should be given for homework that is not completed.
3. Use the following time limit for homework: 10 minutes per grade (third graders get 30 minutes, twelfth graders get 120 minutes).

STRUCTURES FOR STUDENT SUCCESS

Now is your chance with your leadership team, after all of the discussions and readings woven into the activities above, to outline three guidelines to improve homework and/or grading practices at your school or in your district. You may want to start with a larger change such as eliminating all Ds and Fs (Corbett and Wilson, Article 8) or having all homework be used for formative assessment *only*. If you want to start smaller, then you may want to provide time limits for homework or have teachers give a separate "effort" grade for assignments. In either case, stick to *three* or fewer guidelines:

School-wide Guidelines to Improve Homework and/or Grading Practices

1.

2.

3.

Index

About the Authors

Kim Marshall was a sixth-grade teacher, central office curriculum director, and elementary principal in the Boston Public Schools for thirty-two years. Since 2002, Kim has provided one-on-one coaching for principals, mostly in New York City in affiliation with New Leaders, a non-profit that recruits, trains, and supports urban principals.

In addition, Kim consults, speaks, and teaches courses for school leaders, with a special focus on teacher supervision and evaluation, time management, the effective use of student assessments, and (in collaboration with Jay McTighe and Associates) curriculum unit design.

Kim is the author of a number of articles and books, including *Rethinking Teacher Supervision and Evaluation* (Jossey-Bass, second edition, 2013). He also produces The Marshall Memo, a weekly summary of helpful articles for principals, teachers, superintendents, and other educators (www.marshallmemo.com). Kim is married and has two children, both teachers.

Jenn David-Lang has worked in the field of education for more than twenty-five years. Currently, she runs THE MAIN IDEA, an annual subscription service that provides monthly summaries of compelling books and professional learning ideas to school leaders throughout the world (www. TheMainIdea.org).

Jenn founded THE MAIN IDEA in 2007 upon witnessing that many school leaders who were consumed with the day-to-day responsibilities of running their schools had no time for their own professional development.

When Jenn is not up to her ears in books, she offers a wide range of consultation, including: designing and providing workshops for leaders and teachers, coaching leaders, and conducting school evaluations. In prior years, Jenn received her administrative license and Ed.M. from the Bank Street College of Education, served in a variety of administrative and consulting positions, founded and directed a nonprofit to support urban middle school students, served as an adjunct instructor in education, and taught both math and English at the middle and high school levels.

Jenn's husband is a guidance counselor in the New York City schools, and they have two children attending public schools.

Made in the
USA
Middletown, DE